ИЧЧ

PROPERTY AND THE CONSTITUTION

Property and the Constitution

Edited by
JANET McLEAN
Director, New Zealand Institute of Public Law
The Victoria University of Wellington

·HART·
PUBLISHING
OXFORD – PORTLAND OREGON
1999

Hart Publishing
Oxford and Portland, Oregon

Published in North America (US and Canada) by
Hart Publishing
c/o International Specialized Book Services
5804 NE Hassalo Street
Portland, Oregon
97213-3644
USA

Distributed in the Netherlands, Belgium and Luxembourg by
Intersentia, Churchillaan 108
B2900 Schoten
Antwerpen
Belgium

Distributed in Australia and New Zealand by
Federation Press
John St
Leichhardt
NSW 2000

Hart Publishing Ltd is a specialist legal publisher based in Oxford, England.
To order further copies of this book or to request a list of other
publications please write to:

Hart Publishing Ltd, 19 Whitehouse Road, Oxford, OX1 4PA
Telephone: +44 (0)1865 434459 or Fax: +44 (0)1865 794882
e-mail: mail@hartpub.co.uk

British Library Cataloguing in Publication Data
Data Available
ISBN 1 84113–055–9 (cloth)

Typeset by Hope Services (Abingdon) Ltd.
Printed in Great Britain on acid-free paper
by Biddles Ltd, Guildford and Kings Lynn.

Foreword

by

Lord Cooke of Thorndon

Baroness Thatcher would not enjoy this book. It may be inferred that none of the dozen contributors would for a moment entertain seriously her dictum that there is no such thing as society. Without immediate access to *The Downing Street Years* or *Woman's Own* I cannot comment on whether the severity of that apparently simplistic view was convincingly qualified by the context. By contrast, however, no contributor could conceivably be accused of over-simplification and all are concerned throughout with the *social role* of the concept of property.

A range of points are tellingly made. Some of the more accessible ones might be roughly summarised as follows, with their principal proponents identified. But these are only starting points leading to much more developed theses to which a foreword cannot attempt to do justice.

'Property' can loosely be used to mean that which is the subject of property but, more accurately, the term denotes a relationship between a person and an asset, carrying rights in that asset on the strength of which it can reasonably be said that the person owns it or shares in its ownership. While the details of these rights within particular states obviously vary and may be of great complexity (Geoffrey Samuel), the recognition and preservation of substantial rights of this kind is a necessity of civilisation (J. W. Harris). A division into public and private property is artificial. Property may be used not merely as a restraint on government, but as an instrument of government, by attaching certain public obligations to private control; and it is socially dangerous to assume that governments have a natural right to privatise everything (Janet McLean). The limitation of property rights is as important as their recognition (Kevin Gray and Susan Francis Gray, in a par-ticularly informative paper highlighting North American jurisprudence on the rise of privately-controlled shopping malls and residential estates).

Although property as such was deliberately omitted from the New Zealand Bill of Rights 1990 because of a fear of generating disputes, there are advan-tages in constitutionalising property: then it is revealed as a right standing alongside others and requiring to be reconciled with them. It is not something precedent to all other human rights, as the common law is sometimes seen to suggest (Gregory Alexander and Andre van der Valt). Thus family rights may influence the scope of property (Tom Allen). And I cannot resist the thought that the majority decision of the House of Lords in *Hunter v Canary Wharf Limited*[1] may be less defensible in the light of the incorporation of the

---

[1] [1997] 2 All E.R. 426.

European Convention on Human Rights into United Kingdom domestic law.

Some of the papers have a special New Zealand significance. Jeremy Waldron, a distinguished New Zealand expatriate academic lawyer based at Columbia University, warns against trying to redress unjust acquisitions of property in the past by redistributions working equal injustice in the present; but he draws a rejoinder from M. M. Goldsmith to the effect that this is no excuse for leaving an established wrong untouched. In more specific terms Alex Frame points to the paradox that the catalyst for the current resurgence of Maori communal property was the vogue for privatisation of assets previously held by the Crown; while John Dawson in an account of the Ngai Tahu settlement demonstrates how dramatic has been that resurgence. Already Ngai Tahu and Tainui have become major players in the New Zealand economic scene. And the Maori share of fishing quota is solid testimony to a genuine, if belated, acceptance of the fiduciary duty owed by a colonising power to an indigenous people.

In the main the contributors represent various shades of liberal opinion, but Michael Robertson argues for a frankly socialist approach. If anything is missing from this collection, it is an unrepentant and unqualified market philosophy of property. The most vivid phrase in the book comes from a non-contributor, Jeremy Bentham, who is quoted by Jeremy Waldron: '. . . our property becomes part of our being, and cannot be torn from us without rending us to the quick'. It was this truth that led the Privy Council, in a case which I had forgotten but has been unearthed by Tom Allen, *Fok Lai Ying v Governor in Council*[2], to hold that a right to full compensation does not prevent a compulsory acquisition from being arbitrary. As to what justifies a compulsory acquisition or a limitation of rights, perhaps in the end it is all, as lawyers like to say, a question of fact and degree—though philosophy such as is expounded here may help to shape solutions.

Janet McLean, with the indispensable financial support that she acknowledges in her preface, succeeded in assembling at a conference in Wellington a select team of specialists, mainly from outside New Zealand (Durham, Cornell, Exeter, Cambridge, Greenwich, Oxford, Kent, New York, South Africa). This was something of a triumph of logistics, but it was more. Having written a number of forewords to New Zealand law books, I can say that what distinguishes this one is that it presents the carefully considered and thought-provoking work of authors whose professional lives are centred, at least in part, on examining concepts in depth. I congratulate Janet McLean on her initiative. It has led to a compilation appropriate in quality and the subject matter to the emphasis traditionally placed by this University on constitutional study. The book will be enduring evidence of her outstandingly constructive service as Director of the New Zealand Institute of Public Law.

Law School,   Robin Cooke
Victoria University of Wellington
May 1999

[2] [1997] 3 L.R.C. 101.

Contents

Preface

The papers in this collection, were presented at a conference held in Wellington on 17 and 18 July 1998 under the auspices of the New Zealand Institute of Public Law at the Faculty of Law, Victoria University of Wellington. Geoffrey Samuel and Tom Allen made their contributions to the topic after the event.

Bringing people from different parts of the globe together for a couple of days is often a difficult and demanding task. In this, I was fortunate to have the financial assistance of the Victoria University Foundation and the New Zealand Law Foundation, and accommodation and support from the Law Faculty at Victoria University. I was the happy recipient of encouragement and advice from Michael Taggart, Stuart Anderson, the Rt Hon. Justice Keith, Dr Alex Frame and Alison Quentin-Baxter. Thanks also go to Victoria Russell and Fiona Stuart for their help in preparing the papers for publication, and to the law libraries at Victoria and Otago Universities. Most of all, I am grateful to Denise Blackett, the administrator of the Institute, for the characteristically thoughtful, efficient and committed way in which she contributed to the organisation of the conference and to the preparation of the papers for publication.

The contributors have, without exception, been supportive of and enthusiastic about this project—and in many cases had to come thousands of miles to attend the conference. I thank them, and Lord Cooke of Thorndon for agreeing to write the Foreword.

Janet McLean
Director
New Zealand Institute of Public Law

List of Contributors

Tom Allen is a Senior Lecturer, Department of Law, University of Durham.

Gregory S. Alexander is a Professor of Law, Cornell University.

John Dawson is a Senior Lecturer, Faculty of Law, University of Otago.

Alex Frame is a Barrister and Senior Lecturer, Victoria University of Wellington.

Maurice M. Goldsmith is a Senior Lecturer in Philosophy, Victoria University of Wellington and formerly Professor of Political Theory at the University of Exeter.

Kevin Gray is a Fellow of Trinity College and a Professor and Dean of Law, the University of Cambridge.

Susan Francis Gray is a Senior Lecturer in Law, the University of Greenwich.

Jim Harris is a Fellow, Tutor and Professor of Law, Keble College, Oxford.

Janet McLean is a Senior Lecturer in Law and Director of the New Zealand Institute of Public Law, Victoria University of Wellington.

Michael Robertson is a Senior Lecturer, Faculty of Law, University of Otago.

Geoffrey Samuel is a Professor of Law, Kent Law School, University of Kent.

Jeremy Waldron is the Maurice and Hilda Friedman Professor of Law, and Director of the Center for Law and Philosophy, Columbia University in the City of New York.

Andre van der Walt is a Professor of Private Law, the University of South Africa.

Table of Cases

1

Property as Power and Resistance

JANET McLEAN*

I. INTRODUCTION

Property has always had a public dimension in at least two separate and related senses—as a means to distribute power; and as a means of resistance against governmental power. That is, property can be regarded both as a method of conferring authority and as a counterpoise against such authority. Many of the essays in this collection will focus on the latter, evaluating the various rationale (in terms of both positive and negative liberty) for the constitutional protection of private property and deriving therefrom the proper constitutional limits of government authority over such property. Among these explanations of the constitutional role of private property, for example, is the view that property offers a means of resistance against a tyrannical democratic majority, and also confers on people the independence necessary for proper citizenship. In this introductory chapter I want to relate the idea of "property as authority" to "property as resistance" in a slightly different way. Property regarded as resistance, as defining a private zone of autonomy, tends to dominate contemporary discussions. But what of the use by governments, or their agents, of property as a means of exercising authority: pursuing public policy objectives by divestment or conferring property on "private" bodies as partial agents for the state? Should the *Crown* as *owner* be able to enjoy property both as a means of exercising authority and as creating a zone of autonomy or means to resist interference? Under those circumstances, what is the proper analysis of the governmental/proprietary distinction? And what does it mean for property to enjoy the epithet "public"?

The Romans traditionally separated *imperium* from *dominium*—the former being the power to govern, and the latter being the power of ownership.[1] Such a distinction resonates with the much later Lockean understanding of property as a neutral de-politicised instrument detached from obedience to a sovereign.

* Thanks to Michael Robertson, Michael Taggart, Tim Mulgan, Stuart Anderson, Ingo von Münch and the students in my 1998 honours seminar at Victoria University of Wellington. My theme is taken from the discussion in Geoffrey Samuel, *The Foundations of Legal Reasoning* (Antwerp, Maklu, 1994), p. 246.
[1] Geoffrey Samuel discusses how the Roman conception was modified by English customary law in Chapter 3, below.

Imperium is a public matter and *dominium* a private one. The distinction accords too, with classical Austinian understandings about governance by legislated command and delegated authority. In modern constitutional law terms we thus consider the sovereign's power to regulate to be a public law matter and the Crown's power to hold property to be defined by private law—the Crown having the same powers in this regard as a natural person.[2]

But there are other strongly competing visions of governance. The struggle of ownership and ruler-ship to free themselves of each other is one of the great themes of Medieval English legal history. Medieval views about property thoroughly conflated property and authority. The Crown was sovereign over the whole of England because, according to the fiction, it had once owned all the lands.[3] The tenure system had the effect of emphasising social, economic and thus political relationships between persons and property. Even as late as the eighteenth century, Crown Charters would not distinguish between grants of property and delegated public powers—or even speak in those terms: property itself was the instrument of governance. And later the statutory (mainly utility) corporations of the early nineteenth century would be referred to as "little Commonwealths" or "little Republics" using "private" property to further the work of governments.[4]

The separation of *imperium* from *dominium* then, was never complete. It is equally difficult to sustain in the modern state. Governments pursue their goals through the use of economic instruments, by contracts, and by imposing conditions on the distribution of government largess.[5] Property settlements between governments and indigenous peoples restore particular titles and rights to property and at the same time quite deliberately raise expectations that something like sovereignty is being conferred or restored.[6] The increasing interpenetration between public and private institutions and capital,[7] has obscured both the question of "who" governs and "how" they govern with consequences for the operation of democratic values.[8] And it gives rise to a tension: when *imperium* and *dominium* are located in a single institution—how can one reconcile property as authority and property as resistance? Why should governments, or their agents, enjoy property protections (a zone of autonomy) designed to protect property holders from governments?

---

[2] Such a doctrine is not uncontroversial among public lawyers—a matter to which I shall return.

[3] K. McNeil, *Common Law Aboriginal Title* (Oxford, Clarendon Press, 1989), p. 108.

[4] M. J. Horwitz, *The Transformation of American Law 1870–1960* (New York, Oxford University Press, 1992), p. 65; G. S. Alexander, *Commodity and Propriety* (Chicago, University of Chicago Press, 1997), p. 198-199.

[5] C. Reich, "The New Property", (1964) 73 *Yale L J* 733. See also G. S. Alexander, "The Concept of Property in Private and Constitutional Law: the Ideology of the Scientific Turn in Legal Analysis", (1982) 82 *Col L R* 1545; T. Dantith, "Regulation by Contract: The New Prerogative", (1979) *Current Legal Problems* 41.

[6] See Chapter 10 below by John Dawson, and Chapter 11 below by Alex Frame.

[7] The expression is Carol Harlow's: see, "'Public' and 'Private' Law", (1980) 43 *Mod L Rev* 241, 257.

[8] See in particular Chapter 12 below by Michael Robertson, and Chapter 2 below by Kevin and Susan Gray.

Let me introduce some of the issues by a more detailed illustration. New York City was founded in a series of pre-revolutionary charters from the Crown which granted it title to land and special franchises.[9] In the eighteenth century it governed not so much by the income from such property but by cajoling and enticing others to build city amenities by way of land swaps, special licences and other tagged grants. Most lucrative were the grants of water lots given in exchange for restrictive covenants, affirmative obligations and special responsibilities (such as to construct wharves and public spaces in addition to streets at front and rear). Such a method was risky, inefficient and likely corrupt—but it avoided the need for public financing, a public bureaucracy, the raising of taxes, or direct regulatory powers. There was a certain reciprocity—"public" institutions had private rights and so private individuals had public obligations. And, importantly, New York City enjoyed autonomy. Its power to dispose of its estate was not a delegated one, nor dependent on state grant—it held rights against the State of New York and the Federation. As such it inhabited an intermediate zone between what we would now consider to be public and private—an idea to which I and others shall return.[10]

The "new governance" sweeping much of the globe, is oddly, if not wholly, reminiscent of this era. The political difficulties of raising taxes, a profound sense that governments are not good at "running things" (that central agencies do not have the information or skills to manage such services), and an urge to deregulate (to retreat from the use of *imperium*—at least of a command and control type) have led to the widespread use of some of the same techniques. Modern governments also resort to persuasion, consultation and other informal methods of achieving their goals. And, as in the eighteenth century, property held by governments is not so much important for the revenue it might earn, but for the ways it might be deployed to achieve policy outcomes. In this political context, the widespread use of powers of eminent domain to further majoritarian interests at the expense of a few or individual property-holders seems unlikely.[11] More likely is that governments will *divest* themselves of property to further their policy goals, or delegate the power of eminent domain to other private entities which have lost their "public" hue. Similarly, governance by delegated command is less likely than contracting out functions and encouraging self-regulation. Legislative activity will often involve the creation of *new* forms of rights by establishing trespass rules and exclusive rights of user—and calling these "*property*"—for example, pollution rights, tradeable fishing rights and the

---

[9] For a fascinating study see H. Hartog, *Public Property and Private Power: the Corporation of the City of New York in American Law*, 1730–1870 (Chapel Hill and London, University of North Carolina Press, 1983). See also the review by C. Rose, "Public Property, Old and New", (1985) 79 *Nw ULR* 216.

[10] See in particular Chapter 2 below by Kevin and Susan Gray which refers to "quasi-public property".

[11] Except in cases involving historical injustice—see the discussion of the South African constitutional property clause in Chapter 6 below by Andre van der Walt and Chapters 8 and 9 below by Jeremy Waldron and Maurice Goldsmith, respectively.

like.[12] Significantly, the last of these strategies, potentially creates rights (resis-tance) against the state. Now, as in eighteenth century New York City, the view that governments themselves should do little but make others do what they ought, is the prevailing public policy requiring active governmental intervention of a particular kind.[13]

The comparison between eighteenth century New York City and "the new managerialism" is, however, incomplete. In its new incarnation, there is no acknowledgement of the essential exchange which was the fulcrum of the old—special privilege for public obligation. Indeed, governments resile from the notion that they grant privileges, for that would be to admit of governmentally created competitive advantage at a time when governments are striving to appear neutral. Such privilege has too much of a feudal quality. In modern times we tend to think of property as resistance, not as privilege or as a means of achieving sovereign will. Nevertheless such privileges do exist either *de facto* or *de jure*, and often can be found in the details. In New Zealand, for example, (where there is little or nothing by way of utility regulation) private utility com-panies jealously defend the interests of their shareholders as the sole focus of their endeavours against charges of social irresponsibility. However, under complicated provisions of resource management law, the same companies enjoy powers of eminent domain.[14] These provisions confer the status of "government work" on certain activities by specified bodies, providing, for example, for the construction of roads and transmission lines. Among other things, such provi-sions would seem to indicate that serving the public interest is a core function of such "network utility operators" rather than an incidental or additional one. The habit of strictly distinguishing between *imperium* and *dominium* and pub-lic and private does not leave conceptual space for such a middle ground of activity, either for publicly or privately-owned bodies. As Stuart Anderson has suggested, a return to an ambiguous hybrid category of institutions—such as that which the Victorians understood—may help in an analysis of today's new agencies.[15]

---

[12] See J. W. Harris, *Property and Justice* (Oxford, Clarendon Press, 1996), Part I.

[13] See for a discussion of the Canadian context, H. Arthurs, "'Mechanical Arts and Merchandise': Canadian Public Administration in the New Economy", (1997) 42 *McGill LJ* 29. Such types of intervention, he suggests, encourage the growing tendency to "see ourselves as rights-bear-ing individuals rather than members of a community, as operating at odds with the state rather than as its beneficiaries, as seekers of personal redress through litigation rather than as agents of social improvement through political activity" (at 45).

[14] The Resource Management Act 1991, s. 166 confers network utility operator status on certain utility providers. By s. 186, approved "requiring authorities" are empowered to apply to the Minister of Lands to compulsorily acquire property. If successful, the project has the status of "gov-ernment work" for the purposes of the Public Works Act 1931. Though the criteria in the Resource Management Act 1991 do not specifically include a public purpose test, the Public Works Act definition of "government work" does.

[15] S. Anderson, "Municipal Corporations go to Market", unpublished commentary. See also H. Schieber, "Public Rights and the Rule of Law in American Legal History", (1984) 72 *Calif L Rev* 217, 225.

Public lawyers have responded to these developments in a number of ways: by extending the law of judicial review to certain private bodies, by suggesting that there should be a separate public law of tort and contract, by extending human rights and information privacy protections to private bodies, by the proliferation of new complaints mechanisms, and by the statutory imposition of social goals on otherwise commercial enterprises (the latter with mixed success).[16] At the core of much of this debate is the question of what difference, if any, it makes for property to be privately rather than publicly owned. What exactly are the limits of autonomy of action in this "private" zone? It is to this question I would presently like to turn. Let us begin with the first part of that comparison. What is the situation of the Crown as owner?

II. THE CROWN AS OWNER

So strong is the private property paradigm, that one typical response is that the government's proprietary rights are in no way different from those of a private owner.[17] Some property indeed appears to be closely analogous to private property, giving rise to similar powers of exclusion in the owner or its agents. A Minister of the Crown, for example, is able to exclude people as trespassers from her offices at Whitehall much the same as any other corporate officer.[18] Indeed, in early medieval times the Crown's property was regarded as private property belonging to the King and so could be dealt with according to his wants and appetites. The risk of kings alienating vast tracts of territory to raise funds, however, soon became apparent.[19] Concern about such alienations threatening the basis of sovereignty itself eventually resulted in two related distinctions: between the King and Crown; and between Crown property which is alienable and that which is inalienable. By the later middle ages the "Crown" was taken as something separate from the king and as representing the "body politic".[20] Hence the King's "personal" property could be conceived as separate from the property of the realm. Pollock and Maitland describe "Crown property" as the "original endowment of the kingship" so designated at the time "settlement of the Conquest was completed and . . . registered in the Domesday Book".[21] These

---

[16] See generally, M. Taggart (ed.), *The Province of Administrative Law* (Oxford, Hart Publishing, 1997) and especially, M. Taggart, "State-Owned Enterprises and Social Responsibility: a Contradiction in Terms?", [1993] *NZ Recent L Rev* 343; J. McLean, "Contracting in the Corporatised and Privatised Environment", (1996) 7 *PLR* 223.

[17] See the discussion of Justice La Forest's comments in *The Queen* v. *Committee for the Commonwealth of Canada* (1991) 77 D L R (4th) 385, 402 by Gray and Gray, pp. 28–29.

[18] The example is from Jim Harris, above n. 12, at p. 104.

[19] e.g., Richard II was alleged to have acted in dishersion of the Crown of England by alienating the Isle of Oleron.

[20] Sometimes the "Crown" was taken to personify the Crown estate itself as it passed from father to son. See further, E. H. Kantorowicz, *The King's Two Bodies: A Study in Medieval Political Theology* (Princeton, Princeton University Press, 1957).

[21] F. Pollock and F. W. Maitland *History of English Law* 2nd rev. edn. (1968) pp. 383–384.

properties, they considered to be permanently annexed to the kingly office and as such inalienable.

In this they reflected the now often unfashionable idea that a core of Crown property is the basis of government.[22] A modern restatement of such a view is captured in the German basic law guarantees governing recent privatisations. The Federal Republic cannot divest itself of property so as to deprive itself of the ability to achieve the basic agreed ends of government. Such a core might be considered "public property" in its broadest sense.

The German government then, has encountered *constitutional* impediments to privatisation programmes.[23] Constitutional amendments were required for the vesting of the postal and telecommunications services in private companies and even of the federal railways in a state-owned corporation.[24] This approach has no counterpart in the British or New Zealand constitutional arrangements in relation to privatisation. There are no timely processes (parliamentary or otherwise) with which to assess the prices offered for state assets, or to ensure that the proceeds of such sales are applied for declared purposes such as to retire debt.[25] There are no legal means or processes with which to assess the ends of government or the strategic assets needed to perform those functions—except, that is, as defined by the government of the day in legislation, or simply by the exercise of the prerogative.[26] The process of divestment, at least in common law jurisdictions, is not troubled by any transcending notion of "the state". The democratic deficit should be obvious.[27] Tyrannous majorities may divest as well as acquire property. In this area of "Crown property" at least in British or British-derived constitutions one might be forgiven for thinking that private property is indeed strongly analogous to Crown property. Such an asymmetry between controls on acquisition as opposed to divestment may become all the

[22] The idea has not been lost by Maori in New Zealand—see especially Chapter 10 below by John Dawson.

[23] See further on the German Constitution, Chapter 5 below by Gregory Alexander.

[24] See for example G. Püttner, "Constitutional Limitations on Privatisation" in E. Riedel (ed.), *German Reports on Public Law* (Baden-Baden, Nomos Verlagsgesellschaft, 1998), pp. 66–76. In both cases guarantee clauses were introduced (Arts 87e and 87f I Basic Law). The latter requires the Federation to ensure a basic supply of post and telecommunication services throughout the whole country. See for a comparison of the British and French experiences of privatisation, C. Graham and T. Prosser, *Privatising Public Enterprises* (Oxford, Clarendon Press, 1991).

[25] See, for example, M. Taggart, "Book Review" of C. Graham and T. Prosser, *Privatising Public Enterprises* (Oxford, Clarendon Press, 1991), (1993) 4 *PLR* 271, 273. He relates that French politicians were required by statute to retire debt whereas in New Zealand between 1984–1991 of the $9.7 bn raised from asset sales, only an estimated $450 million was applied to reducing long-term debt.

[26] For example, in 1989, the New Zealand government's policy of selling Crown assets including land, necessitated the publication of a legal opinion as to whether the Crown was required to have legislative approval to do so (see Legislation Advisory Committee, *Departmental Statutes*, Report No. 4 (Wellington, Ministry of Justice 1989) Appendix 2). The opinion concluded that with the exception of certain lands acquired by the government under a particular enactment, the Crown in its corporate capacity could sell land without legislative authorisation. As it transpired, many asset sales required an incidental legislative act such as repeal or amendment of related legislation.

[27] See T. Dantith, "The Executive Power Today: Bargaining and Economic Control" in J. Jowell and D. Oliver, *The Changing Constitution* (Oxford, Clarendon Press, 1985), pp. 174, 177–182.

more exaggerated given collective action problems and the normative resilience of property which Jeremy Waldron discusses later in this volume.

There are then, no grand constitutional principles to help us think about the nature of Crown property, but there is some guidance to be found in the details of the common law. Not only did it consider that the Crown owned a sovereign core of property, but (and this may be a different thing) that the Crown also held property in a default sense: all property must be owned by someone and in the event that no particular person or group has a stronger proven claim, that "someone" is the Crown or sovereign.[28] The common law defined what the Crown could grant of these properties, in effect limiting what could be owned, and distinguishing between the Crown's property holdings as proprietor and as regulator or protector of the public.[29] *Imperium* and *dominium* can be distinguished even within a property concept. The case of navigable rivers is illustrative.

Limitations on Crown powers in the Magna Charta[30] evolved into the principle that the sovereign holds title to lands under navigable waters in two capacities—as the governmental authority charged with protecting the rights of the public and as the proprietary owner of subjacent land with the right to grant to individuals any private property interest which did not interfere with public rights.[31] That is, whether the subjacent lands were owned by the king or a private person, the public's right to navigation applied to all tidal waters.[32] The effect was that what normally the king could grant for his personal interest or profit, could not in this case be granted free of paramount public rights. In America the idea that some state-owned property is held in trust for the public as beneficial owner would later evolve into the public trust doctrine.

The doctrine has always been controversial[33] and I do not mean to go into the details here except to make a few general points.[34] First, there is a dispute about whether the doctrine proscribed alienation of subjacent land altogether. In some

---

[28] See also Arts 399 and 400 of the Civil Code of Lower Canada.

[29] This distinction is explored in Chapter 10 below by John Dawson in relation to property settlements with indigenous people.

[30] These dealt with the removal of fishing weirs which obstructed upstream fishing rights and navigation.

[31] M. L. Rosen, "Lands Under Navigable Waters: The Governmental/Proprietary Distinction", (1982) 34 *U Fla L Rev* 561, 566.

[32] Sir Matthew Hale confirmed this view in *De Jure Maris* 1716 cap IV and extended such rights to non-tidal waters , see above n. 31, at 568–569.

[33] Both before and after Elizabeth I declared the Crown *prima facie* owner of the shore to the high-water mark there were contested claims to exclusive property rights over navigable waters; see e.g. *A-G* v. *Emerson* [1891] AC 649.

[34] See further H. Schieber, above n. 15; M. Selvin, "The Public Trust Doctrine in American Law and Economic Policy 1789–1920", [1980] *Wisconsin L Rev* 1403; C. Rose, "The Comedy of the Commons; Custom, Commerce, and Inherently Public Property", (1986) 53 *U Chi L R* 711; G S Alexander, above n. 4, at pp. 271–277; L. Butler, "The Commons Concept: An Historical Concept with Modern Relevance", (1982) 23 *Wm & Mary L R* 835; J. Sax, "The Public Trust Doctrine in Natural Resource Law: Effective Judicial Intervention", (1970) 68 *Mich L Rev* 471; R. Lazarus, "Changing Conceptions of Property and Sovereignty in Natural Resources: Questioning the Public Trust Doctrine", (1986) 71 *Iowa L R* 631.

American states the English common law doctrine was interpreted as restricting ownership of subjacent land to the state governments. Such a view is not surprising given that in early times the governmental and proprietary concepts were not commonly distinguished.[35] To enforce public rights over private land, by *jus publicum*, or dominion (now often referred to as the "police power") would have been, and still is, a risky business. If a state actively governs by means of its own property, sooner or later it will encounter conflicts between its uses of property and the uses of others. It may have suited governments then, for political reasons, to accept impediments on their own property ownership—and hence more easily impose similar impediments on private owners. Lazarus suggests that the public trust doctrine was the public property analogue to private property concepts such as "qualified property" and "property affected with a public interest". As itself an impediment on Crown's use of property, it provided "the sovereign with a ready answer to claims of the sanctity of private property rights at a time when governmental power was itself rooted in its own property holdings".[36] The private property analogues to the public trust doctrine are matters to which I shall return.

Secondly, there is dispute as to whether the prohibition on alienation applied to the legislature as well as the king. A number of scholars have contended that while the king could not alienate such land free of its subordination to public trust rights of navigation and fishing, the legislature could do so.[37] One explanation was that the legislature (unlike the Crown) is "the same thing as the public itself".[38] There is a sense here that the commons (such as the air, running water, navigable rivers) is conceived not as a system of "no ownership" (which the Crown holds in default), but rather of joint ownership (which the Crown holds as representative for the body politic) with a requirement for agreement about its management.[39]

Thirdly, the doctrine suggests that the common law envisages a concept of non-exclusive ownership which could be applied to both publicly and privately

---

[35] There was a tendency to obscure questions of jurisdiction and proprietary right.

[36] Lazarus, above n. 34, at 701.

[37] In his 1826 treatise on tidelands, for example, Joseph Angell discussed the Crown's ownership of waterway "trust" lands and comes to this conclusion (see the excellent discussion in C. Rose, *Property and Persuasion: Essays on the History, Theory and Rhetoric of Ownership* (Boulder, Westview, 1994), pp. 119–122). Lazarus concurs with this view, above n. 34, at n. 20, as does Sax, above n. 34, at 476. Cf. *Arnold v. Mundy* 6 NJL 1 (1821) to the effect that even the legislature may be limited in its power to dispose of Crown lands.

[38] For the difficulties of conceiving of the legal personality of the Crown see J. McLean, "Personality and Public Law Doctrine", (1999) 49 *U Toronto LJ* 123 reviewing D. Runciman, *Pluralism and the Personality of the State* (Cambridge, Cambridge University Press, 1997).

[39] See G. A. Cohen, *Self-ownership, Freedom and Equality* (Cambridge, Cambridge University Press, 1995). As Cohen asks (at p. 83): "Why should we not regard the land, prior to A's appropriation, as jointly owned, rather than, as Nozick takes for granted, owned by no one? When land is owned in common, each can use it on his own initiative, provided that he does not interfere with similar use by others: under common ownership of the land no one owns any of it. Under joint ownership, by contrast, the land is owned by all together, and what each may do with it is subject to collective decision". (I am grateful to Tim Mulgan for this reference.)

owned property.[40] Even subjacent land which *has* been granted to private ownership is affected by public rights under the state's protection.[41] And while it is
a matter of further controversy whether the public trust doctrine could be
enforceable by the public at large, other common law actions were available to
protect rights of common pasture, fishery and rights of way.[42] Indeed, title to
lands subject to common use was usually vested in private parties because prescriptive rights could be acquired more readily over private than over public
land (where possession of the Crown was presumed).[43]

To return to the original question, does it matter whether property is publicly
or privately owned? Crown or state property does not by definition constitute
"public property". Some state-owned property is closely analogous to private
property, with similar elements of exclusivity. The older common law understanding that there is a core of state property essential for governance and which
cannot be alienated is not clearly reflected in the English constitution. However,
there is common law authority to the effect that in certain circumstances the
state's rights over property as owner are restricted by its responsibilities to protect the public. The Crown does not hold such property as a "natural person"
might do, but must (according to Lord Hale's view of the *publici juris*) offer "the
public" the same protection as vested rights holders. Moreover such public
rights attach to both publicly and privately-owned property. It is to the private
property analogue of the public trust doctrine I would now like briefly to turn.

III.   PRIVATE PROPERTY WITH PUBLIC PURPOSES

Public rights over private property have been able to be acquired by a number
of different means: by grant, implied grant and prescriptive use. According to
the common law then, restrictions on the uses of private property could be
imposed from above (the state, or organised public) and below (the unorganised
public). My present concern is the former types of restrictions. How should we
analyse the situation in which government actively pursues its policy by conferring privileges on privately-owned entities, and the like, to do the government's
work? Should that use of private property enjoy full property protections?
Should the manner of regulation (by the use of a property regime) immunise the
activity from public controls?

[40] See Harris, above n. 12, at p. 109 n. 27.

[41] The doctrine is said to have its antecedents in the concept of *res communes* which Bracton introduced into the common law in the mid-thirteenth century. He considered the shores of the sea as common to all and inalienable, which view was later confirmed by legislation. In Roman law there were
four types of non-exclusive ownership: *res universitatis* (belonging to corporate bodies); *res sacriae* or
religiosae (sacred buildings); *res publicae* (common to all people such as rivers, ports); and *res nullius*
(belonging to no one). See further D. R. Coquillette, "Mosses From an Old Manse: Another Look at
Some Historic Property Cases About the Environment", (1979) 64 *Cornell L R* 761, 801.

[42] For example, the writs of praecipe and questus est to protect rights of use and the assize of
novel disseisin for the invasion of rights on common land (see Coquillette above n. 39, at 806).

[43] McNeil, above n. 3, at pp. 94, 105; L. Butler, above n. 34, at 860, 861.

Before such activities commonly became nationalised, the common law said no. It considered certain businesses to be affected by the public interest. This private law analogue to the public trust doctrine was originally used to protect the privileges of corporate interests. Grantees of exclusive interests, according to the doctrine, do not hold them merely for their own benefit, but also for the benefit of the public and trade. The doctrine would attach to *de jure* and *de facto* monopoly situations: where there was one facility licensed by the Crown, or there was only one facility available which enjoyed a dominant position. The doctrine included public utilities, common carriers and railways; traditionally regulated businesses such as inns cabs and mills; and industries which although not public at their inception, had become such.[44]

The doctrine later became a justification for legislative price-fixing (which I am not advocating here). What I think is useful and interesting about it, is its classification of certain property as hybrid. It effectively separates the elements of *dominium* and *imperium* even within privately-owned property—thereby creating the kind of quasi-public property which Gray and Gray will discuss.

IV. CONCLUSION

Many of the doctrines which I have briefly traversed have fallen into decline and disuse over a period in which much of the relevant property has been publicly-owned. Certain public expectations and intuitions about the "public" nature of certain property have remained. It is telling, for example, that in New Zealand, claims by Maori under the Treaty of Waitangi have mainly been successful over property which could be described as *res communes*.[45] Empowering Maori to manage access to and the use of such resources under the terms of the settlements exploits the ambiguous nature of the governmental/proprietary distinction— such ambiguity as has itself been encouraged by the programme of privatisation.

I am far from certain whether these doctrines as formerly stated will properly serve modern needs. I wish merely to raise the prospect that hybrid categories of property may be useful in thinking about regulation and accountability given the prevailing the techniques of governance. Down-sized governments, deregulation, and use of eighteenth century techniques to govern, shift the focus for public lawyers from the *ultra vires* doctrine and traditional command and control techniques for expressing sovereign will to the nature of property regimes and their uses in pursuing public policy. Public lawyers like myself have much to learn from others in this regard—as the chapters which follow will demonstrate.

---

[44] See further, M. Taggart, "Public Utilities and Public Law" in P. Joseph, *Essays on the Constitution* (Wellington, Brookers, 1995); P Craig, "Constitutions Property and Regulation", [1998] *PL* 538, and Chapter 2 below by Gray and Gray.

[45] See Chapters 10 and 11 below by John Dawson and Alex Frame respectively. Jeremy Waldron (Chapter 8) and Maurice Goldsmith (Chapter 90are more concerned with questions which arise, for example, in relation to the disposal of 99- year renewable leases held by private owners from Maori, over high country sheep farms.

2

Private Property and Public Propriety

KEVIN GRAY AND SUSAN FRANCIS GRAY[1]

The shifting relationship between the domains of the public and private has posed, for lawyers and social philosophers, one of the enduring themes of inquiry of the late twentieth century. In a heavily formative contribution to this dialogue, Stanley Benn and Gerald Gaus observed during the 1980s that "despite its best efforts", even "the liberal world view cannot always sustain a consistent and clean cut between what is public and what is private".[2] Instead Benn and Gaus were to advocate a continuum-based understanding of the public/private divide, adopting the general position that a starkly dichotomous view of the public/private distinction is nowadays increasingly impossible to sustain.

The present chapter seeks to explore—somewhat unusually within the area of property relationships—the perception that notions of "public" and "private" operate, not dichotomously, but continuously across a spectrum in which adjacent connotations shade easily into one another. Such a suggestion should, in fact, perturb our public lawyers rather less markedly than our private lawyers. For it is the public lawyer who has had to grapple, in recent years, with the steady extension of judicial review of administrative action to cover the decision-making functions of bodies which can only tenuously be described as public in origin.[3] In this context the intricately graded nature of public/private terrain is already well recognised. It is, however, the private lawyer (immersed in the fields of contract, commerce and property) who is inevitably more puzzled by the threatened fragmentation of the public/private distinction. For many private lawyers it remains heretical to suppose that "publicness" and "privateness" are separated, not by a conceptual chasm of large political significance, but by incremental stages which imperfectly conceal the fluid or interpenetrating nature of these long cherished legal categories. But then, again, it is always salutary to remember that yesterday's unthinkable thought quite often becomes the orthodoxy of tomorrow.

---

[1] Thanks for advice, assistance and critical comment are owed to many, including Tim Bonyhady, Kurt Iveson, Janet McLean, Patrick Troy, Andrew von Hirsch, David Wills and Peter Zawada.

[2] "The Public and the Private: Concepts and Action" in S. Benn and G. Gaus (eds), *Public and Private in Social Life* (London and Canberra, Croom Helm), 1983, p. 25.

[3] See e.g., R v. *Panel on Take-overs and Mergers, ex parte Datafin plc* [1987] QB 815.

I. PROPERTY THEORY

For years both lawyers and lay persons have shared one lazy, but rather wide-spread, belief—that there exists a unitary concept of property, unqualified in scope and ungradable in intensity. And, if we thought about the concept at all, we have been prone to regard this undifferentiated notion of property as capable of existence in both a *public* and a *private* form.

One unwitting source of much of the mythology about property may have been William Blackstone, who argued that the "right of property" comprised: [4]

> "that sole or despotic dominion which one man claims and exercises over the external things of the world, in total exclusion of the right of any other individual in the universe".

Writing in the mid-eighteenth century, Blackstone described the common law concept of property as essentially assertive, oppositional and exclusory. Property was a solid, reassuringly three-dimensional concept, resonating with its own unmistakable message for the world at large: property seemed to be absolute, unequivocal and quite possibly cosmic in its implications.

Modern property theory has long disavowed such naive accounts of the human or socially constructed phenomenon of property. Most property theorists nowadays accept the idea that "property" is not a thing or resource, but rather a power relationship.[5] As Justice Lionel Murphy once said, "property is not the land or thing, but is *in* the land or thing".[6] The term "property" is simply an abbreviated reference to a quantum of socially permissible power exercised in respect of socially valued resources. Furthermore, it is beginning to be agreed that the power relationship implicit in "property" is not *absolute* but *relative*: there may well be *gradations* of "property" in a resource; and the amount of "property" which various persons may be accorded simultaneously in the same resource can be calibrated from a maximum value to a minimum value. Far from being a monolithic notion of standard content and invariable intensity, "property" has come to be viewed as having an almost infinitely divisible and commensurable quality.[7]

Deeper reflection throws up one further embarrassment which is much overlooked even in expert legal discourse. It is, in fact, almost impossible to attribute much meaning to the supposed distinction between *private* and *public* property, at least so long as "property" is conceived to be a thing or resource. It is extraordinarily difficult to identify any genuine instances of "public property", in the sense of resources collectively owned by the citizenry in their capacity as

---

[4] See W. Blackstone, *Commentaries on the Laws of England* (Chicago, University of Chicago Press, facsimile edn. 1979) II, p. 2.

[5] See K. J. Gray, "Property in Thin Air", (1991) 50 *Cambridge LJ* 252, 294.

[6] *Dorman* v. *Rodgers* (1982) 148 CLR 365, 372.

[7] K. J. Gray and S. F. Gray, "The Idea of Property in Land" in S. Bright and J. Dewar (eds), *Land Law: Themes and Perspectives* (Oxford, Oxford University Press, 1998), pp. 15–16.

citizens.[8] In the strict common law tradition even government-owned property is regarded, technically, as still subject to "private ownership". Thus when in 1991, in *The Queen* v. *Committee for the Commonwealth of Canada*,[9] the Supreme Court of Canada was called to rule upon public access to a government-owned airport terminal concourse, Justice La Forest was driven to agree that the government's proprietary rights were in no way different from those of a private owner.[10] Some of the embarrassment is, of course, relieved by the recognition that "property" is not, in any true sense, a thing or resource as such but rather a socially endorsed *power-relationship* in respect of things and resources. This reinterpretation of property as a species of power seems at first to render it easier to distinguish between public and private property—until one bears in mind another of the points made by Justice Murphy. As Murphy was wont to say, "[t]he distinction between public power and private power is not clear-cut and one may shade into the other".[11]

Thus "property" in any given resource is also, in several important respects, a "spectrum" concept. The "property" accorded to any particular person in respect of any particular resource is identifiable as a point located across a spectrum of differing intensities of socially approved user control. And the allocation to various actors of differing quantums of "property" in the same resource depends ultimately, yet fundamentally, upon collective perceptions of the social permissibility or public merit attributable to various kinds of competing user of the resource in question. In this way a deep subtext of "propriety" has always pervaded the social and legal definition of "property".[12] Indeed the language of "property" may have much more in common with "propriety" than with entitlement; and the notion of a "property right" may have more to do with perceptions of "rightness" than with any concept of enforceable exclusory title.

The trouble is that modern case law has not uniformly incorporated or internalised this understanding of the deep structure of property. The common law still tends to articulate the notion of property in terms of raw exclusory power.[13]

---

[8] So-called public highways and waterways may provide a closer approximation to "public property", although even here the classification is imperfect. In relation to such resources, see the suggestion that the rights of the public are generally unqualified and absolute. As Lord Wilberforce indicated in *Wills' Trustees* v. *Cairngorm Canoeing and Sailing School Ltd.* 1976 SLT 162, 191, "once a public right of passage is established, there is no warrant for making any distinction, or even for making any enquiry, as to the purpose for which it is exercised. One cannot stop . . . a pedestrian on a highway, and ask him what is the nature of his use."

[9] (1991) 77 DLR (4th) 385.

[10] Ibid., at 402*e*.

[11] *Gerhardy* v. *Brown* (1985) 159 CLR 70, 107.

[12] See K. J. Gray, "Equitable Property", (1994) 47(2) *Current Legal Problems* 157, 183, 207–208.

[13] See Lord Camden CJ's classic statement that "[b]y the laws of England every invasion of land, be it ever so minute, is a trespass. No man can set his foot upon my ground without my licence" (*Entick* v. *Carrington* (1765) 19 Howell's State Trials 1029, 1066, 2 Wils KB 275, 291, 95 ER 807, 817). Even today "[t]he right to exclude strangers is an ordinary incident of ownership of land" (Deane J. in *Gerhardy* v. *Brown* (1985) 159 CLR 70, 150). The exclusionary prerogative of the landowner is widely believed to derive from a "fundamental element of the property right" (Justice Rehnquist in *Kaiser Aetna* v. *United States* 444 US 164, 179–180, 62 L Ed 2d 332, 346 (1979)). See also Justice Marshall in *Loretto* v. *Teleprompter Manhattan CATV Corp.* 458 US 419, 435, 73 L Ed

According to this absolutist theory, the landowner enjoys an unqualified prerogative to determine—no matter how arbitrarily, selectively or capriciously—who may have access, and on what terms, to "his" or "her" land.[14] As a general principle, the landowner is possessed of uncontrolled discretion to exclude any person from trespassing on private property.[15] Under a nineteenth century English doctrine, often attributed to *Wood* v. *Leadbitter*,[16] permissions to enter land are acknowledged to be revocable at the will of the landowner without any prior notice,[17] without any requirement of objectively reasonable cause[18] and without any obligation to proffer a rationally communicable explanation, either before or after, for any particular act of exclusion.[19] In the absence of some extraordinary plea of necessity[20] or some other overriding constraint imposed by statute or common law,[21] the landowner simply enjoys an unchallengeable discretion to withhold or withdraw permission to enter.[22]

An ancient territorial imperative accordingly receives the supportive sanction of the civil law. Unconsented intrusion into, or presence upon, another's land is generally actionable as trespass, with consequences which range from the award of money damages to the granting of injunctive relief (and the possible imprisonment of the trespasser for contemptuous breach of the terms of the latter). For the most part, the common law engages in no subtle gradation of the exclusory powers inherent in ownership: the rule of peremptory exclusion makes no distinction between the species of property to which it may relate. In its strict conventional form the common law rule applies indifferently to domestic dwellings,

---

2d 868, 882 (1982); *Coco* v. *The Queen* (1994) 179 CLR 427, 438; *R* v. *Somerset County Council, ex parte Fewings* [1995] 1 WLR 1037, 1050H–1051B; *Newbury D C* v. *Russell* (1997) 95 LGR 705, 713; *Jacque* v. *Steenberg Homes Inc.* 563 NW2d 154, 159–160 (Wis 1997).

[14] See e.g., Justice Ritchie in *Colet* v. *The Queen* (1981) 119 DLR (3d) 521, 526.

[15] K. J. Gray, *Elements of Land Law*, 2nd edn. (London, Butterworths, 1993), pp. 893-899.

[16] (1845) 13 M & W 838, 844-845, 153 ER 351, 354. For a more detailed description of the symbolic significance of this decision, see K. J. Gray, "The Ambivalence of Property" in G. Prins (ed.), *Threats Without Enemies* (London, Earthscan Publications, 1993), pp. 155–156.

[17] *Lambert* v. *Roberts* [1981] 2 All ER 15, 19d. Rules of natural justice are traditionally inapplicable to the selective grant of access to privately-held land (see *Heatley* v. *Tasmanian Racing and Gaming Commission* (1977) 137 CLR 487, 511; *Russo* v. *Ontario Jockey Club* (1988) 46 DLR (4th) 359, 362).

[18] See e.g., *Austin* v. *Rescon Construction (1984) Ltd.* (1989) 57 DLR (4th) 591, 593; *Russo* v. *Ontario Jockey Club* (1988) 46 DLR (4th) 359, 364; *Plenty* v. *Dillon* (1991) 171 CLR 635, 655; *Jacque* v. *Steenberg Homes Inc.* 563 NW2d 154, 159–160 (1997).

[19] See *Russo* v. *Ontario Jockey Club* (1988) 46 DLR (4th) 359, 361.

[20] See K. J. Gray and S. F. Gray, "Civil Rights, Civil Wrongs and Quasi-Public Space", (1999) EHRLR 46, 53–4.

[21] In most modern jurisdictions, of course, the power to control access is subject to legislation prohibiting discrimination on grounds of race or gender. Certain other limitations—irrelevant for present purposes—may now be imposed by common law doctrines of contract and estoppel (see *Elements of Land Law*, above n. 15, at pp. 312–368, 909–914).

[22] See *Madden* v. *Queens County Jockey Club Inc.* 72 NE 2d 697, 698 (1947) ("The question posed . . . is whether the operator of a race track can, without reason or sufficient excuse, exclude a person from attending its races. In our opinion he can; he has the power to admit as spectators only those whom he may select, and to exclude others solely of his own volition, as long as the exclusion is not founded on race, creed, color or national origin").

crowded urban spaces and vast tracts of Australian outback. Nor, in general, has the common law troubled to differentiate, in terms of the exclusory power, between various kinds of landowner, whether private, corporate or governmental. The prerogative of property is, in its way, both total and totalitarian.

II. IDEOLOGICAL CROSS-CURRENTS

It is a central tenet of the present chapter that such property conceptualism, whilst it may have made sense in the social and political circumstances of a bygone era, no longer wholly accords with the reality of modern conditions. The ideology of property as uncontrolled exclusory power is nowadays just as untenable as is the dichotomous distinction between the domains of the private and the public.[23] Both conceptual structures nowadays threaten fundamental values of community and democracy. Both imperil important freedoms of expression, association and movement. Both place in hazard those critical, but fragile, social values which are summed up in irreducible notions of fairness and respect for human dignity.

The present chapter is thus directed, initially, towards an examination of the viability of property as raw exclusory power, for this characterisation of property lies at the heart of an intensely significant contemporary debate which reaches to the root of our social arrangements for co-operative living. It may not be going too far to suggest that the theme of exclusion will bulk large in the social history of the next 25 or 30 years; that fairly huge outcomes will turn on whether we attribute continued vitality to the unqualified exclusory function of "property" or choose instead to fashion our property thinking to accord with more inclusive, more integrative visions of social relationship. We may be facing a fork in the road ahead—and we must take one direction or the other. Are we to reinforce a steadily growing culture of exclusion or should we, instead, take steps to generate a rather different climate of community? The "exclusion question" mirrors—indeed epitomises—one of the more profound problems of social philosophy with which we have to engage during the foreseeable future.

Nor should it surprise us that debate in this area cuts incisively into our ideologies of property, into personal perceptions of wealth, autonomy and the purpose of social relationships. Against a backdrop of deepening disenchantment with government, the "exclusion question" throws a sharp focus upon an increasingly fierce confrontation between the social ethics of self-reliance or self-interest and a competing philosophy of co-operative or communitarian value. At stake are rival perceptions of the political good—of the balance to be maintained between individual and community interests. As Tim Bonyhady once put it, in a passage now widely cited across the common law world,

---

[23] See e.g., *Bock* v. *Westminster Mall Co* 819 P 2d 55, 60 (Colo 1991) for a refutation of the "simplistic division of the universe into public and private spheres".

"property may be better understood, both historically and legally, as the result of a balance struck between competing individual and collective goals, the private and the public interest".[24] In striking this balance, we are each, in our respective jurisdictions, beginning to reach the point where we must make some kind of significant election between the self-regarding entrenchment of individual advantage and the promotion of rather different life patterns of "connectedness"[25] which consciously strive for the maintenance of some degree of social cohesion and mutual regard.

And the choice is, of course, made even more complex by the fact that the recent past has exposed many of us to heavily formative, if sometimes subliminal, ideological motivations which now cut across each other in glorious confusion. In roughly chronological order, the post-war period has witnessed a quite extraordinary movement towards the legal curtailment of unaccountable public power, the arrival of unprecedented levels of general consumer affluence and, now, the emergence of the deregulatory state—all of which developments exert strong influences upon the "exclusion question".

The curtailment of unaccountable public power

The first development—the curtailment of unaccountable public power—is, of course, symbolised in the acknowledgement throughout most common law countries of a remarkable regime of judicial review of administrative action. Over the past three decades this jurisdiction has eloquently underscored, within an integrative and egalitarian post-war context, our sharply lowered levels of tolerance for any brute exercise of unreasoned public power—our collective distaste for any abuse of right in derogation of the legitimate expectations of the relatively disempowered. Above all, the advent of judicial review has embedded in the collective mind-set an expectation of enhanced standards of rationality across wide ranges of decision-making—the subjugation of official authority to an inner morality of deliberative due process.[26] In the public domain even low

---

[24] T. Bonyhady, "Property Rights" in T. Bonyhady (ed.), *Environmental Protection and Legal Change* (Sydney, Federation Press, 1992), p. 44.

[25] See E. T. Freyfogle, "Context and Accommodation in Modern Property Law", (1988–1989) 41 *Stan L Rev* 1529, 1530 et seq.

[26] A legitimate expectation of reasoned communication—as distinct from a mere liability to be acted upon—increasingly provides a core element in modern prescriptions for fair treatment of one's fellow citizens as autonomous moral agents. This notion, which in more recent times featured heavily in the writings of Lon Fuller (see L. Fuller, *The Morality of Law* (New Haven, Yale University Press, 1964), pp. 162–163, 186) carries a resonance of an earlier Kantian or dignitarian view of the moral significance of the individual. Thus, it is argued, "rights to interchange" are intrinsic to a proper recognition of a person's humanity just as the interposition of explanatory procedures conduces ultimately to the fairness of all decisional processes involving an individual's welfare or liberty (see e.g., E. L. Pincoffs, "Due Process, Fraternity, and a Kantian Injunction" in J. R. Pennock and J. W. Chapman (eds), *Due Process Nomos XVIII* (New York, New York University Press, 1977), p. 172; L. Tribe, *American Constitutional Law*, 2nd edn. (New York, Foundation Press, 1988), p. 666; *Feiner v. New York*, 340 US 315, 327, 95 L Ed 295, 304 (1951); K. J. Gray and S. F. Gray, above n. 20, at 59–60).

concentrations of power can no longer be divorced from a pervasive recognition of accompanying responsibility.

The advent of consumer affluence

The second development—the arrival of an era of consumer affluence—has conferred upon large sections of the population a hitherto unknown freedom to accumulate wealth, to indulge a range of personal preferences in matters of lifestyle, and to construct highly individualist visions of the good life. But, ironically, the affluent society has also mobilised a different sort of power, which previously had little meaning when the exigencies of economic survival substantially precluded the possibility of consumer selection and material accumulation. For the ordinary individual citizen exclusory strategies have become, for the first time, a viable general response to the challenge of social interaction: most people now own something worth excluding others from. The new affluence has thus brought not only the power to control one's immediate environment through the active exercise of choice, but also the power—in response to a very basic human instinct—to exclude others from access to the hard won fruits of individualist endeavour. In this private arena we now find power unaccompanied by any more broadly related decisional responsibility, for here power is associated only with the priority automatically accorded to the protection and exclusive enjoyment of self-determined individual preferences.

The privatisation of social, economic, and therapeutic functions

Thirdly, and most recently, what we call in England the Thatcherite revolution has seen a massive transfer to the privatised sector of social, economic and therapeutic functions previously performed by agencies of the state.[27] And, again, this development has exerted another huge effect upon the balance of power, reallocating significant control over access to certain resources, benefits and facilities in the direction of private actors whose primary concern is not so much the promotion of a welfare or public service ideal but rather the generation of a corporate profit. But if the consumer revolution did nothing to inspire social solidarity, this latest shift of power has gone far towards eroding what little communitarian sentiment existed amongst us. Only 15 years ago Michael Ignatieff was able to observe the social worker, the nurse, the volunteer tending to the needs of the less privileged—as he said, "in my name"—drawing the conclusion that: [28]

---

[27] See e.g., C. Bolick, "Thatcher's Revolution: Deregulation and Political Transformation", (1995) 12 *Yale J on Reg* 527.

[28] M. Ignatieff, *The Needs of Strangers* (London, Chatto & Windus, 1984) p. 10.

"[i]t is this solidarity among strangers, this transformation . . . of needs into rights and rights into care that gives us whatever fragile basis we have for saying that we live in a moral community".

Shortly afterwards, however, Thatcher was to declare famously that there was "no such thing as society"[29]—and she may turn out to have been more correct than even she thought. With the advent of the deregulatory state we find that essential social and economic functions have now become substantially uncoupled from broader notions of public responsibility. Decisional responsibility in the exercise of deregulated power is owed only impersonally to the corporate entity of the privatised agency or utility.

III.   THE QUASI-PUBLIC DIMENSION OF PROPERTY

It is largely against the background of such developments that the present chapter seeks to explore the middle-ground which lies between dichotomous perceptions of property as either "public" or "private". For most of the last 100 years or so the jurisprudence of this middle-ground—the domain of the "quasi-public"—has been strangely neglected, even though it is clear that the "quasi-public" dimension of property was once widely recognised as a highly relevant category in earlier Anglo-American legal thinking.[30] It is, of course, beyond doubt that many of today's property relationships—most notably in respect of the inner sanctum of the family home—are resolutely biased towards the "private" and absolutist end of the proprietary spectrum; and it may even be that certain genuinely "public" instances of property relationship still survive. But in other areas of the law of property the acknowledgement of an analytic category of the "quasi-public" has acquired a new contemporary relevance by offering an escape from the significant dangers which inhere in the gathering culture of social exclusion.[31]

This revival of the jurisprudence of "quasi-public" property owes much to a recognition that the public/private distinction is marked, not by any clean break, but rather by a multitude of finely intercalated distinctions or gradations. Accordingly, it has been argued that, in the field of modern property relationships, there is no unbridgeable gulf between public and private law; that private property is never truly *private*[32] and rarely truly *absolute*.[33] Particularly in view

---

[29] See M. Thatcher, *The Downing Street Years* (London, Harper Collins, 1993), p. 626.

[30] See, above n. 20, at 88–9.

[31] For earlier advocacy of the quasi-public dimension of property analysis, see Gray, above n. 12, at 172–181.

[32] Gray, above n. 5, at 303–304; above n. 12, at 211.

[33] "A man's right in his real property of course is not absolute. It was a maxim of the common law that one should so use his property as not to injure the rights of others . . . [T]he maxim [expresses] the inevitable proposition that rights are relative and there must be an accommodation when they meet. Hence it has long been true that necessity, private or public, may justify entry upon the lands of another" (*State v. Shack* 277 A2d 369, 373 (1971)). See also Justice Black in *Marsh v. Alabama* 326 US 501, 506, 90 L Ed 265, 268 (1946).

of the social and legal primacy now accorded to various claims of civil liberty or human right,[34] it has become increasingly apparent that the quantum of an owner's "property" in any resource is intrinsically curtailed by parameters of a broadly moral or social character.[35] On this view the limits of property comprise simply "the interfaces between accepted and unaccepted social claims."[36] "Property" in a hatchet has never, for example, implied any right to bury the hatchet in a neighbour's head: indeed property rights and personal rights have always coalesced in a large degree.[37] Considerations of public propriety serve constantly, if normally silently, to define or qualify the prerogatives of private property. In this sense, it can be rightly claimed that all property has a public law character and that the entire fabric of our public social order is crucially subtended by the *restrictiveness*, rather than the *amplitude*, of the supposedly private regime of property.

Of course, the strengthening perception that property is a relative phenomenon, moulded by collective visions of the social good, poses an inevitable threat to the viability of the common law model of property as raw, untrammelled, individually exercised exclusory power. Any absolute claim of decisional control over property is destined to violate a range of those more highly-rated human interests and values which ultimately underpin our recent understanding of the institution of social democracy. Foremost amongst these important, but vulnerable, social goals are vital freedoms of association and assembly, movement and expression. Moreover, given that public decision-making is nowadays exposed to increasingly strict scrutiny, it begins to appear strangely inconsistent that similar principles of at least procedural propriety have not more markedly infiltrated certain reaches of the private law of property. Indeed it seems rather odd that public power should be increasingly subjected to restraint, whilst private power—supremely evidenced in the exercise of rights of property—substantially escapes analogous social control.[38]

The foregoing observations about the rejuvenation of quasi-public property jurisprudence may now be tested within three different, perhaps unlikely, contexts. Each context concerns some ever more common mechanism of social exclusion. Each of these exclusory mechanisms brings into collision countervailing territorial and social instincts. Each throws into opposition deep desires

---

[34] Note, for instance, the recent enactment in England of the Human Rights Act 1998.

[35] "It has always been one of the fundamental features of a civilised society that exclusory claims of property stop where the infringement of more basic human freedoms begins . . . The law of property has always said much more than is commonly supposed about the subject of human rights" (Gray, above n. 12, at 211). As the Supreme Court of New Jersey observed in *State* v. *Shack*, 277 A2d 369, 372 (1971), "[p]roperty rights serve human values. They are recognised to that end, and are limited by it".

[36] Justice Murphy in *Dorman* v. *Rodgers* (1982) 148 CLR 365, 372.

[37] "[T]he dichotomy between personal liberties and property rights is a false one" (Justice Stewart in *Lynch* v. *Household Finance Corp.* 405 US 538, 552, 31 L Ed 2d 424, 434–435 (1972)).

[38] K. J. Gray, above n. 12, at 211–212. See also H. Woolf, "Public Law—Private Law: Why the Divide?", (1986) *PL* 220, 238; G. Borrie, "The Regulation of Public and Private Power", (1989) *PL* 552, 561–564.

for exclusive control over a defined patch of territory and also for harmonised co-existence in some form of interactive, interdependent human society.

The shopping mall or civic commercial centre

Within the Anglo-American world, part of the debate over the socially accept-able parameters of private property has come to focus, curiously, upon the large shopping malls or civic commercial centres which are so prevalent a feature of our modern urban lifestyle. Such premises are commonly the subject of private ownership vested in large corporate concerns, yet the apparent liberality of their inclusive invitation to the general public renders it extremely questionable whether the exercise of supposed rights of ownership in this context is properly classifiable as occurring within a purely "private" zone. The private owner of the mall is, often, a property development corporation financed by generous local government subsidy and by investment capital drawn from countless citi-zens' pension and insurance funds. Does this kind of "private" owner really enjoy an unqualified exclusory prerogative in respect of access to the mall precincts? The precise scope of the power to exclude unwanted strangers from the common areas of such contemporary marketplaces has, accordingly, become a significant and symbolic test of the limits of private ownership; and virtually every major jurisdiction throughout the Anglo-American world has now had experience of fiercely contested mall access litigation.[39] Particularly where unrestricted access provides a gateway for leafletting, solicitation and other forms of democratic consultation, the issue of mall access has come to impinge upon the highly sensitive freedom to interact and communicate with a self-selected audience of one's peers. Quite apart from highlighting questions of expressive opportunity, the mall access problem also places an increasingly direct scrutiny upon the legitimacy of the exclusion of those whose presence is somehow deemed inimical to the commercial process.[40]

Albeit privately owned, the modern shopping centre has, of course, a pro-foundly public dimension. It has rightly been said that "access by the public is the very reason for its existence"[41]—and not merely for the purpose of con-

---

[39] See, most notably, *Harrison* v. *Carswell* (1975) 62 DLR (3d) 68 (Supreme Court of Canada); *PruneYard Shopping Center* v. *Robins* 447 US 74, 64 L Ed 2d 741 (1980) (US Supreme Court); *CIN Properties Ltd* v. *Rawlins* [1995] 2 EGLR 130 (English Court of Appeal).

[40] The current preoccupation with the shopping mall issue coincides with a spate of litigation in the USA and elsewhere whose scarcely spoken objective is to "sweep [the city's] commercial zones clear of homeless people and other social pariahs" (Pregerson CJ (dissenting) in *Roulette* v. *City of Seattle* 78 F3d 1425, 1435 (1996)). For evidence of strong concerns to evict the indigent peremptorily from such locations as public libraries, public parks, railway stations and city sidewalks, see e.g., *Kreimer* v. *Bureau of Police for Town of Morristown* 958 F2d 1242 (3rd Cir 1992); *Pottinger* v. *City of Miami* 810 F Supp 1551 (SD Fla 1992); *Streetwatch* v. *National Railroad Passenger Corp.* 875 F Supp 1055 (SDNY 1995).

[41] *Schwartz-Torrance Investment Corp.* v. *Bakery and Confectionery Workers' Union, Local No 31* 394 P2d 921, 924 (Supreme Court of California, 1964), citing *Lombard* v. *United States* 373 US 267, 10 L Ed 2d 338 (1963).

sumer purchase.[42] The comfortable layout of the shopping mall, with its extensive provision of seating, fountains, open-plan cafes, entertainments and exhibitions, affords much of the aspect of a socially valuable, cultural or artistic meeting-place.[43] Nowadays such complexes frequently incorporate the local library, a post office or bank and various local government-run public information outlets. The location effectively provides the equivalent, in an enclosed format, of a city square or public park,[44] civic venues which, in the common law tradition, have long been viewed as affected by some public trust guaranteeing free access for all.[45] Indeed, the civic function of the shopping mall, in affording a potential venue for expressive activity, has frequently prompted American courts to assert that there is a link between the protection of reasonable shopping mall access and the "interest of a free society in the highly placed value of open markets for ideas".[46]

It is equally often the case that the modern mall or civic commercial centre provides a place of solace for the disadvantaged, the over-burdened, the elderly and the oppressed of society. The open areas of these complexes may well embody what Frank Michelman has termed a "civic common", that is, "a site that not only accommodates cerebral exchanges of ideas but, at the same time, generates a supportive good that we may call civic sociability, an aspect of what others have recently been calling 'social capital'.[47] It is not irrelevant that in England, for instance, shopping malls nowadays serve as a common meeting-place for the unemployed, the depressed and the discouraged. In recent times the importance of this function of the average mall has been intensified by the widespread closure of government-funded medical and therapeutic institutions and their replacement by largely ineffective policies of "care in the community". Ironically, there is a sense in which Thatcher's "care in the community" strategy can be made to work only if down-town shopping malls are caused to remain open to all-comers as a haven or retreat in times of loneliness or trouble. In the

---

[42] There is substantial evidence that, in late twentieth century culture, shopping has itself become a recreational activity—"the new American pastime" (*Wilhoite* v. *Melvin Simon & Associates Inc.* 640 NE2d 382, 385 (1994)). See W. S. Kowinski, *The Malling of America* (New York, William Morrow, 1985); J. D. Lord, "The Malling of the American Landscape", in J. A. Dawson and J. D. Lord (eds), *Shopping Centre Development: Policies and Prospects* (London, Croom Helm, 1985), p. 209; M. Crawford, "The World in a Shopping Mall" in M. Sorkin (ed.), *Variations on a Theme Park: The New American City and the End of Public Space* (New York, Hill & Wang, 1992), p. 8.

[43] See e.g., *Shad Alliance* v. *Smith Haven Mall* 484 NYS 2d 849, 851, 859 (AD 2 Dept 1985); *City of Jamestown* v. *Beneda* 477 NW2d 830, 838 (ND 1991).

[44] *City of Jamestown* v. *Beneda*, above n. 43, at 837–838.

[45] See e.g., Justice Roberts in *Hague* v. *Committee for Industrial Organization* 307 US 496, 515, 83 L Ed 1423, 1436 (1939).

[46] *City of Jamestown* v. *Beneda* 477 NW2d 830, 835 (1991), citing *International Society for Krishna Consciousness* v. *Schrader* 461 F Supp 714, 718 (1978). See also *Alderwood Associates* v. *Washington Environmental Council* 635 P2d 108, 117 (1981) (Supreme Court of Washington); *Bock* v. *Westminster Mall Co* 819 P2d 55, 62 (Colo 1991).

[47] F. Michelman, "The Common Law Baseline and Restitution for the Lost Commons: A Reply to Professor Epstein", (1997) 64 *U Chi L Rev* 57, 61. "The cathedrals of private commerce have indeed evolved into civic and social fora of large public significance" (K. J. Gray and S. F. Gray, above n. 20, at 56).

England which lies beyond the affluent South-East, the population of the typical shopping mall is further swelled by the presence of a small army of low-income teenage mothers, truanting schoolchildren and disoriented youths, all ill-served by failing systems of nursery care, public education and employment training.

The *dramatis personae* of the shopping mall or civic commercial centre is now virtually complete. But does the "private" owner of such premises retain the traditionally unqualified common law privilege to exclude or eject strangers arbitrarily, without reason assigned, from the common parts of the commercial area? Are we still dealing here with a purely private power unconstrained by requirements of rationality or natural justice? Does, say, the unproven or subjectively perceived threat of crime or other disturbance override the need for objectively rational justification of peremptory ouster?[48] Is it simply the case that a property owner may extrude individuals quite selectively (merely because they look like trouble) or even entirely capriciously (without any showing of reasons good or bad)?

The response to such questions suddenly touches upon a number of fundamental issues relating to the social and political ecology of modern urban space. Not only does the debate highlight the difficulties of reconciling lifestyles of compulsory leisure with the pressing demands of public safety and civil liberty.[49] It throws a fresh perspective on what some have termed a "new feudalism [where] huge tracts of property and associated public places are controlled—and policed—by private corporations".[50] At stake here is the delineation of significant areas of regulatory authority. The development of "mass private property"[51] has meant that much public social life is now conducted on

[48] The exigency of situational crime prevention in places of public resort is sometimes believed to provide strong endorsement of the traditional common law trespass rule. It has been suggested that intensive access control, entry screening and proactive surveillance and management often afford key techniques of situational prevention, even though such exclusion strategies effectively target merely those who fit certain predetermined risk profiles (see e.g., C. D. Shearing and P. C. Stenning, "Private Security: Implications for Social Control", (1982–1983) 30 *Social Problems* 493, 503–504; M. Crawford, "The World in a Shopping Mall", above n. 42, at 27; R. V. Clarke, "Situational Crime Prevention" in M. Tonry and D. P. Farrington (eds), *Building a Safer Society: Crime and Justice: A Review of Research* (Chicago, University of Chicago Press, 1995), p. 91; R. White, "No-Go in the Fortress City: Young People, Inequality and Space", (1996) 14(1) *Urban Policy and Research* 37, 42).

[49] On the attractiveness of the modern shopping mall or centre to young people who lack neighbourhood leisure facilities and the money to purchase alternative forms of entertainment, see R. Shields, "The Individual, Consumption Cultures and the Fate of Community" in R. Shields (ed.), *Lifestyle Shopping: The Subject of Consumption* (London, Routledge, 1992), p. 110; R. White, "Street Life: Police Practices and Youth Behaviour" in R. White and C. Alder (eds), *The Police and Young People in Australia* (Cambridge University Press, 1994), p. 111.

[50] C. D. Shearing and P. C. Stenning, above n. 48, at 503. See also L. Sandercock, "From Main Street to Fortress: The Future of Malls as Public Spaces—OR—'Shut Up and Shop'", (1997) 9 *Just Policy* 27, 28.

[51] The term "mass private property" has been loosely used by criminologists and other social scientists to characterise "huge, privately owned facilities . . . [including] shopping centers . . . enormous residential estates . . . equally large office, recreational, industrial, and manufacturing complexes, and many university campuses" (Shearing and Stenning, above n. 48, at 496.)

premises which are privately owned. Accordingly, in such locations, the *protection of private property* has started to coalesce with the *preservation of public order*, raising important questions about the appropriate balance between public and private strategies of policing and about the effectiveness of the constitutional protection of individual liberties. Within these zones it becomes highly arguable that the privatisation of social space has in fact "relocate[d] the power to define and maintain order . . . from the state to property developers".[52] Indeed, some already see the exercise of stringent corporate control over the domain of the shopping mall as threatening an important element of pedestrian democracy—as symbolising the "decline of urban liberalism" and "the end of what might be called the Olmstedian vision of public space".[53] At the very least, it is painfully clear that the proactive policing of newly privatised urban space intensifies the social exclusion of the marginalised and disadvantaged, with consequent damage to the overall harmony of community relationships.[54]

Consider now the latest English contribution to this branch of jurisprudence. In *CIN Properties Ltd. v. Rawlins*[55] CIN Properties, the owner of a shopping mall which dominates the centre of the market town of Wellingborough, purported to impose a lifetime ban upon any further entry within mall precincts by a named group of locally resident, mostly unemployed youths, of whom the majority were black. This prohibition *sine die* followed a confused history of alleged conflict between the youths and the private security firm which patrolled the mall, although an attempted prosecution of the youths for disorder offences broke down for want of evidence and no charge of misconduct (or other rational ground of eviction) was ever made out against them.[56]

It is not necessary for present purposes to suppose that the young men in question were possessed of either deeply attractive personalities or imperturbable temperaments, but the effect of their exclusion was permanently to cut off their access to the commercial and other facilities contained within the shopping centre and even to preclude their seeking employment in their home town's

---

[52] M. Davis, "Less Mickey Mouse, More Dirty Harry: Property, Policing and the Modern Metropolis", (1994) 5(2) *Polemic* 63, 64. For further influential and critical reference to "what is now a nationwide trend toward the privatization of public property", see Chief Judge Posner in *Chicago Acorn, SEIU Local No 880 v. Metropolitan Pier and Exposition Authority*, 150 F3d 695, 704 (1998).

[53] M. Davis, "Fortress Los Angeles: The Militarization of Urban Space" in M. Sorkin (ed.), above n. 42, at p. 156. (Frederick Law Olmsted was the American architect and landscaper who notably extolled the democratic virtues—"the harmonizing and refining influence"—of shared public space (Davis, ibid., at p.156)). See also K. Iveson, "Putting the Public Back into Public Space", (1998) 16(1) *Urban Policy and Research* 21 .

[54] See R. White, "Young People and the Policing of Community Space", (1993) 26(3) *ANZJ Crim* 207, 216; R. White and A. Sutton, "Crime Prevention, Urban Space and Social Exclusion", (1995) 31(1) *Australian and New Zealand Journal of Sociology* 82, 90.

[55] [1995] 2 EGLR 130. For a more detailed examination of this decision, see Gray and Gray, above n. 20.

[56] There was, predictably, an alleged background of racial abuse by the private security firm and of intimidatory behaviour by the youths.

primary work location.[57] Two weeks after the abortive criminal trial CIN Properties obtained injunctive relief to reinforce the privately imposed ban on entry. The youths became subject to a lifelong civil sanction, entirely disproportional to any possibly perceived threat of harm, which exposed them to the risk of imprisonment for contempt should they ever re-enter an extensively demarcated no-go zone in the middle of their own town.

The stance adopted by CIN Properties seemed to resonate with the feudal possibility that, consistently with common law principle, one private actor might even today, on invoking the threat of indefinite incarceration, exile a group of citizens arbitrarily and permanently from the centre of their home town.[58] Was it really the case that an unchallengeable private exercise of a property power could nowadays restrict public access to a large part of a town centre?[59] Yet, in *CIN Properties Ltd.* v. *Rawlins*,[60] the English Court of Appeal unanimously overturned a county court ruling that members of the public, subject only to a requirement of "reasonable conduct", had an "equitable" or "irrevocable" right to enter and use the shopping mall during its normal opening hours.[61] The Court of Appeal declared CIN Properties to have been perfectly entitled—however arbitrarily—to withdraw the implied invitation enjoyed by the defendant youths (as indeed by all members of the public) to enter the shopping centre. The House of Lords later denied leave to appeal, and the European Commission of Human Rights declined to intervene, not least because the United Kingdom had never ratified the guarantee of liberty of movement contained in Protocol No. 4, Article 2 of the European Convention for the Protection of Human Rights and Fundamental Freedoms.[62]

---

[57] The property owner's denial of access to the shopping centre thus impaired the youths' ability to perform one of the essential preconditions of their receipt of state benefit—that of being available for all forms of paid employment.

[58] For reference to the "internal exile" which Charles Reich once feared might become the fate of the unconventional and the unwaged, see "The Individual Sector", (1990–1991) 100 *Yale LJ* 1465, 1467.

[59] The spectre of the "company town" (see *Marsh* v. *Alabama* 326 US 501, 90 L Ed 265 (1946)) has returned. Many of the New Town Development Corporations—established in England by central government during the 1970s and 1980s in order to stimulate the generation of urban areas—spent the late 1980s and 1990s selling off their assets to private companies. For example, in 1987 Postel Properties Ltd. purchased most of the town centre of Washington, Co Durham, from the Washington Development Corporation. Postel Properties Ltd. has recently banned single-issue campaigners from protesting within the town precincts against the closure of a local playing field site, a move which is currently the subject of a petition to the European Commission of Human Rights (see *Washington First* v. *United Kingdom*, filed 30 October 1998).

[60] [1995] 2 EGLR 130, 134J.

[61] Interim judgment of Mr Recorder Philip Cox QC, 6 January 1994, Birmingham County Court, Transcript, 15.

[62] *Mark Anderson* v. *United Kingdom*, Application No. 33689/96, (Decision as to admissibility dated 27 October 1997) (see [1998] EHRLR 218). The applicants' most realistic opportunity of success rendered unavailable, the Commission proceeded, by a majority, to declare inadmissible the complaint that the applicants had been deprived of freedoms of peaceful assembly and association guaranteed by Article 11. The Commission pointed out cautiously that the Convention case law on Article 11 had not, to date, indicated that freedom of assembly "is intended to guarantee a right to

The approach of the Court of Appeal in *CIN Properties Ltd.* v. *Rawlins* stands in remarkable contrast to that now adopted in other parts of the common law world. Many jurisdictions have come to question whether, in a crowded modern urban environment where recreational, associational and expressional space is increasingly at a premium, an unanalysed, monolithic privilege of arbitrary exclusion is still entirely tenable.[63] It seems somehow legally unattractive that the private owner of a shopping centre should be empowered to exclude someone "simply for wearing a green hat or a paisley tie" or because he or she has "blond hair, or . . . is from Pennsylvania"[64] or is ugly[65] or unsightly?[66] Have we really reached the stage where privatised police power—ever more common in the modern context[67]—is unchallengeable and lies beyond the reach of legal scrutiny?

In recent years, in a movement which has slowly gained momentum across the common law world, courts have begun to demarcate certain kinds of location, including shopping malls and civic commercial centres, as "quasi-public" spaces, to which all citizens must be allowed access on a non-discriminatory basis and from which they can be evicted only for good cause.[68] Unlike, say, the domestic curtilage, such locations, although nominally subject to private ownership, have been so opened up to public use, through general or unrestricted invitation, that they can no longer be regarded as strictly private areas.[69] The

pass and re-pass in public places, or to assemble for purely social purposes anywhere one wishes". The Convention freedom of association was likewise ruled irrelevant on the ground that it comprised a highly purposive right "for individuals to associate 'in order to attain various ends'".

[63] Indeed closer analysis of the history of the Anglo-American trespass rule tends to suggest that this rule is not, and perhaps originally never was, quite so absolutist as has been widely supposed (see Gray and Gray, above n. 20, at 85–9).

[64] *Brooks* v. *Chicago Downs Association Inc.* 791 F2d 512, 514, 518 (1986). See Chief Justice Laskin in *Harrison* v. *Carswell* (1975) 62 DLR (3d) 68, 70 ("an extravagant position").

[65] For disapproving reference to "an 'ugly' rule" of exclusion from a library, see *Kreimer* v. *Bureau of Police for Town of Morristown* 765 F Supp 181, 194 (DNJ 1991).

[66] In May 1997 Miss Eilene Kadden, an overweight American wearing leggings which had been purchased in Harrods of London, claimed to have been thrown out of Harrods for contravention of the store's dress code, an allegation which she later construed as a form of "sizeism" (see *The Times*, 21 May 1997 (p. 1) and 15 December 1997 (p. 5)). She is reportedly suing Harrods, motivated by the belief that it "is appalling [Harrods] feels it can pick and choose its customers".

[67] For an account of the growing concern aroused by private policing, see "Private Police and Personal Privacy: Who's Guarding the Guards?", (1995–1996) 40 *NYL Sch L Rev* 225.

[68] The terminology of "quasi-public" property is now widely and explicitly used by American courts in relation to the large shopping mall or retail outlet (see e.g., *Sutherland* v. *Southcenter Shopping Ctr Inc.* 478 P2d 792, 800 (1970); *State* v. *Marley* 509 P2d 1095, 1104 (1973); *Corn* v. *State* 332 So2d 4, 8 (1976); *People* v. *Wilson* 469 NYS2d 905, 908 (1983); *Shad Alliance* v. *Smith Haven Mall* 462 NYS2d 344, 348 (1983), 484 NYS2d 849, 857 (AD 2 Dept 1985); *Cox Cable San Diego Inc.* v. *Bookspan* 240 Cal Rptr 407, 411 (1987); *Planned Parenthood Shasta-Diablo Inc.* v. *Williams* 16 Cal Rptr 2d 540, 543 (Cal App 1 Dist 1993); *City of Helena* v. *Krautter* 852 P2d 636, 639 (Mont 1993); *State* v. *Woods* 624 So2d 739, 740 (Fla 5th DCA 1993), rev den 634 So2d 629 (Fla 1994); *Rivers* v. *Dillards Dept Store Inc.* 698 So2d 1328, 1332 (Fla App 1 Dist 1997)).

[69] Such perceptions have a far from modern provenance. Three centuries ago Chief Justice Hale pointed out that private property, when "affected with a public interest, . . . ceases to be *juris privati* only" (Hale, *De Portibus Maris*, 1 Harg L Tr 78). Hence emerged a theme, of pervasive significance in Anglo-American jurisprudence, that private property becomes clothed with a public

implied liberality of the outreach to the public has caused the land to lose its purely private quality and become instead "private property having an essential public character".[70] It is acknowledged accordingly that access to such "quasi-public" premises must be governed by an overarching doctrine of reasonableness which gives effect to a new morality of social community. In short, the common law's conventional rule of arbitrary exclusion has started to give way to a rather different rule under which the private owner of quasi-public premises may exclude members of the public only on grounds which are objectively and communicably reasonable.[71]

The genesis of this shift of common law paradigm is often taken to have been Chief Justice Laskin's famous dissent in *Harrison* v. *Carswell*.[72] Here the Chief Justice of Canada voiced incredulity that the common law could have remained "so devoid of reason" as to tolerate the "whimsy" of entirely capricious exclusion from such "quasi-public"[73] locations as the shopping mall.[74] Laskin's dissent certainly opened up a new area of common law debate, highlighting as it did a deep distrust both of the process of purely subjective, unreasoned determination and of the excessive power thereby conferred upon the owners of land. However, in castigating claims of absolute exclusory power in quasi-public places as an "abusive exercise of rights",[75] Laskin merely echoed a view already being expressed in adjacent jurisdictions that such "tremendous power . . . cannot be the law because it is dictatorial in nature and no one can be invested with that sole power".[76]

interest when used in such manner as to make it "of public consequence" and "affect the community at large" (Chief Justice Waite in *Munn* v. *Illinois* 94 US 113, 126, 24 L Ed 77, 84 (1877)). See also *Allnutt* v. *Inglis* (1810) 12 East 527, 542, 104 ER 206, 212; *Mobile* v. *Yuille* (1841) 3 Ala (NS) 140, 36 Am Dec 441, 444.

[70] *R* v. *Layton* (1988) 38 CCC (3d) 550, 568. See also Justice Powell in *Central Hardware Co* v. *National Labor Relations Board* 407 US 539, 547, 33 L Ed 2d 122, 128 (1972); Chief Justice Laskin in *Harrison* v. *Carswell* (1975) 62 DLR (3d) 68, 73. In describing modern shopping malls in *New Jersey Coalition Against War in the Middle East* v. *JMB Realty Corp.* 650 A2d 757, 761, 772–773 (NJ 1994), the late Chief Justice Wilentz affirmed that "We know of no private property that more closely resembles public property . . . The predominant characteristic of the normal use of these properties is its all-inclusiveness . . . The invitation to the public is simple: 'Come here, that's all we ask. We hope you will buy, but you do not have to, and you need not intend to. All we ask is that you come here. You can do whatever you want so long as you do not interfere with other visitors' . . .'".

[71] See e.g., *R* v. *Asatne-Mensah*, 1996 Ont CJ LEXIS 1959 (8 May 1996) ("Land, of a public function and character, presumptively clothes persons with the privilege and licence of attendance. The absolute right of exclusion, retained to the private citizen, . . . is whittled away . . .").

[72] (1975) 62 DLR (3d) 68, 73–74. Justices Spence and Beetz joined in Chief Justice Laskin's dissent.

[73] The headnote in *Harrison* v. *Carswell*, but curiously no other part of the report, uses the terminology of "quasi-public" character in relation to the shopping centre.

[74] "To say in such circumstances that the shopping centre owner may, at his whim, order any member of the public out of the shopping centre on penalty or liability for trespass if he refuses to leave, does not make sense if there is no proper reason in that member's conduct or activity to justify the order to leave" ((1975) 62 DLR (3d) 68, 73).

[75] *Harrison* v. *Carswell* (1975) 62 DLR (3d) 68, 74–75.

[76] *People* v. *Wolf* 312 NYS2d 721, 724 (1970). See also *H-CHH Associates* v. *Citizens for Representative Government* 238 Cal Rptr 841, 852–854 (1987).

The modern elaboration of constitutional principle in the USA has witnessed the emergence of a similarly restrictive view of the right to exclude from premises affected with a public interest. Whilst American courts have not accepted that the Federal Constitution (and particularly its First Amendment protection of the freedoms of religion, speech, press and assembly) mandates any general right of public access to private property,[77] many courts have nevertheless been happy to fashion, often from the more expansive provisions of state constitutions,[78] a generous right of reasonable access to quasi-public locations. These locations have varied from facilities such as community libraries[79] and university campuses,[80] to shopping malls and large retail outlets,[81] camps for migrant farmworkers,[82] and large railway stations.[83]

Even without reference to constitutionally protected civil rights, other American courts have reached similar conclusions simply by declaring that the *common law itself* no longer entitles the owner of quasi-public premises arbitrarily "to exclude anyone at all for any reason".[84] In reverting to a recognition of a "common law right of reasonable access",[85] such courts have emphasised

---

[77] "[T]he First Amendment does not create an absolute right to trespass" (*Armes* v. *City of Philadelphia* 706 F Supp 1156, 1164 (ED Pa 1989)). For the general principle, see *Brown* v. *Louisiana* 383 US 131, 166, 15 L Ed 2d 637, 659 (1966); *Lloyd Corp. Ltd.* v. *Tanner* 407 US 551, 569–570, 33 L Ed 2d 131, 143 (1972); *Hudgens* v. *National Labor Relations Board* 424 US 507, 519–520, 47 L Ed 2d 196, 206–207 (1976); *Frisby* v. *Schultz* 487 US 474, 484–485, 101 L Ed 2d 420, 431–432 (1988). A famous exception relates to the case of the "company town" (*Marsh* v. *Alabama* 326 US 501, 90 L Ed 265 (1946)), where a private owner was deemed to be "performing the full spectrum of municipal powers" and therefore to stand "in the shoes of the State" (see *Lloyd Corp. Ltd.* v. *Tanner* 407 US 551, 569, 33 L Ed 2d 131, 143 (1972)).

[78] See *PruneYard Shopping Center* v. *Robins* 447 US 74, 81, 64 L Ed 2d 741, 752 (1980), affirming *Robins* v. *PruneYard Shopping Center* 592 P2d 341 (1979) (Supreme Court of California).

[79] *Kreimer* v. *Bureau of Police for Town of Morristown* 958 F2d 1242, 1255 (3rd Cir 1992); *Brinkmeier* v. *City of Freeport* 1993 US Dist LEXIS 9255 (2 July 1993).

[80] *State* v. *Schmid* 423 A2d 615 (1980). See also *Commonwealth* v. *Tate* 432 A2d 1382 (Pa 1981).

[81] *Alderwood Associates* v. *Washington Environmental Council* 635 P2d 108 (1981) (Supreme Court of Washington); *Citizens To End Animal Suffering And Exploitation Inc.* v. *Faneuil Hall Marketplace Inc.* 745 F Supp 65 (D Mass 1990); *State* v. *Cargill* 786 P2d 208 (1990); *City of Jamestown* v. *Beneda* 477 NW2d 830 (ND 1991); *Bock* v. *Westminster Mall Co* 819 P2d 55 (Colo 1991); *Lloyd Corp. Ltd.* v. *Whiffen* 849 P2d 446 (Or 1993) (*Whiffen II*); *State* v. *Dameron* 853 P2d 1285 (Or 1993); *State* v. *Woods* 624 So2d 739, (Fla 5th DCA 1993), rev den 634 So2d 629 (Fla 1994); *New Jersey Coalition Against War in the Middle East* v. *JMB Realty Corp.* 650 A2d 757 (NJ 1994); *Fred Meyer Inc.* v. *Casey* 67 F3d 1412 (9th Cir 1995); *Safeway Inc.* v. *Jane Does 1 through 50*, 920 P2d 168 (1996); *Stranahan* v. *Fred Meyer Inc.* 958 P2d 854 (1998).

[82] *State* v. *Shack* 277 A2d 369 (1971); *Freedman* v. *New Jersey State Police* 343 A2d 148 (1975); *Baer* v. *Sorbello* NJ Super AD, 425 A2d 1089 (1981).

[83] *Streetwatch* v. *National Railroad Passenger Corp.* 875 F Supp 1055, 1059–1061 (SDNY 1995).

[84] *Uston* v. *Resorts International Hotel Inc.* 445 A2d 370, 373 (1982) (Supreme Court of New Jersey). See also *Cummins* v. *St Louis Amusement Co.* 147 SW2d 190, 193 (Mo Ct App 1941); *Rockwell* v. *Pennsylvania State Horse Racing Commission* 327 A2d 211, 213–214 (Pa 1974); *Toms* v. *Tiger Lanes Inc.* 313 So2d 852, 854 (La Ct App 1975), cert den 319 So2d 443; *Bonomo* v. *Louisiana Downs Inc.* 337 So2d 553, 558–559 (La Ct App 1976); *Marzocca* v. *Ferrone* 461 A2d 1133, 1137 (NJ 1983).

[85] *Hoagburg* v. *Harrah's Marina Hotel Casino* 585 F Supp 1167, 1173 (1984). In effect, some courts in the USA have simply accepted that the doctrine of *Wood* v. *Leadbitter* above, n. 16, is now merely a curiosity of legal history, having been overtaken by the steady evolution of the common law (see *Uston* v. *Resorts International Hotel Inc.* 445 A2d 370, 374 (NJ 1982); *Marzocca* v. *Ferrone* 453 A2d 228, 232 (NJ Super AD 1982); *Brooks* v. *Chicago Downs Association Inc.* 791 F2d 512, 519 (1986)).

the heightened duty of the landowner "not to act in an arbitrary or discriminatory manner"[86] towards persons who enter premises which, for his own economic reasons, the landowner has opened up for general public access.[87] This duty of reasonableness has particular application in cases where the landowner supplies a service or facility to the public in conditions of "virtual monopoly"[88] or where the landowner, by the open profession of a common or public calling, has effectively estopped himself from making arbitrary derogations from the inclusiveness of his invitation.[89] On these bases American courts have been able to assert the existence of a right of reasonable access to a range of facilities extending from ski resorts[90] and casinos[91] to gasoline service stations[92] and airport,[93] bus[94] and railway terminals.[95]

For its part, the Supreme Court of Canada ruled in 1991 in favour of a right of reasonable public access to an airport terminal concourse, holding that such premises bore the earmarks of a "public arena"[96] and were "in many ways a

[86] *Uston* v. *Resorts International Hotel Inc.* 445 A2d 370, 375 (NJ 1982). "Where an organisation is quasi-public, its power to exclude must be reasonably and lawfully exercised in furtherance of the public welfare related to its public characteristics" (*Matthews* v. *Bay Head Improvement Association*, 471 A2d 355, 366 (NJ 1984)).

[87] The most forthright statement of this principle is still Justice Black's assertion in *Marsh* v. *Alabama* 326 US 501, 506, 90 L Ed 265, 268 (1946), that "[t]he more an owner, for his advantage, opens up his property for use by the public in general, the more do his rights become circumscribed by the statutory and constitutional rights of those who use it". This dictum is now increasingly cited in the shopping mall jurisprudence (see e.g., *Corn* v. *State* 332 So2d 4, 6–8 (1976); *Lloyd Corp. Ltd.* v. *Whiffen* 849 P2d 446, 451 (Or 1993) (*Whiffen II*); and, perhaps most significantly, *Stranahan* v. *Fred Meyer Inc.* 958 P2d 854, 873, 875–876 (1998)).

[88] See Lord Ellenborough CJ in *Allnutt* v. *Inglis* (1810) 12 East 527, 538, 540, 104 ER 206, 211; *Munn* v. *Illinois* 94 US 113, 126, 24 L Ed 77, 84 (1877).

[89] The primary historical instance is that of the common innkeeper who is neither entitled to select his guests nor justified in applying any ground of exclusion or discrimination which is itself unreasonable. The innkeeper must admit all comers, subject to good behaviour, to such accommodation as remains available (see YB 39 H VI fo 18, pl 24 (1460); *White's Case* (1558) 2 Dyer 158b, 73 ER 343, 344; *Calye's Case* (1584) 8 Co Rep 32a, 77 ER 520; *Anon* (1623) 2 Roll Rep 345, 81 ER 842, 843; *Newton* v. *Trigg* (1691) 1 Show 268, 269, 89 ER 566; *Lane* v. *Cotton* (1701) 12 Mod 472, 484, 88 ER 1458, 1464–1465; *R* v. *Ivens* (1835) 7 C & P 213, 219, 173 ER 94, 96–97; *Markham* v. *Brown* (1837) 8 NH 523, 31 Am Dec 209, 210; *Robins & Co* v. *Gray* [1895] 2 QB 501, 503–504; *Lamond* v. *Richard* [1897] 1 QB 541, 547; *Said* v. *Butt* [1920] 3 KB 497, 502; *Bellaney* v. *Reilly* [1945] IR 542, 557–558). For classic and explicit curial recognition of the "quasi public" function of the common innkeeper, see e.g., *Slaughter* v. *Commonwealth* (1856) 54 Va 767, 777; *De Wolf* v. *Ford*, 86 NE 527, 529 (1908).

[90] *Dalury* v. *S-K-I Ltd.* 670 A2d 795, 799–800 (Vt 1995).

[91] *Uston* v. *Resorts International Hotel Inc.* 445 A2d 370, 373–375 (NJ 1982); *Hoagburg* v. *Harrah's Marina Hotel Casino* 585 F Supp 1167, 1173 (1984); *Campione* v. *Adamar of New Jersey Inc.* 643 A2d 42, 52 (NJ Super L 1993); *State* v. *Morse* 647 A2d 495, 497 (NJ Super L 1994).

[92] *Streeter* v. *Brogan* 274 A2d 312, 315–317 (1971).

[93] *Jamison* v. *City of St Louis* 828 F2d 1280, 1283 (8th Cir 1987). See also *International Society for Krishna Consciousness* v. *Schrader* 461 F Supp 714, 718 (1978).

[94] *Wolin* v. *Port of New York Authority* 392 F2d 83, 90 (1968).

[95] *Streetwatch* v. *National Railroad Passenger Corp.* 875 F Supp 1055, 1061–1062 (SDNY 1995). See also *In re Hoffman* 434 P2d 353, 356 (1967); *People* v. *Bright* 526 NYS2d 66, 72 (1988); *People* v. *Pratt* 625 NYS2d 869, 873 (NY City Crim Ct 1995); *Rogers* v. *New York City Transit Authority* 680 NE2d 142, 147–148 (NY 1997).

[96] Justice L'Heureux-Dubé in *The Queen* v. *Committee for the Commonwealth of Canada* (1991) 77 DLR (4th) 385, 426 f. See also *R* v. *Asatne-Mensah*, 1996 Ont CJ LEXIS 1959 (8 May 1996) ("a forum imbued with many characteristics associated with public places").

thoroughfare"[97] or "contemporary crossroads",[98] a "modern equivalent of the streets and by-ways of the past".[99] Such areas, declared Chief Justice Lamer, were held by their owner in a "quasi-fiduciary" capacity[100] and could not therefore be closed off from reasonable public access.[101] As Justice McLachlin explained, the safeguarding of civic rights of access and communication within these areas was integrally linked with the "pursuit of truth, participation in the community and the conditions necessary for individual fulfilment and human flourishing".[102] It was, said Justice McLachlin, only through "the encouragement of a tolerant and welcoming environment which promotes diversity in forms of self-fulfilment and human flourishing" that the Court could recognise "the role of expression in maximising human potential and happiness through intellectual and artistic communication".[103] Similar fulfilment-based arguments could, in fact, be advanced in support of a reasonable access rule in respect of local parks and leisure centres, sporting facilities, community colleges, cinemas and theatres, and may even extend to justify a right of reasonable recreational access to privately held areas of wild country.

Although the development of overriding rights of reasonable access to quasi-public property is far from uniform or complete throughout common law jurisdictions, even sceptical observers have begun to acknowledge the way in which recent thinking "blurs the line between the public and nonpublic forum".[104] Slowly but surely private property is being required to reach some accommodation with a public morality which gives effect to minimum standards of democratic community.[105] Ownership "does not always mean absolute dominion"[106] and, indeed, there is nothing new about the notion that a landowner's "autonomy interest must be accommodated with the interests of the public".[107] As

---

[97] *The Queen* v. *Committee for the Commonwealth of Canada* (1991) 77 DLR (4th) 385, 396*h* per Chief Justice Lamer, Justices Sopinka and Cory concurring.

[98] Ibid., at 430*g* (Justice L'Heureux-Dubé).

[99] Ibid., at 459*g* (Justice McLachlin).

[100] Ibid., at 393*d*.

[101] Ibid., at 393f. (Chief Justice Lamer). See *R* v. *Asatne-Mensah* above n. 96, although here the court confined the principle to the terminal concourse as distinct from its vehicular approaches and roadways. See also *R* v. *Trabulsey* (1995) 97 CCC (3d) 147, 157.

[102] (1991) 77 DLR (4th) 385, 457*d*.

[103] (1991) 77 DLR (4th) 385, 457*h*. It was Lon Fuller who identified as the "central indisputable principle of what may be called substantive natural law" the requirement to "[o]pen up, maintain, and preserve the integrity of the channels of communication by which men convey to one another what they perceive, feel, and desire" (see L. L. Fuller, *The Morality of Law* (New Haven and London, Yale University Press, 1964), p. 185 et seq.).

[104] *Chicago Acorn, SEIU Local No 880* v. *Metropolitan Pier and Exposition Authority* 150 F3d 695, 703 (1998) (Chief Judge Posner).

[105] See, for instance, the way in which the Full Court of the Australian Federal Court has recently upheld "the application of community standards" in determining the scope of a statutory category of "reasonable excuse" for trespass (*Mark* v. *Henshaw* (1998) 155 ALR 118, 120 (invasion of battery hen farm by animal rights protesters)).

[106] *Marsh* v. *Alabama* 326 US 501, 506, 90 L Ed 265, 268 (1946) (Justice Black).

[107] *Hudgens* v. *National Labor Relations Board* 424 US 507, 542, 47 L Ed 2d 196, 220 (1976) (Justice Marshall, citing *Munn* v. *Illinois* 94 US 113, 126, 24 L Ed 77, 84 (1877)). As, for instance,

community mores infiltrate ever deeper into the heartland of private property, it becomes increasingly clear that the decisional prerogatives attached to such property may be more limited than was once supposed. The mere incidence of "naked" proprietary title can no longer control the allocation of basic civic entitlements.[108]

Some indication of an emerging acceptance of the right not to be unreasonably excluded from quasi-public places can be gained from the fact that much of the focus of American commentary has now shifted away from the primary issue of principle towards the secondary issue whether the recognition of quasi-public access rights comprises a "taking" requiring the payment of compensation to the affected property owner.[109] By a process of lateral thought, it is even beginning to be asked whether, if the citizen has an access entitlement to such fora as shopping malls for free speech purposes, similar rights of access may be claimed in support of expressive freedom on privately owned and controlled areas of the electronic media and cyberspace.[110] It is even tempting for some to argue that internet service providers are a modern successor to the common carrier and should be subject to a rule of reasonable access for all.[111]

But let us return, for the moment, to *terra firma*. Some will, of course, see the increasing segregation of the affluent and the indigent in modern cities as both morally offensive and socially dangerous. The process of arbitrary exclusion from "quasi-public" places not only imposes significant limitations on freedom of movement;[112] it controverts the instinctive impulse that "the right to move freely about one's neighborhood or town . . . is indeed 'implicit in the concept

---

the Supreme Court of California indicated in *Robins* v. *PruneYard Shopping Center* 592 P2d 341, 347 (1979), "the public interest in peaceful speech outweighs the desire of property owners for control over their property".

[108]   This tenet lay deep at the heart of the US Supreme Court's ruling in *Marsh* v. *Alabama* 326 US 501, 509, 90 L Ed 265, 270 (1946). For more contemporary reference to this "enduring principle", see *In re Lane*, 79 Cal Rptr 729, 457 P2d 561 (1969); *Allred* v. *Shawley* 284 Cal Rptr 140, 142 (Cal App 4 Dist 1991); *New Jersey Coalition Against War in the Middle East* v. *JMB Realty Corp.* 650 A2d 757, 777 (NJ 1994).

[109]   See e.g., *Stranahan* v. *Fred Meyer Inc.* 958 P2d 854, 863–865 (1998). See also R. Epstein, "Takings, Exclusivity and Speech: The Legacy of PruneYard v. Robins", (1997) 64 *U Chi L Rev* 21. For a denial that any compensable taking has occurred in the present context, see *PruneYard Shopping Center* v. *Robins* 447 US 74, 82–85, 64 L Ed 2d 741, 753–754 (1980); *New Jersey Coalition Against War in the Middle East* v. *JMB Realty Corp.* 650 A2d 757, 779 (NJ 1994); F. Michelman, above n. 47.

[110]   See D. E. Steinglass, "Extending PruneYard: Citizens' Right to Demand Public Access Cable Channels", (1996) 71 *NYU L Rev* 1113; D. J. Goldstone, "A Funny Thing Happened on the Way to the Cyber Forum: Public vs Private in Cyberspace Speech", (1998) 69 *U Colo L Rev* 1, 40 et seq.

[111]   It is not irrelevant that in the USA the early telephone and telegraph companies were classified as common carriers (see e.g., *Munn* v. *Illinois*, above n. 69, *Notes on US Reports*, 27). See, however, *Religious Technology Center* v. *Netcom On-Line Communication Services Inc.* 907 F Supp 1361 (ND Cal 1995); *CompuServe Inc.* v. *Cyber Promotions Inc.* 962 F Supp 1015, 1025 (1997).

[112]   *Pottinger* v. *City of Miami* 810 F Supp 1551, 1580–1581 (SD Fla 1992) ("Like the anti-sleeping ordinances, enforcement of the challenged ordinances against homeless individuals significantly burdens their freedom of movement. It has the effect of preventing homeless people from coming into the City").

of ordered liberty'".[113] Above all, the uncompromising enforcement of trespass law in quasi-public areas may be thought to violate that most fundamental of rights—"the right to be let alone".[114] Yet our next mechanism of social exclusion provides a context in which "the right to be let alone" is asserted most vigorously, not by those who seek entitlement to quasi-public access, but rather by those whose concern it is to exclude the public from access to a very specific kind of territory.

The enclosed or gated residential community

We have already strayed into the second of the zones of exclusion which form the subject matter of this chapter. Many of the themes adumbrated in relation to shopping mall access are likewise relevant to the enclosed or gated residential community, although it is probably fair to say that curial analysis of this more recent exclusionary phenomenon still remains at a less advanced stage of development. It will suffice here merely to flag some of the emerging challenges presented by the device of the walled residential enclave.

This second context of strategic exclusion revolves around the tendency, increasingly prevalent in the USA but known also elsewhere, for private home owners to unite behind modern defensive palisades in closed or semi-closed residential associations.[115] Within such areas the citizen may live essentially free from the constant fear of assault, burglary or other social disorder, the territory of the community being sanitised of potential wrongdoers and protected, by one means or another, from unconsented intrusion. Once inside the walls of the community, the association member need no longer be reminded daily of the deadweight of poverty and human misery so clearly apparent on the public sidewalk nor be caused to despair of the ineffectualness of government in combatting the emanations of social ill. Indeed, the overt orderliness of the enclosed community may actually be intensified by covenanted compliance on the part of community members with exacting—if not oppressive—schemes of local regulation aimed at enforcing heightened standards of residential amenity and security.[116]

---

[113] *Lutz* v. *City of New York* 899 F2d 255, 268 (3d Cir 1990).

[114] For Justice Brandeis this entitlement was "the most comprehensive of rights and the right most valued by civilized [people]" (*Olmstead* v. *United States* 277 US 438, 478, 72 L Ed 944, 956 (1928)). See also *Streetwatch* v. *National Railroad Passenger Corp.* 875 F Supp 1055, 1065 (SDNY 1995).

[115] For an account of the historical context of common interest communities, see W. S. Hyatt, "Common Interest Communities: Evolution and Reinvention", (1998) 31 *J Marshall L Rev* 303.

[116] See e.g., *State* v. *Panther Valley Property Owners Association* 704 A2d 1010 (1998), which involved a legal challenge to a gated community's practice of imposing its own traffic rules regarding excessive speed and careless driving by means of private violation notices and monetary penalties ultimately enforceable by lien upon the homes of defaulting community members. For a description of other onerous features of covenanted burdens within the community context, see e.g., D. J. Kennedy, "Residential Associations as State Actors: Regulating the Impact of Gated Communities on Nonmembers", (1995–1996) 105 *Yale LJ* 761, 762–763.

A substantial literature has now emerged to describe the operation of controlled or gated residential associations. Such associations have proliferated throughout the USA with dramatic speed, with well over 30 million Americans now estimated to be living within some form of community structure, of whom more than 8 million reside within gated and guarded enclaves.[117] The fastest growing residential communities in the nation, it has been said, "are private and usually gated, governed by a thicket of covenants, codes and restrictions".[118] In perhaps its most extreme form, the protective structure comprises a fully gated community, with its own shops and services, patrolled by guards, dogs and helicopters—the spectre of "Fortress America".

Quite clearly the essence of the enclosed residential community lies in the general and arbitrary exclusion of non-members from unconsented entry upon the premises of the community. It is striking, however, that gated communities, although nominally private property, throw up many of the same challenges to policy and ideology which are raised by the problem of shopping mall access. The role of confrontational security personnel in denying general or unannounced access inevitably exposes an awkward tension between the demands of pedestrian democracy and the supposed prerogatives of private proprietary control.[119] Is the condominium, through the agency of its local security patrol, entitled quite arbitrarily to withhold or withdraw permission to enter the community's premises or to communicate with its residents? The policing of the gated community—which may itself have been built over a pre-existing infrastructure of public streets and walkways—generates exactly similar concerns as in the shopping mall case about the proper borderline to be maintained between the public and private regulation of urbanised space.[120] Ultimately these and many analogous issues regarding the governance of the enclosed residential association point towards an underlying ambivalence as to the degree of privacy which can genuinely attach to the property rights comprised within the homeowners' association model.

Whatever their merits in insulating members from the apprehension of crime and other forms of social discomfort, gated communities have begun to accu-

[117] See e.g., H. Rishikof and A. J. Wohl, "Private Communities or Public Governments: 'The State will make the Call'", (1996) 30 *Val U L Rev* 509, 514; P. M. Wald, "Looking Forward to the Next Millennium: Social Previews to Legal Change", (1997) 70 *Temple L Rev* 1085, 1107.

[118] T. Egan, "Many Seek Security in Private Communities", *NY Times*, 3 September 1995, A1 (noting that the number of private community associations is expected to double by 2005). Another estimate suggests that 25 per cent to 30 per cent of Americans will live in such residential community associations by early in the next century (see S. Siegel, "The Constitution and Private Government: Toward the Recognition of Constitutional Rights in Private Residential Communities Fifty Years after Marsh v. Alabama", (1998) 6 *Wm & Mary Bill of Rts J* 461, 465).

[119] See, for instance, the practice adopted by some residential associations in the USA by which pedestrian access to gated streets is charged at a rate of $3 in order, effectively, to exclude the very poor (see D. J. Kennedy, above n. 116, at 771).

[120] See e.g., *State v. Panther Valley Property Owners Association* 704 A2d 1010, 1014 (1998) (above n. 116) where concern was expressed that "coextensive enforcement of [traffic rules] by a private entity may be inimical to the public good and safety of the public".

mulate their fair share of critical appraisal. David Kennedy has declared that "the harms imposed on society by residential associations are significant" and has suggested that the courts "should consider curtailing" the power of these associations over nonmembers.[121] Enclosed associations have been blamed by Kennedy and others for accelerating and accentuating the flight of middle class Americans to the safety of the suburbs, thereby abandoning the city centres to become wastelands inhabited by muggers and hoodlums. The result, it is said, is the fragmentation of the metropolitan areas and the destruction of shared values based on sentiments of social solidarity and "the experience of otherness".[122] The "secession of the successful", as these demographic and cultural changes have been termed,[123] is now credited with promoting a generally diminished sense of civic responsibility. On this view, protected residential communities merely serve to foster the perception that "one's duties consist of satisfying one's obligations to private property".[124] Exclusive communities and gated neighbourhoods "exacerbate the schism between the rich and the poor".[125] Some commentators, perhaps most notably Jerry Frug of Harvard University, have accordingly called for the reversal of this trend towards social alienation by means of active urban strategies of "community building" based on motivations which are more intensely organic, inclusive and integrative.[126] Indeed— significantly in our last context—the new urbanists want to make public spaces the "focal points of neighbourhood life".[127]

The gated community clearly raises concerns which, once again, make it feasible to draw upon the civic ideology of "quasi-public" space. Attention here is focused, of course, upon the permissibility of reasonable general access to the common parts of enclosed residential communities.[128] Already one American commentator has voiced the thought that common interest developments, particularly of the gated or fortified variety, are "neither fully private nor public", and that their activities "should not be considered 'private' and thus presumptively

---

[121] D. J. Kennedy, above n. 116, at 763.

[122] See J. Frug, "The Geography of Community", (1996) 48 *Stan L Rev* 1047, 1050, 1062–1064.

[123] Labor Secretary Robert B. Reich, *NY Times*, 20 January 1991, #6 (Magazine) 16, 42, quoted by Kennedy, above n. 116, at 777.

[124] E. McKenzie, *Privatopia: Homeowner Associations and the Rise of Residential Private Government* (New Haven, Yale University Press, 1994), p. 196. One particularly strong fear is that the residents of privately financed communities will lack any incentive to vote for schemes of taxation which redistribute their income for the purpose of expenditure on public services outside the walls of their enclave.

[125] E. A. Welle, "Public Service: Opting Out of Public Provision: Constraints and Policy Considerations", (1996) 73 *Denv U L Rev* 1221, 1232–1233.

[126] J. Frug, "The Geography of Community", above n. 122, at 1092; "City Services", (1998) 73 *NYU L Rev* 23, 35–39.

[127] J Frug, above n. 122, at 1092.

[128] In *Laguna Publishing Co* v. *Golden Rain Foundation of Laguna Hills* 182 Cal Rptr 813, 827 (1982) a Californian Court of Appeal stressed that, in relation to the gated community in question, "although the public generally is not invited, there is a substantial traffic into Leisure World of a variety of vendors and service persons whom the residents of Leisure World do invite in daily to accommodate the living needs of a community this large".

beyond the reach of 'public' policy".[129] Certainly, as the academic literature readily confirms, there is an increasing level of disquiet about the way in which dichotomous perceptions of the public/private distinction improperly shield the privatised regulatory structure of enclosed residential developments from evaluation against more general social ideals and democratic values.[130]

That matters of public interest may abridge the operation of private property rights has always been apparent in the characteristically American solicitude for a range of expressive freedoms protected by the First Amendment of the United States Constitution. In this connection it is interesting to observe the incipient emergence of a case law jurisprudence which, in this slightly different context, begins to mirror many of the features of the jurisprudence on shopping mall access to which we referred earlier.

A key issue relates to the entitlement of non-members to communicate for peaceful purposes with members of an enclosed or sheltered housing development. Thus, for instance, American courts have upheld the right of door-to-door petitioners to have access to a planned retirement community.[131] Such a community has frequently been considered the equivalent of a municipality,[132] with the result that the corporate officers of the community could not, without creating "a political 'isolation booth'", bar what they knew to be a "bona fide political endeavour".[133] More recently, American courts have drawn explicitly upon the potent analogies of the "company town" and the regional shopping centre[134] in order to preclude gated communities from placing arbitrary and discriminatory prohibitions on the delivery to community residents of various kinds of unsolicited newspapers and advertising materials[135] and political literature.[136] This curial stance not only confirms the historic American inclination

---

[129] E. McKenzie, "Reinventing Common Interest Developments: Reflections on a Policy Role for the Judiciary", (1998) 31 *J Marshall L Rev* 397, 404–405.

[130] See e.g., D. J. Kennedy, above n. 116; S. Siegel, above n. 118.

[131] *State v. Kolcz*, 276 A2d 595, 599–600 (1971).

[132] See S. Siegel, above n. 118, at 476–490.

[133] 276 A2d 595, 600.

[134] See *Laguna Publishing Co v. Golden Rain Foundation of Laguna Hills* 182 Cal Rptr 813, 825–827 (1982), where a gated community was described as having "peculiar attributes . . . which in many ways approximate a municipality [and] bring it conceptually close to characterization as a company town" (see *Marsh v. Alabama*, above n. 59). In *Laguna Publishing* the Court, whilst acknowledging that, unlike a shopping mall, the gated community does not offer unlimited public access, still thought the *PruneYard* jurisprudence on shopping mall access to "define certain concepts to build on" in reaching its decision (see *PruneYard Shopping Center v. Robins*, above n. 39 US, affirming *Robins v. PruneYard Shopping Center* 592 P2d 341 (1979) (Supreme Court of California)).

[135] *Laguna Publishing Co v. Golden Rain Foundation of Laguna Hills*, 182 Cal Rptr 813, 826–832 (1982). It is debatable, however, whether an individual community member has a right to insist on the inclusion of her own advertising material or personal statement in a gated community's dedicated newsletter or bulletin board (see *William G Mulligan Foundation for the Control of First Aid Squadders and Roving Paramedics v. Brooks* 711 A2d 961, 967 (1998)).

[136] *Guttenberg Taxpayers and Rentpayers Association v. Galaxy Towers Condominium Association* 686 A2d 344, 347 (1995), 688 A2d 156, 159 (NJ Super L 1996) ("A level playing field requires equal access to this condominium because it has become in essence a political 'company town'").

that a household's reception of externally generated literature should "depend upon the will of the individual master of each household, and not upon the determination of the community".[137] It also displaces "a needless and exaggerated insistence upon private property rights incident to such communities" where such insistence is "irrelevant in preventing any meaningful encroachment upon private property rights and results in a pointless discrimination which causes serious financial detriment to another".[138]

The critical balance between the private and public aspects of residential association rights was highlighted, most significantly, in *Citizens Against Gated Enclaves* v. *Whitley Heights Civic Association*.[139] Here an association of homeowners living in Whitley Heights, an affluent, beautiful and historic neighbourhood in the Hollywood Hills of Los Angeles, reached an agreement with the City authorities which purported to withdraw Whitley Heights streets and sidewalks from general public use. The association was to be allowed to place gates on the streets in order to restrict access to residents of the houses inside the gates, to their invitees and to operators of emergency vehicles. The gates were duly installed at a cost of several hundreds of thousands of dollars charged to and paid by the relevant homeowners.

Shortly after the construction of the gates began, a number of residents living outside the gated area formed a protest group, under the inspired acronym of CAGE (Citizens Against Gated Enclaves), in defence of their claim to use the proposed gated area for such purposes as commuting to work and jogging. They sought an injunction requiring the removal of the gates and this injunction was granted and duly affirmed on appeal. The appellate court declared that, although it understood "the deep and abiding concern of the City and [the homeowners' association] with crime prevention and historic preservation", it doubted that the state legislature would have had any desire to "permit a return to feudal times with each suburb being a fiefdom to which other citizens of the State are denied their fundamental right of access to use public streets within those areas".[140] In the absence of express authorisation by the legislature, the Court accordingly refused to endorse any foreclosure of general access to the area concerned.

As self-defensive residential communities begin to spring up in other parts of the common law world, it seems likely that *Citizens Against Gated Enclaves* v. *Whitley Heights Civic Association* will be frequently cited in support of a more

---

[137] Justice Black in *Martin* v. *City of Struthers* 319 US 141, 87 L Ed 1313, 1316 (1943). See also *Walker* v. *Georgetown Housing Authority* 677 NE2d 1125, 1127–1128 (Mass 1997). It remains, of course, open to the individual householder, by notification to the supplier, to prohibit the delivery of unwanted publications (see *City of Fredonia* v. *Chanute Tribune* 638 P2d 347, 349–350 (1981); *Tillman* v. *Distribution Systems of America Inc.* 648 NYS2d 630, 635–636 (AD 2 Dept 1996)).

[138] *Laguna Publishing Co* v. *Golden Rain Foundation of Laguna Hills* 182 Cal Rptr 813, 826 (1982). (The court pointed out that the gated community's normal screening procedures would still apply to the delivery personnel who sought to supply newspapers to the doorstep of individual community residents (182 Cal Rptr 813, 830)).

[139] 28 Cal Rptr 2d 451 (Cal App 2 Dist 1994).

[140] 28 Cal Rptr 2d 451, 457.

expansive understanding of the public or civic dimensions of privately held urban space.

The privatised public service utility

We turn now, briefly, to a third context in which, during recent years, the distinction between public and private domains appears to have become somewhat blurred. This context concerns a mechanism which conduces toward a different sort of social exclusion, and it may be that the analytic category of the "quasi-public" still has an important role to play in resolving the tensions which have emerged.

Our third context relates to the operation of the privatised public service utilities which have lately burgeoned throughout the modern deregulatory state. Regardless of their nominal classification, such utilities now occupy an entirely ambivalent position somewhere across the spectrum extending between poles of publicness and privateness: they are public in origin, private in form, and quasi-governmental in function. The day may soon be coming when the internal discipline of "quasi-public property" jurisprudence will be required to control the commercial activities of at least some of these supposedly private corporatised agencies. This will be particularly the case where such bodies attempt to assert an untrammelled exclusory power as incidental to their new proprietary prerogatives, for such a claim may be deeply inimical to important civic values of community and democracy.

The difficulty is precisely this. One frequent, but largely unobserved, consequence of our modern passion for privatisation and deregulation has been to skew or dislocate the process of compulsory acquisition of land. The exercise of eminent domain for supervening community purposes is, of course, a phenomenon well known to us all. Most have little difficulty in accepting that the state, in the name of all citizens, may call on one or more individuals, in extreme circumstances and in return for just compensation, to yield up some private good for the greater good of the whole community. Were it postulated, however, that one citizen, X, might enjoy a *private* power of compulsory acquisition over the land of another citizen, Y, for the purpose of X's own personal gain, the suggestion would normally attract the sternest, most sceptical, scrutiny.[141] Yet

---

[141] Within Commonwealth jurisdictions the closest approximation to privately activated compulsory purchase probably arises in connection with statutory measures which enable a court to order the creation of certain rights of user over privately owned servient land in favour of privately owned dominant land. Such statutory innovations are, however, severely limited in scope (see e.g., Access to Neighbouring Land Act 1992, s. 1; Property Law Act (British Columbia (RSBC 1979, c 340)), s. 32; Property Law Act 1974 (Queensland), s 180; Conveyancing and Law of Property Act 1884 (Tasmania), s. 84J). The Queensland statute, perhaps the best known example of such legislation, demands that it be "consistent with the public interest that the dominant land should be used in the manner proposed" (Property Law Act 1974, s. 180(3)(a)), a proviso which has been restrictively applied (see e.g., *Ex parte Edward Street Properties Pty Ltd.* [1977] Qd R 86).

something awfully like this can now happen in the context of some of our privatised utilities. Many privatised commercial concerns, having functioned formerly within the public sector, retain indirectly the substantial economic advantage of the statutory powers of compulsory purchase once vested in their predecessors. Such powers are now exercisable even though their effect is inevitably to diminish the wealth or amenity of one private citizen and even though the substantial beneficiaries of such acquisition will be the corporate persona of the privatised utility and those other private citizens who are its equity shareholders.

One example will suffice. In England let us suppose that citizen Y owns a house which stands low on the slopes of a beautiful valley. The Environment Agency—the body statutorily entrusted with the stewardship of the nation's water supplies[142]—determines that, in an effort to combat the national water shortage, this valley (including Y's land) should be compulsorily acquired for the purpose of constructing a new reservoir. Towards this end the Environment Agency exercises its power of acquisition under the Water Resources Act 1991,[143] although the Agency has, of course, neither the resources nor the expertise to engage in the massive capital investment of reservoir construction. Instead, the Environment Agency simply utilises another of the statutory powers within its armoury[144] and franchises the construction and subsequent profitable operation of the reservoir to the Blankshire Water Company.

Until relatively recently the Blankshire Water Company used to function within the public sector as the Blankshire Water Board, but following flotation—if that is the right word here—now exists as a privatised utility whose shareholders comprise citizen X and numerous others. Citizen Y is forced from his cherished home, while citizen X laughs all the way to the bank with his handsome dividend returns. Citizen Y receives the usual derisory under-value for relinquishing his principal capital asset, while citizen X looks forward to the substantial capital gain which will undoubtedly accrue on the eventual sale of his shares. The social consequence is one of double exclusion: Y is excluded, *first*, from his own land[145] and, *second*, from full participation in the commonwealth of benefits to which his status as citizen should (and once did) entitle him. He is compelled, in effect, to contribute disproportionately to the water company's profits and to enhance the dividends and ultimate resale gains received by its distant and faceless shareholders.

It is strongly arguable that there is room here for the revitalisation of another "quasi-public property" classification, with the more far-reaching judicial

---

[142] Water Resources Act 1991 (England), ss. 2(1)(a), (2), 19(1). See Environment Act 1995 (UK), s. 2(1)(a)(i).

[143] Water Resources Act 1991 (England), s. 154(1). See Environment Act 1995 (UK), s 2(1)(a)(iv).

[144] See Water Resources Act 1991 (England), s. 20(2)(a). See Environment Act 1995 (UK), s 2(1)(a)(i).

[145] See, for instance, the bitter dissents provoked by the decision of the Supreme Court of Michigan in *Poletown Neighborhood Council* v. *City of Detroit* 304 NW2d 455 (1981), which effectively authorised the expropriation of the elderly Polish-American population of a Detroit suburb in order to clear a site for a new assembly plant for General Motors Corporation.

surveillance of corporate activity associated with this jurisprudence.[146] In, for instance, the scenario outlined above, the critical question is not whether, in principle, citizen Y should be immune from the requirement of personal sacrifice in the face of a greater community need—clearly he deserves no such immunity. Often, however, the more critical question will be whether the privatised water company has targeted the Environment Agency's compulsory purchase powers on Y's land, not because this land provides, in environmental terms, the *best* site for a reservoir, but rather because—usually for reasons of geomorphology—it represents the *cheapest*, albeit ecologically detrimental, option for reservoir construction. There is today—in this context and in many analogous settings—an overwhelming case for the exercise of close judicial control in the public interest over the "private" proprietary operations of the new corporate utilities. Only in this way can the danger be averted that proprietary power may become divorced, on a grand scale, from wider conceptions of social responsibility.

It is tantalising to recall that the terminology of "quasi public property" enjoys a venerable history in this very context. The phrase "quasi public property" was actually used in the American case law of the late nineteenth century and early twentieth century precisely to characterise the assets of private companies regulated by the courts in the public interest.[147] Examples of such assets were provided by the telephone systems,[148] irrigation networks,[149] railroad, turnpike and canal companies[150] and grain elevators,[151] which were so essential to the development and continuing success of a large-scale agrarian economy. Under cover of this attribution of quasi-publicness American courts were, for a period of some 50 years or so, accustomed to assert an important measure of supervisory control—of socially rational oversight—in respect of the activities of even those companies which charged the public a toll for the provision of their services.

To the present day American courts still tend to scrutinise with fierce vigilance any proposal that eminent domain be asserted in order to effect a compulsory purchase from one private actor for the benefit of another. Constitutionally permissible "taking" must be for a public purpose and if it appears that the primary beneficiary of a taking is not the public, but rather a private party (whether individual or corporate), the exercise of the power of eminent domain is apt to be castigated as an "attempt by a private entity to use

---

[146] For an analogous argument, based on early common law doctrines in respect of common callings and monopolies, that the operations of privatised utilities require strong judicial control, see M. Taggart, "Corporatisation, Privatisation and Public Law", (1991) 2 *PLR* 77, 105–106.

[147] For early use of the "quasi-public" classification in this context, see *Slaughter* v. *Commonwealth* (1856) 54 Va 767, 776.

[148] *State* v. *Nordskog* 136 P 694, 695 (1913).

[149] *Imperial Irrigation Co* v. *Jayne* 138 SW 575, 585 (1911).

[150] *Miners' Ditch Co* v. *Zellerbach* (1869) 37 Cal 543, 577, 591, 99 Am Dec 300, 306, 319; *People* v. *Illinois Cent Railway Co* 84 NE 368, 373 (1908).

[151] *In the Matter of Swigert* 6 NE 469, 475 (1886); *People* v. *Illinois Cent Railway Co* 84 NE 368, 373 (1908).

the city's taking powers to acquire what it could not get through arm's length negotiations".[152]

IV. CONCLUSION

The central contention of this chapter has been that certain areas of private property are today sufficiently affected by a public interest as to merit a new form of control—an increasing form of vigilance—in that same public interest. The infiltration within traditionally private law domains of something akin to public law controls may in fact provide a key to the preservation of those intangible and fragile values which alone assure freedom from widespread exploitation, exclusion and social alienation.

Three areas of private law particularly susceptible to the application of public interest controls have been identified: all three stand to benefit from the heightened discipline imposed by the analytic category of the "quasi-public". The jurisprudence of quasi-public property not only mediates the relationship between public and private; it also serves to infuse the decisional processes of private property with a crucial sense of social responsibility and public accountability. Accordingly, each of the areas discussed in this chapter pinpoints a growing need for careful judicial surveillance over forms of sovereignty which can so easily mutate into the dehumanising assertion of arbitrary, unreasoned power. Never before have constraints of public propriety had so much to contribute towards the formulation of our conceptions of supposedly private property. The immediate challenge is to distinguish, not between starkly dichotomous categories of "private" and "public" property, but between that property which lies within an inherently private domain and those gradations of "quasi-public" property whose acknowledgement is increasingly integral to the well-being of a civil society.

---

[152] *City of Lansing* v. *Edward Rose Realty Inc.* 481 NW2d 795, 798 (Mich App 1992), affd 502 NW2d 638, 645–647 (Mich 1993). See also *Shizas* v. *Detroit* 52 NW2d 589, 592–596 (1952); *Wilmington Parking Authority* v. *Land With Improvements*, 521 A2d 227, 234–235 (Del 1986); *City of Center Line* v. *Chmelko*, 416 NW2d 401, 404–407 (Mich App 1987).

3

The Many Dimensions of Property

GEOFFREY SAMUEL

The idea of a public dimension to private property law is, for the comparative lawyer, a creative idea capable of providing a range of insights not just into the precariousness of the public and private divide but more generally into the strengths and weaknesses of traditional legal science. Yet, as an idea, it is itself plagued by what might be termed an epistemological ambiguity. It is indeed challenging in the way that it forces lawyers to look beyond the categories within which they work and research. Yet the idea of a public dimension to private property implies that the knowledge context is little more than two-dimensional in its complexity. This is misleading. Private property indeed has a constitutional dimension, but this constitutional dimension is so fragmented and complex when translated into legal institutions and concepts that it might be better to talk in terms of multi-dimensions. Put another way, when theorising about property the comparatist might be better served if he or she draws an analogy with theorising about time. In the eighteenth and nineteenth centuries philosophers thought that they had captured time, rather as legal and political thinkers thought they had mastered and axiomatised property.[1] Yet time returned as an enigma to haunt the contemporary scientific community.[2] Might the same be said of property? Just as time is progressively invading the realms of all the physical sciences in ways that are shattering the old certainties,[3] might property be seen as a notion that is continuously and relentlessly undermining the traditional forms of representing legal knowledge?

I. TWO MODELS OF PROPERTY

In order to investigate the modern dimensions of property in Western legal thought, one must start out from the two models that underpin it. The first is the Roman conception. The distinguishing feature of this model is the unitary notion of ownership (*dominium, proprietas*) which gave expression to an exclusive power (*potestas*) relationship between a person (*persona*) and thing (*res*).[4]

---

[1] Cf. *Code civil*, art, 544.
[2] B. Piettre, *Philosophie et science du temps* (Paris, Presses Universitaires de France, 1994) p. 117.
[3] Ibid., p. 120.
[4] J.2.4.4.

This power relationship was all-embracing in that it represented not just the most complete form of power that one could have over a thing,[5] but also a relationship which absorbed all aspects and interests with respect to the *res*.[6] The philosophical and epistemological implications of the basic idea ought never to be underestimated. The emphasis was on the individual person and the individual thing as a social structure functioning in a zone—private law (*ius privatum*) – which of itself endowed the *potestas* bond with little or no correlative proprietary obligations. Once a plaintiff seeking repossession of his thing was found to be the owner, the judge had to order the thing to be handed back to the plaintiff.[7] There was no discussion about whether he deserved, in some social sense, to be the owner of the disputed *res*. Property owners were not, however, actually free to act as they pleased with their property. For the notion of ownership found itself in a dialectical relationship with another fundamental form of power, the power to govern (*imperium*).[8] This second form of power attached to all public offices and operated within a legal zone, public law (*ius publicum*), that was independent from private law.[9] Thus slaves had public law remedies against cruel masters[10] and magistrates had a range of public law powers and remedies in respect of land and buildings.[11] These powers had the practical result of encouraging owners, in order to enhance their own interests, to take account of the interests of their neighbours.[12]

The second model is the feudal conception of property. This model differs from the Roman one in a number of important ways. First feudalism made a fundamental distinction between land and moveable property. Such a distinction was not without meaning in the Roman model. Land has obvious physical and economic features that distinguish it from moveable things. But the legal relationship, in structural terms, between a person and a plot of land was in the Roman model exactly the same as the relationship between a person and a chalice. This feudal distinction between land and what became known as chattels (from the Norman French word *chatel*) represented a quite new dichotomy. The idea of "fixed" and "non-fixed" property had the effect of emphasising a social, economic and thus political relationship between person and land that made any distinction between a private law of property and a public law of command (*imperium*) meaningless. *Dominium* brought with it its own *imperium* and thus the law of property, in as much as it centred on land, was in feudal thinking a form of public law.[13] The second difference between the feudal and Roman models is to be

---

[5] The Romans specifically recognised *dominum* as a form of *potestas*: D.50.16.215.

[6] A.-M. Patault, *Introduction historique au droit des biens* (Paris, Presses Universitaires de France, 1989), p. 17.

[7] D.6.1.9.

[8] D.2.1.3.

[9] D.1.1.1.2.

[10] D.1.6.2.

[11] See e.g., D.39.1 and D.39.2.

[12] A. Borkowski, *Textbook on Roman Law*, 2nd edn. (Oxford, Blackstone, 1997), pp. 160–161.

[13] W. Ullmann, *Law and Politics in the Middle Ages: an Introduction to the Sources of Medieval Political Ideas* (Ithaca, Cornell University Press, 1975), pp. 216–218; R. C. van Caenegem, *An*

found in the idea that feudal law did not envisage the control of land in terms of a unitary and absolute bond which embraced and absorbed the physical land itself. Instead the feudal model was based on the idea that a range of different people could each have a different interest in a single piece of land. The key concept was seisin.[14] And while, at first sight, seisin can be compared with the Roman concept of possession—both gave expression to a quasi-factual relationship with property—it was not a notion that expressed a factual bond between person and physical thing. It represented a legitimate power to draw profit from land.[15] The third difference largely results from the first two. Feudal property lawyers did not conceptualise the law of property in terms of physical things (*res*); they saw it as consisting of a range of different legal "rights" (*iura*) divorced from the actual physical thing itself.[16] "Where Rome conceived only a single right and a single master", observes Professor Patault, "medieval law juxtaposed different masters and a plurality of owners within the limits of the capital".[17]

When the two models of property law are compared it is tempting to conclude that the Roman structure is the least complex. However a more detailed investigation of Roman thinking reveals some complications. The Romans may not have made too much of the distinction between land and moveables, but they recognised a subtle and fundamental dichotomy within the notion of a *res* that was to have profound implications for legal thinking. Things, so Gaius tells us, can be classified into two kinds. There are tangible things (*res corporales*) such as land, clothes, gold and the like which can be touched and thus exist both in fact and in law.[18] Equally, however, there are intangible things (*res incorporales*); these are things which exist only in law and encompass for example an inheritance, a right of way over someone else's land and obligations.[19] Now once one introduces the idea of an intangible thing that can exist only in law one is both raising legal thinking to a new level of subtlety and introducing a new dimension of complexity. This complexity is partly evident from within the law of property in as much as the notion of *dominium* must logically extend to a *res incorporalis*. How can one have an independent proprietary relationship with an object that exists only in law? One can of course maintain the abstract structure between *persona* and *res*, yet the more one tries to define the nature of the object owned the more one is forced back to the notion of ownership itself. Ownership is no longer a relationship of power over an object which has its own

Historical Introduction to Western Constitutional Law (Cambridge, Cambridge University Press, 1995, pp. 1–6; R. C. van Caenegem, "Government, Law and Society" in J. H. Burns (ed.), *The Cambridge History of Medieval Political Thought c.350–c.1450* (Cambridge, Cambridge University Press, 1988), pp. 178–180.

[14] On which see S. F. C. Milsom, *Historical Foundations of the Common Law*, 2nd edn. (London, Butterworths, 1981) 120–122.
[15] Patault, above n. 6, at p. 21.
[16] Ibid., p. 22.
[17] Ibid., p. 24.
[18] G.2.13.
[19] G.2.14.

independent existence as a physical reality (*dominium*); it becomes dependent upon other areas of private law actually defining the object (*proprietas*). This rebounds upon ownership in as much as this unique relationship represents a bond between owner and object which is given expression in the law of actions by an action against the thing itself. An owner could reclaim what is his by an *actio in rem* and in early Roman law, as Gaius informs us, the thing itself (or some representative part of it) had to be in court.[20] Of course some forms of intangible property could be made to depend upon the existence of a physical thing. Thus the holder of a right of use in another's physical thing would lose his object (right of use) the moment the physical thing was destroyed.[21] However with regard to a contractual debt—a *res incorporalis* as Gaius specifically recognises—the situation verged on a contradiction.[22] A contractual debt was defined entirely by the law of obligations and an obligation was given its own quite separate remedy of an *action in personam*. Just as one does not use an *actio in rem* to reclaim what is *owed* because the creditor does not *own* money in the debtor's possession, so one does not use an *actio in personam* to recover property *owned* by the claimant since *nec enim quod nostrum est nobis dari potest* (what is ours cannot be conveyed to us).[23] Yet if a contractual debt is a *res*, then it would seem to follow logically that it is capable of being owned.[24] Owning and owing would appear to contradict within a single dimension.

Such contradictions did not seem to worry the Roman jurists to whom definitions were always dangerous.[25] Nevertheless the inherent complexities within the Roman model were to prove troublesome when the two models of property law clashed in late medieval Europe. What makes modern European property law complex is not just the internal symmetries of Roman law or feudal law, but the relentless and continuous attempt to impose the Roman model on the customary systems during the centuries that followed the rediscovery of Roman law in the eleventh century. The Glossators and the Post-Glossators had an unsurpassed knowledge of the Roman source materials and for them law as a concept and legal science (*scientia juris*) was equivalent to Roman law.[26] However, the society in which they lived was anything but Roman.[27] The

---

[20] G.4.16–17.

[21] J.2.1.26; D.7.1.2; D.5.3.16.8.

[22] G.2.14.

[23] G.4.4.

[24] This was specifically recognised in the case of a dead person's estate (*hereditas*) which was considered a *res* in itself capable of being claimed by an *actio in rem* even with respect to the personal obligations contained in the estate: D.5.3.25.18.

[25] D.50.17.202.

[26] For a discussion of the methods of the medieval jurists see O. F. Robinson, T. D. Fergus and W. M. Gordon, *European History: Sources and Institutions*, 2nd edn. (London, Butterworths, 1994), pp. 42–71; Ullmann, above n. 13, at pp. 83–116; J. W. Jones, *Historical Introduction to the Theory of Law* (Westp.ort, Greenwood Press, 1970), pp. 11–21; F. Wieacker, *A History of Private Law in Europe* (trans T Weir, Oxford, Oxford University Press, 1995), pp. 28–46, 55–61.

[27] Although economic revival and change and the increasing influence of Roman law were leading to the marked decline of feudalism: van Caenegem, *Historical Introduction*, above n. 13, at 76–78.

existence of a central state was not a feature of feudal Europe and, accordingly, the distinctions to be found in the *Institutes of Justinian* and in the *Digest* between public and private law and between property and obligations had little immediate impact in any kind of empirical sense.[28] Seisin was both a property and an administrative structure, just as contract was at one and the same time a proprietary, obligational, commercial and a political instrument.[29] For its part, seisin translated into Roman concepts only by deforming both seisin and the Roman model.

This Roman model was of course more complex than a mere structure for ownership. In addition to *dominium*, the medieval jurists found in the Roman sources two other proprietary relationships capable of existing between a person and a thing. The first was possession which represented a factual—or in truth a quasi-factual—relationship between *persona* and *res* and which differed from ownership not just in substance[30] but also in respect of the remedy available.[31] The second was the *ius in re aliena*, that is to say a "right" (*ius*) in respect of property belonging to another. Ownership in Roman law may have been an all-embracing and unitary institutional relationship, but this did not mean that an owner could not divest himself of the use of his thing or the fruits that the *res* produced.[32] The Glossators and Post-Glossators were thus faced with some extremely subtle questions when it came to translating feudal structures into Roman concepts. Was seisin a possessory relationship or was it just a *ius* in land? Was one form of feudal holding superior to others allowing the application of the label of *dominium* in turn endowing the owner with the right to the *rei vindicatio* (the real remedy protecting ownership)? Indeed were there different kinds of *dominium*—for example a *dominium utile* as opposed to a *dominium directum*?[33] If there were different kinds of ownership, could one be superior to all the others, a kind of "super real right"?[34] Was the relationship of possession itself a *ius* or was it something quite different? Indeed what was the relationship between *ius* and *dominium*: was ownership a *ius* or was it a form of *potestas* that was quite different?

These questions were to give rise to an extraordinarily rich literature focusing around a whole range of conceptually based Latin legal terms.[35] The bringing together of the two models of property was, however, to have a restrictive result in as much as the extraordinary flexibility of the feudal notion of property relations was inevitably to be curtailed once the Post-Glossators had succeeded

---

[28] F. Zenati and T. Revet, *Les biens*, 2nd edn. (Paris, Presses Universitaires de France, 1997), p. 31.

[29] Patault, above n. 6, at p. 43.

[30] D.41.2.12.1 (Possession has nothing in common with ownership).

[31] D.43.16.1pr-1; D.43.17.1.2; and see generally Borkowski, above n. 12, at pp. 167–169.

[32] In fact the Roman jurists recognised that such "rights" in another's property amounted to the divesting of a portion of ownership: D.7.1.4.

[33] Zenati and Revet, above n. 28, at p. 134.

[34] Ibid.

[35] See in particular Zenati and Revet, above n. 28, at pp. 133–135.

in Romanising customary law.[36] Seisin gradually slipped towards simple Roman possession, but not without leaving a certain chaos in property thinking which is still being felt in modern civil law.[37] For its part, then, the Roman model also suffered; notions such as *dominum* and *possessio* were "tortured" and "deformed" and ended up by failing to reflect the social, economic or political reality of the time.[38] This unreality was, to some extent, to continue right up to the *Code civil* in that when it came to re-establishing the Roman model in France in the aftermath of the Revolution some feudal notions, such as the distinction between moveable and immovable property, remained rooted in legal thinking.[39] Such a distinction was, of course, a realistic one in medieval society; but in a commercial and capitalist economy, in which everything was reducible to money, the original Roman model in many ways was more relevant.

II. PROPERTY RIGHTS

Yet there was a further and more serious complication. At the end of the Middle Ages the notion of *ius* itself was undergoing a metamorphosis. In the Roman sources themselves a *ius* represented a substantive legal "connection"[40] giving rise to entitlements in the law of actions; the term gave expression to an objective view of law where individuals were related one to another through various legal *iura*.[41] The source of *iura* was, in the classical period at any rate, the existence of Roman society itself.[42] Moreover the existence of a *ius* was never in itself, at least in the classical period, adequate to express a legal claim. Such claims were still focused around the *actio* and thus in discussing questions of liability the jurists always posed the question of whether or not an action would be available.[43] This epistemological and ideological view was to change during the era of the Post-Glossators as a result not just of juristic reinterpretation of Roman concepts but of the nominalist revolution associated with the late medieval philosopher William of Ockham.[44]

The nominalist revolution was, for its part, rooted partly in the methods of the medieval scholastics, whose work is characterised, *inter alia*, by

[36] Patault, above n. 6, at pp. 44, 104–105.
[37] Ibid., p. 114.
[38] Ibid., pp. 104–105.
[39] CC art 516; Patault, above n. 6, at 117.
[40] M Villey, *La formation de la pensée juridique moderne*, 4th edn. (Paris, Montchrestien, 1975), p. 651. And see in particular D.1.1.12.
[41] D.1.1.11.
[42] The power of command (*imperium*) was transferred to the emperor by the Roman people as a whole via the *lex regia*: D.1.4.1pr. The text implies that it is the existence of society itself which generates the sovereignty; another text (D.1.1.1.4) on the *ius gentium* (law of nations) suggests that it is the mutual relations between those living as a group which generates *iura*: *ubi societa ibi ius*.
[43] A good example involving the invasion of a property *ius* is D.9.2.50.
[44] On which see Villey, above n. 40, at pp. 199–210. But cf. R. Tuck, *Natural Rights Theories: Their Origin and Development* (Cambridge, Cambridge University Press, 1979), pp. 22–23.

distinctiones, and partly in the actual juristic methodology of the Romans themselves. The scholastic approach was to impact on philosophy and epistemology
in that it encouraged not just a different way of viewing the world—of viewing
"reality"—but a new approach to methodology. As Alain Laurent has
observed:[45]

> "the individualist paradigm began to take shape in the epistemological field, then in
> the 'sociological' and ethical, in opposing itself to the then dominant realist and holis-
> tic philosophy of Saint Thomas [Aquinas]. Ockham used the notion of the *individuum*
> as "the object of an original and empirical intuition of reality necessarily individual
> and one'."

The individual is a unique and separate being who lives only through himself.
The Church and the town no longer existed as "realities" but were simply names
to express a collection of individuals. Such thinking also found support in the
Digest in as much as the terms "thing" and "person" actually forced lawyers into
reflecting on the nature of these entities.[46] The political birds (so to speak) that
took wing in this nominalist revolution, finally came home to roost in the celebrated ideological statement of Margaret Thatcher that "there is no such thing
as society". There "are individual men and women and there are families".[47]

This increasing focus on the individual as the source of society entailed a refo-
cusing of the notion of *ius*. Aided by some texts dating from the final period of
the Roman empire,[48] the notion of a *ius* became more subjective. It absorbed the
Roman institution of the *actio* to become a term capable of expressing not just
a legal relation but a legal entitlement. Yet by developing into an entitlement it
subtly changed from being a legal relation to being a legal object. This was particularly evident in respect of the *iura in re*. The person who had a *ius* in respect
of a thing belonging to another had no direct *ius* to the *res corporalis* itself since
only the owner had this unique legal relation; what he had was in effect a *ius* to
a *ius in re*.[49] This contradiction was exacerbated by the theorising with respect
to ownership itself. The Glossators in searching to reconstruct Roman law,
were faced with the problem that the sources disclosed no actual definition of
dominium. They thus set about trawling the source materials in order to give the
term some substance and they arrived at the conclusion that the contents con-

[45] A. Laurant, *Histoire de l'individualisme* (Paris, Presses Universitaires de France, 1993), p. 23.
[46] See in particular D.5.1.76; D.41.3.30.
[47] *Women's Own*, 31 October 1987. Note on this point the observation of M. Rheinstein: "With
eighteenth century Enlightenment the individualizing view of society began to be preponderant. In
the French Revolution the new ideology became official. The nation was to be *une et indivisible*. The
state was now clearly conceived to be composed of individual citizens. The intermediate groups of
manor, guild, estate, province were swept away; the municipalities were made subdivisions of the
state government. But one group, intermediate between the state and its individual citizens was left
intact: the family": "The Family and the Law", *International Encyclopedia of Comparative Law*,
(New York, Oceana) Vol. IV, Ch. 1, para. 15.
[48] See in particular J.4.6pr (and D.44.7.51) where it is stated that an action is nothing else but a
ius of pursuing in law what is owed to one.
[49] Zenati and Revet, above n. 28, at pp. 273–275.

sisted of an entitlement to use the thing, to its fruits and to alienate it.[50] Now there is certainly authority in the *Digest* for this extraordinary piece of detective work.[51] However it has to be remembered that the medieval jurists could only view this authority through their own feudal model in which such entitlements were divorced from the physical *res* itself. And thus they arrived at the conclusion that the substance of *dominium* consisted of *iura*; that is to say ownership comprised of the *ius utendi, ius fruendi* and *ius abutendi*.[52] These *iura* were thus "objects" which could be granted by an owner to another.

The theorising did not stop there. The question arose as to the legal nature of *dominum* as a legal relation in itself. Was it something quite different from a *ius* or was it simply a *ius*? This question was a vital one. For the moment the Post-Glossators concluded that *dominum* was a *ius*,[53] they had created a model in which the term *ius* was invested with a form of *potestas*. And this merging of *ius* and *dominium* resulted in a situation whereby all *iura* became property entitlements in the sense of an active power to revindicate.[54] In other words, when a *ius* became a subjective entitlement to an object it brought with it the implicit entitlement to succeed in a law of actions sense; once the *ius* (right) had been proved, the judge had to find for the right-holder.[55] The effect, then, of the nominalist revolution, together with the bringing together of *dominum* and *ius*, was to establish the modern subjective right.[56]

This had two important effects. The first, inside the law of property, was to re-emphasise once again the distinction between *res corporales* and *res incorporales*;[57] individualism dictated that the starting point for thinking about property was the exclusive bond between a person and a thing.[58] "Property" (*proprietas*) came to express both the physical thing and the idea of a single owner.[59] However this re-emphasis could only be expressed through the conceptual language of the Roman and the feudal models combined since the contents of the *res corporalis* had been reduced by the Post-Glossators to rights (*ius utendi, ius fruendi* and *ius abutendi*). Thus the *Code civil* ended up by defining ownership as the *right* to enjoy and dispose of things in the *most absolute manner*.[60] The second effect, beyond the borders of the law of property, was to re-orientate legal science. The birth of the modern subjective right imposed upon legal analysis in general a property paradigm. All rights (*iura*) are rights *to*

---

[50] Patault, above n. 6, at p. 110.
[51] See e.g., D.5.3.25.11.
[52] Patault, above n. 6, at pp. 22–23.
[53] Ibid., pp. 109–110.
[54] Tuck, above n. 44, at p. 16.
[55] Cf. D.6.1.9.
[56] Tuck, above n. 44, at p. 28; Zenati and Revet, above n. 28, at pp. 245–246.
[57] See *Code civil*, arts 527–529.
[58] Patault, above n. 6, at pp. 219–220.
[59] This is true even in the common law: see *Sale of Goods Act 1979* (UK) ss. 16–18 which talks of transferring the "property" in goods. *Proprietas* can thus mean either ownership (*Code civil* art. 544) or the thing itself (*Code civil* art. 644): Patault, above n. 6, at p. 219.
[60] *Code civil* art 544 (emphasis added).

something. This "something" in turn had the effect of extending the institution of the *res*—in particular the *res incorporalis*—beyond the category of "goods" (*bona*) to include "rights" (*ius incorporale*) themselves.[61] In Roman law it was difficult to envisage a *ius* independent either of some tangible thing—thus even a servitude had need of a physical object—or of some carefully defined *in personam* obligation. In contemporary legal thinking, however, a subjective right has the capacity at one and the same time to create, to define and to endow a normative entitlement to its own object. Thus one can have a "right" (for example a usufruct) in a "right" (since moveables include *res incorporales*).[62]

Such a development can perhaps be envisaged within its own law of property dimension without too much difficulty. However, when seen within the structure of the modern codes, a number of fundamental contradictions emerge if one continues to insist on a two-dimensional view of law as a set of normative propositions hierarchically arranged. If ownership is the right to enjoy and dispose of a thing in the most absolute manner, how are owners to be socially constrained—or, more realistically (given the political climate of Napoleonic France),[63] how is a *dirigiste* government to function? The answer is to be found in the second limb of the French definition of ownership which limits the exercise of ownership only to a usage not prohibited by statute or by regulations.[64] In other words the *Code civil* indicates clearly that *imperium* will trump *dominium*. This fundamental limitation to the right of an owner does not at first sight appear as a contraction since the Roman model clearly separates public from private law. Public law deals with the interests (*utilitates*) of the state, while private law is concerned with the interests of individuals.[65] Yet the moment one brings into the equation the notion of an "interest" one is immediately adding a new dimension to the model: for an "interest" is a notion that can function entirely outside of the world of *iura* and of established legal categories. It is, as François Ost observed, an omnipresent notion which by its very imprecision subverts the established categories, concepts, mechanisms and principles of the law.[66] Statute and regulation may for example limit the liberty of owners to exercise their property rights in certain defined ways, but what if, more generally, it is against the "public interest" for an owner to exercise a property right in a way not actually covered by some public law text? Equally questions can be posed about the relationship between the "commercial interest" and the "public interest". To what extent should freedom of information, or indeed freedom of speech, be curtailed in the "interest" of a private owner? More generally, when do "economic interests" become "public interests" and when is it in the

---

[61]   Zenati and Revet, above n.28, at p. 246.

[62]   *Code civil* art. 581.

[63]   J.-L. Halpérin, *Histoire du droit privé français depuis 1804* (Paris, Presses Universitaires de France, 1996), p. 37.

[64]   *Code civil* art 544.

[65]   D.1.1.1.2.

[66]   F. Ost, *Droit et intérêt: volume 2: entre droit et non-droit: l'intérêt* (Bruxelles, Facultés universitaires Saint-Louis, 1990), pp. 9–19.

"public interest" to give special protection to the economic interest of a private person or body?

These questions can of course emerge as straight-forward constitutional or private law cases and, as such, be analysed within the traditional rule-hierarchy. Yet it is often these kinds of litigation problem that illustrate the dimensional gaps that exist between the great rational concepts of "rights" and "duties" on the one hand and the established categories like "public" and "private" on the other. One particular gap that has long plagued the Roman model of law actually results from the individualistic orientation of the *persona* and *res* structure. If property belonging to an individual is wrongfully interfered with by another, then the law of actions—these days to be found in codes of procedure—is not short of remedies. But what if it is property in the public realm that is wrongfully damaged or misappropriated? The Roman sources indicate clearly that the model could eventually be adapted to deal with this kind of problem. Towns and some other corporate bodies were finally treated as *personae* and could thus sue or be sued in their own right;[67] and the state itself could be represented in court via institutions like the *fiscus*.[68] In the later civil law, offices such as the *ministère public* were developed to represent the public interest in legal proceedings.[69] Nevertheless, as Mauro Cappelletti has observed:[70]

"more and more frequently the complexity of modern societies generates situations in which a single human action can be beneficial or prejudicial to large numbers of people, thus making entirely inadequate the traditional scheme of litigation as merely a two-party affair".

In turn this makes the Roman dichotomy between public and private law "too simple to reflect present realities".[71] For:[72]

"between the individual and the state there are numerous groups, communities, and collectivities which forcefully claim the enjoyment and judicial protection of certain rights which are classifiable neither as 'public' nor 'private' in the traditional sense."

III.   PROPERTY INTERESTS

Professor Cappelletti has a point of course. Yet an investigation into the dimensions of property law ought to reveal that the problem is not simply one of outdated categories and procedures. The very notion of a property right, as this brief survey of the history of the Roman model has hopefully indicated, implies structures that go to the root of what can only be called the epistemological

---

[67] D.50.16.16.

[68] J.-L. Mestre, *Introduction historique au droit administratif français* (Paris, Presses Universitaires de France, 1985), pp. 106–108.

[69] See generally J. Volff, *Le ministère public* (Paris, Presses Universitaires de France, 1998).

[70] M. Cappelletti, *The Judicial Process in Comparative Perspective* (Oxford, Clarendon Press, 1989), p. 271.

[71] Ibid., p. 273.

[72] Ibid.

foundation of law. The Roman model is centred on the individual, but an individual controlled and constrained by a public law in which *imperium* is always in a state of tension with *dominium*.[73] This model of property will never, then, become outdated as such since it represents a powerful epistemological and ideological starting point. What must be kept in mind however is that it is not the only relevant model. Now the feudal structure, in as much as it represents a static economic and political system founded on land, is clearly of little relevance. But if the concept of land is replaced by that of an interest it does become feasible, as indeed Cappelletti seems to recognise, to talk about a "return to feudalism".[74] The interest of the sovereign can become eclipsed by the interests of powerful intermediary groups. Thus just as one can talk of the interests of this or that individual, so one can refer to the interests of this or that class, such as for example the "interests of consumers".[75] Just as there were once different "rights" (*iura*) of different people in a single plot of land, so today there are different interests in play with respect to a single *res* (using the term in its widest Latin sense). And these different interests can have at one and the same time a private and a public law dimension. For example, a clause in a bill in France to give protection to trade unions (organisations defending of course the interests of employees) against claims for damages in tort by employers (representing the commercial interest) was struck down as unconstitutional.[76] Even at the level of the individual the plurality of interests can be complex. Thus a contract between A and B may well have property implications for C, D and E, not actual parties to the *iuris vinculum*. Not surprisingly, the "interests" of these third parties have given rise to much case law in Europe.

There is no doubt whatsoever that the Roman model was biased against such intermediary groups, for a text in the *Digest* talks of them being tightly controlled.[77] Yet the notion of an "interest" as a quasi-descriptive legal concept is not post Roman. It was used as a means for turning damage into damages[78] and it acted as a control device for defining those who could avail themselves of an *actio*.[79] Indeed there is one text that specifically links the *actio* to the *interest*.[80] This dimension to the Roman model was lost when the law of actions, the third institutional sub-division of *ius* in Gaius' institutional plan,[81] essentially failed

---

[73] J. Ellul, *Histoire des institutions: 1–2/L'Antiquité* (Paris, Presses Universitaires de France, 6th ed. 1984) 477–478.

[74] Cappelletti, above n. 70, at 297.

[75] See e.g., French *Code de la consommation* art 421–1.

[76] *Conseil Constitutionnel* 22.10.1982; [1982] RDCC 61 (extracted in B. Rudden, *A Source-book on French Law*, 3rd edn. (Oxford, Clarendon Press, 1991), p. 72). One should note how the constitutional court talked of it belonging to the state to produce special regimes aimed at "reconciling the interests in play".

[77] D.3.4.1pr.

[78] See e.g., D.9.2.21.2; D.19.1.1.

[79] See e.g., D.45.1.38.17.

[80] D.19.1.1.

[81] H. F. Jolowicz, *Roman Foundations of Modern Law* (Westport, Greenwood Press, 1978), pp. 61–81.

to survive the disappearance of the formulary system.[82] The later evolution of *ius* into the subjective right served only to confirm the loss of the "third dimension". It did not seem to make any logical sense to have an independent system of remedies and the famous distinction between actions *in rem* and *in personam* became a distinction between two kinds of right.[83] Procedure, in the civilian model, thus remains divorced from codes of subjective rights with the result that the conceptual role of an interest in legal thought remains analytically obscure.[84]

However, if one leaves the civil law tradition for the common law, the dimensional richness of pre-codification thinking can be fully recaptured. As Villey once observed, common lawyers were spared the reductionism of the Humanist and Enlightenment legal scientists.[85] The general point to be made, of course, is that feudalism remains particularly important for Western law in that it provided the context for the development of a customary system that was to resist the effects of Romanisation. The English common law is the result of the survival of a system of customary law that was to be found in northern Europe before the reception of Roman law. The influence of feudalism thus introduced a number of complexities into legal thought that have survived in the common law tradition. Perhaps the most important, at least for the property lawyer, is the fundamental distinction between land and other property; moveable goods were not as such subject to a regime of *in rem* remedies and thus were not differentiated from "obligational" claims such as debts. Indeed a claim in debt was as "proprietary" as a claim in detinue for a specific item of property in another's possession; one was a chose in action while the other was a chose in possession.[86]

Of course the distinction between moveable and immovable property is not, as we have seen, confined to the feudal model and given the obvious physical differences, such a classification might cause little surprise.[87] Yet it was not a fundamental distinction in Roman law itself. Certainly, it seems that land was something that could not be stolen, although there was some uncertainty about this;[88] but as a physical object (*res corporalis*) capable of supporting a legal relationship with a person there was no necessary reason why land should be given special treatment. Land was a *res* and the distinction between immovable and moveable property was simply one distinction amongst many. What makes the distinction important within the feudal model is that land was not envisaged as

[82] For a discussion of changes in legal procedure in Rome see Borkowski, above n. 12, at pp. 63–83.

[83] Jolowicz, above n. 81, at pp. 78–81.

[84] See generally Ost, above n. 66.

[85] Villey, above n. 40, at 700.

[86] J. H. Baker, *An Introduction to English Legal History*, 3rd edn. (London, Butterworths, 1990), pp. 441–442; F. H. Lawson and B. Rudden *The Law of Property*, 2nd edn. (Oxford, Clarendon Press, 1982), p. 20; M. Bridge, *Personal Property Law*, 2nd edn. (London, Blackstone, 1996), pp. 3–6.

[87] *Code civil* art. 516.

[88] D.47.2.25pr.

being the subject of a unique legal relationship between person and thing. The public and private aspect to land rested upon a customary legal regime that was entirely alien to the one to be found in the *Corpus Iuris Civilis*. "Ownership belongs to a flat world in which rights in land or other forms of wealth are dependent upon no authority except the state", observes Milsom, but feudal tenure "belongs to a smaller world in which there is no need and no room for abstract ideas like ownership".[89] In continental Europe this smaller world became enlarged with the reception of Roman law; the feudal land law was transformed, via the Roman law of actions, into a world of *dominium utile* and *domininium directum*.[90] In England, however, there was no reception and as a result English land law remains, relative to the codes, unique.

The distinction between moveable and immovable property is, then, the *summa divisio* of English property law. However, it is not expressed in this way. Rather than immovable property one talks in terms of real property and this category is to be contrasted with personal property. This language of "realty" seems more Roman than feudal and to an extent it is; real property was property originally protected by a real action (*in rem*) whereas personal property was protected only by an *actio in personam*.[91] But there the similarity ends since the real actions of the early common law were very different in procedural form from the Roman *actio in rem* and they responded to concepts that were feudal rather than Roman.[92] All land since 1066 was owned (in the Roman sense) by the Crown and accordingly all lesser titles could not be based on *dominium* as such. Medieval English land law was based, instead, upon seisin.[93] The person seised of land did not therefore own the land as such; he held it within a feudal hierarchy which had at its head the king. However land could also be held for a term of years under a "contract" outside of the strict feudal hierarchy. Such transactions are now called leases and by statute are true property rights;[94] but originally they granted neither real nor possessory rights in the land and thus, in the language of Roman law, were mere contracts.[95] They were commercial rather than feudal transactions in that the principal use was to secure a loan.[96] Later a lessee's possession under a lease came to be protected and this was achieved, *inter alia*, both by a "real" action (that is to say an action for the recovery of the possession) and by the action of trespass (the two actions may have had a common origin).[97] A claim for damages could be brought against anyone who wrongfully invaded the lessee's possession. The action for damages based

---

[89]   Milsom, above n. 14, at p. 100.

[90]   J.-P. Lévy, *Histoire de la propriété* (Paris, Presses Universitaires de France, 1972), p. 45.

[91]   P. Stein, *Legal Institutions: The Development of Dispute Settlement* (London, Butterworths, 1984), p. 165.

[92]   Ibid., pp. 167–168.

[93]   See F. H. Lawson, "Common Law" in *International Encyclopedia of Comparative Law* (New York, Oceana), Vol. VI, Ch. 2, Part II (J. C. B. Mohr), para. 29.

[94]   Law of Property Act 1925, s. 1.

[95]   Lawson, above n. 93. See also Milsom, above n. 14, at pp. 152–157.

[96]   Baker, above n. 86, at p. 338.

[97]   Milsom, above n. 14, at pp. 154–155.

upon trespass, however, was not a proprietary action in the Roman sense, although its main purpose was to protect possessors of property; it was as much a claim in the law of obligations since it was an action for damages based upon a wrong. Indirect interferences with land from noise or pollution were, equally, remedied by an action based upon a wrong. This was the action for nuisance and even today remains based upon an interest in land.[98] Remedies were thus central to the understanding of property "rights" in English law, but these remedies, if viewed from the position of the Roman model, were neither truly *in rem* nor classically *in personam*. They were remedies protecting the use and enjoyment of land and this use and enjoyment is expressed today in terms of an "interest".

English real property law is not, however, to be understood entirely from the position of legal actions since the complexity of feudal ideas found expression in a conceptual model as well as via remedial claims. Such a model was necessary since feudal titles to land could be granted by one person to another not only for life but also for shorter periods or for successive periods, subject perhaps to various conditions.[99] The central concept in this model is the notion of an "estate" which is an abstract entity between the holder or holders of land and the land itself. It represents the temporal aspect of land—a "fourth dimension"[100]—capable of being divisible between various holders but remaining, metaphysically speaking, as a single whole. Estate is thus a more rarefied and flexible idea than the notion of an "interest" (even although one talks today of various interests in land) in that it was designed to take account of the past and future as well as the present. Again there is a Roman element to this term in as much as it is derived from the Latin word *status* and once reflected the idea of a person's status in relation to a piece of land. In a sense, then, the term "estate" is a concept straddling the law of persons and the law of things. However in operation it was far removed from Roman thinking in that several people can enjoy at one and the same time "ownership" rights in the same piece of property and each of these rights is separately alienable. It is not, therefore, the *res corporalis* that is alienated (that was, and in theory remains, impossible since all land is owned by the Crown); it is the estate, a *res incorporalis*, that is the thing that is alienated.[101]

In the past, the number of estates that were capable of being recognised by the common law was unlimited since feudal and other interests did not have to be reconciled with, and conceptualised according to, the Roman model. Thus, as Lawson has pointed out:

> "there was nothing to prevent the development of limited interests of a non-feudal kind which were not confined to the very restricted list found in Roman law".

---

[98] *Hunter* v. *Canary Wharf Ltd.* [1997] AC 655.
[99] See e.g., Stein, above n. 91, at pp. 166–167.
[100] Lawson and Rudden, above n. 86, at p. 88.
[101] Patault, above n. 6, at pp. 33–34.

There was no *numerus clausus* of such interests and: [102]

"what happened was that a novel but strictly logical form of legal grammar was evolved, conformity to which was essential if such limited interests were to be validly created".

This grammar is now on a statutory basis and as such, given the disappearance of feudalism, it may be tempting to apply the Roman model of ownership. This is dangerous as Lawson has shown in his comparative analysis. Although the whole estate may be thought of as the whole quantum of interest in the land ("that for which the full capital value of the land would be paid by a purchaser"), [103] such a whole estate, called the "fee simple", is fragmentable. In civil law, ownership, as we have seen, is the coming together of the *ius utendi, fruendi* and *abutendi*; but the fee simple of the common law, while in one sense the nearest thing to ownership, is "a fragmentable quantum of interest". And this fee simple: [104]

"has, more than any other factor, made it both impossible and superfluous to attempt to rivet what a Common Lawyer would consider the oversimplified notion of ownership on the common law system of real property law".

This, once again, is why English lawyers talk less in terms of ownership and more in terms of interests.[105]

Interest is also a useful notion because, as we have seen, it attaches with ease to the legal remedy (*actio*). One can thus think in terms of property interests protected by the law of actions. At this level, however, one must not just think of the remedies provided by the common law courts; it is equally important to take account of the equitable relief furnished by the Court of Chancery. For example P contracts with S for S to sell to P a piece of land. At law P will have no legal rights in the land itself (*in rem*) until the property is conveyed, but if the court of equity will grant specific performance of the contract could it not be said that P has an *equitable* right in the land? Or, put another way, can one talk in terms of a recognised *equitable interest*? Such interests are recognised as subsisting in English property law with the result that property "rights" are never just a matter of substantive law; they can be created and (or) extended by the law of actions. Thus a right of way over another's property can be created in equity simply by an owner of land giving the impression to a neighbour, who accordingly acts to his detriment, that he has such a right.[106]

Of course by far the most important property right created by equity is that arising out of a trust. From its earliest days the Court of Chancery recognised that the contents of ownership could be split: the right to enjoy (*ius utendi*) could be vested in one person (the beneficiary) while to right to administer and

---

[102] Lawson, above n. 93, at para. 35.
[103] Ibid., para 38.
[104] Ibid.
[105] See e.g., Lawson and Rudden, above n. 86, at pp. 40–64.
[106] *Crabb* v. *Arun District Council* [1976] Ch 179.

to alienate (*ius abutendi*) could be vested in another. When analysed from the position of the codes, the main difficulty facing the civil lawyer is to decide what kind of right the beneficiary has under a trust. Is it a *ius in rem* or is it only a *ius in personam*? The question has given rise to much literature in the Anglo-American world,[107] but it would be idle for the comparatist to spend too much time on this question as a matter of form. For notions like *dominium* and *in rem* have to be treated with great care in the context of the common law system. In the civil law, relationships between *persona* and *persona* (obligations) or between *persona* and *res* (property) can be seen—often misleadingly—as flat or two-dimensional. This is not really true of the common law where legal relations have to be appreciated not only through the prism of remedies but also on occasions through a number of specific and all-embracing equitable doctrines such as estoppel and the protection of the *bona fide* purchaser. It may be, of course, that equity will then "extend" the interest protected by the remedy to something more akin to a "right". Yet what needs to be stressed is that the English law of property cannot be understood in terms of a flat two-dimensional world. It operates within a multi-dimensional model where, to use the language of the Roman model, an *actio in personam* can be based upon a *ius in rem* [108] and rights can be defeated by interests.[109]

Take for example the notion of "tracing" in equity. This has been described as an *actio in rem* for money[110] and thus in one sense involves language and concepts familiar to any jurist from anywhere in Europe. Yet at whatever level one operates there are problems for the civilian. The idea of a revindication action for money in another's patrimony is impossible for most civil lawyers since ownership passes on delivery and certainly passes if money becomes mixed with other coins. Equally the description of tracing as neither a claim nor a remedy, but a "process", introduces a procedural (or substantive?) tool that has little meaning in traditional legal science.[111] It is, accordingly, by no means easy to analyse equitable property rights through the Romanist language of *iura in rem*, *actiones*, *dominium* and so on. Rights, remedies and interests are fragmented ideas to be reconstructed within particular factual situations and attaching to particular institutions and concepts adapted or even developed to suit particular empirical situations. Perhaps the only point of contact is that such tracing remedies are now motivated by the principle of unjust enrichment. Yet even here there is a comparative problem. In the civilian world the law of unjust enrichment belongs to the law of obligations, not to the law of actions *in rem*.

---

[107] Lawson and Rudden, above n. 86, at p. 58.
[108] See e.g., *Lipkin Gorman* v. *Karpnale Ltd.* [1991] 2 AC 548.
[109] See e.g., *Miller* v. *Jackson* [1977] QB 966.
[110] F. H. Lawson, *Remedies of English Law*, 2nd edn. (London, Butterworths, 1980), pp. 147–160.
[111] Millet L J in *Boscawen* v. *Bajwa* [1995] 4 All ER 769, 776–777.

IV. LAW OF PERSONS AND LAW OF THINGS

The English feudal model differed from the Roman model in another important way. Royal power via the *curia regis* developed its own system of exceptional jurisdictions to deal with matters that impinged upon the king's interest. However this system was not open as of right to the population.[112] In order to gain access to the royal courts a complainant had to obtain an administrative "ticket" called a "writ" and these writs were based upon model factual situations which were gradually extended only on a case by case basis.[113] The conceptual foundation of these writs did not follow the Roman structure or mentality. Certainly there was a reliance on a law of actions (the writ system was called the forms of action) and the common law courts were prepared to offer a revindication remedy for land (writ of right).[114] But many of the other writs such as debt, detinue, trover and nuisance were both *in personam* and *in rem* in nature;[115] they grew out of the facts of late medieval English society and not out of some revered law book.[116] This system survived in form up until the nineteenth century. A series of major procedural reforms during this period revolutionised the court structure and the forms of action were replaced with a system of pleading less formal in style.[117] However in substance the common law remained attached to the distinction between land and moveable (personal) property with the result that personal property problems were handled by remedies that were categorised under "tort".[118] And, according to the codes, tort (delict) belongs to the law of obligations.

In fact the feudal background, together with the forms of action, has introduced into the area of moveable property a certain subtlety in the form of the relationship of bailment which is in some ways analogous to the doctrine of estates in land.[119] As such, it again transgresses, in the language of the Roman model, the law of persons and the law of things. The transfer of possession in a chattel will of itself give rise to obligations and these obligations belong in sub-

---

[112] Baker, above n. 86, at pp. 16–18.

[113] Ibid., pp. 63–67; R. C. van Caenegem, *The Birth of the English Common Law*, 2nd edn. (Cambridge, Cambridge University Press, 1988), pp. 29–30. Note in particular Milsom's comment: "But plaintiffs could not get to the court without a chancery writ, and the formulae of the writs, most of which were highly practical responses to the needs of thirteenth-century litigants, became an authoritative canon which could not easily be altered or added to . . . The common law writs came to be seen as somehow basic, almost like the Ten Commandments or the Twelve Tables, the data from which the law itself was derived": Milsom, above n. 14, at p. 36.

[114] But cf. van Caenegem, *Birth*, above n. 113, at p. 44.

[115] Milsom, above n. 14, at pp. 6–8, 119–122, 260–261, 263, 275, 278, 398–399.

[116] Ibid., 43–44; R. C. van Caenegem, *Judges, Legislators and Professors* (Cambridge, Cambridge University Press, 1987), pp. 124–126.

[117] Baker, above n. 86, at pp. 80–81. For the background to these reforms see G. Wilson, *Cases and Materials on the English Legal System* (London, Sweet & Maxwell, 1973), pp. 1–12, 18–22, 33–34, 47–48, 345–348.

[118] Torts (Interference with Goods) Act 1977 (UK).

[119] Lawson and Rudden, above n. 86, at pp. 95–97.

stance not only to the law of property rather than to the law of obligations,[120] but also, in part, to the law of persons. In form bailment rights and duties are given expression via remedies in tort; yet these remedial rights are attached not to the property relationship as such but to the status of "bailee" and "bailor".[121] The relationship of bailment looks as if it owes much to the Roman contracts *re* and it may well be that the common law was influenced by Roman thinking.[122] Nevertheless it cuts across civilian thinking in that it has the effect of introducing into a whole range of commercial and consumer transactions a property (*in rem*) dimension that is both independent of, yet linked to, the law of rights *in personam*.

Feudalism, then, had the effect of blurring the boundary between the law of persons and the law of things. Feudal positions such as that of the serf were as much a matter of status as obligation and this prompted Maine to observe that "the movement of the progressive societies has hitherto been a movement from status to contract".[123] Roman law, it might be said, was the means of releasing the employee from serfdom to liberty of employment. Now the absence of a reception of Roman law in England did not of course result in employees remaining shackled within a law of persons. What it did do was to impede analysis along Roman institutional lines until the nineteenth century with the result that distinctions between contract, tort and status were by no means clear by the time the railways were invented and developed.[124] The notion of a bailee or of a common carrier could be said to be as much a question of status as of contract.[125] As Graveson has observed, the:[126]

> "Common Law until the early nineteenth century was a law of relationships, many of status, some of less than status, and upon those relationships of status vicarious liability was founded".

The result is that the modern English private law is in many respects a mixture of persons, things, actions and obligations; it lacks the symmetry of the codes because it transgresses such a symmetry. Accordingly, although the persons and things distinction can be applied to the common law in as much as legal personality and status are both established concepts, it is necessary on occasion to abandon such architecture when it comes to the understanding of some of the English case law.

Take two examples. In *Stevenson* v. *Beverley Bentinck*[127] the question arose as to whether an innocent purchaser of a car, which turned out to have been on

---

[120] *Building and Civil Engineering Holidays Scheme Management Ltd.* v. *Post Office* [1966] 1 QB 247, 261.
[121] Torts (Interference with Goods) Act 1977 (UK), s. 2(2).
[122] *Coggs* v. *Bernard* (1703) 92 ER 107.
[123] H. Maine, *Ancient Law* (1861, Oxford ed. 1939), p. 141.
[124] R. H. Graveson, *Status in the Common Law* (London, Athlone, 1953), pp. 38–40.
[125] A. W. B. Simpson, *A History of the Common Law of Contract* (Oxford, Clarendon Press, 1975), pp. 206–207, 231–234.
[126] Graveson, above n. 124, at p. 41.
[127] [1976] 1 WLR 483.

hire-purchase, was a "private purchaser" within the meaning of statute. According to the Court of Appeal it was a question of status. It is not a valid argument for a "trade or finance purchaser" to claim that he had purchased such a vehicle in his capacity as a private purchaser; if he works as a trade and finance purchaser then that is a category to which he automatically belongs. Status was accordingly used directly to solve a property problem. A similar approach can be discerned in the more recent case of *Waverley Borough Council* v. *Fletcher*[128] which involved a dispute about the possession, and in reality ownership, of a medieval brooch which a member of the public had found in a public park while using a metal detector. The dispute arose because the use of such detectors was prohibited by the local authority. The Court of Appeal held that the council had the better possessory title to the brooch because, in using the metal detector, the finder had turned himself into a trespasser. In effect, then, the finder's status of "trespasser" directly affected his possessory claim. Of course neither the tort of trespass nor the tort of conversion belongs to the law of persons as such. Yet at the level of reasoning one can see an intermixing of concepts in as much as the standing of a party is directly determining the relationship between *persona* and *res*. Or, put another way, possession, and those entitled to possession, is close to being on occasions a question of status.

Waverley Borough Council v. *Fletcher* has the extra dimension of being, in part, a public law case in as much as it involved a local authority. Yet status as a legal category brings its own dimensional problems into property law: for although it is, according to the civilian model, very much part of private law, it clearly has a constitutional dimension. Few would argue today that the status of women with regard to family property is a matter having no constitutional implications. This public law dimension may not be evident at first sight in the tort of conversion cases involving disputes between finance companies and hire-purchasers. But the class of "private purchasers" is very much in the tradition of distinguishing between the interests of consumers and the interests of professionals. Special groups are being accorded property rights denied to other groups. A constitutional dimension to property has thus been exposed simply through the use of status as part of the common law reasoning model.

In some property cases the constitutional dimension can become particularly evident if the law of persons dimension is of such a nature that it brings into play the Convention for the Protection of Human Rights and Fundamental Freedoms. For example, in claims by commercial organisations for the return of embarrassing leaked documents, the interests in respect of the *res* (leaked document) can become quite complex. The procedural, property and constitutional rights to be found in such cases often depend upon what interest the court chooses to emphasise.[129] Will it be the commercial interest of the company capable of being expressed, for example, via their property right in the docu-

---

[128] [1996] QB 334.

[129] See e.g., *X Ltd.* v. *Morgan Grampian Ltd.* [1991] 1 AC 1; cf. *Goodwin* v. *United Kingdom* (1996), pp. 22 EHRR 123.

ment or will it be the interest of employees to "whistle blow"? Will it be the interest of the press, or individual journalist, in reporting newsworthy behaviour of say the directors of the company or will it be the interest of the public in general in learning about such behaviour (and more indirectly in having a free press)?[130] An added complexity to this kind of problem is that an appeal to the "public interest" allows the court to "downgrade" the case from one of principle to one of fact. Such an approach not only permits a court to side-step an inconvenient precedent,[131] but avoids any discussion of the issue in terms of rights. Ought a property right to take precedence over the constitutional right of a journalist to protect his or her sources? One is, it might be said, choosing the "feudal" over the "Roman" model.

This kind of "feudal interests" approach, using this term as a means of expressing dimensional complexity, can extend in English law to what the civil codes would see as a right to dignity. Such an interest, in the French Code civil, is not a patrimonial right even although its invasion may on occasions give rise to an action in the law of obligations. It is a right that attaches directly to the person and is thus placed within the Book dealing with the Law of Persons.[132] This goes far in excluding economic interests while, at the same time, giving expression to a right that transcends the private and public divide (which is particularly strict in France).[133] Even in the civil law, therefore, there is a certain dimensional complexity to the dignity interest. This complexity is even greater in the common law for two reasons. First because the common law, lacking the structure of the Roman model, does not have a clearly defined boundary between the law of persons and the law of things. All non-contractual damages actions end up in the law of tort and as problems to be analysed in terms of existing causes of action. This means that personality interests often get treated as if they were property problems.[134] Secondly, because, as one might expect of the "feudal model", it is analysed as a problem of competing interests. For example medical treatment such as an operation or sterilisation can be given only when the patient consents, yet what if the patient is unconscious? If the operation is not urgent it is probably the case in many Western systems that consent cannot be implied even if such an operation would be in the interest of the patient.

---

[130] "No public interest is served in shielding this source from exposure. The information leaked by this source and published on 28 May 1997 was in any event planned for authorised publication by the plaintiff on 3 June. Rather than serving a public interest, it appears that the prior and premature disclosure and publication of the draft accounts served a private purpose of the source or a private purpose of the defendant in securing a scoop...": Mummery LJ in *Camelot Group plc v. Centaur Communications Ltd.* [1998] 2 WLR 379, 392.

[131] "I am conscious that [the European Court of Human Rights] reached different conclusions on the same facts but this is a no more surprising legal phenomenon than this court concluding that a particular course of conduct amounted to negligence when the court of first instance concluded that the very same course of conduct did *not* amount to negligence": Schiemann LJ in *Camelot Group plc v. Centaur Communications Ltd.* [1998] 2 WLR 379, 388.

[132] *Code civil* art. 16.

[133] V Saint-James, "Réflexions sur la dignité de l'être humain en tant que concept juridique du droit français", [1997] *Recueil Dalloz*, Chron 61.

[134] See e.g., *Khorasandjian v. Bush* [1993] QB 727.

However if the operation is required as a matter of life-or-death necessity it imme-diately becomes possible to argue that the interest in preserving the life of the patient implies of itself consent. The doctor must act in the "best interests of his patient".[135] Matters become difficult, of course, if the patient is known to belong to a religious faith that has a strict rule prohibiting say a blood transfusion. In this situation the whole consent issue is resolved, in English law at least, by reference to the interests in play. And so in a case involving the question of whether or not an emergency blood transfusion could be given to a person brought up as a Jehovah's Witness, Lord Donaldson MR reasoned as follows:[136]

> "This situation gives rise to a conflict between two interests, that of the patient and that of the society in which he lives. The patient's interest consists of his right to self-determination – his right to live his own life how he wishes, even if it will damage his health or lead to his premature death. Society's interest is in upholding the concept that all human life is sacred and that it should be preserved if at all possible. It is well established that in the ultimate the right of the individual is paramount. But this merely shifts the problem where the conflict occurs and calls for a very careful exam-ination of whether, and if so the way in which, the individual is exercising that right. In the case of doubt, that doubt falls to be resolved in favour of the preservation of life for if the individual is to override the public interest, he must do so in clear terms".

This introduction of the "public interest" into the consent problem is, how-ever, more ambiguous than it might at first seem. Lord Donaldson uses it in terms of preserving life. But what if such preservation of life turns out to be eco-nomically expensive in a society where resources are limited? Might it not be in the "public interest" to terminate life?

This problem emerges in the controversial Tony Bland case.[137] Bland was left in a condition known as "persistent vegetative state" (PVS) as a result of the Hillsborough football ground tragedy and according to standard medical opin-ion there was no chance of him ever regaining consciousness. The parents of Tony Bland held the view that their son would not have wanted to be left in this condition and they thus supported the hospital when it sought a declaration that it would be lawful to turn off the life support machine. Although the judges in all three courts were in no doubt about the moral and ethical dimensions in issue, they quickly fixed onto the idea of the unconscious person's "best inter-ests". A patient in a state of unconsciousness had two distinct rights: the right of self-determination and the right to be treated in a way that is in his or her best interests.[138] Having set up the "best interests" structure it was relatively easy to arrive at the conclusion that it would both respect the dignity of the *persona* and be in his (its) best interests that medical treatment be discontinued. Lord Mustill did admit that the "distressing truth which must not be shirked is that . . . he has

---

[135] *In re F (Mental Patient: Sterilisation)* [1990] 2 AC 1.
[136] *Re T* [1992] 3 WLR 782, 796.
[137] *Airedale NHS Trust* v. *Bland* [1993] AC 789.
[138] See Butler-Sloss in *Bland*, above n. 137, at pp. 816–817.

no best interests of any kind".[139] Yet this had the effect of allowing attention to shift off the *persona* and consent and onto the "interests of the community". "Threaded through the technical arguments addressed to the House were strands of a much wider position", said Lord Mustill, "that it is in the best interests of the community at large that Anthony Bland's life should now end". For the "large resources of skill, labour and money now being devoted to Anthony Bland might in the opinion of many be more fruitfully employed in improving the condition of other patients, who if treated may have useful, healthy and enjoyable lives for many years to come".[140] As far as he was concerned, this was a question that could only be answered by Parliament; yet, despite his personal conviction, Lord Mustill has gone far in articulating the legal route by which compulsory euthanasia could be legally justified were it ever to be in the "public interest". In the common law tradition, patrimonial interests can so easily become the dominant consideration both in private and in public law. Consent as a state of mind is, no doubt, an important point of focus in determining liability of the hospital. Yet its construction is often formulated out of the building block of an "interest". Such a concept is useful because it appears to be descriptive and thus the House of Lords appears to be giving effect to Tony Bland's subjective desire to die. The cynic might claim, however, that it is the "best economic interest" of society that has the most influence when it comes to constructing and reconstructing states of mind.

V. TOWARDS A NEW EPISTEMOLOGY OF PROPERTY

Economic interest is typical of the new language of property—a language that transcends the public and private divide.[141] Yet how is this new language to be reconciled with the traditional models of property law? The late Professor Lawson never underestimated the complexities to be found in both models of property law.[142] However perhaps his great insight was to suggest that in order to understand the feudal model it was necessary to move into a "fourth dimension". This is evidently a creative model in which to conceptualise the complexity of English land law and, in addition, it is an idea that can be extended beyond land law to property law in general. Indeed, given the undoubted public law, law of persons and law of obligations dimensions to property, Professor Lawson's model ought perhaps to be adapted to law as a whole. That is to say, the idea of envisaging law in terms of a flat two-dimensional hierarchy of systematically arranged linguistic propositions is no longer adequate to give expression to the complexities of legal thought. Ownership, possession, real

---

[139] Above n. 137, at 897.
[140] Ibid., at 896.
[141] A. Jacquemin and G. Schrans, *Le droit économique*, 3rd edn. (Paris, Presses Universitaires de France, 1982), pp. 34–51.
[142] F. H. Lawson, above n. 93, at Vol. VI, Ch. 2, Part VIII.

rights, personal rights, rights as a concept, actions, legal categories and so on cannot be represented in a two-dimensional form and this is why it is not unreasonable to claim that legal science has moved beyond the "axiomatic stage" of development. It is, perhaps, now in a "post-axiomatic" stage where the aim is not to reduce the complexity of law but to embrace it.[143] What Professor Lawson has provided is the outline of an epistemological model that can do just this.

The strength of such a multi-dimensional model is that it could reconcile within a single structure *in rem, in personam, ius publicum* and interest relationships. Property interests could function in a world of rights, remedies and sovereignty without contradiction in as much as different logical relations could be confined within their own dimension.[144] In other words, such a model would be capable at one and the same time of representing not just the various levels of legal science—empirical categories, rational (institutional) categories, rights and duties. It could equally encapsulate the seemingly descriptive notions such as interests, damage, fault and the like. In particular, then, a multi-dimensional model is required if "interests", "rights" and remedies are to be conceptualised in ways that avoid contradiction.[145] Now such contradictions were something the Natural Lawyers and Pandectists sought specifically to eliminate from their two-dimensional and highly abstract systems.[146] Yet what this chapter has tried to emphasise is that even the civilian model of property is, in its historical essence, too complex in its structure to be able to succumb to such reductionism. The relationship between personality rights, real rights (*iura in rem* and *in re*), personal rights (*iura in personam*) and constitutional rights, seemingly given expression by the formal symmetry of the codes, can so easily be undermined by the notion of property itself. Does "property" include "rights" with the result that one can have a right to a right? Do rights such as dignity have a patrimonial dimension that allows them to be reduced to an economic interest capable of being assessed in damages? What of the relationship between rights (*dominium*) and sovereignty (*imperium*): is this rendered partly, if not completely, meaningless by the European Convention of Human Rights? Can new status groups have rights as effective and as strong as those attaching to the individual *persona*? And if so do these rights represent a public or a private interest? The truth, of course, is that these conceptual contradictions within legal thinking are what endows legal discourse with its analytical richness. They give law its flexibility in the face of social facts. And if social fact is never reducible to two-dimensions, then it is not unreasonable for the epistemologist to conclude that a knowledge model of property—of law—might need to be more complex than a civil code.

---

[143] G. Samuel, "The Impact of European Integration on Private Law—A Comment", (1998) 18 *Legal Studies* 167.

[144] These ideas are developed in more depth in G. Samuel, *The Foundations of Legal Reasoning* (Antwerp, Maklu, 1994).

[145] See e.g., G. Samuel and J. Rinkes, *Law of Obligations and Legal Remedies* (London, Cavendish, 1996), pp. 353–356.

[146] F. Wieacker, above n. 26, at pp. 343–344.

It is this complexity that suggests an analogy with time. How is time to be represented in a scientific model? The traditional vision is of an arrow in which time flies or flows in a linear and uniform way. Such a model is extremely valuable, of course. It conforms very closely to the commonsense of the individual human acting as a central point in a world in which uniformity of movement seems a natural law. Yet when it comes to representing space and time in terms of mathematical models difficulties soon emerge between the common sense notion of time and the representation of time at the level of theory. Einstein avoided some of the contradictions that emerged from the uni-dimensional view of time as an arrow by refusing to accept the model itself.[147] For him time was to be seen within a multi-dimensional model where past, present and future did not exist in linear form but in different dimensions. Within such a model the past might be rediscovered at some point in the future.[148] Of course drawing an analogy between law and time has its dangers. Indeed the history of science is littered with transformations that proved illegitimate;[149] and legal science itself has had its own share of futile epistemological analogies the effects of which still continue to infect legal thinking. The analogy with time is drawn here, therefore, only as a symbol and not as a conceptual device;[150] it is used as a symbol to provoke a change in the symmetry of knowledge representation. That such a change is desirable is of course a matter of debate. But there is one great practical advantage for the comparative property lawyer in transgressing the traditional symmetry of the model in which the dimensions of law have been represented. It becomes possible to rethink the various European models of law within a single, if complex, structure and this, in turn, could provide an opportunity to stimulate further the debate about legal harmonisation.[151]

[147] Piettre, above n. 2, at p. 37.
[148] Ibid., pp. 70–72.
[149] A. Virieux-Reymond, *Introduction à l'épistémologie*, 2nd edn. (Paris, Presses Universitaires de France, 1972), pp. 71–72.
[150] For the difference see A. Leroux and A. Marciano, *La philosophie économique* (Paris, Presses Universitaires de France, 1998) p. 33.
[151] Cf. P Legrand, "European Legal Systems are not Converging", (1996) 45 *ICLQ* 52; "Against a European Civil Code", (1997) 60 *Mod LR* 44.

4

Is Property a Human Right?

J. W. HARRIS

Every term in the question I have chosen for the title to this chapter is the subject of philosophical and jurisprudential controversy. What is a "right"? What is it about any particular right that warrants attaching to it the epithet "human"? How can any facet of human experience be separated out from all else that happens to us in such a way that it can be said to found a human right? If people disagree about such matters, by what argumentative procedure can it be established that something or other "is" a human right? How could the notion of property fit the bill? What, after all, is "property"? I shall argue that all these questions intersect. If taken together, the answer to each unravels in the light of answers offered for the others.

In the first part of my book *Property and Justice*[1] I addressed the last of these questions—what is property? I concluded that there is no "true" meaning of this term, that is, one which transcends all contexts in which the question might be raised. I offered a definition tailored to a particular project, that of deciding whether property institutions can be justified and, if so, what features they ought to incorporate. That was the project pursued in the second half of the book. I shall in this chapter apply the conclusions I reached about property's justifiability to the question: "Is Property a Human Right?"

In the next section I offer a definition of property which, I contend, reflects the structural features of property institutions—the ways in which the bits interconnect. It also reflects, I think, a wide swathe of legal and lay property talk, although I have freely invented terms so that important distinctions become more precise. In the third section I argue that certain more expansive definitions of property should be rejected. In the fourth section, I investigate, briefly, the nature of rights in general and human rights in particular. The fifth section argues against a strong conception of a human property right derived from historical-entitlement theories of justice. The sixth section advances the view that there is a background moral right to property, which has some carry-over effect for the presumptive and qualified moral status of existing property-holdings. In that special (and relatively weak) sense, property may be said to be a human right.

---

[1] J. W. Harris, *Property and Justice* (Oxford, Clarendon Press, 1996).

I. WHAT IS PROPERTY?

"Property" designates those items which are points of reference within, and therefore presupposed by, the rules of a property institution—namely, trespassory, property-limitation, expropriation and appropriation rules. Such items are either the subject of direct trespassory protection or else separately assignable as parts of private wealth (or both).

Therefore, "property" comprises (1) ownership and quasi-ownership interests in things (tangible or ideational); (2) other rights over such things as are enforceable against all-comers (non-ownership proprietary interests); (3) money; and (4) cashable rights. In addition, some legal systems recognise protected non-propertyholdings and/or communitarian property, neither of which are internal to property institutions. The foregoing is my definition of property. I shall now seek to explain and justify this definition.

The last 20 years have witnessed a burgeoning of philosophical interest in the nature and normative foundations of property.[2] Running through much of this literature is the following ambivalence. Sometimes the term "property" is taken to refer to an institution, and sometimes it is treated as synonymous with the word "ownership". In the former sense, "property" refers to any system of rules and principles governing the use and allocation of resources; and it is said that we may distinguish three ideal-typical varieties: common property; collective property; and private property. In the latter sense, the notion of "property" is to be explained, or exploded, by asking whether there are any necessary and sufficient conditions for establishing that anyone "owns" something. This ambivalence is important for our present inquiry. We might be seeking to discover whether human beings have a right that their community introduce or maintain a property institution of a particular type, or whether anyone has a right to own a particular resource.

I contend that the ambivalence should be transcended in the following way. Property is an institution in which ownership interests are important, but not the only, items. The stereotypical conceptions of common and collective property have no counterparts in real property institutions. On the other hand, every property institution includes common and collective features.

[2] L. C. Becker, *Property Rights: Philosophic Foundations* (London, Routledge and Kegan Paul, 1977); "The Moral Basis of Property Rights" in J. R. Pennock and J. W. Chapman (eds), *Property: Nomos XXII* (New York, New York University Press, 1980); A. Ryan, *Property and Political Theory* (Oxford, Blackwell, 1984); A. Reeve, *Property* (London, Macmillan, 1986); J. Waldron, *The Right to Private Property* (Oxford, Clarendon Press, 1988); S. R .Munzer, *A Theory of Property* (New York, Cambridge University Press, 1990); J. Grunebaum, *Private Ownership* (Routledge and Kegan Paul, 1986); S. Buckle, *Natural Law and the Theory of Property: Grotius to Hume* (Oxford, Clarendon Press, 1991); M. J. Radin, *Reinterpreting Property* (Chicago, University of Chicago Press, 1993); J. Christman, *The Myth of Property* (New York, Oxford University Press, 1994); J Penner, *The Idea of Property in Law* (Oxford, Clarendon Press, 1996). See also the essays collected in *Property: Nomos XXII*, above; and E. F. Paul, F. D. Miller and J. Paul (eds), *Property Rights* (Cambridge, Cambridge University Press, 1994).

Another ambivalence to be found in the philosophic literature relates to materiality. "Property", whether conceived of as an institution or as ownership, is primarily explicated in terms of land and chattels. Intellectual property may not get a look in. More important is the fluctuating approach towards money, especially money in the form of monetary claims. If we wish to know whether property is a human right, intangible forms of property cannot be left out.

Added to these two ambivalences we find a degree of scepticism about ownership—and hence about "property", when "property" is treated synonymously with "ownership". One source of this scepticism is an illegitimate deduction from two highly influential seminal works. The first is Hohfeld's reduction of rights in *in rem* into "multitital" *in personam* claim-rights, privileges, powers and immunities.[3] The second is Tony Honoré's listing of the incidents of the "liberal concept of full individual ownership".[4] Following these leads, it is widely accepted that ownership ("property") comprises a bundle of detachable rights. That being so, some have concluded that it is pointless (or impossible) to attribute any sense to the notion of ownership.

At its worst, this scepticism takes the form of what I have called "totality ownership".[5] For a person to be owner of a thing, it would have to be true that she was at liberty to do absolutely anything she liked with it. Now it can easily be shown that there are restrictions on the use of even ordinary chattels. No one may use a hammer to hit people or break windows. Therefore, no one ever owns a hammer, or anything else. Totality ownership is a conception never deployed by any property institution. It is an invention of sceptics, put up to be knocked down. I call it an "Aunt Sally" concept.

Another source of scepticism about ownership ("property") derives from the pedagogic priority of land law within common law academies. The doctrine of estates, it is said, dispenses altogether with the concept of ownership. Added to that are the manifold complexities introduced into resource holdings by trust law, company law, and all the other institutional structures which separate control over material objects from allocation of intangible wealth. Where is any single notion of property ("ownership") to be found within all this diversity?

If, on these sceptical accounts, property means nothing in particular, of course it cannot be the subject of a human right. Constitutional provisions which suppose that it is, should be unmasked as open season invitations to courts to give any rights they choose the status of "property".[6]

---

[3] W. N. Hohfeld, *Fundamental Legal Conceptions as Applied in Judicial Reasoning* (New Haven, Yale University Press, 1919), p. 71 et seq. I have discussed Hohfeld's analysis in *Property and Justice*, above n. 1, at pp. 120–125.

[4] A. M. Honoré, "Ownership" in A. G. Guest (ed.), *Oxford Essays in Jurisprudence* (London, Oxford University Press, 1961). A revised version of the essay appears in Tony Honoré, *Making Law Bind: Essays Legal and Philosophical* (Oxford, Clarendon Press, 1986), pp. 161–192. I have discussed Honoré's list of incidents in *Property and Justice*, above n. 1, at pp. 125–130.

[5] Above n. 1, at pp. 132–138.

[6] See Ackerman's approach to constitutional theory, discussed in the next section.

My answer to such scepticism is as follows. There is no univocal, singular concept of ownership, applicable to all resources at all stages of social and legal development. Instead, property institutions include a spectrum of ownership interests. We need to display the interactions between this spectrum and the different types of rules to be found in property institutions, as well as indicating the space left for non-ownership items. The overall analysis has to be institution focused.

Foundational to all property institutions are the twinned, and mutually irreducible, notions of trespassory rules and the ownership spectrum. By "trespassory rules", I mean any rules imposing obligations on all members of a society, other than some specially excepted individual or group, not to make use of a resource without the consent of that individual or group. The most hallowed such trespassory rule embodies the commandment "Thou shalt not steal". Legal trespassory rules may be supported by criminal or civil sanctions. Most of them are negative bans on intermeddling; but they may take the form of positive requirements to restore. In modern property institutions such rules are applied to ideational entities, as well as to chattels and land. Hence we speak of "intellectual property".

If we suppose that some resource—the Antarctic continent, Shakespeare's plays—ought not to be the subject of any trespassory rules, we have concluded that it ought not to come within the purview of a property institution. We may express this conclusion by referring to such things as "common property" (in the strict sense of that expression). Subject to what is said below about cashable rights, trespassory protection is a necessary condition for it to be true that the mantle of property is thrown over any resource. However, it is not a sufficient condition. Supposing we think that all persons, other than special licence-holders, should be prohibited from meddling with transplantable human organs or human embryos and gametes, but at the same time that the licence-holders themselves should not be free to act as owners in relation to these things.[7] Again we have concluded that these resources ought to fall outside the purview of property. For such things I have coined the term "protected non-property-holdings".

Propertihood emerges, pre-eminently, from a combination of trespassory rules and the ownership spectrum. This spectrum consists of ownership interests which display three characteristics. First, they all involve a juridical relation between a person (or group) and a resource. Secondly, the juridical relation consists of an open-ended set of privileges and powers. Thirdly, they authorise self-seekingness on the part of the favoured individual or group. Legal dogmatists may choose to reserve the term "ownership" or "dominion" for the upper end of the spectrum and to apply other labels to items lower down—as civil law systems traditionally do. The substantive operation of property institutions,

---

[7] As is the case with the regulatory regimes set up in the United Kingdom by the Human Organ Transplants Act 1989 and the Human Fertilisation and Embryology Act 1990.

however, requires that we mark these three similarities between all ownership interests. Title conditions of one kind or another vest ownership interests in individuals or groups so that they slot into the protection of trespassory rules. Despite much juristic speculation to the contrary, questions of absolute or relative title have nothing to do with ownership.

Ownership interests presuppose trespassory rules. If nothing could be stolen (or otherwise wrongfully interfered with), nothing could be owned. Trespassory rules establish the perimeter of ownership interests. Since it is no wrong for you to look at my house as you pass by, ownership of it does not include an exclusive power to control its aesthetic enjoyment. Nevertheless, the content of ownership interests cannot be derived by spelling out all relevant trespassory rules. It is both tortious and criminal if I kill or torture your cat. Whether you have a *prima facie* privilege to do either of these things depends on how we understand the applicable ownership interest.

Ownership interests are logically primitive organising ideas. They are not finite bundles of rights. They comprise open-ended sets of use-privileges, control-powers and, usually, powers of transmission. We deploy them, subliminally, in countless daily interactions. If I own a book, no one will ordinarily question my liberty to scribble in it, use it to prop up a table leg, or do any number of unlistable things with it; nor my powers to control a similarly open-ended set of uses by others; nor my powers to sell it or give it away to any of an unlistable class of persons.

The ownership spectrum ranges from "mere property" to "full-blooded ownership". Someone vested with mere property has no transmission powers and his use-privileges and control-powers may be considerably circumscribed, whilst still being open-ended. There are many things which a statutory tenant of a dwelling may not do with it; but the things which she may do, or permit others to do, are open-ended.[8] Full-blooded ownership of things entails a relationship between a person (or group) and a thing such that he (or they) have, *prima facie*, unlimited privileges of use or abuse over the thing, and, *prima facie*, unlimited powers of control and transmission, so far as such use or exercise of power does not infringe some property-independent prohibition.

A property-independent prohibition is one which is addressed to all persons, irrespective of whether they own anything. I commit a battery if I bash you over the head with a cosh. It is relevant neither to guilt nor to sentence whether or not I owned the cosh. Unlike the Aunt Sally concept of totality ownership, full-blooded ownership never implies, even *prima facie*, any privilege to break property-independent prohibitions.

---

[8] Ownership terminology has been employed in the House of Lords to tenancies, no matter how short their duration, as a way of characterising that "exclusive possession" which is the hallmark of an estate in land. "The tenant possessing exclusive possesssion is able to exercise the rights of an owner of land which is in the real sense his land, albeit temporarily and subject to certain restrictions": Lord Templeman in *Street* v. *Mountford* [1985] AC 809 at 816.

Property-independent prohibitions are to be contrasted with three types of rule which play an important part within modern property institutions, namely, property-limitation rules, expropriation rules and appropriation rules. All of these presuppose ownership interests. In the case of a property-limitation rule, some positive or negative mode of using a thing, which would otherwise be privileged to someone by virtue of her ownership interest in it, is negated by the imposition of a corresponding negative or positive duty; or the exercise of a power, otherwise inherent in ownership, is qualified or curtailed. Nuisance and planning law contain examples. Expropriation rules divest owners, against their will, in favour either of the state (taxation, compulsory purchase, fines and criminal forfeiture), or of private persons (damages, bankruptcy, divorce transfer orders). Appropriation rules are sometimes the counterparts of expropriation rules, and sometimes apply to assets which, but for their impact, would be ownerless (intestacy rules, finders-keepers' rules).

Trespassory rules and the ownership spectrum constitute the base of any property institution, the combination of property-limitation, expropriation and appropriation rules, its scaffolding. Various juristic traditions have distilled entities which mask these common features. Land law in common law systems is especially opaque. We convey (or create or show title to) estates, never ownership. Yet that which a person may do, or permit others to do, with land in which she has an estate turns entirely on the ownership interest which is the incident of that particular estate. So much is presupposed by the plethora of property-limitation rules which apply to landowners; and by those expropriation and appropriation rules which apply to the whole of a person's wealth, whatever its resource-substructure.

Universal outworks of modern property institutions include non-ownership proprietary interests (easements, servitudes, mortgages), and quasi-ownership interests (public property of all kinds). Both are protected by trespassory rules.

Whereas ownership interests comprise the three elements of resource-relation, open-endedness and authorised self-seekingness, non-ownership proprietary interests exhibit the first and third, but not the second; and quasi-ownership interests the first and second, but not the third. Public agencies do not "own" resources vested in them in the same sense that private individuals do. The content of the juridical relation is a combination of privileges and powers modelled on those of a comparable private ownership interest and other features derived from the particular public function for the discharge of which the resource is vested in the agency. The holder of a quasi-ownership interest cannot, as an ordinary owner may, respond to any criticism of the use made of a resource: "The thing is mine to do with as I please".

I apologise for this invention of labels, but I think the distinctions I have drawn are important and that familiar legal terminology is not adequate for the job. Take, for instance, debates about whether information of various kinds ought, or ought not, to be property. Suppose we think that some kinds of information should be freely accessible to all. There ought to be no bans on its use in any circumstances. Then it is excluded from all proprietary conceptions—"common property". Or we might decide that information stored in databases relating to an individual should be protected from use by anyone save for specified (listed) purposes. We then surround it with trespassory protection, but confer privileges and powers modelled on ownership interests on no one. Those in whom the databases are vested are entrusted with protected non-property-holdings. In this situation, we might think that the individual concerned should have a defined access right, to be used at his absolute discretion, and enforceable against whoever is holding the database—a non-ownership proprietary interest.

Suppose we thought that the media should be banned from publishing sensitive information about a person's private life, save to the extent that the person agreed to it. Thus far, we reserve to the person mere property in the information. It is a quite distinct question whether we should, as well, confer on him something like full-blooded ownership, enabling him to make money through exclusive control of the information. For that, if he decides to put details of his private life in the public domain, the media ban would still apply—so that no one could publish the information except someone to whom he gave (or sold) the privilege of doing so.

Take the case of commercial information. We might suppose that useful research and development would only be pursued if an enterprise is granted trespassory protection over the information it collects. Then we may grant it an ownership interest, but one specifically limited to that which is needed to provide the necessary incentive. That is unlikely to match the sort of full-blooded ownership we take people to enjoy in respect of chattels. The monopoly should not be timeless. There might be open-ended powers to control uses of the information by commercial rivals, but perhaps not as regards uses which reflect political rights. If the enterprise in question is state-owned, we may concede a quasi-ownership interest on incentive grounds, but one which builds in the discharge of important public functions.[9]

Money is property. When it takes the form of physical cash—coins and banknotes—trespassory protection obviously applies. It is special in two ways. First, whilst transmission powers may be excluded in the case of ownership interests in other resources, that is conceptually impossible for cash. Money would not be money if it could not be spent. Secondly, use-privileges are of small moment. Unless there is some property-limitation rule debarring defacement of currency I may, for what it is worth, turn coins I own into ornaments, or paper my walls with my banknotes. But what matters about owning money is the wealth-potential it affords in buying other resources or services.

Compare cashable rights—choses in action, like bank balances and company shares. Common lawyers and French lawyers call them "property" ("propriété"), whilst the Germans and now the Dutch do not. Cashable rights do not accord those vested with them any use-privileges at all. However, they are

---

[9] For discussion of information as property, see *Property and Justice*, above n. 1, at pp. 341–351.

transmissible as part of a person's private wealth. For that reason, expropriation and appropriation rules have come to be applied to them—they are subject to bankruptcy law and to garnishee orders in the enforcement of judgments; and intestacy rules apply to them in much the same way as they apply to anything else owned by the deceased. Explicit provision is made for their transmission in German and Dutch law too; and hence, as Wolfgang Mincke has pointed out, the fact that those systems reserve the term "property" ("eigentum", "eigendom") for the ownership of material resources is a difference in juristic dogmatics, not in substance.[10]

It was by virtue of their assignability, not their trespassory protection, that cashable rights were originally brought within the purview of expropriation and appropriation rules. Once propertihood is conferred upon them for that reason, direct trespassory protection may follow. In modern English law, choses in action can be the subject of theft. However, there may in other systems be cashable rights which are not granted specific trespassory protection but yet do come within the scope of expropriation and appropriation rules. Arguably, that is true of business goodwill in English law. Hence, although there has never been a property institution without trespassory rules, there may be particular property items which are not accorded trespassory protection. Accordingly, I suggested in the definition at the beginning of this section that proprietary status needs to be defined in the alternative. A right (or collection of rights) is proprietary either if it is the subject of trespassory rules, or if it is assignable as part of a person's private wealth.

For completeness I must add a semi-proprietary conception which has recently sprung into prominence in several common law jurisdictions. I call it "communitarian property". It concerns the title to land of indigenous populations within the structure of a later-imposed property system.

Trespassory rules may protect the ownership interest of two or more persons, of an unincorporated group, or of a juristic person. Joint, group and corporate owners are free, *prima facie*, to make such uses of their assets as they jointly or collectively decide, within whatever property-limitation rules apply to all owners. The general law lays down the framework governing both joint disposal and internal division of joint, group or corporate property. "Communitarian property", in contrast, refers to a spontaneously evolved category of holding. So long as it survives, it receives external trespassory protection from a property institution, but without intrusion into its internal regulations. It is a form of property of the greatest historical importance, but one which, for better or for worse, has been largely eclipsed in modern societies.[11] As we shall see, powerful

[10] W. Mincke, "Property: Assets or Power? Objects or Relations as Substrata of Property Rights" in J. W. Harris, *Property Problems: From Genes to Pension Funds* (London, Kluwer Publishing International, 1997), pp. 78–88.

[11] See P. Vinogradoff, *Outlines of Historical Jurisprudence* (Oxford, Oxford University Press, 1920), pp. 321–343. P. Grossi, *An Alternative to Private Property: Collective Property in the Juridical Consciousness of the Nineteenth Century* (trans L. Cochrane, Chicago, University Chicago Press, 1981).

arguments may be advanced for the view that this form of property is the subject of human rights.

II.   WHAT PROPERTY IS NOT

The definition offered at the beginning of the last section will not serve all purposes. When the term "property", or some related term, is employed dispositively within a common law, statutory or constitutional rule, there may be acceptable reasons for adopting some other definition. However, any globalised extension of the concept obfuscates important distinctions. In *Property and Justice* I argued that this is the case in respect of four projects of property-concept expansion.[12] I shall in this section try to show how this is especially true in relation to putative human rights.

Economic analysis

In accordance with one style of economic analysis of law, all rights are potentially property rights. The reason lies in the idea of "internalising externalities".

According to economic analysis, the efficient solution to any question of how a resource should be used is the one which all involved would value most. Were transaction costs zero, that position could be achieved collectively on a market in which all bid. It would take account of the effect on other people which anyone's use of the resource may have—an externality. Given real transaction costs, the problem of "hold-outs" and so forth, such negotiations are often impracticable. A property regime allocating ownership of resources to individuals is then to be preferred. Owners may bargain for payment in respect of beneficial externalities and be held accountable for harmful ones. In that way, externalities will be internalised.

The concept-expansive crunch comes when "resources" are taken to include everyone's bodily and mental capacities. Collectively bargained decisions about how people should use these resources being often impracticable, we may allow people rights in respect of these capacities which they can bargain not to exercise. If we do that, we have internalised the externalities enjoyed or suffered by others when persons use their bodies and minds. Hence, these rights should also be styled "property" rights.[13] On this view, a woman's right not to be raped is a

---

[12] Above n. 1, at pp. 145–163.

[13] A. A. Alchian and H. Demsetz, "The Property Rights Paradigm", (1973) 33 *Journal of Economic History* 16. G. Calabresi & A D Mellamed, "Property Rules, Liability Rules and Inalienability: One View of the Cathedral", (1972) 85 *Harv LR* 1089. Calabresi and Mellamed add, by way of qualification, that, as well as being a right which the holder is free to agree not to exercise, it must, to be a "property entitlement", also be protected either by criminal sanctions or by civil injunctive relief. See generally, Y Barzel, *Economic Analysis of Property Rights* (Cambridge, Cambridge University Press, 1989).

property right.[14] Denial of sex imposes externalities. The "efficient" solution would be one reached by negotiations between all women and those seeking sexual access to their bodies.[15] Happily, the economic analysts find this impracticable and accordingly recommend that externalities be internalised by giving women this "property" right.

In practice, those who advocate this extension of property terminology do not employ it consistently, but constantly slip into more traditional terms. But in any case, we might conclude that uses of a person's bodily and mental capacities should not, even in principle, be placed at the service of those who would pay most for them on a notional market. We may very well suppose that the right not to be raped is a human right, even if we think that property is not.

Macpherson's property rhetoric

C. B. Macpherson offered a different argument for using "property" as the label for certain aspirational rights. He advocated an egalitarian society in which everyone would enjoy those income and political rights needed for "a fully human life"; and designated them all "property" rights.[16] There would be this rhetorical advantage in so describing them. Persons otherwise unwilling to agree to the advocated rights could be moved to do so if we call them "property rights", thanks to the "prestige" which attaches to that label.[17]

I suggest that this rhetorical strategy is wholly implausible. Arguably, in modern political culture "human rights" has more prestige than "property". Be that as it may, anyone who does not accept that the proposed rights are human rights is unlikely to change her mind because their advocate attaches the "property" epithet to them.

Reich's new property

Charles Reich offered a more plausible suggestion for designating nondiscretionary welfare entitlements "property" rights, when he called for a "new property".[18] Reich offered the following diagnosis of changed relationships between governments and citizens in modern Western societies. Large holdings of private wealth used to provide centres of independent initiative. With the growth of the "public interest state", much wealth is allocated in the form of

[14] Calabresi and Mellamed, "Property Rules", above n. 13, at 1125–1127.

[15] For criticism of the application of market analysis to such a context, see M. J. Radin, *Reinterpreting Property*, above n. 2, at pp. 201–202.

[16] C. B. MacPherson, "Capitalism and the Changing Concept of Property" in E. Kamenka and R. S. Neale (eds), *Feudalism, Capitalism and Beyond* (Canberra, Australian National University Press, 1975) 119–122; *Property: Mainstream and Critical Positions* (Oxford, Blackwell, 1978), pp. 205–206.

[17] MacPherson, above n. 16, at p. 122.

[18] C. A. Reich, "The New Property", (1964) 73 *Yale LJ* 733.

"government largesse"—welfare benefits, government contracts, subsidies, and so forth. The discretionary power to award, withhold or terminate largesse threatens independence. As far as possible, the discretionary element should be removed. Reformed largesse would take the form of entitlements. It would secure independence comparable to that which private property formerly secured and, in that sense, would constitute "new property".

Nothing would have been changed in the substantive proposal if Reich had entitled his article "A Call for a Property Substitute" rather than "The New Property". Property-labelling has, it seems, done little to promote the proposed reform.[19]

Even if there were sound public law strategic reasons for calling reformed largesse "property", we would still need to be clear that it is not property in the traditional sense. Suppose we think that there are human rights to non-discretionary welfare payments. It would be a distinct question whether they should be cashable rights. Should the entitled person be empowered to anticipate his benefits and trade them for other things? Should they be subject to expropriation rules—form part of his bankruptcy estate, be attachable by his judgment creditors? Of course, money once paid over in discharge of such entitlements is property. I suggest that more confusion than light is achieved if we describe the entitlements themselves as "property", unless we really wanted them to take the form of cashable rights.

Ackerman's constitutional theory

Bruce Ackerman recommends that the concept of property be extended to cover all liberties to use things, specifically in the context of the "takings" clause of the Fifth Amendment to the United States Constitution—"nor shall private property be taken for public use, without just compensation".[20] He recognises that judges usually adopt an "ordinary observer" approach to this clause: they assume that there is a conventionally-accepted sense in which people own resources. Ackerman condemns this attitude by invoking ownership scepticism on the basis of what I earlier referred to as "totality ownership". The law never assigns to any single person "the right to use anything in absolutely any way he pleases"; and hence "it risks serious confusion to identify any single individual as the owner of any particular thing".[21] That being so, no restrictive sense can be attributed to the word "property". Instead, we should approach the clause from the perspective of a "scientific policymaker"—one who aspires to solve all problems by attributing to the legal system a single comprehensive view of the

---

[19] See W. Van Alstyne, "Cracks in the 'New Property': Adjudicative Due Process", (1977) 62 *Cornell LR* 445.

[20] B. A. Ackerman, *Private Property and the Constitution* (New Haven, Yale University Press, 1977).

[21] Ibid., pp. 26–27.

just society. The *prima facie* scope of the clause should extend to all restrictions of "any user right",[22] such as speed limits.[23]

Now since all legal restraints may be infringed by using things, it follows that the takings clause empowers courts to declare any of them unconstitutional if they run counter to the scientific policymaker's conception of the just society. On such a constitutional theory, all the other amendments in the Bill of Rights are surplusage.

Transferring the theory to the general field of human rights would have this consequence. Every legal prohibition is a taking of property. It therefore becomes conceptually incoherent to argue (as some might wish to do) that, whereas freedoms of speech and assembly are human rights, "property" is not.

There are more important things than property—matters which are more uncontroversially the proper subject of human rights. Whatever the merits of expansive definitions in other contexts (and I doubt they are great), we will have no suitable focus for the present discussion unless we adopt an understanding of the concept of property which roughly reflects lawyers' ordinary use of the term. That my definition seeks to do.

III. WHAT ARE HUMAN RIGHTS?

A moral right arises when some facet of the right-subject's well-being is, *prima facie*, a sufficient reason for the introduction or maintenance of one or more social (or legal) rules. "Well-being" includes both activities which the right-subject may wish to engage in and states of affairs which are of value to the right-subject. Natural rights are such moral rights as allegedly follow from the interaction between the formal and substantive requirements of just treatment and the facts of the world. Human rights are such moral rights as are claimed, for whatever reason, to be due to all human beings.

In the foregoing definitions I have jumped several jurisprudential and philosophical hurdles. There is a long-standing controversy about the concept of a right. On the one side stand those who support an "interest" theory of rights.[24] Opposed are the supporters of a "choice" theory.[25] I am not convinced that the word "right" stands for a univocal concept—that, because it is a word, it must have the same meaning within and outside the law. I can appreciate the advantages of reserving the term, within the law, for the correlative to those duties which are waivable at the choice of a subject. I nevertheless consider that an

---

[22] Ibid., p. 28.

[23] Ibid., pp. 124–125.

[24] See, e.g., N. MacCormick, "Rights in Legislation" in P. M. S. Hacker and J. Raz (eds), *Law, Morality and Society: Essays in Honour of H L A Hart* (Oxford, Clarendon Press, 1977); and J. Raz, *The Morality of Freedom* (Oxford, Clarendon Press, 1986), pp. 165–192.

[25] See, e.g., H. L. A. Hart, *Essays on Bentham: Studies in Jurisprudence and Political Theory* (Oxford, Clarendon Press, 1982), pp. 164–188; and H. Steiner, *An Essay on Rights* (Oxford, Blackwell, 1994), pp. 59–74.

interest conception is to be preferred if what we have in mind is the moral standing of a subject to insist that some legal or social rule should be introduced or maintained.

Not all facets of a person's well-being (her interests) constitute even *prima facie* reasons for rules. A person may be a non-smoker and also have an aversion to pineapple juice. She might maintain that her health is a facet of her well-being which constitutes a sufficient reason for the introduction of a property-limitation rule banning owners of restaurants from serving non-smokers on the same premises as smokers—that her health founds a moral right. But she would hardly claim that the facet of her well-being constituted by her taste in beverages is any reason for a rule restricting the supply of pineapple juice (even if such a restriction would make it more likely that her preferred beverages would be readily available). Taste does not found moral rights.

Natural rights theorists suppose that, the world being what it is, and just treatment being what it is, there are facets of well-being which everywhere and always found certain moral rights. Such rights are then natural rights. If they apply to all human beings, they are also human rights. They might also extend to animals. It might be claimed, for example, that causing excruciating pain to animals falls outside just treatment of them, that it is demonstrable that using them in a particular way causes them excruciating pain, and that therefore this aspect of their well-being does, and always has, supported rules prohibiting such usage.

It is possible to be sceptical about the whole idea of natural rights. There are two obvious sources of such scepticism. One might deny the possibility of any metaphysical or other basis on which an abstract and ahistorical conception of just treatment could be erected. Or one might argue—as communitarians do—that treatment is not something to be accorded to atomistic individuals conceived of as standing apart from their communities. Rather, a community's culture is (at least partly) constitutive of the human person so that any rights he or she may have are contingent on that culture.[26]

Do human rights fare any better than natural rights in the face of such scepticism? One way in which it might be suggested that they do is that they rely merely on convention. The modern world abounds in international treaties in which such rights are proclaimed.[27] If anyone is sceptical, just refer him to the texts.

[26] See M. J. Sandel, *Liberalism and the Limits of Justice* (Cambridge, Cambridge University Press, 1982); M. Walzer, *Spheres of Justice: a Defense of Pluralism and Equality* (New York, Basic Books, 1982); A. MacIntyre, *After Virtue: a Study in Moral Theory*, 2nd edn. (Notre Dame, University of Notre Dame Press, 1984); C. Taylor, *Sources of the Self: The Making of the Modern Identity* (Cambridge, Harvard University Press, 1989). For discussion of these themes, see A. Buchanan, "Assessing the Communitarian Critique of Liberalism", (1989) 94 *Ethics* 852; S. Gardbaum, "Law, Politics, and the Claims of Community", (1992) *Mich LR* 685; S. Avineri and A. De-Shalit (eds), *Communitarianism and Individualism* (Oxford, Oxford University Press, 1992).

[27] See R. P. Claude and B. H. Weston (eds), *Human Rights in the World Community*, 2nd edn. (Philadelphia, University of Pennsylvania Press, 1992); R. Beddard, *Human Rights and Europe*, 3rd edn. (Cambridge, Grotius Publications, 1993).

That response would be too quick. Champions of human rights suppose that they are genuine moral rights.[28] They are considered to be cross-cultural in scope. An entire political regime may be condemned for riding roughshod over human rights. It is their supposed moral content which guides both those who draft, and those who interpret, documents tabulating human rights.

In any case, we could find no answer to the question "Is property a human right?" simply by consulting the texts of treaties and constitutions, since they diverge on the matter. Both common law and civil law systems have for centuries given some recognition to the principle that government should not expropriate the private property of citizens without paying compensation. The takings clause of the United States Constitution, to which reference has already been made, is the most famous embodiment of this principle in a constitutional text. Property has played a pivotal role in the development of American constitutionalism.[29] The recently enacted constitution of the Republic of South Africa lists property rights among its fundamental rights, although the scope of the provision was the subject of considerable controversy.[30] A different view has been taken in Canada. When the Canadian Charter of Rights and Freedoms was introduced into the constitutional law of Canada in 1982, drawing on the experience of American and European bills of rights as well as the common law, no specific protection of "property" was included, even though such a clause had been contained in the earlier Canadian bill of rights. The charter mentions rights to "life, liberty and security of the person", but not property; and this omission appears to have caused the Canadian Supreme Court no difficulty in articulating a coherent view of constitutionally protected basic rights.[31]

When the European Convention for the Protection of Human Rights and Fundamental Freedoms is incorporated into United Kingdom law, we will have a right to property set out in a constitutional text. Protocol 1 to the Convention provides, in Article 1:

> "Every natural or legal person is entitled to the peaceful enjoyment of his possessions. No one shall be deprived of his possessions except in the public interest and subject to the conditions provided for by law and by the general principles of international law."
>
> "The preceding provisions shall not, however, in any way impair the right of a state to enforce such laws as it deems necessary to control the use of property in accordance with the general interest or to secure the payment of taxes or other contributions or penalties."

The case law of the European Court of Human Rights and the decisions and reports of the European Human Rights Commission confirm that this provision

---

[28] See E. Kamenka and R. S. Neale (eds), above n. 16. C. S. Nino, *The Ethics of Human Rights* (Oxford, Clarendon Press, 1991).

[29] J. Ely, *The Guardian of Every Other Right: A Constitutional History of Property Rights* (New York, Oxford University Press, 1992).

[30] See M. Chaskalson, "Stumbling Towards Section 28: Negotiation Over the Protection of Property Rights in the Interim Constitution", (1995) 11 *South African Journal On Human Rights* 222.

[31] See E. R. Alexander, "The Canadian Charter of Rights and Freedoms in the Supreme Court of Canada", (1989) 105 *LQR* 561, at 588–593.

does indeed presuppose a "right to property". "Possessions" has been held to include, as well as ownership of land, chattels and cash, also intellectual property and what I have called "cashable rights" and "non-ownership proprietary interests". The court has interpreted the article as requiring a balancing test between the public and private interests, wherein a wide "margin of appreciation" must be accorded to states' legislatures. Broad questions of social and economic policy are properly comprised within the "public interest", provided measures respect "proportionality". Findings of violation have been few.[32]

Compare this article with the other rights enunciated in the Convention and its protocols—to life; not to be tortured or enslaved; to liberty and security of the person; to fair trials; not to be subjected to retrospective punishment; to respect for privacy; to freedom of thought, conscience and religion; to freedom of expression; to freedom of peaceful assembly; to marry and found a family; to education; not to be imprisoned for debt; to liberty of movement. Two differences stand out. First, the property right is the only one expressly conferred on "legal" as well as "natural" persons. Second, the other rights have a degree of transparent universality which the property right lacks. We all have bodies which may be killed, tortured, enslaved or imprisoned. Anyone may choose to join in political controversy, to take part in family life, to adopt a religion, or to change her place of residence, and so on. All these things may plausibly be said to advance facets of well-being which are more or less the same for all. But a person's "possessions" vary enormously in the extent to which they contribute to well-being, and some people may have none at all.

The first difference may be explained in the following way. Legal persons, not being human beings, cannot be the bearers of human rights. Nevertheless, the "possessions" of human individuals include certain cashable rights which are constituted by juristic invention through the machinery of incorporation—shares, debentures, and so forth. The Convention confers the property right upon legal persons as a derivative measure for enforcing human rights over such hived-off portions of wealth.

The second difference is not so easily explained. Exercise of some of the other rights may, on occasion, conflict with other people's rights. Indeed, the Convention bristles with qualifications. But if maintenance of one's property-holdings, no matter how disproportionately great, is conceived of as a human right then this is a right which, by its very nature, arms its right-subject with power to dominate the lives of others. Ownership includes powers of control over access to that which is owned. Owners of enterprises and of family dwellings, in particular, have *prima facie* powers, by virtue of their ownership, to control vital aspects of the life-chances of their employees and dependants.[33] More generally, in an increasingly overcrowded world all of us may suffer from decisions taken by owners because of their deleterious environmental conse-

---

[32] See F. Jacobs and R. White, *The European Convention on Human Rights,* 2nd edn. (New York, Clarendon Press, 1995) Chap. 14.

[33] See Harris, above n. 1, at pp. 264–275.

quences. "The peaceful enjoyment of his possessions" no doubt contributes to the well-being of an owner, but it may be the means of damaging the well-being of his fellows. Since "possessions" covers anything from immense riches to the clothes someone stands up in, how could it be supposed that the well-being of all humans makes "enjoyment" of all possessions a universal right?

IV. HISTORICAL-ENTITLEMENT THEORIES OF JUSTICE

If it could be shown that there is a sound moral foundation underpinning full ownership of all the property-holdings we encounter in modern societies, no matter how disparate they may be, then property is as much a human right as any of the other rights listed in the European Convention. If that can be established, then forcibly taking property from whoever holds it to meet others' needs (via redistributive taxation) is unjust. So are most restrictions on ownership powers designed to prevent owners dominating others' lives, or imposed for more general environmental reasons. That there is such a moral foundation is claimed by those historical-entitlement theorists of justice who derive their inspiration from the fifth chapter of John Locke's *Second Treatise of Government*.[34]

Scope of the theories

According to a historical-entitlement theory of justice, a resource is held by natural right if its owner derives title, by successive transfers, from one who originally appropriated some un-owned thing in a just way. Theorists are often imprecise about what counts as an initial appropriating act. Roughly, either it is simple first occupancy or it is that plus some infusion of labour on the appropriator's part. Successive transfers include sales and *inter vivos* gifts and, for most historical-entitlement theorists, also bequests.[35]

In deciding whether an original appropriation was just, variations are offered on Locke's requirement that there must be "enough and as good" left for others.[36]

[34] R. Nozick, *Anarchy, State and Utopia* (Oxford, Blackwell, 1974), pp. 150–183; M. N. Rothbard, "Justice and Property Rights" in S. L. Blumenfeld (ed.), *Property in a Humane Economy* (La Salle Open Court, 1974), pp. 101–120; R. A. Epstein, "Possession as the Root of Title", (1979) 3 *Georgia LR* 1221–1243; *Takings: Private Property and the Power of Eminent Domain* (Cambridge, Harvard University Press, 1985); H. Steiner, above n. 25, chs 3 and 6.

[35] Nozick, *Anarchy, State and Utopia*, above n. 34, at p. 238. Rothbard, "Justice and Property Rights", above n. 34, at p. 114. Epstein, *Takings*, above n. 34, at pp. 304, 347. Nozick has subsequently suggested that the right of bequest should not extend to property which the testator has himself inherited—R. Nozick, *The Examined Life: Philosophical Meditations* (New York, Simon and Schuster, 1989), pp. 30–31. Steiner argues that there is no moral right of bequest at all, so that all assets of deceased persons are ownerless and available for appropriation – above n. 25, at pp. 250–258.

[36] J. Locke, *Second Treatise of Government*, 3rd edn. (G. W. Gough (ed.) Oxford, Blackwell, 1976) ch. v, s. 27.

Philosophical accounts are usually set in an imaginary state of nature. Since we do not know, in most cases, when resources now subject to property-holdings were first transformed from being un-owned to being owned, any application of a historical-entitlement theory to the real world will, in practice, deploy presumptions in favour of the status quo.

A pure historical-entitlement account would restrict just claims to own resources in the following way. The claimant must herself have appropriated un-owned things (in whatever manner the theory stipulates as just appropriation), or must have derived title by successive transfers from such an appropriator. Re-allocation from one who now holds a resource in favour of a claimant must be made when, but only when, the claimant can show an original or derived title while the present holder cannot. Such an account leaves yawning gaps. If a property-owner dies intestate, do her assets join the class of ownerless things available for appropriation by the first-comer? How does one occupy, or mix one's labour with, intangible property—cashable rights and intellectual property? How do communal goods, held by public agencies in the form of quasi-ownership interests, get into the act?

Within the literature historical-entitlement theories seldom come pure. Consequentialist considerations are prayed in aid. This is so throughout Richard Epstein's celebrated critique of the US Supreme Court's interpretation of the takings clause. He maintains, for example, that even proven past injustices should not be remedied by requiring present holders to disgorge in favour of claimants who derive title from original appropriators, because such a programme would impede productivity and public peace.[37] Even Robert Nozick is constrained to invoke consequentialist arguments. He deals with the Lockean "enough and as good" proviso in the following way. So long as the appropriation did not (and continues not to) make other people worse off, all things considered, than they would have been had it not occurred (or were not still insisted on), then the appropriation is just; and in making this comparison one may take into account all the familiar incentive and market-instrumental advantages of private property institutions.[38]

Quite apart from practical problems of implementation, the normative foundations of the entire process are open to powerful objections. Why should we accept that occupancy, with or without labour, of that which was previously un-owned entails a unilateral power to subject other people to trespassory obligations banning them from all contact with the resource without leave of the appropriator? If successive transferees step into his shoes, that power enables him to impose an eternal sequence of trespassory rules on all generations of mankind. Can a single appropriative act have such consequences for a never-ending normative universe?

---

[37] Epstein, *Takings*, above n. 34, at pp. 346–349.
[38] Nozick, above n. 34, at pp. 175–182.

The alchemy deployed by historical-entitlement theorists to deal with these problems is dogmatic insistence on a supposedly uncontestable and supra-temporal concept of ownership. Ownership just must comprise, not merely unlimited use-privileges and control-powers, but also unlimited powers of transmission. Original appropriation, at whatever past date it occurred, must have involved that concept of ownership. No normative argument need be supplied to establish these preconceived conceptual truths.

Remove these conceptual props, and the entire superstructure of historical-entitlement theories falls away. Tony Honoré has argued that what he calls "the liberal concept of full individual ownership" is not timeless. Less developed cultures—where original appropriations may have occurred—employ lesser ownership conceptions.[39] I submit that a spectrum of ownership interests applies even within modern property institutions; and that there is no basis, in justice, for a free-standing natural right to full-blooded ownership.[40]

First occupancy

Consider first occupancy. Blackstone is a much-cited advocate of full ownership—"that sole and despotic dominion which one man claims and exercises over the external things of the world, in total exclusion of the right of any other individual in the universe".[41] Yet Blackstone supposed that, in the state of nature, someone who first occupied a determined spot, for rest, shade or the like, "Acquired therein a kind of transient property, that lasted so long as he was using it, and no longer".[42]

Property institutions commonly confer ownership on finders of lost chattels or on those who have been acting as owners of land for a period of time. More generally, first occupancy is treated as a distinct title condition. Such provisions can be supported on consequentialist grounds, but they do not implement natural rights. There are reasons of expediency requiring bright-line rules which always result in a windfall.

The position is more complicated when first occupancy of land has been established by a group rather than an individual. It may be that the group is bound together by cultural and economic ties and that the land is integral to its self-identity. In that case it can claim, not full-blooded ownership, but that special kind of entitlement which I have called "communitarian property".

Such was recognised for aboriginal tribes by the decision of the High Court of Australia in the path-breaking *Mabo* case.[43] The court ruled that, according to the common law of Australia, the "radical title" to land acquired by the

---

[39] Honoré, above n. 4, at 215–226.

[40] Harris, above n. 1, at chs 12 and 13.

[41] W. Blackstone, *Commentaries on the Laws of England,* 16th edn. (Butterworth and Son, 1825) II, 1.

[42] Ibid., II 2, 3.

[43] *Mabo* v. *State of Queensland (No. 2)* [1992] 175 CLR 1.

Crown on settlement was burdened with the "native title" of any aboriginal clan or group which was in occupation of any distinct portion of territory. So long as it persisted, the community's native title had the benefit of trespassory protection against the rest of the world. It was not requisite to show that, internally, the members viewed their relationship to the land as an "ownership" interest. All questions as to the rights of individual members were to be settled, as questions of fact, by reference to the evolving traditions of the group. Native title was not an institution of the common law, but a special defeasible interest which the common law ought in justice to (and therefore did) recognise.

The High Court did not accept the ingenious suggestion of Kent McNeil that any such group acquires title to an ordinary fee simple estate by virtue of prior possession.[44] Adoption of that view would have meant that any tribe of native inhabitants were as free to trade their land (if they all wished to do so) as are the members of any commercial partnership or other unincorporated association.

When the conditions requisite for communitarian property are established, incompatible uses by outsiders may amount to an attack on the community's collective integrity. It may not be able to survive at all if the intrusions go unchecked. If that much can be demonstrated, the community is as entitled to insist upon trespassory rules prohibiting such incompatible uses as is an individual to call for bans on life-threatening attacks. In those rather limited circumstances, first occupancy does establish a natural right—which may be called a group human right—to communitarian property.

Of course, addition of market-instrumental arguments might extend this natural right. Supposing one insists that, to achieve maximum exploitation, all property should be the subject of full-blooded ownership. On that assumption, native first occupants ought to be introduced into a modern system of private property by conferring (or indeed imposing) such ownership upon them. There would be a windfall element if, for example, a group could cash in on mineral rights, by virtue of the fact that their ancestors had once hunted and gathered on the ground. But it would be a windfall of the same kind that accrues whenever a person has occupied land for some limited purpose and thereby acquires a title which enables him to reap the land's development value.

Self-ownership

The favourite method by which historical-entitlement theorists insert labour into the process of original just appropriation is to call in the notion of self-ownership. It is assumed that a single concept of full-blooded ownership must apply, not only to all external resources, but also to the subject herself. I have summarised the liberal version of the self-ownership argument in the following four steps:

---

[44] K. McNeil, *Common Law Aboriginal Title* (Oxford, Clarendon Press, 1989).

(1) If I am not a slave, nobody else owns my body. Therefore;
(2) I must own myself. Therefore;
(3) I must own all my actions, including those which create or improve resources. Therefore;
(4) I own the resources, or the improvements, which I produce.

I contend that there is a *non sequitur* between steps 1 and 2. From the fact that nobody else owns my body, it does not follow that I own myself. Instead, nobody owns me. Since the abolition of slavery, human beings are removed altogether from the field of property.[45]

My suggestion has caused disquiet, because self-ownership has been a staple of philosophical speculation for 300 years. It is argued that the rights which people have over their bodies just must be called "self-ownership". What must be stressed, however, is that, for this version of original just appropriation to work, it would have to be the case that the same concept of ownership—namely, full-blooded ownership—is being employed in steps 2, 3 and 4.

Distinguish two contexts in which appeals may be made to self-ownership.[46] The first raises the question whether a person's rights over her own body are limitless. Supposing a "bodily-use libertarian" wishes to claim that they are. The subject ought to be free to sell herself into life-long sexual or industrial servitude, to engage in duelling, or to do, or permit to be done, with or to her body anything that can enter the imagination. The bodily-use libertarian might found all these claims on the "fact" that people own themselves.

The second context is this. When people own external resources, should they be free to make any uses they please of them, and be exempt from redistributive taxation, environmental controls, and so forth? A "property-libertarian" might answer yes; and found his view on the "fact" that resource-ownership derives from self-ownership, and "ownership" in both contexts is (by conceptual necessity) full ownership.

If we build a univocal concept of ownership into these two areas of controversy in that way, it becomes conceptually incoherent for anyone to be a bodily-use libertarian, on the one hand, but not a property-libertarian, on the other—and vice versa. You cannot disapprove paternalist constraints on what people may do with their own bodies, and also be a socialist. You cannot be a conservative paternalist over body-use, and also a thorough-going capitalist. Furthermore, it would be a conceptual necessity that, at whatever age one supposed that children ought to be allowed to own toys, that would be the point at which they should be free to confer sexual favours over their bodies.

I suggest that the two contexts should not be clamped together in that way. It is only the philosophically in-bred notion of self-ownership which gives colour

---

[45] Above n. 1, at pp. 184–197.
[46] There is a third, which concerns ownership of separated bodily parts. I have argued that it is both unnecessary, and also liable to prove too much, to invoke self-ownership in that context, as well as in the two mentioned here—see *Property and Justice*, above n. 1, at pp. 351–361.

to such false compression. The rights we do have over our bodies are more fundamental human rights than any there may be over external resources.

V.   A BACKGROUND PROPERTY RIGHT

If we have human rights in respect of our bodies and our political freedoms, how do we get from there to any claim to have such rights over external resources? I attempted to answer that question in Part II of *Property and Justice*. I began with a minimalist conception of justice, and ended with a moral background right to property.

The minimalist conception of justice comprises three elements: First, natural equality—if treatment of a certain kind is due to one person, X, nothing less is due to another person, Y, merely on the ground that Y is an inferior type of human being to X. Secondly, the value of autonomous choice—human agency is an ineliminable preconception of justice. Thirdly, the banning of unprovoked invasions of bodily integrity—homicides, assaults and forcible detentions are *prima facie* natural wrongs correlating with natural rights.

The background right is vested in every citizen of a modern state. It requires both that a property institution should be in place, and that a mix of property-specific justice reasons be taken into account, where relevant, in any question of distribution or property-institutional design. Justice reasons are "property-specific" if they support holdings of ownership or quasi-ownership interests in land, chattels, ideas, money or cashable rights; or non-ownership proprietary interests, or property-limitation, expropriation and appropriation rules, respecting such resources.

Central importance should be accorded to the property-freedom argument, the most celebrated exposition of which is to be found in Hegel's *Philosophy of Right*.[47] Ownership interests confer open-ended use-privileges, control-powers and (usually) powers of transmission and thereby augment ranges of autonomy. All such property freedoms are valuable. However, none of them is sacrosanct. Domination-potential constitutes a constant counterpoise, since the property freedoms of X may always potentially entail illegitimate power to dominate the life-chances of Y.

There are, as well, three property-instrumental arguments arising from incentives to create wealth, valuable markets, and the independence from governmental control associated with private holdings of wealth. The latter two, like the property-freedom argument itself, are distributionally blind. Their impact must be assessed against the following distributive considerations.

Every property institution is built upon trespassory rules binding all non-owners. For such rules to carry moral force the society in which a property institution holds sway must, one way or another, shoulder the burden of meeting all

[47] G. W. F. Hegel, *Elements of the Philosophy of Right* (trans H. B. Nisbet, Cambridge, Cambridge University Press, 1991), pp. 73–103.

citizens' basic needs. Furthermore, although there are no free-standing natural rights to full-blooded ownership, substance may be given to the shell of two natural rights based on labour-desert and privacy.

The moral background right requires alteration of property institutions where a conventional solution exists which clearly runs counter to the balance of property-specific justice reasons. However, where this balance leaves some issue indeterminate or subject to good-faith controversy, the conventional solution, if there is one, should usually be retained. In this respect juristic doctrine, as a specialist variety of social convention, has a part to play.

Where the general features of a property institution embody the structure required by the background right, or come close to doing so, most titles to holdings will be, at least *prima facie*, just. Where they do not, reform needs to take account of the principle of justified reliance. That principle should not, however, be invoked indiscriminately. It is based on an analogy with an interpersonal principle. Consequently, for it to be relevant, the community must, in some sense, be credited with having induced expectations. That is not an inference which it will be appropriate to draw whenever an out-moded or unpopular legal provision is repealed or changed.

The mix of property-specific justice reasons and its conventional or juristic interpretation have the consequence that some individual or group can found a superior claim to most of the resources within the purview of a property institution (which are not the subject of quasi-ownership interests vested in public agencies, nor of protected non-propertyholdings, nor of communitarian property). Where that is not the case, a resource is windfall wealth. In that event, equality of resources is the only applicable principle. It requires that, by some appropriate mechanism, the wealth-potential of the resource should be equally divided among the members of a relevant community. This residual role for the principle of equality of resources may operate both in the context of some item of social wealth as to which no member of the wider community has any better claim than any other member (unallocated natural resources); and also as between members of a restricted community who together are entitled as against everyone else (assets left on the breakdown of an association).

VI. CONCLUSION

The background property right is historically situated. It is not a timeless natural right, and so differs in this respect from rights not to be subjected to unprovoked violence to the person. Any past society which managed to do without property cannot be trans-historically condemned on that account. Nevertheless, the background right is now a human right. The well-being of every citizen of a modern state requires that his or her society should maintain a property institution. Everyone would be treated unjustly if his or her society did not afford, at least, the freedom from centralised direction which results from deploying money, full-blooded ownership of chattels, and ownership interests in dwellings.

Moreover, the background right carries over into a presumptive and qualified right to ownership interests of various kinds in other resources, provided that a property institution (in its implementation of the mix of property-specific justice reasons) passes a certain threshold of justice. There can be property institutions imposed by force for the selfish gratification of a dominant group, within social settings where the community's obligations to meet basic needs are flatly disregarded. In such a context trespassory rules protecting holdings do not impose genuine obligations—it is not then wrong to steal, in the way that it is always wrong to commit murder, assault or rape.

I shall assume that modern Western property institutions pass this justice threshold. That being so, the presumptive and qualified entitlement to whatever holdings have arisen is morally sound. Nevertheless, ownership does not have the unqualified moral status it would have were historical-entitlement theories sound, which they are not. Every holding carries force only by virtue of a plausible outcome to the (perhaps changing) balance of relevant property-specific justice reasons. Ownership interests may be properly restricted by property-limitation rules and may also be properly expropriated to fund the discharge by the state of functions which it has rightly undertaken.

Constitutional provisions protecting the right to property should be interpreted in the light of the background right and its presumptive carry-over into specific holdings. Such provisions usually take the form of a qualified immunity from expropriation. Such immunities presuppose the moral background right and its concrete implementation. The first sentence of Protocol 1 (Article 1) of the European human rights convention may be understood in this sense: "Every natural or legal person is entitled to the peaceful enjoyment of his possessions".

Without entering into the constitutional doctrines of any particular jurisdiction, the underlying issues may be stated abstractly in the following way. To begin with, there are property-independent prohibitions addressed to everyone which may happen, incidentally, to deny certain uses of things to owners. In their case, no question of expropriation arises. Either such prohibitions are justifiable restraints on the conduct of all persons (owners included) or they are not. It is a crime for anyone to drive a motor vehicle dangerously. It would be absurd to suggest that those who happen to own cars are thereby subjected to a compensable loss.

A limiting case would be one where a legislator banned all uses of a thing. In effect it would then be depriving persons who owned that type of thing of their ownership interests. There might then be a case for compensation, assuming that the previous state of the law had given rise to reliance interests. It is preferable in such a case if the legislator expressly bans ownership as such—for example, of handguns.[48]

---

[48] See A. Story, "Compensation for Banned Handguns: Indemnifying 'Old Property'", (1998) 61 *Mod LR* 188–206. Story argues that the state can, without payment of compensation, ban or seize

Just taxation is expropriation but contravenes no human right. Whether a property-limitation rule, unaccompanied by compensation, infringes the crystallised background human right turns on what we conceive to be the proper boundary between private and social wealth.

Every property institution discharges the dual functions of controlling use and allocating social wealth. When it delegates control over competing uses of a scarce resource (R) to X by recognising an ownership interest (OI) in X over R, it simultaneously accords to X an item of social wealth associated with the exploitation of the privileges and powers inherent in OI. Suppose that, to further some public goal, an amalgam of privileges and powers (P) is abstracted from OI. The compensation principle is implicated if and only if the mix of property-specific justice reasons which supported X being vested with OI also requires that OI contains P. Compensation then preserves X's allocated share of social wealth even though P has been taken from him.

For compensation to be appropriate it must be the case that X has already invested in R, relying on a conventional understanding (settled at the time of his investment) that the exercise of P was indeed entailed by the balance of property-specific justice reasons. That will not be true in respect of most of the privileges and powers taken from owners by regulations aimed at preserving public health, amenities or the environment.

A modern state which seriously undertook to abolish property altogether would thereby subject its citizenry to the model of soup-kitchen distribution among the destitute, since all allocation of scarce resources and services would be implemented by the rationing choices of some public agency. Hence property, in the scale of human well-being, ranks below life, but alongside liberty. Nevertheless, the holdings vested in any particular person at any particular time are stamped, morally, with a contestable and mutable mix of property-specific justice reasons. Only in that presumptive (and weak) sense do I have a human right to my possessions.

"old property"—that is, property which is "conceptually anachronistic" because it creates, maintains and reproduces relations between people which are no longer recognised as legitimate or morally acceptable by the bulk of the populace. I suggest that this argument is unsound where the postulated consensus did not exist at the time when an owner invested in "old property".

5

Constitutionalising Property: Two Experiences, Two Dilemmas

GREGORY S. ALEXANDER[1]

A remarkable number of nations around the world are currently in the midst of revising their constitutions or writing new constitutions. From South Africa to central and eastern Europe, constitution-making is occurring at a rate virtually unprecedented in world history. Oddly (or, perhaps, predictably) American constitutional lawyers have reacted to this development with amazing indifference. While American constitutional specialists lavish attention on individual political rights in their own country, they have virtually ignored what Bruce Ackerman calls the "rise of world constitutionalism",[2] let alone the development of analogous rights in other countries. This chapter is a modest first attempt at responding to this embarrassing state of indifference.

One of the basic questions that constitution-makers and revisers have to decide is how to treat property. Not all national constitutions, not even all those of liberal democracies, have provisions expressly protecting property. Some countries that are ordinarily classified as liberal democracies have even repealed their constitutional property clauses in recent years.

Assuming that the political leaders of a given country decide to include a clause protecting individual property rights, the relevant questions then become what form the property clause should take and specifically whether property should be deemed a fundamental right. The constitutions of the world's liberal democracies provide a remarkably wide range of examples of property clauses. Even more surprising is the fact that while private property is not treated as a fundamental right in the USA, a highly market-oriented society, it does have that status in social welfare states like Germany.[3] The decision of which of these models to emulate, or indeed whether to create a new model, will have an important consequences for the nation's political, social, and economic order.

[1] I am deeply grateful to Andre van der Walt, of the Faculty of Law at the University of South Africa, for invaluable comments and suggestions. All errors, of course, remain mine alone.

[2] B. Ackerman, "The Rise of World Constitutionalism", (1997) 83 *Va L Rev* 771.

[3] See D. P. Currie, "*Lochner* Abroad: Substantive Due Process and Equal Protection in the Federal Republic of Germany", (1989) *S Ct Rev* 333, 339.

I want briefly to describe two national experiences of constitutionalising property—those of the USA and the Federal Republic of Germany. These two experiences illustrate two different dilemmas which those who undertake to write or revise a constitution need to bear closely in mind. The USA and Germany are both liberal democracies with market economies. The legal systems of both countries fully recognise the basic institutions of private property and freedom of contract. Finally, both nations' constitutions explicitly treat in some fashion the constitutional status of private property. Beyond these basic points of common experience, however, there are important differences—textual and otherwise—between the two. These differences are worth emphasising because they usefully illustrate different pitfalls of which constitution-makers and revisers ought to be keenly aware, particularly in the new democracies of the world.

The point of this chapter is not to choose any one approach to fixing the constitutional status of property as transnationally optimal. Differences in historical and cultural backgrounds of course will and should influence the approach that any particular nation takes to treating property in its constitution. Still, while there is no cross-culturally superior constitutional approach, there is a limit to how far one should push cultural relativism in evaluating national constitutions. At least all liberal democracies share certain common concerns about their constitutions, not the least because of the commitment to the rule of law ideal, however variable the substantive meaning of that ideal may be. This chapter is written, then, under the conviction that constitutional experiences are not entirely incommensurable and, therefore, that nation-states and their peoples do benefit from studying the constitutional experience of other legal systems.

I. TWO VISIONS OF CONSTITUTIONAL PROPERTY AND TWO DILEMMAS

Broadly speaking, property as a constitutional right may be thought to serve two quite different functions. The first is an individual, or personal function: securing a zone of freedom for the individual in the realm of economic activity. In this role, property is closely connected with individual liberty. This idea of property and liberty as intimately and functionally intertwined is quite familiar, of course, in traditional liberal theory and may be thought to constitute the core substantive meaning of property in the liberal tradition.

The second function that might be recognised is social and public rather than personal and private. It is to serve the public good. This conception does not so much socialise ownership as it conceives the ends which property is to serve as being social. Property is individually owned, and the individual owner possesses considerable discretion regarding its uses. But the basic reason why the institution of property is recognised is to advance the collective good of the society that has recognised it. That is, property is privately owned just insofar as this serves the common welfare, where the common welfare is conceived as more than merely the aggregate of individual preference satisfaction. This conception probably enjoys less explicit recognition in traditional liberal theory, but it is not entirely absent from liberalism. Indeed, it can be attributed even to that paragon of liberal property—John Locke—depending on how one interprets his proviso. It was prominent in eighteenth-century political thought, on both sides of the Atlantic, and remains evident in the twentieth-century liberal discourses of property.

The existence of two conceptions of the core function of constitutional property creates dilemmas for legal systems committed to protecting property through constitutional norms. While the two conceptions are not mutually exclusive, in some instances they will lead to different results. At a minimum they will influence the rhetoric by which courts reach decisions about the reach of the constitutional protection of property. The experiences of German and American courts interpreting their constitutional property clauses illustrate two dilemmas that the existence of the two conceptions of property potentially create. The first, illustrated by the American experience, results from the failure explicitly to define the core purpose or purposes for which private property is constitutionally protected. The second, illustrated by the experience of the German courts, is the failure to establish a hierarchy of purposes where the constitutional scheme does explicitly protect more than one constitutional value for property.

II. PROPERTY UNDER THE AMERICAN CONSTITUTION

Perhaps the most striking feature of the American constitutional treatment of property is that there is no property clause as such. Property is mentioned only in the takings clause of the Fifth Amendment and the due process clause of the Fourteenth Amendment. While both protect property to some extent, the extent of protection is limited. Notably, property is not treated in American constitutional law as a fundamental right. This is likely to strike an outsider as odd, given the enormous weight that American society attaches to property.

The more important provision treating property is the so-called takings clause of the Fifth Amendment. Like the due process clause, its formal text is beguilingly simple. And again like the due process clause, its protection is stated in negative rather than affirmative terms. The clause merely provides that Congress (and, through the operation of the Fourteenth Amendment, the states as well) "shall not take property for public purposes without just compensation". The positive implication of this text, of course, is that government *may* take private property but only under two conditions: first, that the appropriation is for a "public purpose", and, secondly, that the government pays the affected owner "just compensation". In practice, neither of these requirements has been problematic. The first, the requirement of a taking for "public use" only, has been construed by the Supreme Court in recent years to provide very little limitation on the permissible range of purposes for which government may appropriate private property.[4] The second, that the government pay the ousted owner "just compensation" for the property taken, means that the owner is entitled to receive the full market value (though not personal value) for that which she or he has lost. The effect is to give government the power of forced sale in dealing with private property that it deems necessary or suitable for some public purpose.

The assumption implicit in both of these requirements is that there has been a taking of property. Therein lies the core problem with American constitutional protection of property. On the one hand, "takings", it would seem, ought not to be restricted to overt exercises of the power of eminent domain, under which the state formally condemns privately-owned property and pays the owner its fair market value. In the modern regulatory state there would be little substantive protection of property, really, little left of the distinction between the public and private spheres, if the takings clause were confined solely to actions that literally constituted *takings*. So, beginning with a famous decision by Justice Holmes in 1922,[5] at the dawn of the modern regulatory age in the USA, the Supreme Court has developed the doctrine of "regulatory takings". This doctrine, which occupies virtually the entire landscape of takings jurisprudence today, has a notoriously and frustratingly vague scope. Justice Holmes provided little guidance, telling us only that a regulatory action, that is, a purported exercise of the state's general and non-compensable police power, in fact constitutes a compensable taking when it "goes too far". In the more than 70 years since the doctrine's birth, the Supreme Court and lower courts have spilled oceans of ink trying to define where that line is. I will not bore readers with the details of the Court's efforts, but suffice it to say that the Court has been singularly unsuccessful in developing a coherent jurisprudence of regulatory takings. Notoriously, constitutional property is, in the apt word of one commentator, a "muddle".[6] The core reason for this confusion, I wish to argue, is the existence of uncertainty and ambivalence regarding what the primary functions or roles of property are from a constitutional perspective.

An obvious place to begin in analysing the reasons for the state of confusion in American constitutional property jurisprudence is that the text of the Constitution provides no direct or ancillary clues concerning why property is protected. The takings clause is only one part of an amendment that also guarantees individual rights that have little or no apparent relationship to property (protection against self-incrimination, for example). Nor is there elsewhere in the Constitution a super-Constitutional norm, or value, which guides interpretation of subsidiary constitutional values. Hence we are left with history and politics (not that those factors would not importantly influence interpretation

---

[4] See *Hawaii Housing Authority* v. *Midkiff* 467 US 229 (1984).

[5] *Pennsylvania Coal Co* v. *Mahon* 260 US 393 (1922).

[6] C. M. Rose, "*Mahon* Reconstructed: Why the Takings Clause Is Still a Muddle", (1984) 57 *S Cal L Rev* 561.

even if the text were clearer). As Carol Rose and others have shown, a careful look at the history and politics of our takings jurisprudence reveals that both conceptions of property that I have described have been present in our property tradition at least since the adoption of the Constitution.[7]

It may come as a surprise to some to hear that the social role of property—maintaining the proper social order, defined in non-market terms—has achieved any serious recognition in American jurisprudence. There has been remarkably little open debate about what is the core constitutional purpose (or purposes) of property. Most commentators take it as simply given that property serves and always has served one and only one constitutional purpose—securing individual liberty.[8] This unexamined assumption, I want to suggest, is the source of the American dilemma. For the fact is that, at least in relation to property, liberty is an ambiguous concept. It can be—and has been—understood to embrace either of the two functions of property. In English political thought, one conception of the relationship between property and liberty is that associated with Locke; the other is associated with James Harrington, for whom property, liberty, and proper citizenship were inextricably connected. This English background directly influenced American political and legal writers from the time of our Revolution to the present. While the Lockean understanding has enjoyed greater exposure, traces of the Harringtonian (or "proprietarian", as I prefer to call it) tradition have been evident in our legal and political thought throughout American history. The historical tendency has been to assume that the two functions are inevitably complementary. (Initially, this tendency can be traced back to the preoccupation with land and the Founders' assumption that the supply of land in the USA was limitless, mooting any question of conflicts over redistribution of land.) American courts have not settled a single clear meaning of autonomy in relation to property. In particular, the Supreme Court's takings jurisprudence historically has oscillated between the two without apparent recognition of what is occurring. At times, it has embraced the strictly preference-satisfying role, while at others it has implicitly recognised both that role and a proprietarian role.

The inability to acknowledge that American constitutional law in practice has recognised both functions of property has inhibited judges from answering the second question, what is the relationship between the two roles. While these two functions are not inevitably in conflict with each, it does not take a great deal of imagination to see that a basic tension between them exists. Disputes that are most likely to lead to litigation are those in which the personal and the social aspects of property are in conflict. Consequently, a clear view of the con-

---

[7] Rose, above n. 6, at 587–597; W. Treanor, "The Origins and Original Significance of the Just Compensation Clause of the Fifth Amendment", (1985) 94 *Yale LJ* 694.

[8] See e.g., J. W. Ely, *The Guardian of Every Other Right: A Constitutional History of Property Rights* (New York, Oxford University Press, 1992); F. McDonald, *Novus Ordo Seclorum: The Intellectual Origins of the Constitution* (Lawrence, University Press of Kansas, 1985); M. Kammen, *Spheres of Liberty: Changing Perceptions of Liberty in American Culture* (Madison, University of Wisconsin Press, 1986).

stitutional dimension of property requires that one know whether the relevant constitutional regime is intended to recognise only one of these functions or both, and if both, what is the contemplated method for resolving conflicts between them? The failure squarely to confront the first questions leads to kind of confusion that exists in the United States now, where there is no agreement even about the core constitutional values that property serves. The result is that our takings jurisprudence is a mess. This, then, is the first dilemma that results from the existence of these two conceptions of why we constitutionally protect property. I turn now to the second experience.

III. THE DUALISTIC EXPERIENCE: PROPERTY UNDER THE
GERMAN CONSTITUTION

The second experience, that of the German constitution, illustrates a different dilemma. This is the dilemma that occurs when the constitutional order, either textually or as the result of judicial construction, does clearly answer the first question and its answer is to recognise property's pluralism; that is, the constitutional order explicitly recognises that property serves more than one constitutional value. Such a legal system then must confront the second question, which is how to order the multiple values that property serves. In many situations, of course, there will be no conflict among these values; indeed, they will often be mutually reinforcing. But this will not always be the case. In instances where two or more constitutional values that are implicated by property require different treatment of the property interest in question, which is to take priority, and how are courts to know which has greater priority in a given situation? This dilemma is not unique to property, of course. It is perhaps the fundamental dilemma for any and every legal system whose normative order is pluralistic. What is special about the case of constitutional property is that its normative order is, at least in the USA, not usually understood as pluralistic in character. It is, however, in Germany. German constitutional law explicitly recognises both the individual and the social purposes of property. It does not do so, however, in a way that unambiguously establishes a basic hierarchy or a method for establishing one. As a result, the German courts have been left the unenviable task of trying to reconcile the two dimensions, and their experience has not been entirely encouraging. Compounding the predicament, more than one high court has jurisdiction over constitutional property claims, and the different courts, particularly the Constitutional Court and the Supreme Court, have differed over whether the meaning of property is to be defined according to public law or private law tradition. Those two traditions effectively track the two functions that I have identified here.

In many respects, little distinguishes the German constitution's treatment of property from the American approach. Both recognise the legitimacy of the institution of private property, and both explicitly state that while the state may legitimately act in ways that may impair the property owner's interest, the state's power so to act is restricted. Finally, both expressly give the constitutionally injured property owner a right to compensation.

Important differences distinguish the two approaches, however. First, textually, the German constitution, unlike the American, has a single property clause. Article 14 of the *Grundgesetz* is the sole textual provision explicitly treating the relationship between the state and the individual concerning property.[9] The American Constitution has fragmented its treatment of property among multiple provisions, and this has led to confusion about the relationship between the meaning of property under the two provisions.

Secondly, Article 14 expressly recognises the institution of private property. The text is stated in affirmative rather than negative terms. It does not simply say that property shall not be deprived or taken except under certain conditions. Rather, it states, "Property and inheritance are guaranteed". The Constitutional Court has textually interpreted that language as guaranteeing the existence of private property as a legal institution. There is no counterpart to this affirmative language in the American constitution, and, curiously for such a property-conscious nation, no other textual basis for recognising the legitimacy of property as such.

Thirdly, and most importantly for purposes of comparing the German and American constitutions, the German constitution explicitly recognises the social role of property. This is hardly surprising and indeed almost required by the fact that elsewhere (in Article 20) the constitution declares the Federal Republic to be a "social state". Article 14 has to be understood against the background of this important provision. Article 14, section 2 states, "Ownership entails obligations. Its use should also serve the public weal".[10] This is the famous "social obligation of ownership" (*Sozialbindung*) clause of Article 14, and it is this provision on which that I want most to concentrate.

The full text of the social obligation clause does not provide a great deal of guidance regarding its substantive intent. The Anglo-American lawyer might be tempted to construe it to state little or nothing more than the familiar common law idea that private ownership of property is not absolute in the sense that the owner may do literally anything she or he wishes with his property. As even the dimmest law student in the Commonwealth or the USA knows, property rights are not absolute. There is always implicit in the legal concept of private property the obligation not to use your thing so as to interfere with another's legal interests. *Sic utere tuo ut alienum non laedes*, the common law's apophthegm stated. So construed, the social-obligation term would provide little substantive basis for distinguishing the German and American approaches.

---

[9] Other provisions in the Basic Law concerning property do not deal with the scope of individual ownership rights. Articles 134 and 135, for example, are transitional provisions affecting property other than that of individuals. Article 134 deals with the status of property under the Third Reich and provides that Reich property becomes federal property. Article 135 concerns the status of property owned by the several states, or *Länder*.

[10] *Grudgesetz*, art. 14(2).

I will argue that this is not a correct understanding of the place of property in German constitutional law and that the idea of property as a "fundamental right" has a quite different meaning under the German constitution. German constitutionalism does not view the right of property as a matter of protecting subjective preferences. Nor does it recognise property as a basic right for the purpose of blocking legislative or regulatory redistributive measures that frustrate the full satisfaction of individual preferences. It is not, in short, designed to instantiate a neo-classical vision of the minimalist "nightwatchman" state.[11] Its purpose instead is more moral and civic than it is economic. The moral dimension of property is that it is basic insofar as it implicates the values of human dignity and self-governance. The civic dimension is that property is the material basis for realising a pre-existing understanding of the proper social order. Stated differently, the German constitutional right of property is not a Lockean right, but a right that fuses the traditions of Kantian liberalism and civic republicanism. It is a conception of property that elsewhere I have called "proprietarian".[12] By that, I mean that property is protected as a fundamental individual right insofar as it serves the purpose of providing the material foundation for maintaining the proper social order, defined according to a scheme of objective values rather than in terms of the satisfaction of individual subjective preferences.

More basically, the social obligation clause of article 14(2) underscores the sense in which the German constitution is fundamentally different from the American constitution in relation to property. The German constitution is not primarily a classically liberal document; it is a social welfare document. This fact is made strikingly clear in the following statement of the Constitutional Court:[13]

> "The image of man under the Basic Law is not that of [an] isolated, sovereign individual; rather, the Basic Law resolves the conflict between the individual and the community by relating and binding the citizen to the community but without detracting from his individuality".

This "image of man" in turn strongly influences the constitutional treatment of property. It not only underlies the social-obligation clause, it also influences the meaning of the personal aspect of property. That aspect rests not a Lockean idea; it might better be thought of from a Hegelian perspective. The basic idea at work is that the role of this individual right of property is to enable the personal development of the individual. The same idea underlies the provision guaranteeing freedom of occupation as a basic right.[14] Both provisions draw on

---

[11] The best expression of that vision remains R. Nozick, *Anarchy, State and Utopia* (New York, Basic Books, 1974).

[12] See G. S. Alexander, *Commodity and Propriety: Competing Visions of Property in American Legal Thought 1776–1970* (Chicago, University of Chicago Press, 1997).

[13] Quoted in K. Sontheimer, "Principles of Human Dignity in the Federal Republic" in U. Karpen (ed.), *The Constitution of the Federal Republic* (Baden-Baden: Nomos Verlagsgesellschaft, 1988), pp. 213, 215.

[14] See F. Ossenbühl, "Economic and Occupational Rights" in Karpen, above n. 13, at pp. 251, 253–254.

a very different intellectual tradition of personal autonomy than the Lockean tradition. Alan Ryan has aptly labelled that tradition one of "self-development". Explaining the relationship between that tradition and the constitutional role of property in Germany requires some background about the German property clause and its constitutional context.

The background to the German Constitution

Germany as a Sozialstaat

The 1949 German Constitution created not only a *Rechtstaat* (state governed by the rule of law) but, equally important, a *Sozialstaat* (social welfare state).[15] Far from perceiving any tension between these two ideals, the Constitution contemplates that the two are mutually reinforcing. Thus, article 20 defines Germany as a "social federal state", while article 28(1) requires the creation of a legal regime that is consistent with "the principles of a republican, democratic, and social legal state [*sozialer Rechtstaat*]". This does not mean that the Basic Law serves as a complete economic as well as political constitution, but it does create a general framework for the state's responsibility in the economic realm.

The basic substantive idea underlying the *Sozialstaat* is that the government has a responsibility to provide for the basic needs of all its citizens. While the Basic Law embraces a modern version of this idea, its roots extend much further back in German history. It can traced back to the Lutheran idea that the relationship between the prince and his people is one of mutual obligation. The people owe allegiance to the prince, but the prince in turn is obligated to provide for the welfare of his people.[16] This idea is a theme that recurs throughout German constitutional history.

Today, the concept of the *Sozialstaat* embraces not only the responsibility to provide a social "safety net", as that term is understood in the USA, but further, to redistribute wealth. The notion that the public's welfare depends upon assuring that no one lives in poverty and avoiding gross inequalities in the social distribution of wealth, while heretical in most American circles, is relatively uncontroversial in Germany today.[17] As one German legal scholar put it, it is "well-established knowledge" that "the social situation of the people improves, if and so far as everybody shares the results of what has been produced by society".[18]

---

[15] H. W. Koch, *A Constitutional History of Germany in the Nineteenth and Twentieth Centuries* (London, Longman, 1984), p. 26.

[16] See D. P. Kommers, *The Constitutional Jurisprudence of the Federal Republic of Germany*, 2nd edn. (Durham, Duke University Press, 1998), p. 41.

[17] See U. Karpen, *Soziale Marktwirtschaft and Grundgesetz. Eine Einführung in die rechtlichen Grundlagen der sozialen Marktwirtschaft* (Baden-Baden, Nomos Verlagsgesellschaft, 1990), p. 14.

[18] U. Karpen, "The Constitution in the Face of Economic and Social Progress" in C. Starck (ed.), *New Challenges to the German Basic Law* (Baden-Baden, Nomos Verlagsgesellschaft, 1991), pp. 87, 90.

While some have expressed uncertainty whether the commitment to the social welfare state imposes affirmative duties on the state to provide particular benefits to all citizens or merely authorises the state to do so, the majority legal opinion in Germany today is that the state *is* under a constitutional obligation to guarantee a minimal subsistence for individual citizens.[19] At that same time, there is growing realisation in Germany today that there are limits to what the state can realistically provide, and an increasing number of Germans now believe that Germany may have already reached (or indeed exceeded) those limits. Still, there is no sense that the existence of limits undermines that basic commitment to the social welfare state.[20]

Human dignity as the ultimate constitutional value

The commitment to the social welfare state has to be understood in connection with the most basic commitment in the entire German constitution—the commitment to the principle of human dignity (*Menschenwürde*). It is no coincidence that the first article of the Basic Law states that "The dignity of man is inviolable. It is to be respected and safeguarded with the full authority of the State".[21] The German Basic Law views basic rights hierarchically, and the right to human dignity is the bedrock of all other constitutional rights. "Human dignity," the Constitutional Court has unambiguously stated, "is at the very top of the value order of the Basic Law".[22] It is, moreover, regarded as pre-political, objective, indeed, transcendent.

From an American perspective, the core challenge would seem to be reconciling the human dignity principle with the commitment to the *Sozialstaat,* reconciling, that is, article 1 with article 20. To American ears, "human dignity" strongly resonates of the individualist outlook associated with classical liberalism, making the constitutional right negative rather than positive in character. From that perspective, the interventionist character of the *Sozialstaat* might be thought to contradict the commitment to individual human dignity.

From the German perspective, however, this is a false trade-off.[23] The conception of human dignity that article 1 embraces is not that of classical individualism. Individual human dignity exists in a social and economic context. It cannot be fully and meaningfully protected without attending to the concrete conditions in which individuals live. "[I]t is social conditions that determine the

---

[19] K. Sontheimer, "Principles of Human Dignity in the Federal Republic" in P. Kirchhoff and D. P. Kommers (eds), *Germany and Its Basic Law* (Baden-Baden, Nomos Verlagsgesellschaft, 1993), pp. 213, 216.

[20] In 1996 elections in the German *Land* of Baden-Württemberg, for example, the SPD, a center-left party that was then the main opposition party in the German Parliament, campaigned on a platform whose slogan was *"Sozialstaat: Reformen-Ja! Abbau-Nein!"* ("The Social Welfare State, Reform, Yes! Demolition, No!")

[21] *Grundgesetz*, art. 1(1).

[22] 27 BVerfGE 1 (Microcensus case, 1969).

[23] Indeed, article 79 of the Basic Law provides that these two provisions are immune from any constitutional amendment.

extent to which the individual is truly able to safeguard his own human dignity."[24]

The social aspect of human dignity is evident in the German concept of the "image of man", that is, the nature of the human personality. This concept, which is central to the German Constitutional Court's dignitarian jurisprudence, defines the human personality as community-centered. Thus, the Constitutional Court early and explicitly stated that: [25]

> "[t]he image of man in the Basic Law is not that of an isolated, sovereign individual; rather, the Basic Law has decided in favor of a relationship between individual and community in the sense of a person's dependence on and commitment to the community, without infringing upon a person's individual value".

Ernst Benda, the distinguished and influential former president (Chief Justice) of the Constitutional Court's First Senate,[26] has noted that the Basic Law rejects the "individualistic conception of man derived from classical liberalism as well as the collectivist view".[27] Perhaps the most accurate description of this conception of the self is to say that it combines the Kantian injunction against treating people as means rather than ends[28] with a strongly communitarian ontology.[29] There are also strong parallels between the German conception of the relationship between the self and property and the role of property in civic republican thought. Republican theory, like German constitutional theory, valued property as the source of personal independence necessary for proper self-development and responsible citizenship.[30]

The relevance of the constitution's commitment to the *Sozialstaat* for understanding the meaning of property under the German constitution should be apparent by now. The *Sozialstaat* and the principle of human dignity lay the foundation for a particular way of understanding the core purpose of property rights. This theory holds that the core purpose of property is not wealth-maximization or the satisfaction of individual preferences, as the American eco-

---

[24] K. Sontheimer, above n. 19, at p. 215.

[25] 4 BVerfGE 7, 15–16 (Investment Aid Case, 1954).

[26] The Constitutional Court is divided into two eight-member panels, called senates. These have mutually exclusive jurisdiction and membership. In cases of jurisdictional conflict, the two senates meet together as a single Plenum. Each senate is headed by the equivalent of a chief justice; traditionally, the president heads the First Senate, while the vice-president heads the Second Senate. The two-senate structure represents a compromise of an old debate over the character of the Constitutional Court as a legal or a political institution. See generally D. P. Kommers, above n. 16, at pp. 16–18.

[27] E. Benda, W. Maihofer, and H.-J. Vogel, "Die Menschenwürdige", *Handbuch des Verfassungsrechts*, 2 vols. (Berlin, de Gruyter, 1984) I, at pp. 110, 117.

[28] For a rich discussion of the Kantian roots of the German constitutional "image of man" see G. P. Fletcher, "Human Dignity as a Constitutional Value", (1984) 22 *U Western Ontario L Rev* 178.

[29] See D. P. Kommers, above n. 16, at p. 241. The communitarian theories that seem most compatible with the Basic Law's image of man idea are those of Michael Sandel and Charles Taylor.

[30] See J. G. A. Pocock, *The Machiavellian Moment* (Princeton, Princeton University Press, 1975); G. S. Alexander, "Time and Property in the American Civic Republican Legal Culture", (1991) 66 *NYU L Rev* 273.

nomic theory of property holds,[31] but self-realization, or self-development, in an objective, distinctly moral and civic sense. That is, property is fundamental insofar as it is necessary for individuals fully to develop as moral agents and participating members of the broader community.

Property as the basis for human flourishing

The clearest exposition of this self-developmental theory of property was in the famous 1968 *Hamburg Flood Control* case.[32] The case involved a challenge to a 1964 statute enacted by the city-state of Hamburg converting all grassland that the state classified as "dike land" into public property. The statute terminated private ownership of such lands, but it did require that owners be compensated. Several owners of dike land claimed that the statute violated their fundamental right to property under article 14.

The basis of this claim illustrates one major difference between the American and German approaches to constitutionally protecting property. Under the American constitution, assuming that the amount of compensation was adequate (and there was no allegation in the case that it was not), there simply would be no basis for a constitutional challenge at all. The purpose of the governmental measure was to build an effective system of dikes in the wake of the devastating floods that hit Hamburg in 1962—certainly public enough to satisfy our weak "public use" requirement.[33] Under our takings clause, once the publicness of the governmental encroachment and the sufficiency of monetary compensation have been satisfied, there is no basis for constitutionally challenging the measure. Monetary (or other) compensation is always an adequate substitute for the thing itself.

Not so under the German constitution. Article 14 is understood to guarantee not merely monetary value of property but extant ownership itself. The Constitutional Court expressly recognised this in its opinion. It stated, "The function of article 14 is not primarily to prevent the taking of property without compensation—although in this respect it offers greater protection than Article 153 of the Weimar Constitution[34]—but rather *to secure existing property in the*

---

[31] For a modern classical expression of the economic theory, see H. Demsetz, "Toward a Theory of Property Rights", (1967) 57 *Am Econ Rev* 347.

[32] 24 BVerfGE 367 (1968).

[33] The standard datum cited to evidence the weakness of the public-use requirement under the Fifth Amendment's takings clause is *Hawaii Housing Authority* v. *Midkiff* 467 US 229 (1984).

[34] Article 153 of the 1919 Weimar Constitution was the basis for some aspects of article 14 of the post-Second World War Basic Law. A number of important differences existed, however, between the treatment of property under the two constitutions, including the fact that, by not allowing compensated expropriations to be judicially challenged, the Weimar Constitution did not protect the institution of property as such. Compensation was always an adequate substitute for the thing itself. See H.-J. Papier, "Die Eigentumsgarantie des Art. 14 I 1 GG" in T. Maunz and G. Dürig, *Grundgesetz Kommentar* 4 vols (München, Beck, 1993), vol 2, Randnummern 18–23.

On the weakness of basic rights under the Weimar Constitution generally, see V. Götz, "Legislative and Executive Power under the Constitutional Requirements Entailed in the Principle of the Rule of Law" in C. Starck (ed.), above n. 18, at pp. 141, 150–152.

hands of its owner".[35] This is the central meaning of the statement in article 14
I that "[p]roperty [is] guaranteed". Give this view that the Basic Law protects
property itself, not just its monetary equivalent, it is easy to understand why
commentators have stated that property is a more important value under the
German constitution than it is under the American takings or due process
clauses. But what needs to be asked is *why* the German Basic Law protects existing property relationships themselves.

The answer is that German constitutional jurisprudence does not treat property as a strictly market commodity but as a civil, and one may say, *civic* right
as well. The Court in the *Hamburg Flood Control* case made it clear that the
core purpose of property as a basic constitutional right is not solely economic
but moral and political. It stated: [36]

> "To hold that property is an elementary constitutional right must be seen in the close
> context of protection of personal liberty. Within the general system of constitutional
> rights, its function is to secure its holder a sphere of liberty in the economic field *and*
> *thereby enable him to lead a self-governing life*".

The last phrase signals the animating idea behind the constitutional role of
property under the German Basic Law—self-governance. Property is necessary
condition for autonomous individuals to experience control over their own
lives. Without property, they lack the material means necessary for a full and
healthy development of their personality. The Court made the connection
between property and personhood explicit in its opinion. It stated, "[T]he property guarantee under Article 14 I 2 must be seen in relationship to the personhood of the owner—that is, to the realm of freedom within which persons
engage in self-defining, responsible activity".[37]

The Court is here invoking an understanding of the function of property that
in some respects echoes what some recent American scholars, most notably
Margaret Jane Radin and C. Edwin Baker, drawing on Hegel, have called the
"personhood function".[38] As Radin explains, the premise of this understanding
is that: [39]

> "to achieve proper self-development—to be a *person*—an individual needs some con-
> trol over resources in the external environment".

The purpose of legal property rights, then, is to secure the requisite degree
of control—self-determination—as a necessary means of facilitating self-

---

[35] 24 BVerfGE at 400 (emphasis added).

[36] Ibid., at 389 (emphasis added).

[37] 24 BVerfGE at 398. In the immediate case, the court decided that the compensated expropriation of dikelands did not violate the owners' basic right because it satisfied the requirement of Article
14 III 1, that expropriations be made only for "the public weal" (*"Wohle der Allgemeinheit"*). More
specifically, it was not a redistribution of land made for general reasons but an appropriate response
to a particular problem of affecting the public good.

[38] See C. E. Baker, "Property and Its Relation to Constitutionally Protected Liberty", (1986) 134
U Pa L Rev 741, 746–747; M. J. Radin, "Property and Personhood", (1982) 34 *Stan L Rev* 957.

[39] Radin, "Property and Personhood", above n. 38, at 957.

development. The theory is most closely associated with Hegel, but Hegel and his followers were by no means the first or the only political philosophers to explain and justify property rights on the basis (and to the extent of) the proper development of the self. Rousseau, for example, had earlier developed a somewhat similar theory of property that stressed the importance of property to proper and full development of the personality. For Rousseau, private ownership was morally justifiable only to the extent that it fulfilled that function.[40] Later, Mill was to link private property with self-management and the Hegelian idea of, as Alan Ryan has put it, "anchor[ing] a man in a world which outlived him".[41]

As the Constitutional Court's opinion makes clear, the German idea of the constitutional property right shares with the self-developmental tradition a conception of liberty that differs from the classical Anglo-American understanding of that term. Borrowing the distinction made famous by Isaiah Berlin,[42] one can say that German constitutional law, like the Hegelian theory of property and the self, understands liberty in its positive as well as a negative sense, that is, freedom *to* rather than freedom *from*.[43] It may be more accurate to describe the German constitutional conception of liberty, in its relation to property, as blending the positive and negative dimensions. The individual owner's freedom from external interference with his property is valued just because that is a precondition for him to act in a way that is necessary to realisation of the self. Put differently, property and liberty are connected with each other, not solely through a politics of fear of the state, but a politics of enabling self-governance. The point of protecting individual ownership is not to create a zone of security from a powerful and threatening state but to make it possible for individuals to realise their own human potential.

The German constitutional commitments to both human dignity and the *Sozialstaat* strongly influence the way in which the Constitutional Court understands the relationship between property and self-development. The Court views considerations of individual welfare as integrally related to the proper self-development of citizens, not as isolated agents but as members of society. Welfare here is less a matter of guaranteeing that the distribution of wealth throughout society is morally optimal than it is of securing the material conditions necessary for the proper development of individuals as responsible and self-governing members of society.

[40] See generally A. Ryan, *Property and Political Theory* (Oxford, Basil Blackwell, 1984), pp. 49–72.

[41] Ibid., p. 149.

[42] See generally I. Berlin, *Two Concepts of Liberty* (Oxford, Clarendon Press, 1958) *passim*.

[43] It is important to be very careful here, though. It is not clear to what extent public assistance, what we would call welfare benefits, are protected as "ownership" under Article 14. Social security interests in Germany today are so protected, but these accrue by virtue of employment. See generally P. Krause, *Eigentum an subjektiven öffentlichen Rechten* (Berlin, Duncker & Humblot, 1982); F. Ossenbühl, *Festschrift für Wolfgang Zeidler*, Bd 1 (Berlin, W de Gruyter, 1987), p. 625. Similarly, the *Sozialstaatsprinzip* (principle of social justice) of article 20 does not create subjective rights, that is, affirmative claim-rights against the state, but instead establishes a goal for the state to pursue through the legislature. See 27 BVerfGE 253, 283; 41 BVerfGE 126, 153; 82 BVerfGE 60, 80.

Institutional tension: public law versus private law meanings of property

Article 14 has two other important provisions. Section 1 provides that the "content and limits" of the property right "shall be defined by statute". The third section states that property may be taken only for the public good. Takings may be effected:

> "only by or pursuant to a statute regulating the nature and extent of compensation. Such compensation shall be determined by establishing an equitable balance between the public interest and the interests of those affected".

This text, juxtaposed with section 1's statement that the "content and limits [of property] shall be determined by statute", seemingly replicates the American dilemma of distinguishing between compensable takings and non-compensable regulations. The two provisions read together require that courts distinguish between the (non-compensable) social obligation of ownership and the compensable taking of property. Unfortunately, the text of the Constitution provides no guidance as to how that distinction is to be drawn.[44] The result has been that the three high courts which have overlapping jurisdiction over constitutional property issues, the German Constitutional Court (Bundesverfassungsgericht), the German Supreme Civil Court (Bundesgerichtshof), and the German Administrative Court (Bundesverwaltungsgericht), have developed different and at times conflicting approaches to resolving the question. The most important of these tensions is that between the Constitutional Court's conception of property, which differs in significant respects from the private law meaning of property, and the Supreme Court's idea of property, which is basically rooted in the Civil Code. It is this failure to reconcile, institutionally and conceptually, the public-law and private-law traditions of property that explains the confused state of regulatory takings law in Germany.

Property in the Constitutional Court: the primacy of propriety

The Constitutional court's conception of property as the basis for proper self-development has produced two defining characteristics of constitutional property jurisprudence in that court. The constitution's treatment of property, both textually and as interpreted by the courts, is *functionally dynamic* and *socially based*. It is functionally dynamic in the sense that the courts consider social and economic changes that have affected the purposes that particular resources serve over time. An influential treatise on German constitutional law aptly captures this focus on the functional change of property and its relevance to constitutional protection: [45]

---

[44] See R. Dolzer, *Property and Environment: The Social Obligation Inherent in Ownership* (International Union for Conservation of Nature and Natural Resources, Environment Policy and Law Paper No. 12, Morges, Switzerland), p. 18.

[45] K. Hesse, *Grundzüge des Verfassungsrechts der Bundesrepublik Deutschland* 20th edn. (Heidelberg, C F Müller, 1995), p. 192.

"As a basis for the individual existence and individual conduct of life as well as a principle of social order the individual ownership of property has lost its importance.
Modern life is based only to a limited extent on the individual power of disposition as
the basis for individual existence, with respect, for example, to the peasant farm or the
family enterprise. The basis for individual existence is usually no longer private property as determined by private law, but the produce of one's own work and participation in the benefits of the welfare state".

The relevance of functional changes of property to constitutional protection
is illustrated by the *Small Garden Plot* case (*Kleingartenentscheidung*).[46] In that
case the Court struck down a federal statute that severely limited the right of
landowners to terminate garden leases. The historical background of the statute
and changes in social conditions are crucial to understanding the decision. At
one time in German history it was common for large landowners, particularly
on the outskirts of cities, to lease to people who owned little or no land small
plots for the purpose of small gardens. These garden plots were an important
method of feeding the German public. As the dominant means of agricultural
production shifted to large-scale commercial productions, these individual garden plots lost their original social purpose and indeed became something of an
anachronism. The individual landowners in the case wanted to change the use
of their land from agricultural purposes to commercial development because the
amount of annual rent from the leasehold had become insubstantial. They
applied for a permit to terminate the garden lease on their land, but the regulatory agency refused to grant the permit because the federal statute did not recognise this sort of change of circumstances as a permissible basis for terminating
leases. The Court held that the statute was unconstitutional because the magnitude of the restriction on the owner's freedom of use was disproportionate to the
public purpose to be served.[47] While the original function of these garden allot-
ments was to provide a source of food in times of social emergency, the purpose
had by modern times become no more than a source of recreation, a social function that the court regarded as decidedly less weighty than its original purpose.
Comparing the weakness of the new function with the severity of the restriction
on the owners' use, the court had little difficulty in concluding that the statute
was unconstitutional.

The *Garden Plot* case also illustrates the other characteristic of constitutional
property jurisprudence, its perception of private ownership as being "socially
tied", as the Constitutional Court put it. The basis for this conception of private
property as socially obligated is a provision in the Basic Law's property clause
that finds no real analogy in the American constitution. Article 14 II provides,

---

[46] 52 BVerfGE 1 (1979).

[47] The principle of proportionality (*Verhältnismäßigkeit*), although nowhere expressly mentioned in the constitution, is a fundamental aspect of German constitutional jurisprudence. It is
derived from the rule of law ideal (*Rechtsstaatlichkeit*) and has a long history predating the 1949
Basic Law. For a good summary of its origins and role, see D. P. Currie, *The Constitution of the
Federal Republic of Germany* (Chicago, University of Chicago Press, 1994), pp. 307–310.

"Property entails obligations. Its use shall also serve the common good". While the Court has never defined the precise scope of this "social obligation of ownership", it is clear that the clause is understood as something more than the idea expressed in the familiar common-law apophthegm, *sic utere tuo ut alienum non laedes* (use your thing in a way that does not interfere with the legal interests of others). It is intended to express the idea that private property rights are always subordinate to the public interest. This idea was more fully expressed in the original draft of Article 14 II, which stated, "Ownership entails a social obligation. Its use shall find its limits in the living necessities of all citizens and in the public order essential to society".[48] That the social obligation recognised in Article 14 II is broader than the minimal duty to avoid creating a public nuisance is clear from various decisions of the Constitutional Court. The social obligation (*Sozialverpflichtung*) was the basis for the Court's statements recognising the constitutional legitimacy of certain forms of rent control[49] and anti-eviction regulations.[50]

From an American perspective, perhaps the most striking sign of the broad reach of the social obligation is the important *Codetermination* case (*Mitbestimmungsentscheidung*).[51] That case involved a challenge to the constitutional validity of the federal Codetermination Act of 1976, an extremely important piece of legislation regulating the relationship between labour and management in German industries. The act mandates worker representation on the boards of directors of large firms, defined as firms with 2000 or more employees. It further requires that the firm's legal representatives as well as its primary labour director be selected by the supervisory board according to specified procedures and that the board's chair and vice-chair be elected by a two-thirds majority.

The ostensible purpose of the Act was to extend and strengthen worker participation in the governance of business enterprises, a practice that has a long history in German labour-management relations. But anyone who has read James Buchanan and Gordon Tullock's famous book, *The Calculus of Consent*, may be tempted to react sceptically to that explanation. A public-choice analysis of the Act would simply see it as a clear instance of rent-seeking legislation, supported by an obviously well-organised and intensely political interest group. That may indeed have been the real basis for the Act, but the German Constitutional Court did not think so. Squarely addressing the public-choice reading (although not calling it by that term), the Court stated: [52]

> "The Codetermination Act does not promote narrow group interests. Rather, the cooperation and integration served by institutional coparticipation . . . has general

---

[48] R. Dolzer, *Property and Environment: The Social Obligation Inherent in Ownership* (Morges, International Union for Conservation of Nature and Natural Resources, 1976), p. 17.

[49] 37 BVerfGE 132, 139–143 (Tenancy and Rent Control case, 1974).

[50] 68 BVerfGE 361, 367–371 (1985).

[51] 50 BVerfGE 290 (Codetermination case, 1979).

[52] 290 BVerfGE at 372.

importance as a social policy; coparticipation is a legitimate political means of safe-guarding the market economy. It serves the public welfare and cannot be regarded as an unsuitable means for the achievement of this purpose".

The plaintiffs, which included a large number of business firms and employers' associations, attacked the act as a gross interference with their property rights. They argued that the Act violated the constitutional property rights of share-holders and the firms themselves under article 14 of the Basic Law as well as other constitutional guarantees.[53] Rejecting this claim, the Constitutional Court concluded that the Act was merely an exercise of the legislature's power under article 14 I to define the "contents and limits" of property. It did not violate the injunction of Article 19 II that "the essence of a basic right [not] be encroached upon". The court stated that while the Act admittedly reduced the powers of shareholders as members of the supervising board, the restriction "remains within the ambit of the commitments of property owners to society in general".[54] Article 14 II makes clear, the court pointed out, that "use and power of disposal do not remain [solely] in the sphere of the individual owner, but concern also the interests of other individuals who depend upon the use of the [particular] object of property".[55] The magnitude of owners' social commitment under article 14 varies with the social importance of the asset and its contemporary purpose.[56] As the Constitutional Court stated, the social obligation "increase[s] in scope as the relationship the property in question and its social environment as well as its social function narrows".[57] Applying this sliding scale approach, the court reasoned that shareholding: [58]

"ha[s] far-reaching social relevance and serve[s] a significant social function, especially since the use of this property always requires the co-operation of the employees whose fundamental rights are affected by such use".

While the text of article 14 speaks only of "property" and seemingly does not distinguish among various sorts of property, in fact the Constitutional Court has drawn just such qualitative distinctions. The *Codetermination* case and *Small Garden* case, read together, allow one to say that the Court distinguishes among different categories of property, creating a kind of hierarchy among types of resources. The sliding scale approach to evaluating the magnitude of the social obligation and the social function of property is the basis for this ordering of property. This is the primary means by which the court has cabined the social obligation, which otherwise would seem to be the proverbial unruly

---

[53] Other grounds for the challenge included interference with the rights of occupation (article 12) and association (article 9). There is a substantial degree of interrelationship between articles 12 and 14. For a lucid discussion, see F. Ossenbühl, "Economic and Occupational Rights" in *Germany and Its Basic Law*, above n. 14 at 251.

[54] 290 BVerfGE at 371.

[55] Ibid.

[56] Ibid.

[57] Ibid.

[58] 290 BVerfGE at 372.

horse. Greater legislative power is recognised over socially important assets like corporate stock than over small garden plots used for leisure.

The Constitutional Court tests the validity of laws regulating property under Article 14(1)'s general guarantee of property. Since the same section also provides that the legislature determines the "contents and limits" of property, the Constitutional Court basic task in dealing with regulatory measures is to determine whether a regulation merely defines the contents and limits of the property interest or is so intrusive that it violates that basic guarantee. In carrying out that task, the Court has adopted a balancing approach.[59] In the *Kleingarten* case, for example, the Court stated: [60]

> "When making a law in the sense of Article 14, section 1 the legislature has to take into account both elements contained in the constitution, the relationship between constitutionally protected legal positions and the demands of a social system of property ownership; it has to balance the different interests meriting protection".

What the court does under this balancing approach is to examine the extent to which the asset involved has a social rather than a strictly individual function. More specifically, it inquires whether and to what extent other persons are dependent on the use of the owner's property. The greater the degree of dependency, the greater the social function and, correspondingly, the greater the degree of legislative freedom to interfere with the owner's property interest for the purpose of protecting the social role of the asset. This functional analysis, moreover, is dynamic in the sense that the court takes into account changes in the functional purposes that the asset serves.[61] As part of this functional approach, the Constitutional Court has relied on the social obligation clause of section 2 to distinguish among and prioritise various types of property interests according to the social functions they serve. The Court has developed a system for "scaling" the social obligation of ownership (*Abstufung der Sozialpflichtigkeit*) according to the specific interest's relation to the property-holder and its social function. The legislature is given greater freedom to delimit the content of and to define the restrictions on property interests whose functions have greater social relevance. Moreover, the legislature has more latitude to define restrictions on interests that are further removed from the property holder's personal liberty. So, investment-based interests gain less constitutional protection than property interests in one's home. In landlord-tenant relations, for example, rent control and other forms of tenant protection are almost routinely affirmed because the tenant's interest is personal and intimately connected with personal liberty while the landlord's interest usually is strictly economic.[62]

---

[59] See D. P. Currie, above n. 47, at p. 295.

[60] BVerfGE 52, 1.

[61] Ibid. See G. F. Schuppert, "The Right to Property" in U. Karpen (ed.), above n. 13, at pp. 107, 109–110, 114–115.

[62] See e.g., BVerfGE 68, 361 (*Wohnungskündigungsgesetzentscheidung*); BVerfGE 89, 1 (*Besitzrecht des Mietersentscheidung*).

The upshot of these doctrinal practices is that the social-obligation clause imposes a substantial restriction on many sorts of property interests. The Court distinguishes among various types of property interests for the very purpose of giving greater weight to those interests that serve a proprietarian, rather than a strictly economic, function.

Property in the Supreme Court: the primacy of private law

The Supreme Court has developed a quite different approach to analysing constitutional property issues. By way of procedural background, while the Constitutional Court has exclusive jurisdiction to determine whether a government action is unconstitutional, it does not have jurisdiction to award compensation for expropriations. That power is vested in the Supreme Court. As a result, the Supreme Court has had the opportunity to award compensation for expropriation-like governmental actions that the Constitutional Court has held to be constitutionally valid. It has done so on the basis of a very different conception of property than that held by the Constitutional Court. While the Constitutional Court regards the property that is protected and the means of its protection under article 14 to be public law matters, the Supreme Court has been strongly influenced by private law conceptions of property.

The Supreme Court has developed two doctrines with which to analyse the reach of constitutional protection of property. These are the doctrine of "individual sacrifice" (*Sonderopfer*)[63] and the doctrine of "situational commitment" (*Situationsgebundenheit*). The first doctrine is basically a principle of equality of treatment. Under it, the court determines whether the regulation singles out a property owner to bear the burden of the regulatory scheme or instead affects all owners more or less equally in a reciprocal scheme of benefits and burdens. To make this calculus more concrete, the court introduced the second doctrine, the situational-commitment idea. Under this doctrine, the court focuses on the relationship between the affected asset and its physical and social context. If the use which is prohibited by a regulation is one that is incompatible with the asset's "situational commitment", then the regulation is sustained and no compensation is due.[64] The Supreme Court itself, however, has given this "situational commitment" idea varying interpretations,[65] and a number of commentators have condemned it as excessively arbitrary.[66] The primary meaning that the Court has attached to the idea, however, is, in the Court's own words, whether a "reasonable owner, *from an economic point of view*, would use a resource in a particular way".[67] As the italicised phrase indicates, the test

---

[63] See Dolzer, above n. 48, at pp. 19–20.

[64] e.g., BGHZ 23, 30 (*Grünflächenurteil*).

[65] See H. Kube, "Private Property in Natural Resources and the Public Weal in German Law—Latent Similarities to the Public Trust Doctrine?", (1997) 37 *Natural Resources Journal* 857, 867.

[66] See Papier, Art 14, Grundgesetz, Rdnr 335.

[67] BGHZ 54, 293 (*Altes Wasserrechtsurteil*) (emphasis added).

presupposes a conception of ownership that focuses on the economic function of property. This conception is at odds with the conception that the Constitutional Court has used, and as a result the two courts have quarrelled over the appropriate meaning of property.

The most important case in which the conflict between the two courts was evident is the W*et Gravel* case (*Naßauskiesungsentscheidung*), discussed earlier. The Supreme Court there took the view that private ownership of land gives the individual owner the right to put the resource to every conceivable and economically appropriate use. This view was explicitly premised on the private law conception of ownership derived from the Civil Code. The Constitutional Court repudiated that view, taking the position that the conception of ownership that is protected by the Constitution is a public law one, derived from the Constitution itself, not from the Civil Code.[68] On remand, the Supreme Court adhered to its views that the right of economic exploitation was at the core of the concept of ownership and that governmental interference with that right was compensable. It avoided a constitutional crisis by saying, however, that the right to compensation was a matter of customary, not constitutional law. That is, even though a government action may trigger no constitutional right to compensation because the action comes within the purview of Article 14's social-obligation clause, the government may still have to pay compensation as a matter of private customary law.

What this dispute revealed was a deep disagreement over the extent to which Article 14 had replaced the traditional private law understanding about the meaning and scope of property. Even though it is quite clear that Article 14 was intended to create a constitutional concept of property which was not primarily market-oriented in character, traditional private law notions, which did adopt a market conception of property, have persisted in influencing judicial thought and in impeding the full realisation of the social vision underlying article 14.

IV. CONCLUSION

Perhaps the dilemmas that the German and American experiences with constitutional property illustrate are inevitable. The institution of private ownership of property historically has rested on multiple and diverse normative visions, and it does so still to this day. This pluralist and contestable character of private property seems highly unlikely ever to give way to a unitary conception, in which property is understood to serve one and only one purpose. Property seems inherently contestable. So long as it remains so, the questions whether it should be constitutionally protectible, to what extent, and by what means will remain essentially political questions, implicating competing political visions. Ultimately, that is, perhaps, a virtue as well as a dilemma.

[68] For a discussion of this, see A. van der Walt, *The Constitutional Property Clause* (Kenwyn, Juta & Co, 1997).

6

The Constitutional Property Clause: Striking a Balance Between Guarantee and Limitation

A J VAN DER WALT[1]

I. INTRODUCTION

The inclusion of a property clause in a bill of rights is a difficult and controversial matter. Property is not universally regarded as one of the fundamental "human" rights, and its constitutional entrenchment can certainly not be justified on the same basis as the "classic" rights like life, liberty and personal security.[2] Theorists have in fact argued that the constitutional entrenchment of property can even undermine the establishment or the functioning of a democratic society—an argument that is probably largely based on the "muddle" that is said to characterise takings jurisprudence in the USA since the 1980s,[3] and seemingly borne out by the fact that the constitutional protection of property in sections 19 and 31 of the Indian Constitution (1950) precipitated a struggle

[1] Thanks to Marjan Gerbrands for research assistance, to Mike Taggart for providing information on the property proposals in New Zealand, and to Janet McLean of the New Zealand Institute of Public Law for the invitation and for financial assistance to attend the conference. Thanks to Greg Alexander, Tom Allen, Henk Botha, Peter Butt, Johan Erasmus, Danie Goosen, Wessel le Roux, Lawrence Makhubela, Frank Michelman, Jenny Nedelsky, Theunis Roux, Joe Singer, Mike Taggart, Johan van der Walt, Karin van Marle and Laura Underkuffler-Freund for reading an early draft of the article and giving me the benefit of their comments. I take full credit for the remaining errors and shortcomings. Parts of this chapter are based on sections of A. J. van der Walt, *Constitutional Property Clauses: A Comparative Analysis* (Cape Town, Juta & Co, 1999).

[2] Of course, there are theorists who argue that property is such a fundamental right, usually on the basis of some version of natural rights theory. For a recent example in the South African context see C. H. Lewis, "The Right to Private Property in a New Political Dispensation in South Africa", (1992) 8 *SAJHR* 389; for a criticism of these theories, see J. Nedelsky, "Should Property be Constitutionalized? A Relational and Comparative Approach" in G. E. van Maanen and A. J. van der Walt (eds), *Property Law on the Threshold of the 21st Century* (Antwerp, Maklu, 1996), pp. 417–432, 420.

[3] See J. Nedelsky, *Private Property and the Future of Constitutionalism: the Madisonian Framework and its Legacy* (Chicago, University of Chicago Press, 1990); J. Nedelsky (1996) above n. 2, at pp. 417–432; S. Lukes, "Five Fables about Human Rights" in S. Shute and S. L. Hurley (eds), *On Human Rights: The Oxford Amnesty Lectures 1993* (New York, Basic Books, 1993), pp. 19, 38–39; J Donnelly, *Universal Human Rights in Theory and Practice* (Ithaca, Cornell University Press, 1989), p. 27.

between the courts and the legislature that seriously compromised the credibility of the courts, almost destroyed the moral and legal authority of the Constitution and ended in the property clause being removed from the bill of rights altogether.[4] In a number of other jurisdictions, these and other, related considerations and concerns have recently resulted in heated discussions about the wisdom and justification of including a property guarantee in a bill of rights.

The Canadian Bill of Rights (1960) contains a property clause in section 1(a), but this clause has been described as "a relatively feeble and underemployed right"[5] because the Bill of Rights is a normal parliamentary law that can be amended like any other law. After a lengthy debate,[6] reference to the protection of property was omitted from the later Canadian Charter of Rights and Freedoms (1983).[7] In *Attorney-General of Quebec* v. *Irwin Toy Ltd*.[8] it was decided that property cannot be read into section 7 of the Charter by interpretation either: property, having been shut out of the front door, cannot enter by the back door.[9] Reasons forwarded for the decision not to include a property clause in the Charter include the following: the property concept is too open-ended, and a general and unspecific property clause might create the possibility for landowners to oppose almost any land-use or planning regulation on the basis that it effected a "taking" of some incident of property;[10] there are sufficient existing sources of protection (including common law, statutory and constitutional protection) for property, with the result that there was insufficient pressure in favour of the entrenchment of property in the Charter;[11] explicit protection of property is unnecessary because property will be protected as part of the protection of life, liberty and the security of the person in terms of section 7 of the Charter;[12] there is too much controversy about the question

---

[4] The history of the Indian property guarantee is discussed in section III of the chapter below.

[5] See R. W. Bauman, "Property Rights in the Canadian Constitutional Context", (1992) 8 *SAJHR* 344, 350.

[6] A. Alvaro, "Why Property Rights were Excluded from the Canadian Charter of Rights and Freedoms", (1991) 24 *Can J Pol Science* 309 and P. W. Augustine, "Protection of the Right to Property Under the Canadian Charter of Rights and Freedoms", (1986) 18 *Ottawa LR* 67, discuss the reasons for this decision. See P W Hogg, *Constitutional Law of Canada*, 3rd edn. (Scarborough, Carswell, 1992), pp. 779–780 for a brief history. See further P. W. Hogg "A Comparison of the Canadian Charter of Rights and Freedoms with the Canadian Bill of Rights" in G. A. Beaudoin and E. Ratushny (eds), *The Canadian Charter of Rights and Freedoms*, 2nd edn. (Toronto, Carswell, 1989), pp. 1–20. R. W. Bauman, above n. 5, at 344–345, 353 indicates that this debate is not over yet.

[7] When the new Charter was enacted the Bill of Rights (1960) was not abolished, with the result that section 1(a) is still valid, subject to its original limitations. That is why P. W. Hogg above n. 6, ch. 44, especially p. 1031, argues that the Bill of Rights continues to provide at least due-process protection of property, albeit within its limited scope of applicability to federal laws.

[8] (1989) 1 SCR 927.

[9] Contrary to the (probably obiter) earlier statement in *The Queen in Right of New Brunswick* v. *Fisherman's Wharf Ltd*. (1982) 135 DLR 3d 307. See in general Augustine, above n. 6, at 55; D. Gibson, *The Law of the Charter: General Principles* (Calgary, Carswell, 1986), pp. 30–31; P. W. Hogg above n. 6, ch. 33.

[10] R. W. Bauman, above n. 5, at 345, 348.

[11] R. W. Bauman, above n. 5, at 345, 348–352; P. W. Hogg above n. 6, at 705–708.

[12] R. W. Bauman, above n. 5, at 345, 352–354. This assumption was mistaken, as indicated earlier (see *Attorney-General* of *Quebec* v. *Irwin Toy Ltd*. (1989) 1 SCR 927).

whether property is a fundamental right that should be ranked with the "classic" personal and civil liberties;[13] and there are concerns that the constitutional entrenchment of property might frustrate land reform efforts, especially in the context of aboriginal land rights.[14]

When South Africa recently went through the process (twice, in 1993 and 1995)[15] of drafting a constitution for a new, democratic order it was always clear that the new constitution would contain an entrenched bill of rights, but it was not so clear whether the bill of rights should include a property clause. Some of the concerns already mentioned in the Canadian context, as well as other concerns that arose from the unique problems and characteristics of the South African situation, were raised during the preliminary drafting phases of both constitutions, and there were academics and politicians who argued against the inclusion of a property clause.[16] The main concern was that the constitutional entrenchment of property rights would "insulate" existing landholdings against land reform efforts, and so institutionalise or entrench existing imbalances and injustices in the distribution of property. However, eventually

---

[13] R. W. Bauman, above n. 5, at 345.

[14] R. W. Bauman, above n. 5, at 354.

[15] The interim Constitution (1993) was the result of political negotiation and was not drafted by democratically elected representatives, and therefore it provided for its own replacement by a final constitution that would be drafted by properly elected representatives. The interim Constitution was promulgated as the Constitution of the Republic of South Africa 200 of 1993, now replaced by the Constitution of the Republic of South Africa 1996. The final Constitution had to comply with certain constitutional principles (Schedule 4) laid down in the interim Constitution, one of which (Principle II) was that the final Constitution had to include protection for universally accepted fundamental rights, freedoms and civil liberties in an entrenched and justiciable set of provisions. The interim Constitution (s. 71) provided that the final Constitution (and its compliance with the constitutional provisions) had to be certified by the Constitutional Court before it could have any force or effect. The final Constitution was accepted by the Constitutional Assembly on 8 May 1996 and submitted to the Constitutional Court for certification. In the *First Certification* case (reported as *In Re: Certification of the Constitution of the Republic of South Africa, 1996* 1996 (10) BCLR 1253 (CC); 1996 (4) SA 744 (CC)) the Constitutional Court refused to certify the first draft of the final Constitution, mainly because of non-compliance with constitutional principles dealing with the powers of provinces; but the Court rejected objections to the content of the property clause, deciding that there was no accepted universal standard of fundamental rights that necessitated the inclusion of a property clause in the Constitution or that prescribed that such a clause, if included, should have a specific content. Eventually the problems in the first draft were rectified and once the final draft of the Constitution was certified (see *In Re: Certification of the Amended Text of the Constitution of South Africa, 1996* 1997 (1) BCLR 1 (CC)), it came into operation on 4 February 1997. For a discussion see M. Chaskalson and D. Davis, "Constitutionalism, the Rule of Law and the First Certification Judgment: Ex Parte Chairperson of the Constitutional Assembly in re: Certification of the Constitution of the Republic of South Africa 1996 1996 (4) SA 744 (CC)", (1997) 13 *SAJHR* 430–445.

[16] See J. Hund, "A Bill of Rights for South Africa", (1989) 34 *Am J Jur* 23, 31; A. Sachs, "Towards a Bill of Rights in a Democratic South Africa", (1990) 6 *SAJHR* 1 4, 6–8; J. Dugard, "A Bill of Rights for South Africa", (1990) 23 *Cornell Int LJ* 441, 459–460; A. J. van der Walt, "Towards the Development of Post-apartheid Land Law: an Exploratory Survey", (1990) *De Jure* 1, 43; and cf. A. J. van der Walt, "Property Rights, Land Rights, and Environmental Rights" in D. H. van Wyk et al (ed.), *Rights and Constitutionalism: the New South African Legal Order* (Kenwyn, Juta & Co, 1994), pp. 455, 479.

property clauses were inserted in both constitutions,[17] and although it is clear that the property clause in the final Constitution (1996) was drafted with greater care to ensure the legitimacy of land reform and redistribution efforts, the absence of any real political debate about the legitimacy and potential effects of a constitutional property clause suggests the existence of a political compromise that was never open to real debate or negotiation.[18] Objections to the inclusion of a property clause came mostly from the Pan Africanist Congress and from a small group of lawyers in the African National Congress. It is probable that "never again" arguments, based on the role that arbitrary and discriminatory dispossessions and forcible removals played during the apartheid era, moved many people from formerly oppressed and disadvantaged groups to support the inclusion of a property clause in the Constitution, regardless of the fact that the security they wanted for themselves would also provide security for beneficiaries of the apartheid system.[19] In the final analysis, the only function of objections to the inclusion of a property clause in the bill of rights was, during the drafting process, to influence the structure and phraseology of the property clause so as to prevent the complete insulation of private property holdings against land reform and other reform initiatives. In other words, the political debate never really allowed serious consideration of the possibility to exclude the property clause from the bill of rights,[20] and instead participants in the debate were forced to consider ways of both including a property clause in the bill of rights and prevent the complete insulation of property from government interference. The perception that the property clause obstructs and frustrates land reform and redistribution still exists, especially amongst those who think that land reform is not progressing with sufficient speed, but more recently it has also been suggested that the property clause should not be seen in a purely negative light, and that it could perhaps function as a useful instrument for the transformation of property law and of existing patterns of property holding and property use in South Africa.[21] However, regardless of the effect of the property clause, its inclusion in the South African bill of rights seems to be the result of

---

[17] Section 28 of the interim Constitution (1993); s. 25 of the final Constitution (1996). For a general discussion of the property clause in the final Constitution see A. J. van der Walt, *The Constitutional Property Clause: a Comparative Analysis of Section 25 of the South African Constitution of 1996* (Kenwyn, Juta & Co, 1997).

[18] There is strong evidence that the property clause was, to a large extent, both included in the Constitution and drafted on the principle of "consensus by fatigue"; see the revealing description of the drafting process of s. 28 of the interim Constitution (1993) by M. Chaskalson, "Stumbling Towards Section 28: Negotiations over the Protection of Property Rights in the Interim Constitution", (1995) 11 *SAJHR* 222.

[19] See J. Nedelsky (1996), above n. 2, at 421.

[20] Although this possibility was raised, see Constitutional Assembly Theme Committee 4 *Draft Bill of Rights* (1996) 137, where Option 2 reads "No property clause at all".

[21] See A. J. van der Walt, "Towards a Theory of Rights in Property: Exploratory Observations on the Paradigm of Post-apartheid Property Law", (1995) 10 *SAPL* 298. The unique features of the South African property clause and its implications for land reform are discussed in section VI of the chapter below.

political expediency and compromise rather than of deep moral or theoretical debate.

Ireland also went through an exercise in constitutional drafting recently, albeit without the pressure of having to create a new, legitimate constitutional order that characterised the South African process.[22] In Ireland, the main focus of the debate about the property clause in the redrafting of the 1937 Constitution seems to have been on the rationalisation of the existing property clause[23] and on the question whether the clause should be amended to make provision more clearly and explicitly for the legitimacy of police power regulation of property.[24] There was, however, at least some discussion of the question whether the Constitution should contain a property clause, and the majority of the Constitution Review Group proposed that a property clause should be included.[25] This proposal was supported on two grounds: it is necessary and desirable to provide protection against the risk of arbitrary and disproportionate deprivation of property by the state; and the right to property and its inclusion in a bill of rights enjoys international recognition.

In New Zealand, a proposal to include a property clause in the Constitution was recently rejected, I assume not without debate or controversy.[26] From the brief overview of recent constitutional experiences it should be clear that the inclusion of an entrenched property clause in a constitutional bill of rights is not at all self-evident, although thorough moral, philosophical and even political debate about the matter does not necessarily play a very large role in the decision whether to include such a clause or not. Against this background it is justified to revisit some of the most important arguments against the "constitutionalisation of property".

In section II below I set out and discuss a number of objections against the constitutional property clause. These objections, forwarded by Jennifer

---

[22] See *Report of the Constitution Review Group* (1996), 357–367. The Constitution Review Group was appointed on 28 March 1995 to review the 1937 Constitution and prepare a report on areas where amendments to the current Constitution might be desirable or necessary. The report was published in May 1996 and submitted to an all-party committee of the national parliament (Oireichtas) that has to review the Constitution.

[23] The current Constitution of Ireland 1937 contains two separate property provisions in art. 40.3.2 and art. 43 (below n. 24). It is generally said that art. 40.3.2 protects individual property, while art. 43 protects the institution of property: see *Report* (1996), above n. 21, at 358, and cf. *Blake* v. *Attorney-General* [1982] IR 117. This has been the cause of some confusion, and the Constitution Review Group (*Report* at 364) proposed that the two sections should be replaced by a single provision.

[24] The current provisions in the 1937 Constitution do not make a clear distinction between a regulatory deprivation of property and a compulsory acquisition or expropriation of property that requires compensation, and consequently there is some room for confusion about the legitimacy of and requirements for a valid regulatory deprivation of property that does not require compensation. Cf. *Electricity Supply Board* v. *Gormley* [1985] IR 129; *Dreher* v. *Irish Land Commission* [1984] ILRM 94 for examples from either category.

[25] See *Report* (1996), above n. 22, at 360–361.

[26] See in general on the public purposes requirement for expropriation in New Zealand case law M. Taggart, "Expropriation, Public Purpose and the Constitution" in C. Forsyth and I. Hare (eds), *The Golden Metwand and the Crooked Cord: Essays on Public Law in Honour of Sir William Wade QC* (Oxford, Clarendon, 1998), pp. 91, 107–108.

Nedelsky, are the strongest and most consistent theoretical arguments against the constitutional entrenchment of property of which I am aware. In section III below I review the history of the constitutional struggle about property between the Indian courts and the legislature; a history that seems to underline and support Nedelsky's arguments against the constitutionalisation of property. In section IV below I evaluate the Indian example in view of Nedelsky's arguments and attempt to reformulate the problem and some of its causes in more general terms. In section V below I compare this analysis with the experience in Australia, where the courts have found a way around at least some of these problems, without much assistance from the drafters of the property clause. In section VI below I analyse the South African property clause, and argue that the drafters of the South African Constitution (1996) have created textual and structural opportunities (and perhaps a constitutional obligation) for avoiding the problems identified by Nedelsky, without having to rely exclusively on judicial intervention and creativity. Finally, I summarise some conclusions and revisit some of the most important problems, issues and arguments in section VIII.

II. ARGUMENTS AGAINST THE "CONSTITUTIONALISATION" OF PROPERTY

Jennifer Nedelsky developed the strongest and most consistent set of arguments against the "constitutionalisation" of property.[27] She formulated five basic objections to the inclusion of a property clause in the bill of rights: (1) property will be insulated in a regulation-free private enclave; (2) the tendency of property to create and support power inequalities will be reinforced; (3) the entrenchment of property will upset and even invert constitutional hierarchies of rights; (4) constitutional litigation about property will result in a waste of resources; and (5) important issues will be removed from the public sphere and converted into technical legal debates.[28]

The first argument turns on Nedelsky's criticism of the public-private divide and its consequences. She argues that the constitutionalisation of property will reinforce the conceptual divide between public and private and exacerbate the detrimental tendency to insulate property against state interference by entrenching it in a "market" dominated private sphere. In this private sphere, the underlying assumption is that the state should not interfere with property without extraordinary justification, and consequently private property holdings will, at

---

[27] Particularly J. Nedelsky (1990) above n. 3, ch. 6; J. Nedelsky (1996) above n. 2, at 417–432. In this section, I concentrate on Nedelsky's views as they are summarised in above n. 2, at 417–432. I will not consider Nedelsky's discussion and criticism of (mostly philosophical) arguments in favour of the constitutional entrenchment of (existing) property-holdings: see Nedelsky (1996), above n. 2, at 419–422.

[28] Some of these objections are similar to the objections raised in the Canadian, Irish and South African debates referred to earlier.

least in principle, be insulated against regulation.[29] Nedelsky acknowledges that the assumptions upon which the public-private divide and the limited nature of the state's powers in the private sphere are based are widely acclaimed in most Western legal systems in any event: her argument is that the constitutional entrenchment of property reinforces and supports this *laissez-faire* view of the relationship between the state and private property, with the result that property is allowed (with constitutional support) to exist and operate in an increasingly regulation-free zone of private enterprise and "market forces". Nedelsky argues that the myth of property as a pre-political right that predates the civil state and that should therefore be insulated against state control and interference is destructive and antisocial even in liberal democracies. It is particularly pernicious in countries (like South Africa and most post colonial democracies) where the present unequal and unjust distribution of property is so obviously and directly the product of (inequitable) government action and interference that it amounts to hypocrisy to insulate the existing distribution pattern against further (reformist) state intervention. According to this argument, the most obvious result of the constitutionalisation of property is not only to uphold and reinforce the myth of property as a pre-political, fundamentally private matter, but also to institutionalise and insulate from further state action the inequitable results of clearly political, earlier interferences with "private" property relations.

Nedelsky's second argument concerns the well-known concern that property is closely related to power, and particularly that property, given its position in a competitive market-oriented society, creates and supports unequal power structures. Whereas the primary object of constitutional rights must be to foster and promote equality, property relations are a major source of inequality, and consequently the constitutionalisation of property will result in an ongoing tension between the protection of inequality (created by property through the market) and constitutional claims for the promotion of equality.[30] In a market-oriented economic system, the demand for free competition and non-interference means that existing hierarchies of inequality will be left intact and allowed to provide the strong and privileged with structural advantages over the weak and underprivileged. Nedelsky argues that, instead of assisting the general constitutional purpose of either eradicating unjust inequalities or of structuring inevitable inequalities in such a manner that people treat each other with basic respect for human dignity, the constitutional entrenchment of property will assist those with property and opportunities to trade on and exploit the weaknesses of others.

The third argument is related to the second, although it operates on a different level of abstraction. Whereas the second argument is concerned with the

[29] J. Nedelsky (1996), above n. 2, at 422–423.
[30] J. Nedelsky (1996), above n. 2, at 423–424. This argument is elaborated in J. Nedelsky, "Reconceiving Rights as Relationships", (1993) *Rev Const Studies* 20–22; cf. J. Nedelsky (1990) above n. 3, at pp. 204, 205–206, 217.

practical and individual position of the underprivileged and disadvantaged in a system where "market forces" are allowed to regulate the distribution of property, the third argument concerns the theoretical and structural relationship between different rights in the bill of rights. Property does not belong to the first-order values (life, liberty and security of the person) that are usually treated as fundamental constitutional rights, and by constitutionalising property the hierarchy of rights is upset, so that "equality will be held accountable to property" instead of "property being held accountable to equality".[31] This argument assumes that property is a means to the higher values in the constitution and not itself one of those higher values. The argument is, therefore, that the protection of property, in so far as it is important for the protection of the higher values of life, liberty and personal security, can be protected through the constitutional entrenchment of those values: arbitrary or punitive confiscations can be attacked as infringements of liberty or security,[32] or as infringements of equality or of the guarantee of fair administrative action. This accords with the theoretical argument that the list of fundamental human rights in the bill of rights should preferably be short and general rather than extensive and specific,[33] and that it should consequently exclude property.

The pragmatic argument is that the constitutionalisation of property will result in high litigation cost and a waste of limited resources, as lawyers and the courts struggle to determine whether any given government policy that has an impact on property holdings is a violation of property rights or not.[34] This argument is particularly strong in view of Nedelsky's analysis of the complex American takings law: the entrenchment of property in the constitution results in the creation of all kinds of increasingly technical and abstract definitions, distinctions, rules, principles and exceptions that eventually render the issues around property incomprehensible to all but a small number of experts. This results not only in unnecessary litigation and a consequent waste of resources, but also in loss of faith in the basic legitimacy and justice of the system. This argument finds some support in the history of the constitutional struggle about property in India.[35]

The pragmatic argument also ties in with Nedelsky's fifth argument, in the sense that the increasing technicalities of takings law carves the whole discussion out of the public debate about the relationship between the state and private property and turns it into an enclave of "lawyers' talk", of which non-

---

[31] J. Nedelsky (1996), above n. 2, at 424–426. Cf. J. Nedelsky (1990) above n. 3, at pp. 207–209.

[32] J. Nedelsky (1996), above n. 2, at 425. This argument has already failed in Canada; see *Attorney-General of Quebec* v. *Irwin Toy Ltd*. (1989) 1 SCR 927 and cf. above n. 12.

[33] See the argument of S. Lukes, above n. 3.

[34] J Nedelsky (1996) above n. 2, at 426.

[35] This struggle was characterised by a tendency to dissolve real debates about the purpose, nature, importance and implications of the constitutional protection of property and its relation to reformist programmes of state action and intervention in increasingly technical "debates" about the meaning and interpretation of the words used in the property clause. See the discussion of the Indian struggle in section III of the chapter below.

lawyers know and understand nothing. Nedelsky argues that the constitution-alisation of property removes issues that should be central to a public, democratic debate and restricts them to a legal, constitutional sphere that is accessible to a small elite of lawyers only.[36] This stifles much-needed public debate and public participation in the development of policy about the state's role in the conservation of scarce resources, the distribution of wealth and the regulation of individual use of property. Above all, it practically terminates public debate about the relationship between state protection of existing property holdings and other state purposes and programmes, such as land reform, tenant protection, consumer protection, welfare and social security and the availability of housing.

From the discussion above it is clear that "the conception of limited government that is the essence of American constitutionalism" is central to Nedelsky's objections,[37] and in the analysis below I return to the importance of that conception for a discussion of the constitutional entrenchment of property. I return to Nedelsky's arguments in section IV of the chapter below, where I evaluate her arguments with reference to the constitutional struggle that resulted from the entrenchment of property in the Indian Constitution (1950). The history of this struggle seems to offer strong support for Nedelsky's objections to the constitutionalisation of property.

III. INDIA: CONSTITUTIONAL CONFLICT ABOUT PROPERTY

When the Indian Constitution (1950) was adopted, it contained a property clause that consisted of two parts: article 19(1)(f) and article 31.[38] Nehru launched the two property provisions through the constitutional assembly personally, convinced that these clauses and the property rights they protected would not stand in the way of the reforms he had in mind.[39] Nehru believed that

---

[36] J. Nedelsky (1996) above n. 2, at 427–428. Cf. J. Nedelsky (1990) above n. 3, at pp. 211–216. See above n. 35, and cf. section III of the chapter below.

[37] J. Nedelsky (1990), above n. 3, at 203, 224.

[38] Article 19(1)(f) provided that, amongst other fundamental rights, all citizens shall have the right to acquire, hold and dispose of property. Article 19(5) allowed for reasonable restrictions of this right. Article 31(1) provided that no person shall be deprived of property save by authority of law, and article 31(2) that no property shall be dispossessed or acquired for public purposes unless the law in question provides for compensation. Article 31(5) provided for a number of exclusions from the compensation guarantee. This set of provisions was typical for post-colonial "Lancaster House" type constitutions: see A. J. van der Walt, "'Double' Property Guarantees: a Structural and Comparative Analysis", (1998) 14 *SAJHR* 3560; T. Allen, "Constitutional Interpretation and the Opening Provisions of Bills of Rights in African Commonwealth countries" in *Proceedings: African Society for International and Comparative Law*, (1993) vol. 5, pp. 321–340.

[39] The Indian experience enjoyed much attention during the drafting phase of the South African constitution. Two of the most important publications in this regard are J. Murphy, "Insulating Land Reform from Constitutional Impugnment: an Indian case study", (1992) 8 *SAJHR* 362; M. Chaskalson, "The Problem with Property: Thoughts on the Constitutional Protection of Property in the United States and the Commonwealth", (1993) 9 *SAJHR* 388.

the property clause provided no more than a limited protection of property, which included compensation for "petty" compulsory acquisitions, but not for large-scale social engineering schemes which benefited the whole country but affected only a few landowners. In these cases, Nehru argued, compensation should be equitable from the perspective of society rather than that of the individual owner.[40] This view was soon contradicted by the courts, precipitating a conflict between the Indian judiciary and legislature which was to continue for 25 years, and which eventually resulted in the removal of the property clause from the bill of rights. Chaskalson[41] blames this conflict (and the negative effects it had) on the fact that a property clause was included in the constitution in a situation where land and economic reforms were obviously essential; Murphy[42] blames the Indian courts for their inability to develop a suitable, non-confrontational model and framework for constitutional review in a situation where reforms were required. It is possible, therefore, to argue that in either case the decision to include property in the Indian Constitution, in a situation where land and economic reforms were inevitable, was instrumental in causing the constitutional struggle about property. If this is indeed a valid observation, this history provides strong support for Nedelsky's objections against the constitutionalisation of property.

In three early cases that concerned various land and economic reforms,[43] the Indian courts struck down reform laws for being *ultra vires* and hence unconstitutional. Interestingly, the courts refrained from justifying their decisions in these early cases with reference to the property guarantee, preferring to base their decisions on either the equality clause in article 14 or the (general) reasonableness provision in article 19 of the Indian Constitution (1950). All three decisions are regarded as reactionary and anti-reform, but the fact that they relied on constitutional guarantees of equality and reasonableness (and not on the property clause) to block what were basically land reforms is significant.[44] While *Kameshwar Singh* v. *State of Bihar*[45] was still on appeal[46] the constitutional assembly responded to these reactionary decisions by introducing the Constitution (First Amendment) Act (1951), which excluded state acquisitions of "estates" or rights in "estates"[47] and similar forms of land tenure from being declared invalid on the basis of articles 14, 19 or 31[48] of the Constitution,[49] and

---

[40]   M. Chaskalson (1993,) above n. 39, at 390.

[41]   Ibid., at 395. M. Chaskalson's views in this regard coincide with Nedelsky's; see the discussion in section II of the chapter above.

[42]   J. Murphy, above n. 39, at 395.

[43]   *Kameshwar Singh* v. *Province of Bihar* AIR (37) 1950 Pat 392; *Kameshwar Singh* v. *State of Bihar* AIR (38) 1951 Pat 91 (FB); *Charanjit Lal Chowdhury* v. *The Union of India* AIR (38) 1951 SC 41.

[44]   Cf. J. Murphy (1992), above n. 39, at 380–381, M. Chaskalson (1993) above n. 39, at 391.

[45]   AIR (38) 1951 Pat 91 (FB).

[46]   J. Murphy (1992), above n. 39, at 380; the decision *a quo* was handed down on 12 March 1951.

[47]   Defined with reference to the kind of land rights which the Bihar law was aimed at reforming in the first place.

[48]   These sections guaranteed equality, reasonableness and property respectively.

[49]   Article 31A.

ousted judicial review of certain land reform measures.[50] In a nutshell, the First Amendment was intended to prevent repetitions of the 1951 *Kameshwar Singh* decision by ousting the courts' power of judicial review with regard to certain land reform measures.[51] Subsequently, when the appeal in *Kameshwar Singh* was heard, the Supreme Court held[52] that the Amendment indeed protected the reform law from judicial scrutiny, but the majority nevertheless decided[53] that only the quantum of compensation was affected by the ouster of the courts' jurisdiction, and not the requirement of public purposes, and the Court went on to strike down two sections of the reform law for being inconsistent with that requirement. This decision is regarded as a sign of defiance against the reformist intentions of the legislature.[54]

A series of decisions handed down between 1952 and 1956 displayed further signs of judicial defiance, but the judicial resistance to reforms was now based on the property clause and no longer on equality—most decisions turned on the adequacy of compensation. The most important and influential of these decisions is *State of West Bengal* v. *Subodh Gopal Bose*,[55] in which the Supreme Court[56] adopted the surprising view that article 31 must be read as a unit and not disjunctively, with the result that both acquisitions (article 31(2)) and deprivations (article 31(1)) of property were said to require compensation in terms of article 31(2).[57] The effect of the Court taking this position[58] was that the power of the state to introduce non-compensable regulatory limitations of property was restricted severely, while the scope of the compensation requirement in the property clause was increased dramatically[59] to include deprivations of property.[60]

The unanimous decision in *State of West Bengal* v. *Bella Banerjee*[61] represents a further stage in the development of the Supreme Court's reactionary position

---

[50] Enumerated in the Ninth Schedule to the Constitution: see art. 31B.

[51] See, with regard to the First Amendment, V. N. Shukla, *The Constitution of India*, 5th edn. (Lucknow, Eastern Book Co, 1969), pp. 142–143, 148–150.

[52] In *State of Bihar* v. *Kameshwar Singh AIR* (39) 1952 SC 252.

[53] On the basis of what Patanjali Sastri CJ at 263 [9] described as "such weak arguments as over-taxed ingenuity could suggest".

[54] J. Murphy (1992) above n. 39, at 381; M. Chaskalson (1993), above n. 39, at 391. Eventually, the Constitution (Seventh Amendment) Act (1956) was promulgated to overturn that part of the majority decision in *State of Bihar* v. *Kameshwar Singh* that dealt with public purpose in terms of the theory of colourable exercise of legislative power. See J. Murphy (1992), 381–382 for a discussion and criticism of the decision and of the amendment, cf. V. N. Shukla (1968), above n. 51, at pp. 150–152.

[55] 1954 (5) SCR 587.

[56] Patanjali Sastri, C.J., ibid. at 593–619.

[57] See V. N. Shukla, above n. 51, at p. 146; J; Murphy (1992), above n. 39, at 366.

[58] Which was followed by the majority (Mahajan J at 122–133 [2]-[39]) in *Dwarkadas Shrinivas* v. *The Sholapur Spinning & Weaving Co Ltd*. AIR (41) 1954 SC 119.

[59] Cf. V. N. Shukla, above n. 51, at p. 145; J. Murphy (1992,) above n. 39, at 367.

[60] The extension of the compensation requirement was not limited to non-acquisitive "regulatory takings", as it is known in American case law, but probably included all deprivations of property, whether their effect was acquisitory or not.

[61] AIR (41) 1954 SC 170.

on the property clause. In this case the Supreme Court[62] decided that the Constitution does provide leeway for the legislature to determine the principles upon which compensation has to be calculated, but that the courts nevertheless had the jurisdiction to determine whether all the elements that make up "the true value of the property" have been considered and whether irrelevant matters have been included. In this decision, the Supreme Court defied the efforts of the legislature to oust the Court's jurisdiction with regard to compensation for acquisitions, and it adopted the view that compensation that did not relate to the full value or just equivalent of the property acquired could be struck down by the Court for being unreasonable. This became the accepted view of the Indian Supreme Court under Patanjali Sastri CJ, and it survived all reform efforts until the mid-1970s.[63]

The approach of the Supreme Court in *Subodh Gopal Bose* was followed in *Saghir Ahmad* v. *The State of Uttar Pradesh*,[64] where the Court held that a deprivation of property was no different from an acquisition of property as intended in article 31(2) of the Constitution, and therefore required compensation. In view of the absence of provision for compensation the law, which was clearly intended as a regulatory law in terms of the police power rather than an acquisitive law in terms of the power of eminent domain, was declared unconstitutional.[65]

The reactionary decisions handed down between 1952 and 1956 shifted the conflict between the Supreme Court and the legislature away from the sphere of equality and into the sphere of property rights: the conjunctive reading of article 31(1) and 31(2) eradicated the distinction between non-compensable deprivations of property and compensable acquisitions of property; and the reading of compensation as full equivalent or true value of the property effectively frustrated the government's apparently quite legitimate constitutional discretion to determine that compensation should be calculated with due reference to the circumstances of each individual acquisition. The legislature responded to these decisions with the Constitution (Fourth Amendment) Act (1955), which streamlined and rephrased article 31 in such a way that the reactionary decisions were overturned. The Fourth Amendment made it clear that the conjunctive reading of article 31(1) and 31(2) (followed since the *Subodh Gopal Bose* decision) was mistaken: article 31(2) applied to acquisitions of property against compensation and article 31(1) to non-acquisitive, non-compensable regulatory limitations of property in terms of the police power. Furthermore, the Amendment inserted an ouster clause into article 31(2), so that no law could be declared invalid on the

---

[62] Patanjali Sastri CJ, ibid. at 172 [2], [5]–[6].
[63] Cf. V. N. Shukla, above n. 51, at pp. 147, 156; J. Murphy (1992), above n. 39, at 374–375; M. Chaskalson (1993), above n. 39, at 191.
[64] 1955 (1) SCR 707.
[65] Cf. T. Allen, "Commonwealth Constitutions and the Right Not to be Deprived of Property", (1993) 42 *Int & Comp LQ* 523 at 530, 532 on the *Saghir Ahmad* case.

basis of inadequate compensation in terms of article 31(2).[66] The most important effect of the Fourth Amendment was that the possibility of providing for non-acquisitive, non-compensable regulatory limitations of property was restored, and the range of compensable acquisitions was restricted.

Between 1956 and 1970 the courts again responded to the ouster clause in the Fourth Amendment in a series of decisions aimed at re-establishing their jurisdiction with regard to the question of compensation. The first important case was *Kochuni* v. *States of Madras and Kerala*,[67] where Subba Rao J[68] gave a surprising new twist to the Sastri Court's reading of article 19 and article 31. The Fourth Amendment, he argued, has made it clear that only article 31(2) applied to acquisition of property, and that the deprivation mentioned in article 31(1) referred to deprivations resulting from the non-acquisitive regulation of property. This means that deprivations of property in terms of article 31(1) had to be judged together with article 19, and more particularly article 19(5), which provided that restrictions on property had to be reasonable. The distinction between article 31(1) and 31(2) brought about by the Fourth Amendment was used, therefore, to establish a new connection between article 19 and article 31(1) and so create a new basis, namely reasonableness, for the Court's jurisdiction over the legitimacy of deprivations of property.[69] The Kochuni decision was followed and applied in *Vajravelu Mudaliar* v. *The Special Deputy Collector for Land Acquisition, West Madras*,[70] where the Court bypassed the ouster clause in the Fourth Amendment (1955). With reference to the earlier decision of the Sastri Court in *State of West Bengal* v. *Bella Banerjee*,[71] it was argued that the Fourth Amendment excluded the jurisdiction of the Court to decide whether compensation was adequate, but the Court still had jurisdiction to decide whether the principles applied to calculate compensation were unreasonable, which would be the case if they were not relevant to the value of the property. Effectively, the Court reclaimed jurisdiction to decide whether compensation was reasonable, although it could not decide whether compensation was adequate.[72] This decision was followed in *Union of India* v. *The Metal Corporation of India Ltd.*[73] and, more importantly, in the famous case of *RC Cooper* v. *Union of India*[74] (also known as the "Bank Nationalisation" case).

In *RC Cooper* v. *Union of India*[75] the Court followed the lead of the decisions in *Kochuni* and *Vajravelu* in investigating the Banking Companies (Acquisition

---

[66] Cf. V. N. Shukla, above n. 51, at p. 143; J Murphy (1992), above n. 39, at 369–370 for a discussion of the Amendment.

[67] AIR (47) 1960 SC 1080.

[68] Ibid. 1096 [33].

[69] Cf. J. Murphy (1992), above n. 39, at 370–371, 384.

[70] AIR (52) 1965 SC 1017.

[71] AIR (41) 1954 SC 170.

[72] See V. N. Shukla, above n. 51, at p. 156; M. Chaskalson (1993), above n. 39, at 392 on the *Vajravelu* case.

[73] AIR (54) 1967 SC 637.

[74] AIR (57) 1970 SC 564.

[75] AIR (57) 1970 SC 564.

and Transfer of Undertakings) Act 22 of 1969, which provided for the national-isation of the major commercial banks.[76] The Court, following the *Vajravelu* decision, held that the principles laid down for the determination of compensa-tion for the acquisition were irrelevant and therefore unreasonable, because the acquisition affected the whole business concern, while the principles laid down for the determination of compensation related to the value of certain of its assets only. The Act was, therefore, declared void in its entirety. This decision precip-itated the final confrontation with the legislature, beginning with the Twenty-Fifth Amendment (1971), which overturned the *Bank Nationalisation* case.[77] Shortly after the *Bank Nationalisation* case was handed down, the Congress Party won a two thirds majority in both houses in the February 1971 elections. The election campaign of the Congress Party was characterised by anti-judicial sentiment and the promotion of social reforms, and soon after the election the new government reacted to the *Golak Nath*[78] and *Bank Nationalisation* cases by promulgating the Twenty-Fourth and Twenty-Fifth Amendments.[79] The Twenty-Fourth Amendment was meant to overrule the *Golak Nath* decision by explicitly making the fundamental rights in the Constitution subject to the amending powers of the legislature, and the Twenty-Fifth Amendment was meant to overturn the *Bank Nationalisation Case* in an attempt to remove the question of compensation from judicial scrutiny altogether. The Twenty-Fifth Amendment removed the duty to pay "compensation" from article 31(2), and replaced it with payment of "an amount". The validity of both these amend-ments was questioned in *Kesavananda* v. *State of Kerala*,[80] where the Supreme Court had one last chance to stand up to the legislature.

In *Kesavanada*, a majority (7 of 13 judges) of the Supreme Court decided that parliament could not abrogate the essential features, the basic structure or framework of the Constitution, so as to change its identity.[81] However, as was stated most clearly in the opinion of one of the majority,[82] the right to property does not constitute one of these essential features—it "does not pertain to the basic structure or framework"—of the Constitution. Consequently, the Twenty-Fourth and Twenty-Fifth Amendments were upheld by the majority. With this decision the Supreme Court finally conceded that its jurisdiction with

---

[76] In effect the Act provided for the taking over of the banking business of the major banks, while leaving their non-banking business to be carried on within certain restrictions.

[77] A separate development that led to the final confrontation was focused on the legislature's power to constantly amend the Constitution whenever a judgment of the Supreme Court didn't suit it. In *IC Golak Nath* v. *State of Punjab* [1967] 2 SCR 762 the majority decided that the amending power of the legislature cannot be used to abridge or take away the fundamental rights that are guar-anteed in the Constitution.

[78] See above n. 77.

[79] See in general M. Chaskalson (1993), above n. 39, at 393.

[80] AIR (60) 1973 SC 1461.

[81] The minority rejected the distinction between essential and non-essential features.

[82] Khanna J at 716–720. See the similar arguments referred to in the introductory section and in the section on Nedelsky's objections above.

regard to the adequacy of reasonableness of compensation was ousted.[83] The Kesavanada decision amounted to a compromise that left the government free to restrict the right of property in the Constitution without completely ousting the courts' jurisdiction regarding the validity of amendments to the Constitution, and this compromise provided a basis on which the conflict over property between the legislature and the courts could be terminated. However, shortly afterwards political difficulties prompted Ghandi to declare a state of emergency,[84] and in the ensuing struggle proposals were mooted to draft a new constitution which would not recognise the courts' power of judicial review at all. This reinforced the Supreme Court's new tendency towards judicial restraint. In the post-emergency elections of 1977 Ghandi's government was comprehensively beaten by the Janata Party, which was in favour of the complete abolition of the constitutional protection of property rights,[85] and which terminated the struggle between the courts and the legislature by the introduction of the Forty-Fourth Amendment (1978). This amendment deleted articles 19(1)(f) and 31 from the fundamental rights in Part II of the Constitution, and replaced them by inserting article 300A in Part XII of the Constitution. Article 300A merely provides that "no person shall be deprived of his property save by authority of law". Being inserted in Part XII of the Constitution, article 300A establishes a constitutional (as opposed to a fundamental) right, which guarantees nothing more than that a deprivation of property requires a valid law that is within the legislative power of the legislature enacting it and that does not violate fundamental rights or other constitutional restrictions.[86] The result is comparable with the position in Canada, where there is no entrenched guarantee of property rights, although an unentrenched constitutional provision ensures that deprivations of property should comply with basic due process requirements.[87]

IV. CONSTITUTIONAL PROPERTY CLAUSE OR GUARANTEE?

Chaskalson's arguments against the adoption of a constitutional property clause in South Africa are based both on his interpretation of the Indian struggle[88] and on what he perceives as the dangers of the American way of thinking about the constitutional property issue.[89] The American way of thinking is also the focal point of Nedelsky's objections against the constitutionalisation of

---

[83] See M. Chaskalson (1993), above n. 39, at 393; J. Murphy (1992) above n. 39, at 376.

[84] On 26 June 1975.

[85] See J. Murphy (1992), above n. 39, at 385–388; M. Chaskalson (1993), above n. 39, at 393–395.

[86] See J. Murphy (1992), above n. 39, at 387.

[87] See the discussion of the Canadian position in section I of the chapter above: s 1(a) of the unentrenched Canadian Bill of Rights (1960) provides due process protection to property rights.

[88] M. Chaskalson (1993) above n. 39, at 389–395.

[89] Ibid., at 395–408.

property,[90] and in this section of the chapter I attempt to identify and describe the problem with constitutionally entrenched property as it emerges from the Indian history and from Nedelsky's discussion of the American way of thinking about property in the constitution. For the sake of the argument, I assume (without analysing or arguing the point) that Nedelsky's objections are determined by the American paradigm she describes, although her arguments are certainly supported by the history of the Indian struggle.

My thesis is that, although Nedelsky describes a specifically American history and its legacy in her analysis of the relationship between private property and constitutionalism, and although her objections focus on and are determined by the *laissez-faire* and free market assumptions that dominate significant parts of jurisprudence and academic commentary on constitutional property issues in the USA,[91] her objections are not based on purely parochial considerations. Instead, I will argue, with reference to the Indian history, that Nedelsky's objections are not restricted to a specific jurisdiction or to a particular constitutional context. Her objections against the constitutionalisation of property[92] revolve around and derive their energy from a centripetal force that may well be present and influential in different countries: free-market, minimalist-state libertarianism and the barrier it erects between the public and private spheres, thereby insulating private property from state regulation in all but the most extraordinary circumstances. In *laissez-faire* libertarian discourse, every issue is determined by the implications of the public-private division: the exercise of limited government powers in a clearly demarcated public sphere, the domination in the private sphere of "market forces", the role of the (common) law in distinguishing public issues from private interests. This theme is the connection between Nedelsky's objections and the history of the Indian property clause: at the root of the constitutional struggle between the Indian Supreme Court and the legislature was a fundamental difference of opinion about the origin and nature of property rights and about the relationship between property rights, constitutionalism and the legitimate exercise of state power. The legislature had a reformist agenda, which required a certain amount of legislative interference with the current property distribution pattern and with existing property holdings; the Supreme Court worked from the assumption that private property was in principle (and justifiably) insulated against state interference, and that the constitutional property clause (again justifiably) reinforced this insulation.

---

[90] Described in section II of the chapter above. Objections against the American approach often emphasise the fact that US case law is seemingly contradictory and hard to understand.

[91] This appears from Nedelsky's analysis, and is nicely illustrated by the title and subtitle of her most important publication on this issue (above n. 3): *Private Property and the Limits of American Constitutionalism: the Madisonian Framework and its Legacy* (Chicago, University of Chicago Press, 1990) (emphasis added).

[92] Summarised in section I above as: (1) property will be isolated in a regulation-free private enclave; (2) the tendency of property to create and support power inequalities will be reinforced; (3) the entrenchment of property will upset and even invert constitutional hierarchies of rights; (4) constitutional litigation about property will result in a waste of resources; and (5) important issues will be removed from the public sphere and converted into technical legal debates.

One can perhaps best describe the change in direction that took place between the Indian decisions in *Kameshwar Singh* v. *Province of Bihar*[93] and *Kesavananda* v. *State of Kerala*[94] in terms of the Indian Supreme Court's realisation that the state not only had the political duty and the legal power to implement land and economic reforms, but that it could and should implement these reforms even if it meant that private property interests had to be affected detrimentally; moreover, this power was not excluded by the existence of the constitutional property clause, but had to be accommodated in its effects. In the terminology of Nedelsky's analysis, one can perhaps say that the Court realised that private property was not insulated against state interference by the mere existence of a constitutional property clause. Of course, and this is a very important qualification, this realisation eventually dawned upon the Indian Supreme Court as a political and not as a constitutional reality: the Court acknowledged as a matter of practical politics that it could only retain its power of constitutional review if it was willing to compromise and sacrifice its jurisdiction over the matter of adequate compensation for compulsory acquisitions of property. Viewed like this, the compromise decision in *Kesavananda* is not a solution to the dilemma described by Nedelsky, but merely a recognition of its existence and a declaration of its fundamental intractability. This seems to underline Nedelsky's point: ultimately, the entrenchment of property in a constitutional guarantee will create an insoluble conflict between the constitutional protection of private interests and the state promotion of the public interest, and the only practicable way of overcoming the conflict is to sacrifice one in favour of the other.

The question is: is there a way out of this dilemma, or is it really a fundamental result of the constitutionalisation of property? Must we see the relationship between private property interests and the public interest in regulating property holdings as a conflict or tension? Nedelsky[95] and Chaskalson[96] argue —and the history of the Indian struggle supports their argument[97]—that the problem is of a fundamental nature and conflict is inevitable, given the decision to entrench the protection of property in a constitutional bill of rights. In other words, once property is constitutionalised the problem can only be avoided by sacrificing either the protection of property as entrenched in the constitution or the state's power and duty to promote the public interest (when necessary at the cost of private property). This point of view is characterised by the (libertarian) assumption that the property clause is nothing more and nothing less than a *fundamental barrier-guarantee*. Existing private property holdings are inevitably insulated from state interference if the property clause means anything at all: the only way out of the dilemma is either to uphold that guarantee at the cost of

---

[93] AIR (37) 1950 Pat 392. See the discussion in section III of the chapter above.
[94] AIR (60) 1973 SC 1461. See the discussion in section III of the chapter above.
[95] See (1996), above n. 2; (1990), above n. 3; cf. the analysis in section II of the chapter above.
[96] See (1993), above n. 39, at 395.
[97] See section III of the chapter above.

state powers, or to sacrifice the guarantee and uphold state powers to regulate the use of property. According to this approach, a property clause is primarily a *guarantee* in the sense of a limit, a barrier between private and public, that upholds and institutionalises the restrictions inherent in the notion of a night-watchman state. As such it invests property itself with a curious, double-sided constitutional character: property becomes both the barrier that insulates the private sphere against the public and the most important rights that are insulated behind that barrier. This view, which features at the heart of Nedelsky's (and Chaskalson's) objections against the constitutionalisation of property, obviously poses a very serious problem for both constitutional and property theory.[98]

Murphy,[99] on the other hand, blames the Indian constitutional debacle on the inability of the Indian courts to come to terms with the constitutional demands of the bill of rights and create a suitable context for constitutional review, thereby suggesting that the problem was not fundamental, and that it could have been avoided or overcome had the courts assumed a different attitude towards the relationship between the property clause and the exigencies of the public interest in the regulation of property rights. This suggestion opens up a new line of inquiry: is it possible that the dilemma of an entrenched property clause, as set out by Nedelsky, can be avoided if the courts assume the right (or a better) framework for constitutional review? If it is possible, what would the differences between the Indian approach and an alternative approach be? Would anything be gained by recognising, as a point of departure, that the property clause cannot simplistically be regarded as a guarantee of existing property holdings? And, if such an alternative framework or approach were possible, what would the implications for Nedelsky's objections be?

Nedelsky herself provides a starting point for this inquiry. She sets out a number of guidelines for the development of a jurisprudence of constitutional property, although she insists that what she describes in these guidelines is the second best option, to be considered when property is already constitutionalised and it is no longer possible to argue that it is best not to constitutionalise property. It is well worth quoting her in full on this point: [100]

> "Finally, how does this all help if property is constitutionalized? The arguments I have laid out can become a guide to the jurisprudence courts can be encouraged to develop. Every effort should be made to persuade judges that the purpose of having property in the constitution is to secure people's relations to material resources against arbitrary,

---

[98] See Nedelsky's objections as they are discussed in section II of the chapter above, and cf. other efforts to overcome the theoretical problems created by this approach: L. S. Underkuffler, "On Property: an Essay", (1990) 100 *Yale LJ* 127–148; L. S. Underkuffler-Freund, "Takings and the Nature of Property", (1996) 9 *Can J Law & Jur* 161–205.

[99] See (1994) 10 *SAJHR* 385 above n. 39, at 395. Murphy's view is supported by H. C. L. Merillat, *Land and the Constitution in India* (New York, Columbia University Press, 1970), p. 124; R. Dhavan, *The Supreme Court of India: a Socio-legal Analysis of its Juristic Techniques* (Bombay, N M Tripathi, 1977).

[100] J. Nedelsky (1996), above n. 2, at 432.

discriminatory incursions and against restructuring of property rights that harm autonomy or dignity in ways unjustifiable in a free, equal, and democratic society. The jurisprudence should start from the assumption that the state creates the regime of property, and that its contours are thus a matter for democratic determination— within the constraints noted above. The jurisprudence should also recognize that legislation and regulation will routinely affect property rights, and that it is only appropriate for courts to become involved when there is an issue of arbitrariness, discrimination, or unjustifiable harm to autonomy or dignity".

At least five principles can be deduced from Nedelsky's guidelines: (1) A jurisprudence of constitutionally entrenched property has to start with the real reason why property is entrenched in the constitution in the first place: to protect people and their relations to property against arbitrary, discriminatory and unjustifiable infringements (and not to insulate existing property-holdings against state action in general). In other words, the starting point has to be that the property clause cannot simply be regarded as a barrier-guarantee in the libertarian sense. (2) The question whether state interferences with property relations are arbitrary, discriminatory and unjustifiable should turn at least in part on whether the harm it causes (to first-order constitutional values like autonomy and dignity) is justifiable in a free, equal and democratic society. This means that the possibility of legitimate state interferences with property is recognised as a matter of principle, and that every infringement of property is judged individually with reference to a substantive, value-oriented standard. (3) The starting point should be that the state creates the regime in which property exists, obtains its value and is protected, with the result that property is always open to on-going democratic determination, within the boundaries already mentioned. This means that the property regime is dynamic, that property-holdings are not isolated against state interference, and that there are certain (constitutional) boundaries within which legitimate state interference can occur. (4) Based on the assumption that property is open to democratic (re-) determination, it is inevitable that property will routinely be affected by normal and legitimate legislation and regulation. (5) Given the boundaries within which democratic determination of property has to be accepted, the courts should only become involved when there is an issue of arbitrariness, discrimination or unjustifiable interference, in other words when the boundaries of legitimate state interference are exceeded in one way or another.

For the rest of my argument in this chapter, I will constantly refer to the contrast between the libertarian, *laissez faire* approach Nedelsky objects to and the approach reflected in her guidelines. The libertarian approach relies on a *guarantee*-oriented view of the constitutional entrenchment of property, with all the attendant assumptions about limited government and the divide that is erected between the public and the private and the supposed reinforcement of this divide by the constitutional property clause. Nedelsky's guidelines for an alternative jurisprudence, on the other hand, describe a *limitation*-oriented approach to the constitutional entrenchment of property, in the sense that it emphasises the fact that property is intrinsically created by and therefore open to further democratic redefinition and regulation, even though the constitutional property clause protects it from arbitrary infringements that are unjustifiable in view of other, higher constitutional values such as human dignity.

Nedelsky insists that property should in principle not be constitutionalised, and that the development of a limitation-oriented constitutional property jurisprudence is only the second best option, but the implication of her guidelines as set out above nevertheless is that, by following these principles, the courts might avoid the dilemma created by an entrenched property clause. The main characteristics of a limitation-oriented property jurisprudence, judging from Nedelsky's principles, would be that it does not treat the property clause as a barrier-guarantee in the libertarian sense, and that it consequently need not sacrifice either the protection of property or the promotion of the public interest. Instead, it attempts to maintain a constitutional tension (or strike a constitutional balance)[101] between the guarantee of existing property-holdings (for the sake of the individual holder of property) and the limitation of individual property rights (in the public interest). If such a jurisprudence were possible, and if it actually succeeded in avoiding at least some of the dangers described in Nedelsky's objections against the constitutionalisation of property, the result seems to be that the objections lose much of their force. After all, if it were possible to entrench property rights in the constitution and still develop a framework for judicial review that avoids the dangers set out by Nedelsky, there would be little point in allowing Nedelsky's objections to influence the decision on whether there should be a property clause or not. The only question, it seems, is whether it really is possible to develop a framework for judicial review and a limitation-oriented jurisprudence of constitutional property that does not treat the property clause as an absolute guarantee which insulates property-holdings against state interference, and that can avoid the dangers on which Nedelsky's objections are based. In a nutshell, if it is possible to develop a constitutional property jurisprudence that avoids Nedelsky's objections the problem is not the constitutional entrenchment of property, but the model of constitutional review in terms of which the property clause is interpreted and applied. In that case the possibility of including a property clause in the constitution cannot be dismissed out of hand.

In the next two sections of the chapter, I analyse two different possibilities in this regard: first, in section V, I discuss an example where the courts developed a framework for judicial review and a constitutional property jurisprudence that strongly resembles the limitation-orientation set out by Nedelsky, without the assistance of a well-drafted property clause. Secondly, in section VI, I discuss an example where a suitable constitutional framework for the development of a

---

[101]   The choice to describe the resulting approach or jurisprudence as either a "balance" or a "tension" can have important philosophical and theoretical implications that I cannot explore here.

limitation-oriented property jurisprudence was created through the drafting of the property clause.

V. AUSTRALIA: INTERPRETATIONAL BALANCE

The Australian property clause appears in a relatively old constitution, and does not offer any textual assistance to the courts for the development of the limitation-oriented constitutional property jurisprudence that is indicated by Nedelsky's guidelines. In terms of age and drafting, this property clause is related to the American Fifth Amendment rather than to any of the typical twentieth-century bills of rights that were drafted subsequent to the Second World War. This makes it particularly interesting to study the case law on this property clause, because the courts recently developed a limitation-oriented jurisprudence that fits in with Nedelsky's guidelines, rather than the guarantee-oriented jurisprudence that Nedelsky objects to and that one might expect in the context of relatively old, nineteenth-century (and therefore possibly libertarian) constitutions.

The Australian Commonwealth Constitution (1900) does not contain a classic, explicit and entrenched bill of rights, and section 51(xxxi) of the Constitution is not a typical property clause at all.[102] The section appears in a provision that outlines the legislative powers of the Australian federal (or commonwealth) parliament, and was intended to ensure that the federal government could acquire property in terms of the power of eminent domain.[103] However, the courts recognise and treat this section as a constitutional property guarantee,[104] and Lane[105] describes the guarantee of just terms as a "Bill-of-Rights provision". The Australian courts have interpreted this section as a

---

[102] Several sources nevertheless mention that there are similarities between s. 51(xxxi) and the Fifth Amendment to the US Constitution: see *Australian Apple and Pear Marketing Board* v. *Tonking* (1942) 66 CLR 77 at 82, where Williams J stated that s. 51(xxxi) "was taken from" the Fifth Amendment, and cf. R. Sackville and M. A. Neave, *Property law: Cases and Materials*, 3rd edn. (Sydney, Butterworths, 1981), pp. 112; P. J. Hanks, *Constitutional Law in Australia* (Sydney, Butterworths, 1991), p. 403.

[103] The provision reads as follows: "The Parliament shall . . . have power to make laws . . . with respect to:. . . (xxxi) The acquisition of property on just terms from any State or person for any purpose in respect of which the Parliament has the power to make laws".

[104] In *Clunies-Ross* v. *The Commonwealth* (1984) 155 CLR 193 (at 193 per Gibbs CJ, Mason, Wilson, Brennan, Deane and Dawson JJ) the provision was described as having "assumed the status of a constitutional guarantee of just terms", which has to be interpreted and applied as a constitutional property guarantee, and this was followed in subsequent cases: see *Peverill* v. *Health Insurance Commission* (1991) 104 ALR 449 per Burchett J at 454; Toohey J in *Health Insurance Commission* v. *Peverill* (1994) 179 CLR 226, 254; Mason CJ in *Mutual Pools & Staff Pty Ltd.* v. *The Commonwealth* (1994) 179 CLR 155, 168; Deane and Gaudron JJ in *Re Director of Public Prosecutions; Ex Parte Lawler* (1994) 179 CLR 270, 284; Mason CJ, Deane and Gaudron JJ in *Georgiadis* v. *Australian and Overseas Broadcasting Corporation* (1994) 179 CLR 297, 303.

[105] P. H. Lane, *A Manual of Australian Constitutional Law*, 4th edn. (Sydney, Law Book Co, 1987), p. 169.

property guarantee in the sense that it provides a constitutional guarantee of the right to receive just compensation ("just terms") for compulsory acquisition of property,[106] as well as a guarantee against arbitrary exercises of the power of expropriation.[107] The double purpose of section 51(xxxi) in both providing and restricting the power to acquire property was confirmed in the important early case of *Bank of New South Wales* v. *The Commonwealth*.[108]

The effect of section 51(xxxi) is, therefore, to guarantee that a compulsory acquisition of property (by the federal government) is only legitimate if it is properly authorised (non-arbitrary) and accompanied by compensation or "just terms". However, the property clause not only guarantees compensation upon acquisition, but extends to the constitutional origin of the power to acquire property. The guarantee therefore also ensures that indirect acquisitions cannot be effected outside section 51(xxxi) in order to escape the just terms requirement. [109] The courts have consistently held that other constitutional powers that involve the acquisition of property have to be exercised within the restrictions imposed by section 51(xxxi). It is said that the constitutional guarantee in section 51(xxxi) "abstracts the power" to supplement the law for the compulsory acquisition of property in any other legislative power.[110] Consequently federal laws for the acquisition of property have to comply with the requirements laid down by section 51(xxxi), even when the acquisition is necessary for the exercise of other constitutional powers [111] (that is, unless the intention is clear that the acquisition was effected under a specific "other head of power" that falls outside the scope of section 51(xxxi)).[112] This exception has been emphasised more strongly in recent case law, and the essence of recent decisions[113] is that not every deprivation of

---

[106] See T. Allen (1993), above n. 65, at 525; P. H. Lane (1987), above n. 105, at 160; P. J. Butt, *Land Law*, 3rd edn. (Sydney, Law Book Co,1996), p. 891; P. J. Hanks above n. 102, at p. 403.

[107] See *Mutual Pools & Staff Pty Ltd.* v. *The Commonwealth* (1994) 179 CLR 155, 168–169 per Mason CJ, at 184 per Deane and Gaudron JJ.

[108] (1948) 76 CLR 1, 349–350 per Dixon J. It is interesting to compare this case with the *Indian Bank Nationalisation* case; see above n. 74.

[109] See *Bank of New South Wales* v. *The Commonwealth* (1948) 76 CLR 1, 349; *Clunies-Ross* v. *The Commonwealth* (1984) 155 CLR 193 at 199; *Peverill* v. *Health Insurance Commission* (1991) 104 ALR 449, 454–455.

[110] *Mutual Pools & Staff Pty Ltd.* v. *The Commonwealth* (1994) 179 CLR 155, 177 per Brennan J; at 169 Mason CJ explains the reason for this principle: "when a power is conferred and some qualification or restriction is attached to its exercise, other powers should be construed, absent any indication of contrary intention, so as not to authorise an exercise of power free from the qualification or restriction".

[111] Such as postal, telegraphic and telephone services, docking facilities, naval and military defence and the provision of lighthouses; all provided for in other subsections of s. 51.

[112] See P. J. Hanks above n. 102, at p. 404; P. H. Lane above n. 105, at p. 163, 164; cf. *Andrews* v. *Howell* (1941) 65 CLR 255. An obvious example of this kind of exclusion is the power of taxation, which clearly does not and cannot fall under the provision dealing with the power to acquire property against compensation.

[113] *Health Insurance Commission* v. *Peverill* (1994) 179 CLR 226; *Mutual Pools & Staff Pty Ltd.* v. *The Commonwealth* (1994) 179 CLR 155; *Re Director of Public Prosecutions; ex parte Lawler* (1994) 179 CLR 270; *Georgiadis* v. *Australian and Overseas Broadcasting Corporation* (1994) 179 CLR 297. Some of these principles have been confirmed and followed in the majority opinion of Brennan CJ, Toohey, Gaudron, McHugh and Gummow JJ in the 'Industrial Relations Act' case

property is recognised as an acquisition of property for purposes of the just terms guarantee in section 51(xxxi). My contention is that this new development transforms the Australian jurisprudence dealing with the property guarantee in section 51(xxxi) from a guarantee-oriented jurisprudence, against which Nedelsky's objections are more or less valid, to a limitation-oriented constitutional property jurisprudence that evades most of Nedelsky's objections.

In the recent decisions already referred to, the High Court of Australia provided a comprehensive explanation of the exclusions from section 51(xxxi).[114] In these decisions, it was reiterated that section 51(xxxi) does not apply to all deprivations of property. First, it has to be shown that a deprivation of property also amounts to an acquisition of property as intended by section 51(xxxi), which means that the deprivation has to be accompanied by a corresponding acquisition of some benefit or advantage, however slight or insubstantial. Without such an advantage there can be no question of an acquisition and section 51(xxxi) does not enter into the picture.[115] However, even when it has been established that a particular deprivation of property also involved an acquisition as meant in section 51(xxxi), the further principle is that not all acquisitions activate the just terms guarantee in section 51(xxxi): a number of exclusions are recognised, and consequently any finding that a specific law or action of the Commonwealth effects an acquisition of property has to be followed by a second inquiry into the question whether the acquisition was an acquisition of property *for purposes of section 51(xxxi)*.[116] An acquisition of property can, according to these decisions, fall outside section 51(xxxi) (and therefore not be subject to the just terms guarantee) for any of a number of reasons: (1) First, the acquisition may be effected in terms of a "different head of power" that is explicitly excluded from section 51(xxxi). An example is the power to impose and regulate the payment of taxes in terms of section 51(ii) of the Constitution.[117] (2) Secondly, an acquisition may be excluded because it forms

(reported as *The State of Victoria* v. *The Commonwealth*; *The State of South Australia* v. *The Commonwealth*; *The State of Western Australia* v. *The Commonwealth*) (1996) 187 CLR 416 at 559.

[114] See *Health Insurance Commission* v. *Peverill* (1994) 179 CLR 226; *Mutual Pools & Staff Pty Ltd.* v. *The Commonwealth* (1994) 179 CLR 155; *Re Director of Public Prosecutions; ex parte Lawler* (1994) 179 CLR 270; *Georgiadis* v. *Australian and Overseas Broadcasting Corporation* (1994) 179 CLR 297.

[115] This is a complicated issue that cannot be discussed in full here. See generally A. J. van der Walt, "Police Power Regulation of Intangible Commercial Property and the Constitutional Property Clause: a Comparative Analysis of Case Law", (1998) vol 2.1 *Electronic Journal of Comparative Law* (EJCL) <http://law.kub.nl/ejcl/21/art2–1.html>; T. Allen (1993), above n. 65. The main principles were laid down in *Health Insurance Commission* v. *Peverill* (1994) 179 CLR 226; *Mutual Pools & Staff Pty Ltd.* v. *The Commonwealth* (1994) 179 CLR 155; *Re Director of Public Prosecutions; ex parte Lawler* (1994) 179 CLR 270; *Georgiadis* v. *Australian and Overseas Broadcasting Corporation* (1994) 179 CLR 297. See further *Australian Capital Television Pty Ltd.* v. *The Commonwealth*; *The State of New South Wales* v. *The Commonwealth* (1992) 177 CLR 106, 165–166 per Brennan J, 196–197 per Dawson J.

[116] This approach suggests a methodology that should be followed when evaluating a possible acquisition in terms of s. 51(xxxi).

[117] See *Mutual Pools & Staff Pty Ltd.* v. *The Commonwealth* (1994) 179 CLR 155.

part of the exercise of another power that is not explicitly excluded from section 51(xxxi), but the exercise of which does not permit of compensation or just terms. An example is a law that permits or effects the forfeiture of property as a penalty upon conviction of a crime in which the property was used[118]—it makes no sense to impose a penalty as part of a legitimate regulatory scheme and then have to pay compensation because the penalty involved an incidental acquisition of the property by the state. (3) A third category of acquisitions that may be excluded involves cases where the acquisition was not the sole or main purpose of the law or action, but was incidental to the taking of reasonable and appropriate measures to promote a different purpose, such as the adjustment or regulation of competing rights, claims and interests of (private) parties in a relationship that requires such regulation as a matter of public interest—a classic definition of an exercise of the police power. An example of this category would be a law that ensures that tax refunds are paid to the party who actually carried the tax burden, even when a different person's contractual right to claim the refund has to be extinguished by law to effect this adjustment.[119] The cases indicate that the just terms guarantee does not apply to such exercises of the police power,[120] even if it involves measures that effect an incidental acquisition of property.

However, in a way this is not new: it is widely recognised that the compensation guarantee does not normally apply to exercises of the police power. The important qualification suggested by these Australian cases is that an acquisition in this third category will only be excluded from the just terms guarantee in section 51(xxxi) if and in so far as the acquisition is *appropriate to and proportionate with the purpose* served by it; if not, the authority of the authorising law falls away and the acquisition will have to be scrutinised in terms of the just terms guarantee.[121] This qualification takes the Australian jurisprudence about the property clause out of the libertarian, guarantee-oriented mode where the

---

[118] In *Ex parte Lawler* (1994) 179 CLR 270 it was held that a law which provides for or effects the forfeiture of property as a penalty for the unlawful use of the property did not effect an acquisition of the property for purposes of s. 51(xxxi), even if the state acquired the property in the process. See the decision of the European Court of Human Rights in the *AGOSI* case (*Allgemeine Gold-und Silberscheideanstalt AG v. United Kingdom* [1987] ECHR Series A Vol 108), where it was said (at 19 [54]) that the behaviour of the owner is a consideration that has to be taken into account to establish whether a fair balance was struck (by the forfeiture) between the individual interests and the public interest.

[119] See *Mutual Pools & Staff Pty Ltd. v. The Commonwealth* (1994) 179 CLR 155, 179. This category offers excellent opportunities for comparison with the German *Contergan* decision BVerfGE 42, 263 (1976).

[120] In *Health Insurance Commission v. Peverill* (1994) 179 CLR 226 at 236, Mason CJ, Deane and Gaudron JJ indicated that the crucial consideration was that the deprivation in question "was effected not only by way of genuine adjustment of competing claims, rights and obligations in the common interests between parties who stand in a particular relationship but also as an element in a regulatory scheme".

[121] See *Australian Capital Television Pty Ltd. v. The Commonwealth of Australia; The State of New South Wales v. The Commonwealth* (1992) 177 CLR 106, 157–162 (Brennan J). This is incidentally also the attitude of the European Court of Human Rights, as is indicated by the *AGOSI* case referred to above n. 118.

property guarantee functions as a barrier that insulates private property against state interference, and immerses the whole issue in a strongly contextual discourse that offers good opportunities for developing a limitation-oriented jurisprudence that escapes Nedelsky's objections. And, even more interesting, the Australian courts developed this limitation-oriented jurisprudence and the proportionality test without any assistance from the structure or phraseology of the property clause.

The cases indicate that a proportionality test has to be employed to determine whether an acquisition of property falls outside the just terms guarantee in section 51(xxxi) because it is incidental to a legitimate action in terms of a different head of power or to a process of adjusting private rights, claims and interests. Two aspects of the decisions in *Mutual Pools*[122] and *Lawler*[123] illustrate this point. It is said that an acquisition of property may be excluded from the guarantee in section 51(xxxi) and justified under a different head of power if the acquisition resulted incidentally from means that are (1) *appropriate and adapted* to serve the non-acquisitory purpose justified under that head of power, and (2) if those means are *reasonably proportionate* to some object or purpose served under the relevant head of power. This means that an acquisition that resulted incidentally from means adopted under a different head of power will not necessarily be justified under that head, and may therefore be judged in terms of the just terms guarantee in section 51(xxxi), if the means adopted to serve the different purpose were not appropriate to it or if the result was disproportionate to the purpose served. This comes very close to the proportionality test used in other jurisdictions[124] to judge whether a limitation of the property guarantee is justifiable and reasonable, and it seems fair to conclude that the proportionality test will play a role when it has to be decided whether a police power regulation of property goes too far and becomes an acquisition of property that is no longer justified under the separate (regulatory) head of power. In *Australian Capital Television Pty Ltd.* v. *The Commonwealth*; *The State of New South Wales* v. *The Commonwealth*,[125] a case that was not decided on the property clause,[126] Brennan J came even closer than in the property cases to formulating a general limitation test in the form of a proportionality test. According to this case:

> "[t]o determine the validity of a law which purports to limit [the right] it is necessary to consider the proportionality between the restriction which a law imposes [on the right] and the legitimate interest which the law is intended to serve".

Furthermore, it was added,[127] proportionality is a question of degree, and:

---

[122] *Mutual Pools & Staff Pty Ltd.* v. *The Commonwealth* (1994) 179 CLR 155, 179 (Brennan J).
[123] *Re Director of Public Prosecutions; ex parte Lawler* (1994) 179 CLR 270, 287 (Dawson J).
[124] Especially Canada, the Council of Europe, Germany and South Africa.
[125] Ibid., at 158.
[126] The case was decided on freedom of communication, although property issues were raised.
[127] (1992) 177 CLR 106, 158.

"[w]hen the boundary of permissible restriction [on the right] is passed, the law imposing the restriction loses the constitutional support of the power which would otherwise be available to support it".

The effect of the proportionality test is that the Australian property clause is recognised as a guarantee against arbitrary and unauthorised acquisitions of property other than on just terms, but at the same time the property clause is not allowed to insulate property-holdings against federal intervention: in any individual case the court determines whether a particular deprivation of property is properly authorised, whether the deprivation amounts to an acquisition of property, whether an acquisition of property falls under and is justified by an exercise of power that is excluded from the compensation guarantee and, ultimately, whether an acquisition of property triggers the compensation requirement in the property clause. All this is done with reference to the legitimate constitutional purpose for which the state action is authorised, the means selected to achieve that purpose, the effect of the state action on the individual property holder and the proportionality between the purpose served and the means selected. Instead of insulating private property against the public sphere, this approach provides protection for property within a specifically constitutional context, with reference to non-privatist notions such as the public benefit of a deprivation, the public purpose for which an action was undertaken, the constitutional authority for state action, and the proportionality between purpose and means that should characterise rational and reasonable state action. Actual loss and the detrimental effect of the loss on the property owner do not by themselves trigger the property guarantee automatically, but are considered as factors that assist the court in determining whether there was an acquisition of property that, taking all relevant factors into account, attracts the compensation guarantee. This approach has to be described as a limitation-oriented constitutional property jurisprudence, and it seems to evade most of the objections raised by Nedelsky.

The analysis of Australian jurisprudence above does not and cannot prove that, given the opportunity, most courts will eventually "come to their senses" and start reading and applying a constitutionally entrenched property clause "properly" and "responsibly". If anything, the trend in recent American jurisprudence points the other way. What the analysis above can indicate is that it is possible, even in a strong libertarian context and without much support from the structure and phraseology of the text, to interpret and develop a constitutionally entrenched property clause in a manner that tends to develop a stronger limitation-orientation in constitutional property jurisprudence instead of the exclusively guarantee-orientation that informs Nedelsky's objections. In other words, the Indian disaster can be avoided if the courts elect to avoid a libertarian approach to the relationship between private property and the constitution. The remaining question is: is it possible to ensure or at least strengthen the chances that the courts will follow this route?

VI. SOUTH AFRICA: STRUCTURAL BALANCE

In this section, I approach the possibility of escaping Nedelsky's objections against the constitutionalisation of property[128] from a different angle. Where the analysis of Australian jurisprudence in the previous section investigated the possibility of evading Nedelsky's objections by developing a limitation-oriented jurisprudence of constitutional property, this section deals with the textual or structural possibility, based on the actual structure or phraseology of the property clause rather than just the initiative of the judiciary, of developing such a limitation-oriented jurisprudence of constitutional property. The example referred to is the South African Constitution (1996), which is of fairly recent origin and in many ways typical of the constitutions of the last couple of decades.[129] In this section, I focus on features of the South African property clause that distinguish it from the Australian example discussed in the previous section: the Australian courts had to develop their limitation-oriented jurisprudence without any assistance from the text of the property clause, but the South African property clause provides strong textual support, and perhaps even the obligation, to develop the kind of limitation-oriented jurisprudence that does not insulate property against the public sphere or from state regulation. This poses the question whether this kind of property clause is more likely to evade Nedelsky's objections, and is therefore less objectionable and more acceptable in terms of Nedelsky's framework; a question to which I return in the concluding section below.

The property clause in section 25 of the South African Constitution (1996)[130] has not yet been the subject of any jurisprudence,[131] and it is difficult to predict

---

[128] See section II of the chapter above.

[129] One obvious issue in the bill of rights would be stronger emphasis on social and economic rights.

[130] I do not discuss the property clause in s. 28 of the now replaced interim Constitution (1993) here. See for a discussion (and in some cases a comparison with the 1996 Constitution) A. Cachalia et al (eds), *Fundamental Rights in the New Constitution* (Cape Town, Juta & Co, 1994); M. Chaskalson (1993) above n. 39; M. Chaskalson, "The Property Clause: Section 28 of the Constitution", (1994) 10 *SAJHR* 131; M. Chaskalson (1995), above n. 18; M. Chaskalson and C. H. Lewis, "Property" in M. Chaskalson et al (eds), *Constitutional Law of South Africa* (Cape Town, Juta & Co, 1996), ch. 31; D. G. Kleyn, "The Constitutional Protection of Property: A Comparison Between the German and the South African Approach", (1996) 11 *SAPL* 402; J. Murphy, "Property Rights in the New Constitution: an Analytical Framework for Constitutional Review", (1993) 26 *CILSA* 211; J. Murphy, "Interpreting the Property Clause in the Constitution Act of 1993", (1995) 10 *SAPL* 107; T. Roux, "Property" in D Davis et al (eds.), *Fundamental Rights in the Constitution: Commentary and Cases* (Kenwyn, Juta & Co, 1997), p. 237; A. J. van der Walt, "Notes on the Interpretation of the Property Clause in the New Constitution", (1994) 57 *THRHR* 181; A. J. van der Walt, above n. 21; A. J. van der Walt, "The Limits of Constitutional Property", (1997) 12 *SAPL* 274. For a discussion of the 1996 Constitution see A. J. van der Walt, *The Constitutional Property Clause: A Comparative Analysis of Section 25 of the South African Constitution of 1996* (Kenwyn, Juta & Co, 1997).

[131] A few cases have dealt with s. 28 of the interim Constitution (1993), though: *In re: Certification of the Constitution of the Republic of South Africa, 1996* (1996) (10) BCLR 1253 (CC); *Transvaal Agricultural Union* v. *Minister of Land Affairs 1996* (12) BCLR 1573 (CC); *Harksen* v. *Lane NO 1997* (12) BCLR 1489 (CC); 1998 (1) SA 300 (CC).

which way the interpretation of the property clause will go. However, even at this early stage one can say that there is strong textual support in section 25 for developing the kind of limitation-oriented constitutional property jurisprudence that can evade Nedelsky's objections to the constitutionalisation of property. The South African Constitution (1996)[132] contains a general limitation provision in section 36 that basically codifies the general limitation notion as stated in section 1 of the Canadian Charter of Rights and Freedoms (1982),[133] together with the further analysis and explication of this notion in the Canadian case of *R* v. *Oakes*.[134] With the assistance of this provision, South African courts can, in principle, develop the same kind of limitation-oriented jurisprudence, based on substantive evaluation of the authority, legitimacy and reasonableness of infringements of property in terms of a proportionality test, as was described with reference to Australia. Section 36 is basically a codified proportionality test, and therefore offers strong structural and textual support for the development of a jurisprudence that casts the constitutional protection and the constitutional limitation of property rights in the form of a proportionality issue. If a constitutional property jurisprudence were to be developed on the basis of the proportionality principle in section 36 of the 1996 Constitution, the limitation orientation of that jurisprudence could potentially be much stronger than in the case of Australia (which has no explicit general limitation clause) or Canada (which has a general limitation clause but no entrenched property clause). Potentially, therefore, the South African Constitution (1996) offers the best structural and textual possibility for the development of a limitation-oriented property jurisprudence, at least as far as the proportionality principle is concerned. Whether this will happen is uncertain, however, since some members of the Constitutional Court have given the impression that they are wary of the general limitation clause and may elect to avoid its application when possible.[135]

---

[132] Section 33 of the interim Constitution contained a similar set of provisions, except that a further requirement (that the limitation had to be necessary) was imposed with respect to certain rights (not including property), and that it was also required that a limitation should not negate the essential content of the right in question. For a general discussion see A. J. van der Walt (1997), above n. 130 ch. 3; A. J. van der Walt (1997) 12 *SAPL* 274, above n. 130; G. Carpenter, "Internal Modifiers and Other Qualifications in Bills of Rights—Some Problems of Interpretation", (1995) 10 *SAPL* 260; I. M. Rautenbach, *General Provisions of the South African Bill of Rights* (Durban, Butterworths, 1995), ch. 6; S. Woolman, "Riding the Push-me Pull-you: Constructing a Test That Reconciles the Conflicting Interests Which Animate the Limitation Clause", (1994) 10 *SAJHR* 60; S. Woolman, "Limitation" in Chaskalson et al (eds), *Constitutional Law of South Africa*, 2nd edn. (Cape Town, Juta & Co, 1998), ch. 12; S. Woolman, "Out of Order? Out of Balance? The Limitation Clause of the Final Constitution", (1997) 13 *SAJHR* 102.

[133] See the discussion of Canadian law in section I of the chapter above.

[134] (1986) 26 DLR 4th 200. The phraseology of s. 36 was paraphrased from the opinion of Chaskalson P in *S* v. *Makwanyane* (1995) 3 SA 391 (CC) 436B-439E.

[135] Especially Sachs J in *Soobramoney* v. *Minister of Health*, KwaZulu-Natal (1998) (1) SA 765 (CC) 783C [54], cf. Langa J in *City Council of Pretoria* v. *Walker* (1998) (3) BCLR 257 (CC) 291 [82]. Indications to the contrary have been given by Goldstone J in *Harksen* v. *Lane* NO (1997) (11) BCLR 1489 (CC) 1512 [53](c); cf. O'Regan J in the same case at 1527 [101], where the limitation clause seems to have been applied more or less consistently.

There is nothing in section 25 of the South African Constitution (1996) that resembles the legislative injunction to define and restrict property in article 14.1.2 and 14.2 of the German Basic Law,[136] and consequently the South African property clause has to be interpreted without that kind of general structural and textual support for the limitation of property by legislation and regulation. However, in another context the South African Constitution (1996) provides stronger structural and textual reasons than the German Basic Law for developing a limitation-oriented constitutional property jurisprudence based on the constitutional legitimacy of statutory limitations of property. Subsections 25(5)–(9) of the Constitution (1996) impose a strong legislative injunction that forces the legislature to develop and adopt laws for the promotion of land reform. These land reform provisions have to be read together with subsection 25(4)(a), which provides that land reform is in the public interest, thereby ensuring that land reform measures will not be attacked or overturned on the basis that they are to the advantage of specific individuals or groups rather than in the public interest or for a public purpose.[137] The land reform provisions in subsections 25(5)–(9) not only authorise the development and promotion of a land reform programme,[138] but create a positive legislative duty that obliges the state to make laws (and take other measures) that will (1) promote equitable access to land for all South Africans,[139] (2) provide security of tenure[140] and (3)

[136] A similar provision might have been unsuitable in the South African context in any event, given the fact that South African property law is largely uncodified.

[137] This provision secures the legitimacy of expropriations for land reform and of other incidental deprivations that result from the land reform programme. The biggest problem is usually the expropriations, since it is often argued that an expropriation for the purpose of restitution or redistribution amounts to taking from X to give to Y, which is not equal to a public purpose.

[138] The land reform programme is said to rest on three pillars: redistribution, tenure reform and restitution. This division is derived from the Reconstruction and Development Programme of the ANC: see the policy document *The Reconstruction and Development Programme: A Policy Framework* (Johannesburg, Umangano Publications, 1994) at 2.4, 19 et seq; as well as the government's *White Paper on Reconstruction and Development* State President's Office (Sep 1994) at 1.3.6, 5, Lead Projects at 48 et seq.; *White Paper on South African Land Policy* Pretoria Department of Land Affairs (Apr 1997) at vi, viii, 9, 10. The three aspects of land reform are now formally sanctioned and controlled by ss. 25(5) (redistribution), 25(6) (tenure reform) and 25(7) (restitution) of the property clause in the 1996 Constitution.

[139] Redistribution is a process whereby land or access to land is given or made available to people who have no land or inadequate land, either for agricultural (subsistence or commercial) or residential purposes. The most important legislative measures implemented so far are the Less Formal Township Establishment Act 112 of 1991, the Provision of Certain Land for Settlement Act 126 of 1993, the Development Facilitation Act 67 of 1995, the Housing Act 107 of 1997 and the Land Reform (Labour Tenants) Act 3 of 1996.

[140] Tenure reform is a process whereby insecure or unsuitable forms of existing land tenure are transformed legally so as to provide better or more suitable rights. This can concern the security of the landholding as such, or the possibility of procuring loans with the land right as security, or any aspect of the tenure under which the land right is held or exercised. The most important legislative measures adopted so far are the Conversion of Certain Rights into Leasehold or Ownership Act 81 of 1988; the Upgrading of Land Tenure Rights Act 112 of 1991; the Development Facilitation Act 67 of 1995; the Land Reform (Labour Tenants) Act 3 of 1996; the Communal Property Associations Act 28 of 1996; the Interim Protection of Informal Land Rights Act 31 of 1996; the Extension of Security of Tenure Act 62 of 1997; and the Prevention of Illegal Eviction from and Unlawful Occupation of Land Act 19 of 1998.

provide for a process of land restitution.[141] In view of this injunction, and of the laws that have been promulgated in terms of it, there is no way that section 25 can be interpreted as a barrier-type property guarantee that insulates existing property-holdings against legislative or other state actions. The land reform subsections of the property clause, read against the reformist backdrop of the 1996 Constitution as a whole, embody a strong interpretive guideline and a strong legislative duty to reform the South African property regime by eradicating the injustices of the past and to promote the constitutional values of equality and human dignity. On the one hand, this injunction clearly implies and assumes the inevitability of state intervention and regulation, with increased (judged against the status quo) deprivations of existing individual property-holdings, in the form of laws that adjust, transform and control the distribution pattern, the content and the limits of property rights. On the other hand, the transformation process clearly has to take place within the framework of the Constitution and the guidelines provided by it: deprivations of property (including expropriations) have to be imposed by way of law of general application that is not arbitrary, and they have to be reasonable and justifiable in view of the values ensconced in the Constitution. In short, there must be a reasonable and justifiable constitutional proportionality between the measures selected to promote the reform of property law and property-holdings and the effect that these measures have on individual property-holders. And, typical for such a value-driven proportionality approach, the validity and legitimacy of interferences with private property must be established with proper regard for the facts and all the relevant circumstances of each individual case, including the history of acquisition and use of property, state subsidies and investment and other factors specified by the Constitution. The compensation provisions in section 25(3) of the 1996 Constitution illustrate this observation very well: although the Constitution guarantees that expropriations are subject to public purpose and payment of compensation, it also specifies that the amount, manner and time of payment of compensation have to be determined with reference to all the circumstances, including a number of factors that are explicitly referred to. Market value is just one of these factors, and has to be weighed up together with others such as the manner of acquisition of the property and the expenditure of state money on it in the past. This allows for an equitable determination that, far from insulating existing property-holdings from reform or redistribution programmes, subjects it to a full consideration of all the factors that constitute and determine the value of the property and the equitable stake of the current owner in it, taking into account all other factors of public concern.

There can be no question that the guarantee-oriented approach to constitutional property, as discussed and objected to by Nedelsky, is impossible to

---

[141] Restitution is a limited process with a limited lifespan, and is aimed at returning specific parcels of land to specific people from whom it had been taken in terms of racially discriminatory laws or practices during the apartheid era. The relevant legislation, which was promulgated in terms of ss. 121–123 of the interim Constitution (1993), is the Restitution of Land Rights Act 22 of 1994.

uphold in the South African constitutional context. The very structure and text of the property clause, in the broader constitutional framework, makes it abundantly clear that such a vision of property is not acceptable in view of the new constitutional order. There can be little doubt that the libertarian, *laissez-faire* barrier-guarantee approach to property is accepted and championed by an influential part of the South African population and legal fraternity,[142] and probably even a substantial part of the judiciary,[143] but even then the conclusion is inevitable that the Constitution requires that the legislature, the courts and South African lawyers should develop property law away from this legacy of the past and towards a different orientation, as spelled out by the Constitution. In a certain sense, the structure and phraseology of section 25 do more than just provide assistance in the judicial development of a limitation-oriented constitutional property jurisprudence: they impose a positive duty upon the legislature and the courts to develop the whole of property law, including private law and customary law, so as to conform with the spirit, purport and objects of the Constitution.[144] This means, unless I am very much mistaken, that section 25 does not and dare not be allowed to stand in the way of regulation and reform, as foreseen and feared by Nedelsky. Far from institutionalising the injustice of existing property-holdings, the South African property clause is the instrument through which the whole property regime and its injustices are to be reformed and transformed. As far as I can see, the development of a proportionality-based, limitation-oriented jurisprudence of constitutional property should play a major role in this process, and although South African lawyers can benefit from comparative studies, the obligation to develop that jurisprudence and to

[142] I use the term advisedly.

[143] See the telling criticism of Sachs J against the underlying patriarchal assumptions of the majority opinion (per Goldstone J) in *Harksen* v. *Lane* NO (1997) (11) BCLR 1489 (CC); 1998 (1) SA 300 (CC) 1534–1535 [123]-[124]. See further A. J. van der Walt, "Tradition on Trial: a Critical Analysis of the Civil-law Tradition in South African Property Law", (1995) 11 *SAJHR* 169–206; A. J. van der Walt (1995), above n. 21. The problem is not necessarily that there is a lack of the political or judicial will to reform, but that the civil law tradition strongly entrenches (a version of) the property-as-barrier-guarantee approach: see A. J. van der Walt, "Ownership and Personal Freedom: Subjectivism in Bernhard Windscheid's Theory of Ownership", (1993) 56 *THRHR* 569–589; A. J. van der Walt, "Marginal Notes on Powerful(l) Legends: Critical Perspectives on Property Theory", (1995) 58 *THRHR* 396–420 for a discussion of some aspects. In his inaugural lecture, A. Cockrell, "The Hegemony of Contract", (1998) 115 *SALJ* 286 developed a similar (if slightly less reformist) argument with regard to the other leg on which "free market" jurisprudence stands, i.e., freedom of contract, or as Cockrell calls it, the hegemony of contract: (at 317)

> "the hegemony of contract is premised on a deep-level commitment to the primacy of market relations. Our belief in the virtues of the market is today so powerful that there will be many doctrinal manifestations of the hegemony of contract where the outcome seems to be acceptable. However, there will also be some sticking points, located at places where our belief in the market runs out. In such contexts, to endorse the hegemony of contract in any simplistic way would involve us in doing a disservice to our underlying political commitments."

[144] See in this regard the concluding sections of A. J. van der Walt, (1995) above n. 21, where a similar argument is developed with reference to the interim Constitution (1993). Cf. the Preamble and ss. 7, 36 and 39 of the 1996 Constitution for an indication of the constitutional values, their transformational importance and the duty to transform South African law.

restructure the property regime in South Africa is much stronger than in Australia, Austria, or Germany.

The fact that there are strong textual and structural reasons and good comparative examples for the creation of a limitation-oriented jurisprudence of constitutional property does not mean that there is any guarantee of success: the South African constitution creates the possibility and the duty to transform property institutions and the framework within which reform can take place, but the work still has to be done. If the courts were to ignore the textual and comparative reasons for developing such a jurisprudence things could still go wrong, much as they have in India. And, if the courts elect to take a different route, it makes no difference whether they do so to protect existing property rights (and sacrifice the transformation of the existing property regime) or to champion the transformation process (and abandon the protection of existing property rights): the result will probably be much the same. Although textual and structural support and injunctions to protect property within a just and equitable system of property rights make it easier for the courts to develop the kind of constitutional property jurisprudence that can escape Nedelsky's objections, they do not provide guarantees that this will indeed happen.

VII. EVALUATION AND CONCLUSIONS

The developments described in this chapter are much harder to evaluate than one might at first think. Superficially, some of these developments seem to refute Nedelsky's arguments against the constitutionalisation of property, but how good are the responses they offer to Nedelsky's objections really? Do these developments support the constitutionalisation of property, or do they merely indicate (as Nedelsky does as a second-best option) that the constitutional entrenchment of property does not have to result in tragedy or disaster, provided the courts develop a suitable framework for constitutional review? To put the question more simply: what do the developments I describe support: the constitutional entrenchment of property, or the development of a proportionality test for constitutional review once property is constitutionalised? The former refutes Nedelsky's arguments; the latter merely underlines her view. If these developments merely support constitutionalisation subject to the development of a suitable jurisprudence, scepticism about the courts' willingness and ability to develop and maintain such a jurisprudence might justify a decision not to risk constitutionalisation. On the other hand, if these developments do support the constitutionalisation of property, the question remains whether they favour a simple and abstract property clause or a long and detailed one.

Despite the difficulties in evaluating the developments I have set out, I think they at least indicate very strongly that Nedelsky's objections against the constitutionalisation of property require more careful examination. To start with the first objection: can one really conclude, on Nedelsky's own evidence and on other examples discussed here, that the constitutionalisation of property has turned property into a regulation-free enclave? With the possible exception of some American cases and the definite exception of some early Indian cases, I think the opposite is true. While it is clearly a major concern of constitutional property jurisprudence that the regulation of property institutions and the use of property should remain possible and viable despite the constitutional entrenchment of property, the result is by and large that courts in most jurisdictions accept, as a matter of fact, that the police power cannot and is not usurped or excluded or even unduly restricted by the property guarantee, except for the provision of due process protection against arbitrary and improper exercises of that power. On the whole, though, Nedelsky's case is overstated on this point, and comparative constitutional experience suggests that the real issue is to establish the theoretical and practical balance between legitimate and arbitrary exercises of the police power, and not to protect it against wholesale abolition.

Nedelsky's second objection is that the constitutional entrenchment of property will institutionalise existing inequalities in the distribution of property and, by implication, power. Clearly, this objection can only be upheld if it is also assumed that the constitutional entrenchment of property insulates existing property-holdings against land reforms or redistribution programmes. And, despite the ostensible support this objection receives from the Indian history set out earlier, comparative constitutional jurisprudence again suggests that this is not the case: courts in many (if not most) jurisdictions accept that even existing and well-established property-holdings are not immune to reform and redistribution. What the property clause usually does is to provide a framework for judicial review within which the constitutional legitimacy and validity of reforms and redistribution programmes can be tested, but to argue that it excludes these reforms wholesale is to overstate the case. In fact, the South African example discussed above suggests the opposite, namely that the constitutional property clause itself may provide the instrument by and through which the whole property system (including existing property institutions and property-holdings) is transformed and reformed. The result is that the constitutionalisation of property does not in itself necessarily imply (or effect, or support) the institutionalisation of existing inequalities in the distribution of property or social power: cases where this was in fact the result of the property clause are the exception rather than the rule.

Nedelsky's third objection was that the constitutionalisation of property will upset the hierarchy of rights in the bill of rights and thereby undermine the promotion and protection of more important rights such as equality. This is indeed an important concern, and it cannot be taken lightly, but the question is whether it supports a general objection against the constitutionalisation of property. Canada is a good case in point: once it has been established that (even legitimate) property interests cannot or are not going to be protected in terms of more general, higher order rights like equality or human dignity, it becomes necessary to reconsider the inclusion of an explicit property clause. In a sense, therefore, this objection is more valid when the bill of rights includes the possibility to protect legitimate property interests in terms of a general protection of higher order rights, but in the absence of such a possibility the objection loses much of its force.

Nedelsky's fourth argument is based on pragmatic grounds, most of which concern the waste of resources through unnecessary property litigation and the resulting transformation of constitutional property law into a overly technical field of "lawyers' talk". Tom Allen[145] makes an interesting and valuable observation on this objection: if the argument based on waste of resources is a pragmatic one, then it has to be evaluated in terms of a pragmatic calculus that also takes into account the possible advantages of the constitutionalisation of property, and experience in many postcolonial Commonwealth jurisdictions suggests that the advantages may sometimes outweigh the costs of litigation in this regard. The most important advantages are both political and economic: the inclusion of a property clause in the constitution is often a political compromise that not only ensures some political and economic stability and security in a process of political transformation,[146] but also makes it possible to reach political consensus on the drafting of a new constitution. This may have an effect on internal political and economic stability and on the possibility of attracting foreign investment, and the benefits that such a compromise brings with it may well outweigh potential litigation costs.

It is not quite as easy to dispose of the second leg of Nedelsky's fourth objection, which was listed as a fifth objection in section II of the chapter above. We will do well, when evaluating the developments in foreign law described above, not to forget Nedelsky's argument that constitutional litigation about property results in a constitutional property discourse characterised by technicalities and elitist lawyer-talk, inaccessible to non-lawyers, that privatises issues and debates about property that should be conducted in the public sphere. An important question is, when evaluating this objection, whether any of the developments described above has the potential of retaining or increasing public debate about the social and political origins of the content, limits and distribution of property; and whether the exclusion of a property clause from the bill of rights will improve matters in any way.

One argument that detracts from the validity of Nedelsky's objection is that, while some kinds of constitutional jurisprudence no doubt entrench property discourse in an unnecessarily technical and non-public debate, other kinds can even enhance the possibility of public debate about property. Part of my objection against a definitional approach in limitation jurisprudence is that such an approach must inevitably reinforce exactly the kind of technical elitism and legalese that Nedelsky objects to—it translates difficult, unclear political

---

[145] In discussion with the author. I am indebted to Tom for this perspective, and grateful for his comments and arguments.

[146] Cf. the remarks on the drafting of the South African Constitution in section I of the chapter above.

debates into misleadingly and temptingly straightforward (albeit technical) legal debates about the meaning and the structural and hierarchical significance of concepts.[147] A truly limitational approach is different. I would not want to make a strong claim with regard to the moral or theoretical merit of the South African constitutional order in this regard, but at least it is conceivable that a public, political debate about property issues remains possible in a context where the constitutional protection of property, the legislative determination of the limits of property and a proportionality test for the legitimacy of limitations of property rights are approached from the text and in the spirit of the South African Constitution (1996). Does this provide a solution to the problems raised by Nedelsky? Clearly, there can be no guarantees, and it would be foolish to think that there is a single, correct approach or answer that, once discovered, can be held onto as a recipe for success. The best one can hope for, I think, is to establish that it is possible to develop a constitutional property jurisprudence, perhaps as part of a framework for judicial review, that offers possibilities for escaping Nedelsky's objections against the constitutional entrenchment of property. If that is possible—and I think that the South African Constitution suggests that it is, without thereby qualifying as the only or the best example available—the next question is how this possibility affects Nedelsky's position.

As was pointed out earlier, Nedelsky insists that her own guidelines for the development of jurisprudence have to be seen as a second-best option, to be followed only when property has been constitutionalised and it is no longer possible or sensible to argue against constitutionalisation. However, I am not convinced by this argument. If property is constitutionalised and Nedelsky's guidelines for the development of jurisprudence regarding constitutional property are followed, it seems to me that a favourable opportunity is created for exactly the kind of public, non-privatist debate about property issues for which Nedelsky strives. If that is possible, what is then the advantage of not having property entrenched in the constitution at all? This raises the question whether the decision to exclude property from the bill of rights solves the problem on which Nedelsky based the fifth objection: is there a better chance for public property debate in the absence of a constitutional property clause? The answer must involve at least two aspects: first, we have to assume that the public debate about property either is satisfactory or can be rendered satisfactory in the absence of a property clause; and secondly, we have to assume that the legal status of property in common law (as amended by legislation) is satisfactory or can be rendered satisfactory in the absence of a property clause.

Consider the first point: Nedelsky's objections are inspired at least partly by the (in my view correct) observation that current social, political and legal debates about property are shaped by the myth that property is a natural,

---

[147] A. J. van der Walt, (1995) 11 *SAJHR* 169–206 above n. 143; A. J. van der Walt (1995) above n. 21; A. J. van der Walt (1993) 56 *THRHR* 569–589, above n. 143; A. J. van der Walt (1995) 58 *THRHR* 396–420 above n. 143, discuss some of the problems with conceptual and structural-hierarchical legal argumentation in the civil law tradition.

pre-political right that should not be interfered with by the state unless it is absolutely unavoidable and clearly in the public interest. Nedelsky's argument is that the constitutionalisation of property (in the USA) reinforced and entrenched this myth. How is this position changed and improved by the absence of a constitutional property clause? Is there any proof that the public debate about property will develop more freely or in another direction if property is not constitutionalised? Is there evidence of a myth-free public debate about the social origins and limits of property in England, or in Canada, where there is no property clause? What little information there is in this regard, given the comparative difficulties, suggests a remarkably similar lack of appreciation of the social and political origins and limits of property in those jurisdictions. If there is a need for a stronger public debate that is not shaped by the myth of private property, I fail to see how the absence of a constitutional property clause will enhance the opportunities for or the quality of such a debate—in fact, I wonder whether the constitutionalisation of property may not, at least in some cases, be the best way of getting a public debate about the social and political origins and limits of property going. I return to this point later.

As far as the second point is concerned, I also fail to see how the myth of natural property—a problem that Nedelsky correctly identifies—is combated by the absence of a constitutional property clause. Without a property clause, the myth of natural property remains, among other places in the strong position it occupies in common law. In fact, the strategy of conceptual severance is probably of private law rather than constitutional law origin and inspiration, relying on private law dogma concerning the incidents or entitlements that constitute property rights and that can be transferred to others. Combined with the myth that private property is a pre-political right that needs to be insulated against state interference, conceptual severance is surely the most important source of the problems with constitutionally entrenched property against which Nedelsky objects. How does the common law get rid of the notion that the legislature is not allowed to interfere with even the smallest incident of a property owner's right? The argument that legislation is the result of democratic decision-making will fail to make an impression in this regard, unless the public view (which is still strongly under the influence of the myth of private property) is changed and it is generally accepted that property was originally created by democratic lawmaking and should therefore be open to further legislative interference. And how will the public view in this regard be changed by the absence of a property clause? If public discussion is still strongly influenced by the myth of private property, as Nedelsky's argument implies (in my view correctly), a strong incentive is required to move public discussion in a different direction. Will the current public discussion about environmental conservation and social security do the trick? In my view no—if anything, public discussion in many Western democracies seems to be strongly opposed to state intervention with private property, and public sympathy with the environmental movement seems in many quarters to have lost some of its momentum of late.

The South African example discussed above offers some interesting perspectives. The South African Constitution (1996) is clearly of a reformist nature and imposes strong reformist and interventionist obligations on the legislature and the judiciary to transform and develop the distribution pattern, nature and institutions of property in accordance with the spirit, purport and objects of the Constitution. This fact alone situates the Constitution and any aspect of the constitutional debate in a public, political discourse, with strong value-laden overtones. Although property is constitutionalised in this context, the property clause must inevitably form part of and be determined by this discourse. Questions concerning the legitimacy of the distribution of property, the social origin and limits of property rights, the legislative and regulatory redefinition and regulation of property rights and the justifiability and legitimacy of state interferences with property institutions and with private property holdings inevitably become part of the public debate, and these questions have to influence the adjudication of any particular property case that comes before a court and of the discussion and framing of legislation that affects property. In view of reformist constitutional provisions[148] these discussions must affect the interpretation, application and development of common law and customary law, for example through the interpretation of common law principles and the application of the *stare decisis* rule, so as to bring all law in line with the Constitution. In a sense, therefore, the Constitution (and the constitutionalisation of property) becomes the instrument or the prism through which all of property law and all property institutions are reformed and transformed to fit a new, value-laden and legitimate constitutional order.

This possibility opens up issues that were not considered by Nedelsky: not only can a substantive and value-oriented constitutional debate about constitutional property avoid the libertarian and privatist guarantee-orientation to which Nedelsky objects, it can act as the catalyst for the transformation of common law, thereby bringing about a much stronger and more fundamental move away from the myth of property as a natural, pre-political right. Of course there are no guarantees – neither foreign constitutional jurisprudence nor the South African Constitution provides guarantees that a limitation-oriented jurisprudence of constitutional (and common law) property will be developed or accepted. But, and this is my point, the absence of a constitutional property clause cannot guarantee that a suitable public debate about property and politics or a suitable limitation-oriented property jurisprudence will develop on the basis of common law either, and the chances of a large-scale revolution in common law property seems to me to be much lower in the absence of a substantive constitutional debate than with it. On the contrary, if the signs of a reactionary flight away from constitutionalism and towards deciding property issues on the basis of common law is anything to go by,[149] I would say that common law

---

[148] The Preamble and ss. 7, 36 and 39 of the 1996 Constitution are examples.
[149] See the opinion of Scalia J in *Lucas v. South Carolina Coastal Council* 505 US 1003 (1992) at B [5]–[6]; and cf. R. Epstein, *Takings: Private Property and the Power of Eminent Domain*

entrenches the myth of private property as a pre-political right, and with it the divide between public and private spheres, much stronger than the property clause does.[150]

So, what are we left with? No easy answers or simple guarantees, unfortunately. Neither the exclusion nor the inclusion of a property clause in the bill of rights can or will guarantee a morally, legally or politically legitimate and equitable system of property institutions and property rights. As in so many other instances, social, political and moral goals will not be protected or promoted automatically through existing legal institutions and procedures, and hard questions about justice and equity will have to be answered and decided the hard way in every individual case.

(Cambridge, Harvard University Press, 1985), p. 57 et seq.; R. Epstein, *Simple Rules for a Complex World* (Cambridge, Harvard University Press, 1995) 53 et seq., 275 et seq.; J. V. DeLong, *Property Matters: How Property Rights are Under Assault—and Why You Should Care* (New York, Free Press, 1997) for examples.

[150] See in this regard A. J. van der Walt, "Un-doing Things with Words: The Colonization of the Public Sphere by Private Property Discourse", (1998) *Acta Juridica* 235.

7

The Human Rights Act (UK) and Property Law

TOM ALLEN*

With the passage of the Human Rights Act, Parliament gave effect in domestic law to the European Convention on Human Rights. Although the Human Rights Act does not give the courts the power to declare legislation invalid or inoperative, it does require them to consider the Convention when interpreting statutes. In addition, it will require public authorities to act in a manner that is compatible with the Convention. The Act is expected to come into force in early 2000, and it has already produced a substantial literature on the impact it is likely to have on British law. This chapter focuses on the impact of the Act on the English law of property.

It begins with a brief overview of the Convention rights that are most likely to have the greatest impact on the English law of property. While it concentrates on the Convention's right to property, it also considers other rights that may have an effect on English property law. The chapter then shifts to a discussion of the principal sections of the Human Rights Act that will give the Convention effect in domestic cases, and it closes with several illustrations of areas of law that may require re-examination in the light of the Act.

I. CONVENTION RIGHTS RELEVANT TO PROPERTY

There is no doubt that the Convention standards apply to many areas of property law. Indeed, since 1966, when the United Kingdom allowed the right of individual petition, it has had to defend legislation covering topics as diverse as the nationalisation of the steel and shipbuilding industries,[1] leasehold enfranchisement,[2] rent controls,[3] planning regulation,[4] and the confiscation and forfeiture of property in relation to the enforcement of criminal law and taxation.[5]

---

* I would like to thank Ian Leigh for his comments on this paper. Any errors are of course my own.
[1] *A, B, C and D v. UK* (1967) 10 *Yearbook* 506 and *Lithgow* v. *UK*, Ser A no. 102 (1986).
[2] *James* v. *UK*, Ser A no. 98 (1986).
[3] *Kilbourn* v. *UK* (1986) 8 EHRR 81.
[4] *Bryan* v. *UK*, Ser A no. 335–A (1995); *Gillow* v. *UK*, Ser A no. 109 (1986); *Buckley* v. *UK* (1997) 23 EHRR 101.
[5] *Handyside* v. *UK*, Ser A no. 24 (1976), 1 EHRR 737; *AGOSI* v. *UK* Ser A no. 108 (1986).

In most of these cases, however, the United Kingdom was successful. Hence, it remains unclear whether the Convention, as applied through the mechanisms of the Human Rights Act, will have a tremendous impact on property law.

Article 1 of the First Protocol: the peaceful enjoyment of possessions[6]

In relation to property, the most important Convention right is contained in Article 1 of the First Protocol, which reads as follows:

> "Every natural or legal person is entitled to the peaceful enjoyment of his possessions. No one shall be deprived of his possessions except in the public interest and subject to the conditions provided for by law and by the general principles of international law.
>
> The preceding provisions shall not, however, in any way impair the right of a state to enforce such laws as it deems necessary to control the use of property in accordance with the general interest or to secure the payment of taxes or other contributions or penalties".

It might be thought that the range of interests protected by the Protocol is quite narrow, since the first sentence only refers to the "*enjoyment* of possessions", and the final sentence allows controls over the "*use* of property". However, the European Court of Human Rights has held that the Protocol applies to other property rights, such as the rights to acquire and dispose of property.[7] It is also clear that "possessions" is not restricted to ownership interests. For example, a security interest in goods is a possession[8] and it now appears that a pending civil claim may also be treated as a possession, but the point is not free from doubt.[9] The Commission has said that social security claims may be treated as possessions, but only if there is a direct link between contributions made by the claimant and the entitlement to the claim.[10] In general, however, a claim is not a possession in the absence of a direct link. In this respect, its position is similar to that of the courts of the USA and many Commonwealth countries.

In *Sporrong and Lönnroth* v. *Sweden*, the European Court stated that Article 1 of the Protocol sets out three rules regarding rights to property: [11]

---

[6] See generally D. J. Harris, M. O'Boyle and C. Warbrick, *Law of the European Convention on Human Rights* (London, Butterworths, 1995); A. J. Van der Walt, "Council of Europe", in *Constitutional Property Clauses: A Comparative Analysis* (Kenwyn, SA, Juta & Co, forthcoming); W. Peukert, "Protection of Ownership under Article of the First Protocol to the European Convention on Human Rights", (1981) 2 *Human Rights Law Journal* 37.

[7] *Inze Case* Ser A no. 126 (1988) (acquisition by intestate succession) and *Marckx Case* Ser A no. 31 (1979), para. 63 (disposition by will).

[8] *Gasus Dosier-Und Fördertechnik GmbH* v. *Netherlands*, Ser A no. 306-B (1995), para. 53.

[9] See *Pressos Compania Naviera SA* (1996) 21 EHRR 301, para. 31; but cf. *National and Provincial Building Society* v. *UK* (1998) 25 EHRR 127; *British-American Tobacco Company Ltd.* v. *The Netherlands*, Ser A no. 331 (1996), *Agneessesns* v. *Belgium* 58 DR 63 (1988) and *A, B and Company AS* v. *Federal Republic of Germany* 14 DR 146 (1978).

[10] See *X* v. *UK* (1970) 13 *Yearbook* 892; *X* v. *The Netherlands* (1971) 14 *Yearbook* 224; *Müller* v. *Austria* [1976] 3 DR 25.

[11] Ser A no. 52 (1982), para. 61.

"The first rule, which is of general nature, enounces the principle of peaceful enjoyment of property; it is set out in the first sentence of the paragraph. The second rule covers deprivation of possessions and subjects it to certain conditions; it appears in the second sentence of the same paragraph. The third rule recognises the States are entitled, amongst other things, to control the use of property in accordance with the general interest, by enforcing such laws as they deem necessary to that purpose; it is contained in the second paragraph".

The function of Rule 1 is somewhat unclear. Wolfgang Peukert argues that it represents an institutional guarantee of private property,[12] but it seems that it imposes a general rule of proportionality against which all interferences with property under the second and third rules must be justified.[13] Rule 2 covers the expropriation of property, and Rule 3 covers matters such as the regulation and limitation of property rights. While the second sentence refers to the "deprivation" of possessions, not every deprivation is a deprivation under the second rule. For example, the confiscation or seizure of property for the enforcement of criminal or tax legislation would be examined under Rule 3 rather than Rule 2, even though the deprivation of property is total.[14] However, it is not always necessary to make a sharp distinction between the second and third rules. In *Sporrong and Lönnroth*, the Court also stated that the three rules are not distinct, and all three reflect the general principle that there must be a "fair balance" between "the demands of the general interest of the community and the requirements of the protection of the individual's fundamental rights".[15] In this respect, the right to property reflects the general idea of proportionality that applies to all Convention rights.

The proportionality test requires the infringement of the applicant's rights to be weighed against the public interest. Under Rule 2, the entitlement to compensation is given considerable weight. Under Rule 3, process has greater weight, since the purpose of many of the measures that fall under Rule 3 would be negated if compensation was payable.[16] However, even under Rule 2, full compensation is not always necessary to achieve a fair balance. For example, in *James* v. *UK*, the Court stated that: [17]

"[l]egitimate objectives of 'public interest', such as pursued in measures of economic reform or measures designed to achieve greater social justice, may call for less than reimbursement of the full market value".

[12] See W. Peukert, above n. 6, at 51–52.

[13] See generally A. J. van der Walt, above n. 6.

[14] *See e.g.*, *AGOSI* v. *UK* Ser A, no. 108 (1986); *Air Canada* v. *UK*, Ser A no. 316-A. In addition, a deprivation that occurs under ordinary principles of private law is also beyond the scope of the Convention: *App No. 11949/86* v. *UK*, (1988) 10 EHRR 149.

[15] Ser A no. 52 (1982), para. 69.

[16] For example, the purpose of forfeiture or tax enforcement measures would be frustrated if compensation had to be paid; accordingly, the emphasis shifts to the procedure by which forfeiture is ordered. See e.g., *Handyside* v. *UK*, Ser A no. 24 (1976) and *AGOSI* v. *UK*, Ser A no. 108.

[17] Ser A no. 98 (1986), para. 54.

Similarly, in *Lithgow* v. *UK*, the Court stated that the complexity of nationalising an industry could justify a departure from the measure of compensation applicable to the typical compulsory purchase of land.[18] Moreover, the "interests of legal certainty" justify a degree of arbitrariness in valuation. In this respect, the Protocol differs from the right to property under the written constitutions of the USA and most Commonwealth countries, where expropriation requires full compensation. Indeed, although *James* v. *UK* and *Lithgow* v. *UK* concern British legislation, Parliament normally entitles expropriatees to full compensation for their property. Furthermore, the English courts generally presume that a simple reference to "compensation" should be read as a reference to full compensation. Hence, it seems unlikely that formal expropriations of property would raise controversial issues under the Convention or the Human Rights Act. Controversy is more likely to arise in relation to indirect or informal "expropriations" of property. This covers situations such as confiscatory taxation and highly restrictive planning laws, which would normally be treated as "controls on use" under Rule 3. Less weight is given to compensation under Rule 3 than to the process by which the national authorities made the relevant decisions. However, in *Sporrong and Lönnroth* the Court stated that it would apply Rule 2 in circumstances where the individual is deprived of all, or substantially all, of the enjoyment of property, even if no formal expropriation occurred.

On Rule 3, the Court has tended to give national authorities greater leeway than it has under Rule 2. It asks whether national authorities considered the applicant's interests in making the decision to interfere with its property rights, but as long as the authorities did consider the applicant's interests, the Court is unlikely to decide against the State.[19] In general, the impact on the applicant must be quite severe for the State to be found in breach of Rule 3. Even so, the Court held against innocent victims of forfeiture and confiscation proceedings in *AGOSI* v. *UK*[20] and *Air Canada* v. *UK*.[21] One case where the decision went in favour of the applicant was *Gillow* v. *UK*.[22] Here, the applicant wished to occupy a house in Guernsey, which he owned and had occupied before letting it to tenants. However, after he left the property, legislation came into effect which restricted the right of residence in Guernsey. His application for a residence permit was refused. The Commission accepted the Government's claim that the restrictions on residency served the public interest, and it stated that the

---

[18] Ser A no. 102 (1986), para. 120–121. See also *Pressos Compania Naviera SA* (1996) 21 EHRR 301, para. 43, on the point that the state may legitimately take into account its financial position.

[19] See e.g., the Commission's opinion in *Bryan* v. *UK* Ser A no. 335–A (1995) (on appeal, the Court only considered Art. 6).

[20] *AGOSI* v. *UK,* Ser A, no. 108 (1986).

[21] Although in *AGOSI*, ibid., para. 54, the Court stated that "[t]he striking of a fair balance depends on many factors and the behaviour of the owner of the property, including the degree of fault or care which he has displayed, is one element of the entirety of circumstances which should be taken into account".

[22] Ser A no. 109 (1986).

standard by which the specific restrictions had to be justified was not as strict as it would be under Rule 2. In a case involving controls on use, it would give considerable weight to the severity of the restrictions imposed, taking into account factors such as the applicant's original purpose for acquiring the property and the suitability of alternative uses. However, while the Commission said that it would ordinarily defer to the judgement of national authorities, in this case the applicant's close personal connection with the house, and the lack of any reasonable alternative use for the house, meant that the prohibition on this occupation of it as his home was a very severe restriction and hence disproportionate.[23]

It can be difficult to predict whether the European Court would evaluate a set of facts under Rule 2 or Rule 3. For example, in *National and Provincial Building Society* v. *UK*,[24] the Court applied Rule 3 to the extinction of the applicant's claim to restitution of money paid on account of invalidated taxes; however, in *Hentrich* v. *France*,[25] the pre-emption of land as part of a scheme for the enforcement of taxes was considered under Rule 2. In this respect, there is a close similarity with the American law regarding the scope of the takings clause of the Fifth Amendment and the due process clause of the Fourteenth Amendment. In general terms, the takings clause corresponds to Rule 2 of Article 1 of the First Protocol, and the due process clause corresponds to Rule 3. In the landmark case *Pennsylvania Coal* v. *Mahon*,[26] the Supreme Court voiced its willingness to treat some types of regulation as takings, for which the Fifth Amendment requires compensation. In practice, the distinction between mere regulation and regulatory takings is very difficult to discern. The Supreme Court has refused to lay down rigid rules on the distinction, as it prefers to take an ad hoc approach to the issue.[27] However, it is clear that the Supreme Court is reluctant to treat regulation as a taking; in particular, regulation must deprive the owner of virtually all the economic value of property before it will be treated as such.[28] The European Court of Human Rights takes a similar approach, as it requires total or near-total deprivation of economic use, even though the principle that Rule 2 does not guarantee compensation in every case, or even full compensation, makes the distinction less important than it is in the USA.

---

[23] The case also went before the Court, where it was held that the Protocol did not apply to Guernsey, because it is a territory for which the United Kingdom is responsible for international relations; hence, an express declaration (which was never made) was required under Art. 4 of the Protocol to apply the Protocol to Guernsey.

[24] (1998) 25 EHRR 127.

[25] Ser A no. 296-A (1995).

[26] 260 US 393 (1922).

[27] See *Penn Central Transp. Co* v. *New York City* 438 US 104, 124 and *Goldblatt* v. *Hempstead* 369 US 590, 594.

[28] *Lucas* v. *South Carolina Coastal Council* 112 S Ct 2886 (1992) is regarded as making the doctrine more generous to property owners, but the diminution of value was almost complete in any case (see W. W. Fisher, III, "The Trouble with *Lucas*", (1993) 45 *Stan L Rev* 1193 and R. J. Lazarus, "Putting the Correct 'Spin' on *Lucas*", (1993) 45 *Stan L Rev* 1411).

When dealing with this issue under the Human Rights Act, British courts must take guidance from the Strasbourg jurisprudence.[29] The question is not entirely new to British judges, however, as it also arises under Commonwealth rights to property. British judges have expressed approval of the principle in *Pennsylvania Coal* in several cases.[30] The most recent statement was made in *La Compagnie Sucriere de Bel Ombre Ltee* v. *The Government of Mauritius*, where Lord Woolf stated that it was not necessary for regulation to reduce property to a "valueless shell" before it would be treated as a compensatable acquisition of property.[31] However, in that case, the Privy Council refused to treat restrictions on a landlord's freedom to deal with land after the expiry of a lease as an acquisition of property. Instead, Lord Woolf said that the restrictions were analogous to a control on use, under Rule 3 of the Protocol. It seems likely, therefore, that British courts would treat regulation as a compensatable deprivation of property only in extreme cases.

Article 6(1): Access to courts

Article 6(1) provides that:

> "In the determination of his civil rights and obligations or of any criminal charge against him, everyone is entitled to a fair and public hearing within a reasonable time by an independent and impartial tribunal established by law".

Many Convention cases on the enjoyment of possessions also involve a claim that Article 6(1) has been breached. For example, a lengthy delay in determining the amount of compensation payable on the expropriation of property could amount to a breach of Article 6(1).[32] Similarly, an adverse decision from a planning tribunal might raise issues under both the First Protocol and Article 6(1).[33]

As explained above, there is some uncertainty over whether private law causes of action should be treated as "possessions" under Article 1 of the First Protocol. Under the constitutional law of many Commonwealth countries, such claims would probably be treated as property, and hence the extinction of the

---

[29]   Section 2(1).

[30]   See e.g., *Belfast* v. *OD Cars* [1960] AC 490, 519, per Viscount Simonds and *La Compagnie Sucriere de Bel Ombre Ltee* v. *The Government of Mauritius* [1995] 3 LRC 494 (PC), 502–506; and see also *Selangor Pilot Association (1946)* v. *Government of Malaysia* [1978] AC 337 (PC-Malaysia), 358, per Lord Salmon (dissenting).

[31]   [1995] 3 LRC 494, 506.

[32]   See e.g., *Ruiz-Mateos* v. *Spain* (1993) 16 EHRR 505.

[33]   See e.g., *Bryan* v. *UK*, Ser A no. 335–A (1995), where the Court stated that a planning inspector's review of an enforcement notice issued under the Town and Country Planning Act 1990 was not, of itself, a hearing by an "independent and impartial tribunal", if only because the Secretary of State has the power to withdraw a case from an inspector at any time (para. 38). However, the availability of an appeal to the High Court, although only on a point of law, ensured that ultimately the applicant would receive a hearing by an independent and impartial tribunal, because the High Court would consider whether the planning inspector had acted independently (paras. 39–47).

claim would be treated as a deprivation of property.[34] Under the Convention, there is some doubt that the Protocol would apply to this situation. However, there is no real doubt that Article 6(1) would apply. *National and Provincial Building Society* v. *UK*, for example, concerned the extinction of claims for restitution of unlawfully imposed taxes: while the Court did not express a view on whether the claims were "possessions" under the Protocol, it did treat the claims as "civil rights" for the purposes of Article 6(1).[35]

A further issue concerns the reference to "civil" rights. As explained above, the Court has stated that social security entitlements are "possessions" under the Protocol only where contributions are directly linked to the entitlement. The Court has also said Article 6(1) does not apply to public law claims; however, in *Feldbrugge* v. *Netherlands*[36] it held that statutory claims to social insurance had both public and private features, but the private features were predominant. The Court indicated that not every social insurance scheme would have a sufficient private element, but it listed several aspects of this particular scheme that cumulatively gave the statutory claims the character of a civil right under Article 6(1). First, "the right in question was a personal, economic and individual right",[37] and the interference with the right affected the applicant's means of subsistence. It did not arise merely from the exercise of a discretionary power, but from a positive statutory right. Secondly, her position was "closely linked" with her private contract of employment, even though the specific right arose under statute.[38] In addition, the scheme operated, in many respects, like a private insurance scheme. In particular, the applicant had contributed to the scheme through deductions from her salary.[39]

Subsequently, in *Salesi* v. *Italy*,[40] the Court suggested that only some of the aspects of the scheme considered in *Feldbrugge* were important. In this case, the applicant argued that a statutory right to social assistance for those unfit to work should be treated as a civil right under Article 6(1). Italy maintained that the applicant's claim to social assistance was a public law claim, because it was not connected with a private law contract and she had not contributed to the scheme. However, the Court stated that "she suffered an interference with her means of subsistence and was claiming an individual, economic right flowing from specific rules laid down in a statute".[41] In *Schuler-Zgraggen v. Switzerland*, the Court commented that, in the light of *Feldbrugge* and similar decisions: [42]

---

[34] See generally T. Allen, *The Right to Property in Commonwealth Constitutions*, ch. 5, 6 (Cambridge, Cambridge University Press, forthcoming), chs. 5, 6.

[35] (1998) 25 EHRR 127. (The Court also found that, assuming that the claims were possessions, there was no violation of the Protocol in any event.)

[36] Ser A no. 99 (1986), paras. 36–40. See also *Deumeland* v. *Federal Republic of Germany*, Ser A vol 100 (1986) paras. 70–74.

[37] Ser A no. 99 (1986), para. 37.

[38] Ibid., para. 38.

[39] Ibid., para. 39.

[40] Ser A no. 257-E (1993).

[41] Ibid., para. 19.

[42] Ser A no. 263 (1993) para. 46.

"the principle of equality of treatment warrant[s] taking the view that today the general rule is that Article 6(1) does apply in the field of social insurance, including even welfare assistance".

While the Court seems to be extending Article 6(1) to some public law claims, its approach is not radically different from that of courts of other countries. In some respects, its approach follows Charles Reich's seminal argument on the "new property".[43] Reich argued that social security and other state benefits had assumed such importance in the lives of most individuals that it deserved protection as property under the Bill of Rights of the United States. In the United States, however, describing an interest as "property" would give it protection under both the takings and due process clauses. This would mean that, under the takings clause, a claim to social security or other benefits could not be extinguished or modified without compensation. This, for the courts in the United States, would go too far, and they have decided that social security and assistance claims should be treated as "property" for the purpose of the due process guarantee of the Fourteenth Amendment, but not for the takings clause.[44] The position under the Convention is similar, although the Court has concluded that these claims are not normally protected as "possessions" under Article 1 of the First Protocol. Instead, they are merely "civil rights" under Article 6.

Article 8: Family life

Article 8 provides that:

"1. Everyone has the right to respect for his private and family life, his home and his correspondence.
2. There shall be no interference by a public authority with the exercise of this right except such as is in accordance with the law and is necessary in a democratic society in the interests of national security, public safety or the economic well-being of the country, for the prevention of disorder or crime, for the protection of health or morals, or for the protection of the rights and freedoms of others".

The right to respect for the home often raises issues that, in English law, might be regarded as issues of property law. Indeed, under the Convention, some cases on Article 8 have also involved issues under Article 1 of the First Protocol. The *Gillow* case is one example. On appeal from the Commission, the Court found that there was no breach of the Protocol (on the basis that the Protocol did not apply to Guernsey), but that there was a breach of Article 8.[45]

Article 8 confers both a negative right to freedom from unreasonable state interference with respect for family life and the home, and a positive right to protection from unreasonable interference by other parties. Hence, in a series of

---

[43] "The New Property", (1964) 73 *Yale L J* 733.
[44] See e.g., *Flemming* v. *Nestor* 363 US 603 (1960).
[45] *Gillow* v. *UK*, Ser A no. 109 (1986).

applications involving the interference caused by noise from Heathrow, the Commission stated that: [46]

> "It has to be noted that a State not only has to respect but also to protect the rights guaranteed by Article 8(1). Considerable noise nuisance can undoubtedly affect the physical well-being of a person and thus interfere with his private life. It may also deprive a person of the possibility of enjoying the amenities of his home".

This was confirmed by the Court in *Lopez Ostra* v. *Spain*, where it held the state responsible for a nuisance caused by a third party's plants because "the town allowed the plants to be built on its land and the State subsidised the plant's construction".[47]

Under English law, the interests in family life and the home are protected under different areas of law, and the degree to which Article 8 challenges the English approach depends on the particular area of law involved. For example, in planning law, the impact of a proposed industrial development on the neighbourhood is likely to be a consideration that the relevant body would be expected to take into account in reaching a decision. As such, judicial review of planning decisions provides some protection for family life and the family home. However, if Parliament allows ordinary procedures to be bypassed, the courts may have no effective power to protect these interests. This is most frequently seen under private Acts, which often confer the authority to engage in activities that would otherwise require planning permission or constitute an actionable nuisance under private law.

Another area where interests in family life and the family home often fail to receive full consideration is the private law of property. In English law, an occupier without possession or title to the dwelling would find it difficult to protect the interests covered by Article 8. In *Hunter* v. *Canary Wharf*, for example, the House of Lords affirmed that mere occupants have no right to bring a claim in nuisance, even if there has been an interference with their family life and enjoyment of their home.[48] Other disputes over dwellings, such as those between the creditor and owner, are framed in a way that excludes family interests from consideration.[49] By contrast, the Convention right to respect of the home is separate from proprietary rights. This has two implications. First, a dwelling can be a "home", under Article 8, even if it is not occupied lawfully. In *Buckley* v. *UK*, the Commission stated that: [50]

---

[46] *Powell* v. *UK*, App No. 9310/81, 9 EHRR 241, 242; see also *Baggs* v. *UK*, App No. 9310/81, 9 EHRR 235 and *Rayner* v. *UK*, App No. 9310/81, 9 EHRR 350. See also *Arondelle* v. *UK*, Report of the Commission, 26 DR 5 (friendly settlement).

[47] (1995) 20 EHRR 277.

[48] *Hunter* v. *Canary Wharf* [1997] AC 655, where the House of Lords rejected the reasoning of *Khorasandjian* v. *Bush* [1993] QB 727 on this point.

[49] See below, on bankruptcy and the family home.

[50] (1995) 19 EHRR CD 20, para. 63. On appeal, the Court agreed (see (1997) 23 EHRR 101, para. 54), but found that refusal to grant planning permission did not violate Art. 8. See also *Gillow* v. *UK*, Ser A no. 109 (1986), where the house was the applicant's "home", even though he occupied it without the requisite planning permission.

"the concept of 'home' within the meaning of Article 8 is not limited to those which are lawfully occupied or which have been lawfully established. 'Home' is an autonomous concept which does not depend on classification under domestic law. Whether or not a particular habitation constitutes a 'home' which attracts the protection of Article 8(1) will depend on the factual circumstances, namely the existence of sufficient and continuous links".

Secondly, ownership or a right to possession of property does not necessarily carry the right to occupy it as a home. In *Velosa Barreto* v. *Portugal*, a landlord who wished to occupy his property as his home argued that Portugal had infringed Article 8 by enacting laws that gave his tenants security of tenure. While the Court acknowledged that Article 8 includes positive obligations, it also stated that: [51]

"effective protection of respect for private and family life cannot require the existence in national law of legal protection enabling each family to have a home for themselves alone. It does not go so far as to place the State under an obligation to give a landlord the right to recover possession of a rented house on request and in any circumstances".

Hence, a landlord who wishes to evict tenants in order to occupy the property as his or her home would be relying on his or her proprietary rights, where the focus would be on the proportionality of any restriction on his or her proprietary rights under Article 1 of the First Protocol.[52]

II.   THE HUMAN RIGHTS ACT AND THE CONVENTION

While the Human Rights Act incorporates the Convention into British law, it falls short of giving the courts the power to declare legislation invalid or inoperative. Instead, the implementation of the Convention by the courts will rely primarily on the obligations imposed by sections 3 and 6.

Section 3: Interpretation of legislation

Section 3 states that "[s]o far as it is possible to do so, primary legislation and subordinate legislation must be read and given effect in a way which is compatible with the Convention rights". As such, it does not represent a radical change in the British approach to protecting rights, as the courts have often stated that they take fundamental rights into account in the interpretation of legislation. In

[51] Ser A no. 334 (1995), para. 24. The Court and the Commission accepted the determination of the Portuguese courts that the landlord already had adequate housing for his family. It is not clear whether the result would have differed if he did not have alternative housing; i.e., whether his proprietary right would have strengthened his Art. 8 claim.

[52] It is unlikely, however, that the Court would treat security of tenure as a disproportionate interference with the landlord's property rights, except in unusual circumstances. See *Spadea and Scalabrino* v. *Italy*, Ser A no. 315–B (1996) and *Scollo* v. *Italy*, Ser A no. 315–C (1996).

particular, there is a presumption that Parliament does not intend to authorise the deprivation of property without compensation, unless the statute contains clear language to that effect.[53] To some extent, this presumption mirrors the protection now provided by section 3 of the Act, when used in combination with Article 1 of the First Protocol. Other presumptions reflect other Convention rights that can relate to property rights: for example, Articles 6 and 8 are reflected in the presumptions that Parliament does not intend to interfere with access to the courts or with family life and the home.[54]

Section 3 of the Human Rights Act also reflects the presumption that Parliament intends to legislate in conformity with the United Kingdom's obligations under international law.[55] Indeed, the Human Rights Act is not the first example of legislation that incorporates fundamental rights under international law. The European Communities Act 1972 indirectly incorporates a right to property, since it incorporates Community law. Although the EC Treaty does not expressly protect a right to property, the European Court of Justice has stated that "respect for fundamental rights forms an integral part of the general principles of law protected by the Court of Justice".[56] As evidence of these general principles, the European Court of Justice looks to the constitutional traditions common to Member States and the international treaties on which the Member States have collaborated or of which they are signatories. The European Convention on Human Rights is the most important example of such a treaty. In the light of the protection of property under both Article 1 of the First Protocol and under the constitutions of many Member States, the Court has declared that: [57]

> "[t]he right to property is guaranteed in the Community legal order in accordance with the ideas common to the constitutions of the Member States, which are also reflected in the first Protocol to the European Convention for the Protection of Human Rights".

Since the European Communities Act 1972 incorporates: [58] "[a]ll such rights, powers, liabilities, obligations and restrictions from time to time created or

[53] See e.g., *A-G* v. *De Keyser's Royal Hotel Ltd.* [1920] AC 508, 542 and *Mayor of Yarmouth* v. *Simmons* (1878) 10 ChD 518, 527.

[54] See *R* v. *Lord Chancellor, ex parte Witham* [1998] QB 575 (DC) (discussed below) and F .A. R. Bennion, *Statutory Interpretation: Codified, with a Critical Commentary*, 3rd edn. (London, Butterworths, 1997), pp. 648–649, 873–876.

[55] Although under section 3, it is clear that the interpretive obligation applies to pre-Convention legislation. It was uncertain whether this was the case previously: *R* v. *Brown* [1994] 1 AC 212, 256 per Lord Lowry. The courts have used the Convention to resolve ambiguities in legislation; however, they tended to use it to confirm the position at common law, rather than to challenge it. See, in particular, *R* v. *Home Secretary, ex parte Brind* [1991] 1 AC 696 (HL), 746 per Lord Bridge and 760 per Lord Ackner; cf. *Rantzen* v. *Mirror Group Newspapers Ltd.* [1994] QB 670 (CA) with *John* v. *Mirror Group Newpapers* [1996] 3 WLR 593, 619 (CA).

[56] *Internationale Handelsgesellshaft* [1970] ECR 1125, 1134.

[57] *Hauer* v. *Land Rheinland-Pfalz* [1979] ECR 3727, 3744.

[58] European Communities Act 1972, s 2(1).

arising by or under the [Community] Treaties", It also incorporates a right to property in areas of British law that are within the scope of Community law.[59]

This is demonstrated by the recent Scottish case, *Booker Aquaculture Ltd* v. *Secretary of State for Scotland.*[60] In this case, the Secretary of State exercised his powers under regulation 7 of the Diseases of Fish (Control) Regulations 1994[61] to order the destruction of all fish belonging to the petitioner, following the outbreak of a disease ("VHS") in his stocks. The Regulations implemented an EC directive for the control of fish diseases.[62] The Secretary of State's policy under the Regulations was to order the destruction of all fish following an outbreak of VHS, although the EC directive did not go so far because it did not require the destruction of fish that were not infected with VHS. The petitioner claimed that he should have been compensated for the destruction of the fish that were not infected, but the Secretary of State took that view that the Regulations did not confer a legal right to compensation and that "the Government's long established policy of non payment of compensation for fish diseases" meant that no ex gratia payment should be made. The Court held that the Regulations fell within the scope of European Community law on the control of fish diseases, and since fundamental rights are part of European Community law, national rules intended to give effect to the general interest pursued by the Community must not constitute, "with regard to the aim pursued, a disproportionate and intolerable interference, impairing the very substance of those rights". Accordingly, the Court held that the Secretary of State had the discretion to apply the disease control measures:

> "in such a way as not to interfere with the fundamental principle of freedom of property further than is necessary for the protection of the interests which those measures were designed to safeguard".

In this case, no consideration was given to the particular circumstances surrounding the outbreak of disease; in particular, it would have been possible to satisfy EC law without ordering the destruction of all of the petitioner's fish. Accordingly, compensation should have been given for fish that did not need to be destroyed to satisfy EC law.

Just how far the courts will take section 3 of the Human Rights Act, particularly in the context of property rights, remains to be seen. At one time, the courts construed statutory powers of expropriation very narrowly. As such, the presumptions of interpretation did not serve the same function as grammatical rules of construction. There are modern examples of cases where courts have used presumptions of statutory interpretation in this way. For example, in *R* v.

---

[59] European Communities Act 1972, s 2(4) "any enactment passed or to be passed, other than one contained in this Part of this Act, shall be construed and have effect subject to the foregoing provisions of this section".

[60] 1998 Greens Weekly Digest 21–1089 (Court of Session, Outer House, 28 May 1998).

[61] SI 1994/1447.

[62] Directive 93/53/EEC.

Lord Chancellor, ex parte Witham,[63] the court strained the language of the Supreme Court Act 1981 in order to limit the Lord Chancellor's power to prescribe fees for issuing a writ in the Supreme Court. The court held that the Lord Chancellor had set the fees so high that he had effectively taken the right of court access from some litigants. Laws J reiterated the principle that general language will not suffice to abrogate a constitutional right and even went as far as saying that the right of access to the courts is so important that it can only be abrogated by express language; that is, it cannot be abrogated by necessary implication.[64]

While *Witham* indicates that section 3 does not introduce a new method of protecting rights, it should be noted that the importance of the presumptions that relate to property has declined in recent years. The presumption that Parliament does not intend to interfere with property rights is treated more as a guideline for ascertaining of the statute's "true" meaning. For example, in *A-G Canada* v. *Hallet & Carey Ltd.*, Lord Radcliffe stated that:[65]

"[t]here are many so-called rules of construction that courts of law have resorted to in their interpretation of statutes, but the paramount rule remains that every statue is to be expounded according to its manifest or expressed intention".

Since the most logical reading of the statute, taken as a whole, suggested that the Canadian authorities had the power to expropriate certain types of property without compensation, no compensation was payable. More recently, in *Secretary of State for Defence* v. *Guardian Newspapers Ltd.*[66] Lord Scarman stated that: [67]

"there certainly remains a place in the law for the principle of construction . . . that the courts must be slow to impute to Parliament an intention to override property rights in the absence of plain words to that effect. But the principle is not an overriding rule of law: it is an aid, amongst many others, developed by the judges in their never ending task of interpreting statutes in such a way as to give effect to their true purpose".

By contrast, the opening words of section 3 make it clear that it is not merely an "aid, amongst many others" for giving effect to the "true purpose" of legislation. Hence, in relation to property, section 3 of the Human Rights Act seems to swing the pendulum closer to the *Witham* approach to interpretation and fundamental rights. As such, it could justify interpretations that do not accord with the "true purpose" of legislation (or, at least not the interpretation that would follow from the application of the ordinary principles of construction).

Section 6: Public authorities

[63] [1998] QB 575 (DC), noted by R. English, "Wrongfooting the Lord Chancellor: Access to Justice in the High Court", (1998) 61 *Mod LR* 245.
[64] [1998] QB 575, 585–586.
[65] [1952] AC 427, 449 (PC) per Lord Radcliffe.
[66] [1985] AC 339 (HL).
[67] Ibid., 363 (dissenting on another point).

In *R* v. *Home Secretary, ex parte Brind*,[68] the House of Lords rejected the argument that public authorities were bound to act in a manner compatible with the Convention. When the Human Rights Act comes into force, this position will be reversed, as section 6(1) provides that "[i]t is unlawful for a public authority to act in a way that is incompatible with a Convention right". Section 7(1) entitles the victim of the unlawful act to bring proceedings against the public authority or to rely on the Convention rights in any legal proceedings. At common law, the victim of unlawful administrative action can petition for an injunction to prevent an unlawful deprivation of property before it occurs. If a deprivation of property or other economic loss has already occurred, it may be possible to claim damages or restitution for any tortious interference with the property. However, there may be cases where no effective remedy is available. In particular, the common law does not recognise a general right to compensation for losses caused by *ultra vires* or invalid administrative acts. For example, unlawful planning decisions may result in economic loss, but there is no general cause of action for recovery.[69] This point has been addressed by section 8 of the Human Rights Act, which states that, where the court finds that an act (or proposed act) of a public authority is unlawful under section 6, the court "may grant such relief or remedy, or make such order, within its jurisdiction as it considers just and appropriate". This includes an award of damages.

Sections 7 and 8 only apply to actions that are unlawful by reason of section 6. However, it is difficult to imagine how an unlawful interference with property would not come within section 6. Article 1 of the First Protocol states that any deprivation of property must be "subject to the conditions provided for by law" and only allows the State to enforce "such laws as it deems necessary to control the use of property". Hence, there may be actions that would be compatible with Convention rights if properly authorised by statute; however, absent such authority, they would be incompatible.

III. ILLUSTRATIONS

The impact of the Human Rights Act on property owners will depend on the nature of assets held and the purpose for which they are held. Large commercial enterprises are likely to rely on the Act for different reasons and in different circumstances than individuals. For individuals, the importance of the Act will probably depend on whether their significant assets are limited to their home and pension, or indeed, if their economic security depends entirely on the state for housing and income support. In the interests of space, we will concentrate

---

[68] [1991] 1 AC 696 (HL).

[69] See *e.g., Dunlop* v. *Woollahra Council* [1982] AC 158 and *Rowling* v. *Takaro Properties Ltd.* [1988] AC 473. There may be a claim for the tort of misfeasance in public office, but as it is necessary to show that the relevant officials knowingly exceeded or abused their powers, such cases are likely to be rare; see *Bourgoin* v. *Ministry of Agriculture* [1986] QB 716.

on the impact of the Act on individuals rather than corporate enterprises, and specifically on the interest held by individuals in a family home. To narrow the examination further, we examine two of the greatest threats to the investment in the family home. The first is an interruption in income, with the consequent threat of bankruptcy. The State seems to be removing itself from any responsibility it once assumed for supporting homeowners who have lost the income necessary to maintain themselves in a privately-owned home. Indeed, there are daily reminders of the need to make private arrangements for retirement, redundancy and disability insurance to cover the threat of the loss of income. One specific problem that this raises is the degree of security in the home, if any, that is given on personal bankruptcy. The second is the threat of a deterioration in the quality of the neighbourhood, as it can jeopardise the quality of life and the value of the home. Planning law, environmental law, land law and tort combine to regulate changes that affect the neighbourhood. In this section, we focus on tort law and the defence of statutory authority.

Illustration I: Bankruptcy and the family home

In most cases, it is in the creditors' interest that the house should be sold, usually as soon as possible. However, a quick sale affects spouses, partners, and dependant children and parents living in the home, and it may contribute to a breakdown in the family itself. Since Article 8 of the Convention protects the right to respect for family life and the home, it is worth asking whether English bankruptcy laws are compatible with these rights. While Parliament did not ignore family interests in drafting the Insolvency Act 1986, it did not include the kind of protective legislation found in many other common law jurisdictions.[70] The failure to include such protection would not, by itself, entitle an evicted family to redress under the Human Rights Act unless there is some ambiguity or discretion in the legislation which the courts could exploit in favour of family rights. However, it seems that the opposite has occurred: the Insolvency Act 1986 does contain provisions that the courts might exploit, but the interpretation of these provisions has almost uniformly ignored family rights to the home. Plainly, this is an area where the Human Rights Act could make a real difference.

Where the bankrupt or his or her family is in occupation, the trustee must apply for an order for possession and sale of the home. There are several different provisions that govern these orders, but the Insolvency Act 1986 directs the court to consider certain common factors when deciding whether to make

---

[70] See K. Gray, *Elements of Land Law*, 2nd edn. (London, Butterworths, 1993), pp. 604–606. Contrast the protection given to the home with the protection given to occupational pension rights, under s. 91(3) of the Pensions Act 1995, which provides that any entitlement or acccrued right to a pension is to be excluded from the holder's estate on bankruptcy (although there is a possibility of an income payments order: s. 91(4).)

the order. [71] There is a degree of security of tenure for one year after the first vesting of the bankrupt's estate in the trustee in bankruptcy, as the court must make such order "as it thinks just and reasonable", having regard to the interests of the creditors, the bankrupt's financial resources, the needs of the children and "all the circumstances of the case other than the needs of the bankrupt". [72] If the bankrupt has a spouse who has occupation rights under the Family Law Act 1996, the court must also consider "the conduct of the spouse or former spouse, so far as contributing to the bankruptcy [and] the needs and financial resources of the spouse or former spouse". [73]

Without going into detail, there may be some question whether the security in the first year satisfies the Convention. In particular, the court is not specifically directed to consider the interests or needs of cohabitees. [74] However, the real difficulties arise after the one-year period expires, because the Act requires the court to assume "unless the circumstances of the case are exceptional, that the interests of the bankrupt's creditors outweigh all other considerations". [75] This was taken from pre-Insolvency Act cases where a trustee in bankruptcy, having succeeded to the interest of a bankrupt co-owner, sought an order for sale of co-owned property. [76] In these cases, the courts stated that they would order a prompt sale unless there were "exceptional circumstances" for a postponement. [77] While the courts often claimed that they balanced commercial and family interests in determining whether circumstances were exceptional, they almost invariably decided that the commercial interests ought to prevail. The leading case was *In re Citro (A Bankrupt)*, where Nourse LJ stated that: [78]

> "it is not uncommon for a wife with young children to be faced with eviction in circumstances where the realisation of her beneficial interest will not produce enough to buy a comparable home. And, if she has to move elsewhere, there may be problems over schooling and so forth. Such circumstances, while engendering a natural sympathy in all who hear of them, cannot be described as exceptional. They are the melancholy consequences of debt and improvidence with which every civilised society has been familiar".

---

[71] The Insolvency Act 1986, s. 335A and the Trusts of Land and Appointment of Trustees Act 1996, s. 14 apply where the bankrupt owns the property with a spouse, cohabitee or other person; the Insolvency Act 1986, s. 336 and the Family Law Act 1996, s. 33 apply where the bankrupt's spouse has occupation rights under the Family Law Act 1996; the Insolvency Act 1986, s. 337 gives the bankrupt occupation rights and provides for orders for sale.

[72] Insolvency Act 1986, ss. 335A(2), 336(4), 337(5).

[73] Insolvency Act 1986, s. 336(4)(b) .

[74] This follows from the Insolvency Act 1986, ss. 335A(2)(b) and 336. While Article 8 of the Convention gives the highest degree of protection to married couples, the Court has recognised that cohabitation is still protected see e.g., *Marckx Case*, Ser A no. 31 (1979).

[75] Insolvency Act 1986, ss. 335A(3), 336(5), 367(6).

[76] Applications were made under the Law of Property Act 1925, s. 30 which has been replaced by the Trusts of Land and Appointment of Trustees Act 1996, s. 14.

[77] See e.g., *In re Citro (A Bankrupt)* [1991] Ch 142 (CA); *In re Bailey (A Bankrupt)* [1977] 1 WLR 278, and see generally Gray, above n. 70, at p. 599.

[78] [1991] Ch 142, 157.

Circumstances were considered exceptional in only one case, but even then, it was primarily because it was the debtor, rather than the creditors, who sought the order for sale.[79]

Although *In re Citro* did not concern the Insolvency Act 1986, Nourse LJ stated that the new provisions did not change the existing position. This has been borne out in several cases. In *Re Raval (A Bankrupt)*[80] and *Judd* v. *Brown (Re Bankrupts)*,[81] the courts were willing to postpone a sale where a forced move would cause serious harm to the health of a family member.[82] However, in these cases, the courts reiterated the principle that even a severe disruption of family life is not a sufficient reason for postponing the sale. Indeed, in *Trustee of the Estate of Eric Bowe (A Bankrupt)* v. *Bowe*,[83] neither the likelihood that the creditors would receive nothing from the sale of the family home, nor the fact that the bankrupt's ex-wife and five children, aged 20, 18, 21, 11 and 10, were all living in the home, were considered exceptional circumstances. The court ordered the sale, even though the proceeds would be used solely to pay the expenses of the trustee in bankruptcy.

Hence, as the law currently stands, the right to respect for family life and the home receives almost no consideration after the one-year period. Whether such a strict limitation is compatible with the Convention is doubtful. According to Article 8(2), limitations must be:

> "necessary in a democratic society in the interests of national security, public safety or the economic well-being of the country, for the prevention of disorder or crime, for the protection of health or morals, or for the protection of the rights and freedoms of others".

While the economic well-being of the country or the protection of the rights and freedoms of others would often justify the sale of the family home (especially after the one-year period), it is difficult to argue that they require a blanket exclusion of the right to respect of the family home in every case, especially since the rights of occupation merely postpone the eventual sale. Even the traditional concern of the courts for the interests of the creditors does not seem to justify the near-automatic eviction of the family. Although the European Court of Human Rights has not had the opportunity to comment on these provisions, it is interesting to note that it has held that legislation conferring security of tenure on tenants does not necessarily infringe the landlord's rights under the First Protocol.[84] Hence, it seems unlikely that the Court would give greater weight to

---

[79] *In re Holliday* [1981] Ch. 405 (CA), where postponement would not have caused any hardship to the creditors.

[80] [1998] 2 FLR 718 (Ch D).

[81] [1998] 2 FLR 360 (Ch D), leave to appeal granted 20 October 1997.

[82] See also *In re Holliday* [1981] Ch 405 (CA); and *Re Ng (A Bankrupt), Trustee of the Estate of Ng* v. *Ng* (1996), [1998] 2 FLR 386 (ChD): no sale would be ordered where trustee has no legitimate reason for applying for the order, or where the sale is clearly not in the interests of the creditors. Cf. *Trustee of the Estate of Eric Bowe (A Bankrupt)* v. *Bowe* (1994), [1998] 2 FLR 439 (Ch D).

[83] [1998] 2 FLR 439.

the trustee in bankruptcy's rights. There is also a strong argument that the real purpose of limiting the right to occupy the home is to punish and deter: the bankrupt must be seen not to enjoy the same lifestyle that he or she had before insolvency, even if the family must suffer as a consequence (and, from *Trustee of the Estate of Eric Bowe (A Bankrupt)* v. *Bowe*, even if the creditors are unlikely to gain anything as a result). Again, it seems doubtful that this could outweigh the Article 8 rights of other members of the bankrupt's family.

Since the current position is based on the interpretation of "exceptional circumstances", it would appear that section 3 of the Human Rights Act will require the courts to regard circumstances as "exceptional" if an immediate sale would infringe Article 8 rights. At the same time, section 3 does not allow the court to ignore statutory language that is clearly meant to have effect; hence, the new interpretation must admit the possibility that there would be at least some cases involving the sale of a dwelling house that do not involve "exceptional circumstances". However, this does not seem to raise any difficulties, for there will be cases where a sale after the one-year period would not infringe the Convention. It seems doubtful, for example, that Article 8 would be infringed by an order for the prompt sale of a home where there are no children and alternative accommodation is readily available.

If the court does conclude that circumstances are exceptional, it is left with little by way of explicit guidance in the Insolvency Act as to how it should deal with the trustee in bankruptcy's application for an order for sale, except that it must make such order as it thinks is "just and reasonable". At this point, the obligation under section 6 of the Act takes over, as the court must decide what is "just and reasonable" and that it is compatible with the Convention. In practical terms, it must decide how long the sale should be postponed, or indeed if any order for sale should be granted. Factors such as the severity of the impact on the family and the availability of alternative accommodation should have greater weight than they do now. Moreover, the court should acknowledge that the right to respect to family life and the home is held by all members of the family, and that a proprietary interest in the dwelling is not necessary for it to be one's "home" under Article 8. Hence, there should be greater consideration of the specific interests of children and cohabitees. For them, eviction from their home should not be merely one of the "melancholy consequences of debt and improvidence".[85]

Illustration II: Tort law, property law and the defence of statutory authority[86]

---

[84] See e.g., *Spadea and Scalabrino* v. *Italy*, Ser A no. 315–B and *Scollo* v. *Italy*, Ser A no. 315–C (1996).

[85] *In re Citro (A Bankrupt)* [1991] Ch 142, 157.

Statutory interpretation has an important effect on the law relating to defences to private nuisance. In those situations where a statute clearly restricts or excludes the right to bring an action for nuisance, there will be little or no scope for applying the Human Rights Act. However, the defence frequently arises by implication from provisions conferring the power to engage in the activities that cause the nuisance. The general principle is that a nuisance that is the inevitable result of exercising a statutory power to carry out specific acts is not actionable.[87] A body that acts under a statutory duty is in an even stronger position, for even if the statute expressly provides that there is no exemption from liability for nuisance, the courts will only impose liability for negligently caused nuisances.[88] Since the availability of the defence relies on the interpretation of the statutory power, section 3 of the Human Rights Act invites a re-examination of this area.

Plainly, the availability of a statutory defence to nuisance does not infringe the Convention unless there is a disproportionate balance between community and private interests. In general terms, the common law of nuisance embodies the principle that interests must be balanced. A nuisance is an unreasonable interference with the plaintiff's proprietary rights, and in determining whether the interference is unreasonable, the courts recognise that[89] "[a] balance has to be maintained between the right of the occupier to do what he likes with his own, and the right of his neighbour not to be interfered with". Nevertheless, there is a fundamental difference between the balance struck by the common law in ordinary nuisance cases and the proportionality test under the Convention. At common law, the community interest is not immediately relevant; in this sense, the common law provides greater protection than the Convention requires. However, the community interest comes into play in the defence of statutory authority, where it seems that the courts accept the legislature's determination that the activity does produce a significant benefit to the community.[90] The principle that the interference should be the minimum necessary to achieve the objective finds some recognition in the common law, since the defence of statutory authority is only available if the nuisance is an inevitable consequence of exercising the statutory power. Hence, it is not immediately obvious that there is any conflict with the Convention, at least in general

[86] See generally G. Kodilinye, "The Statutory Authority Defence in Nuisance Actions", (1990) 19 *Anglo-American L R* 72.

[87] See *City of Manchester* v. *Farnworth* [1930] AC 171, 183 (HL) per Viscount Dunedin.

[88] See *Department of Transport* v. *North West Water Authority* [1984] 1 AC 336, 359–360, per Lord Fraser. In general, English courts tend to find that a provision imposes a duty rather than a power to act, thereby extending the circumstances in which the defence is available: Kodilinye, above n. 86, at 75–79. There are statutes that mitigate the effects of the defence by providing a separate right to compensation, but many statutes do not. While the courts have construed some statutes quite generously, to provide compensation to landowners whose property is affected by the construction of works, there is no general principle that all statutes should be interpreted in this way: see generally K. Davies, "Injurious Affection and Compensation" (1974) 90 *L Q R* 361.

[89] *Sedleigh-Denfield* v. *O'Callaghan* [1940] AC 880, 903 per Lord Wright.

[90] Cf. Kodilinye, above n. 86, at 79.

principle. However, there are elements that the English courts either leave out of the balance or seem to give undue weight.

In particular, in addition to any interference with the individual's rights under the First Protocol, there may be an interference with the owner's Article 8 rights. Although the law of nuisance only seeks to protect proprietary interests, it can indirectly protect family interests. Where it does, the interpretation of statutes that restrict liability for nuisance must take Article 8 into account. This raises one difficult point about the Convention and the defence of statutory authority, since the proportionality of an interference with protected interests depends partly on the availability of procedures for challenging the interferences. In cases of statutory authority, the courts are not in a position to find that Parliament's procedures for allowing participation are inadequate.[91] Moreover, most cases concerning the defence of statutory authority involve private Acts of Parliament, where the parties who ultimately suffer the nuisance may have had no realistic opportunity to intervene in the procedure. The courts regard private Acts as a type of contract between the promoter and Parliament; since the promoter drafts the Act, the courts normally apply the *contra proferentum* rule of interpretation to their construction.[92] While one would expect this rule to restrain the courts from finding implied defences to private law claims, it seems to have been ignored in nuisance cases.

Neither does the current doctrine require the court to ask whether the public benefit could be obtained by reducing the private profit of the defendant. At present, English courts apply the inevitability doctrine as a test of negligence, under which only reasonable precautions must be taken. By contrast, in Canada, the defendant must show that it was "practically impossible to avoid the nuisance" and that there were no "alternate methods of carrying out the work".[93] The standard is higher than the negligence standard applied by English courts. Whether it tips the scales too far in favour of the property owner is uncertain. There may be circumstances where a Canadian enterprise would abandon a project because the cost of preventing the nuisance reduces its profits to the point that it makes commercial sense to transfer their investment to another project. This, of course, could also occur in England, in response to the cost of complying with the negligence standard, but the cost of compliance is lower and so fewer projects would be abandoned. Plainly, there is no simple means of determining whether the Canadian or English doctrine satisfies the proportion-

---

[91] There has been some recognition of the importance of participation in the cases on planning permission as a defence to nuisance: see Pill LJ in the Court of Appeal in *Hunter* v. *Canary Wharf* [1997] AC 655, 669, agreeing with Peter Gibson LJ's comment in *Wheeler* v. *J J Saunders* [1996] Ch 19, 35 that "The court should be slow to acquiesce in the extinction of private rights without compensation as a result of administrative decisions which cannot be appealed and are difficult to challenge".

[92] See *Allen* v. *Gulf Oil Refining Ltd.* [1981] AC 1001, 1020–1021 per Lord Keith (dissenting). Cf. Kodilinye, above n. 86, at 79.

[93] *Ryan* v. *City of Victoria* (SCC) 28 January 1999 and *Tock* v. *St. John's Metropolitan Area Board* (1989), 64 DLR (4th) 620 (SCC), 651, per Sopinka J.

ality test, but where there is doubt over the practical impact of legislative measures—as there is in this case—it seems appropriate to give the benefit of the doubt to the individual and the protection of their Convention rights.

A further question is whether the courts should abandon the current doctrine altogether. This was proposed by La Forest J in the Canadian case, *Tock* v. *St. John's Metropolitan Area Board*, although not accepted by the majority. He stated that: [94]

> "the fundamental issue before the court in a claim for nuisance is not whether the defendant has acted prudently. Rather, the issue for determination is whether, on a consideration of all the circumstances, it is reasonable or unreasonable to award compensation for the damage suffered".

This, according to La Forest J, means that the courts should take into account both the public benefit and private harm caused by the activity in question. If the activity does produce a public benefit, the defendant would not be liable for: [95]

> "those ordinary disturbances diffuse in their effect and having a broad and general impact on the comfort, convenience and material well-being of the public at large".

However, the defendant would be liable whenever its actions brought significant harm inflicted on a small and isolated group of plaintiffs.

Finally, even if the court decides that it must hold that the defence is available to the defendant, section 6 of the Act would be relevant in relation to remedies. The court could consider limiting the defence to petitions for injunctions, thereby allowing the claim for damages to stand.[96] Again, in many cases, this would preserve the public benefit, as it would only shift the cost from one private party to another private party.

IV. CONCLUSIONS

Limitations of space make it impossible to review all aspects of Human Rights Act and Convention that may affect the law of property. However, as a closing comment, the influence of comparative law is worth examining. The Human Rights Act requires the court to consider the jurisprudence of the Strasbourg institutions, but makes no mention of the jurisprudence of the national courts of other member States. British courts may find the comparative method useful,

---

[94] 64 DLR (4th) 620, 643 (SCC). Although all six judges of the panel agreed that the appeal should be allowed, Sopinka J preferred the English view in *Allen* v. *Gulf Oil Refining Ltd.* [1981] AC 1001 and *Tate & Lyle Industries Ltd.* v. *Greater London Council* [1983] 2 AC 509, although he concluded that the damage was not inevitable. In *Ryan* v. *City of Victoria*, 28 January 1999, the Supreme Court indicated that Sopinka J's views should prevail.

[95] 64 DLR (4th) 620, 648: it would not apply to "isolated and infrequent occurrences which inflict heavy material damage on a single victim".

[96] See Davies, above n. 88, at 364–365. Lord Denning MR advocated a similar approach in *Allen* v. *Gulf Oil Refining Ltd.* [1980] QB 156, 168–169, but his proposals were rejected on appeal to the House of Lords (in *Allen* v. *Gulf Oil Refining Ltd.* [1981] AC 1001).

especially since the European Court itself is often guided by national standards. In relation to property rights, comparative law raises several interesting points. For example, the uncertain status of causes of action under the Convention stems partly from the civilian approach to property law. As explained above, while causes in action would be treated as civil rights under Article 6(1), they would not necessarily be treated as possessions under Article 1 of the First Protocol. By contrast, Commonwealth courts have treated such claims as "property" for the purposes of rights to property under Commonwealth constitutions.[97] Perhaps British judges will take note of the differences between civilian and common law conceptions of property, and therefore show more willingness to treat choses in action as "possessions" for the purposes of the Human Rights Act and the Convention. This, of course, would occur only if the British courts took the view that the European Court of Human Rights declares the minimum standard on member States. Whether the British courts will take this view is uncertain, but at least some judges and leading commentators argue that British courts should feel free to impose stricter degree of scrutiny than European Court of Human Rights.[98]

Secondly, the legal systems of some member States give greater importance to the social function of property than Britain. This is particularly true in Germany, as Gregory Alexander points out in his chapter in this book. While there are aspects of the English law of property that recognise the personal connection with specific things, and the importance of property in achieving autonomy and self-governance, the idea does not permeate English law to the same extent as it does German law. In particular, it has had only limited impact in the context of the compulsory acquisition of property and other state-authorised interferences with property. So, for example, there is an implicit assumption that payment of adequate compensation is sufficient to bring about a fair balance between an expropriatee's interests and the public interest.[99] This assumption would not be made so quickly if it were acknowledged that some types of property are not held for economic reasons. The home, in particular, often has

---

[97] See *Georgiadis* v. *Australian and Overseas Telecommunications Corporation* (1994) 179 CLR 297. British judges on the Privy Council have indicated that a broad view of "property" should be taken under Commonwealth constitutions; see, in particular, *A-G The Gambia* v. *Jobe* [1985] LRC (Const.) 556; *Marine Workers Union* v. *Mauritius Marine Authority* [1985] 1 AC 585; [1985] 2 WLR 114; [1985] LRC (Const.) 801; *Government of Mauritius* v. *Union Flacq Sugar Estates Co* [1992] 1 WLR 903.

[98] See generally I. Leigh and L. Lustgarten, "Making Rights Real—The Courts, Remedies and the Human Rights Act" (forthcoming).

[99] See generally D. Farrier and P. McAuslan, "Compensation, Participation and the Compulsory Acquisition of 'Homes'" in J. F. Garner (ed.), *Compensation for Compulsory Purchase: A Comparative Study* (London, The United Kingdom National Committee of Comparative Law, 1975); J. L. Knetsch, *Property Rights and Compensation: Compulsory Acquisition and Other Losses* (Toronto, Butterworths, 1983), p. 59; Australia Law Reform Commission, *Lands Acquisition and Compensation*, Report No. 14 (Canberra, AGPS, 1980), 138; cf. *Fok Lai Ying* v. *Governor-in-Council* [1997] 3 LRC 101 (PC) 113–114: the provision of monetary compensation does not necessarily mean that an interference with one's home is not arbitrary under art. 14 of the Hong Kong Bill of Rights.

a value to its occupants that is not reflected in its market value. Perhaps the introduction of new ideas, via the Human Rights Act, will bring about changes in the English perspective on property law.

8

The Normative Resilience of Property

JEREMY WALDRON[1]

When property rights are in turmoil—as they have been in New Zealand over the last decade or two, as a result of the application of Waitangi principles to disputed land-holdings—it is good to reflect on the basis of the legitimacy of existing structures of ownership. Such reflection may not be politically conclusive, But it is important nevertheless to be able to articulate in legal and moral terms the discomfort that many feel about disrupting existing property arrangements in the name of abstract justice.

Consider this example: X farms a piece of land in the Taranaki, under a long-term lease from the Crown. He and his family and their predecessors in title have been treated for generations as the lawful tenants of the land. But now the legitimacy of the whole arrangement is called in question on the basis of grave irregularities in the original transactions purporting to transfer the land to the Crown from the original inhabitants of the Taranaki. How now should we think about the rights and wrongs of X's position? Or take another example, a little less close to home. The arable land of an agricultural community has been held for generations among a very small group of families, representing (say) less than 15 per cent of the population. The rest either work as farm labourers or in service industries in market towns. Eventually the landless 85 per cent gain political rights, and their representative begins to question the justification of the existing division of land and to call for land reform. And let's say that their critique seems unanswerable on moral grounds. How should we think about the rights and wrongs of the existing landowners in this apparently unjust situation?

In both examples, we are naturally sympathetic to the disruption that any redress of injustice will cause to lives of the farming families (though we temper that of course with equal sympathy for the distress of those whose dispossession constituted the injustice in question). The farmers themselves are likely to be outraged by any demand that they should give up "their" land—even if that demand is made in the name of justice, and even if they are offered some form of compensation. But is there any substance to this outrage and this sympathy? Does it tell us anything about how we should think about property and justice in society? Or should we—who believe in strong justice—simply treat it as the

[1] This article also appears as (1998) 9 *Otago Law Review* 195. We are grateful to the editors for their permission to republish.

squeak of the pips when the lemon is squeezed or, to switch metaphors, the sound of the eggs breaking as a better omelette is concocted. Are the sentiments of those who stand to be dispossessed anything that should give us pause in our enthusiasm for social justice?

These questions raise a whole host of issues in the theory of property, the theory of justice, and the theory of practical politics. In the theory of property, they remind us of the claims of possession and occupancy, the importance of stability and respect for existing expectations, and the role of prescription and similar concepts in the establishment and legitimation of rights. In the theory of justice, they remind us of the notorious difficulties associated with corrective or rectificatory justice, difficulties that surface not only in property, but also in tort law, and to a lesser extent in any body of law where the punishment of wrongs, the compensation of injury, and the vindication of righteous anger is involved. And in the theory of politics, they bring to mind the warnings that political philosophers have often sounded against tearing apart the social fabric in the name of utopian abstractions. One recalls Edmund Burke's advice about the wisdom of preferring tradition, settlement and establishment over our own puny and fragile individual speculations about justice.[2]

Some of these issues I have addressed in the past. I considered some general features of right-based justifications of property in my book, *The Right to Private Property* and I focused there particularly on the Lockean claims of labour and desert and Hegelian claims about the importance of property rights to the integrity of individual personhood.[3] In an article on David Hume, I examined the possibility of a more conservative approach to property that would respect existing equilibria of *de facto* possession and eschew any speculation about the moral basis of property rights.[4] In an article on Immanuel Kant's jurisprudence, I attempted to bring out the importance of the positive law of property, as something that could stand fast in society, in the midst of disagreements about justice.[5] Finally, in a couple of pieces on rectification, I tried to point out some of the more important practical and moral difficulties that confront any attempt to correct historical injustice.[6]

The present chapter will by no means complete the picture: but I want to take this opportunity to add one more piece to the puzzle of how seriously we should take the claims of pure possession, in situations like those laid out in our examples. In this chapter, I want to ask about the relation between existing patterns of property-holdings and the virtues and sentiments that property rights often

[2] E. Burke, *Reflections on the Revolution in France*, in C. C. O'Brien (ed.) (Harmondsworth, Penguin Books, 1969).

[3] J. Waldron, *The Right to Private Property* (Oxford, Clarendon Press, 1988,) esp. pp. 137–253 (Lockean theory) and pp. 343–389 (Hegelian theory).

[4] J. Waldron, "The Advantages and Difficulties of the Humean Theory of Property", (1994) 11 *Social Philosophy and Policy* 85–123.

[5] J. Waldron, "Kant's Legal Positivism", (1996) 109 *Harvard Law Review*, 1535–1566.

[6] J. Waldron, "Superseding Historic Injustice", (1992) 103 *Ethics*, 4–28 and "Historic Injustice: Its Remembrance and Supersession" in G. Oddie and R. Perrett (eds), *Justice, Ethics and New Zealand Society* (Auckland, Oxford University Press, 1992), pp. 139–170.

involve: the sentiment of *belonging*, the condemnation of *theft* and *trespass*, the vice of *dishonesty*, as well as the general sense of *mine and thine*. These are undoubtedly moral sentiments, and they involve powerful thoughts about right and wrong; but it is intriguing that even when the overall morality of some existing set of property rights is called in question, these sentiments tend to associate themselves with the status quo rather than with the moral basis on which the status quo is being criticised. I want to ask why this is, and I want to consider what, if anything, it tells us about the broader enterprise of abstract moral justification and criticism in the area of property rights.

I. HONESTY AND RESPECT FOR PROPERTY

Let me begin with an idea that is deeply embedded in our respect for property—the idea of *honesty*. What exactly is the relation between property and honesty? In times past, "honesty" was used as a general term for virtue or honour, encompassing chastity, generosity, and decorum. But according to the *Oxford English Dictionary* its prevailing modern meaning is "[u]prightness of disposition and conduct; integrity, truthfulness, straightforwardness: the quality opposed to lying, cheating, or stealing".[7] Now, if stealing is one of the things to which the quality denoted by "honesty" is characteristically opposed, then to that extent "property" and "honesty" are correlative terms. To steal is to take somebody's property—that is, an object which, under the rules of property, he has the right to possess—with the intention of permanently depriving him of it (what lawyers call the *animus furandi*). To be disposed not to steal means that one is disposed not to violate the rules of property in this way. To be honest—in this sense of honesty—is to respect the rules of property.

But respect *which* rules of property? The *existing* rules in society, currently in force, however unjust or oppressive? Or the rules of property in so far as they are regarded as fair? "Honesty" also has the meaning of "fairness and straightforwardness of conduct".[8] Does it pull us in two directions here? Is the man who violates an unjust property right with the intention of permanently depriving an undeserving "proprietor" of some goods he "owns" dishonest? Is this even a marginal case for the concept of dishonesty? Or do "honest" and "dishonest" go unequivocally with the positive law of property (leaving it perhaps a further question whether dishonesty is always a vice or always wrong, all things considered)?

If it is a marginal case, then what tends to make a difference at the margin? Is a taking[9] less dishonest depending on its manner, depending on the motive,

---

[7] "Honesty", I 3 d, *Oxford English Dictionary* (Internet Edition).

[8] "Honesty", 2 a, *Webster's Ninth New Collegiate Dictionary* (Springfield, Merriam Webster, 1991), p. 579.

[9] I use "taking" as an entirely neutral term; it refers to any appropriation of occupation of a resource by a person other than the officially designated owner, accompanied by the intention permanently to deprive the official designated owner of the resource, whether that appropriation or occupation is morally justified or thought to be morally justified or not.

depending on the extent of the background injustice, or depending on whether there is an appeal to some alternative set of existing property rights (say, from the past)? Some might say, for example, that there is necessarily something *furtive* or *deceitful* about dishonesty, so that an open taking of something when property rules are contested is to that extent less dishonest. Or they may say that even if the existing allocation of property is unfair, it matters whether or not the taker is motivated by personal greed: though he took from the rich, Robin Hood was not dishonest inasmuch as he gave what he took to the poor. Or, if one "steals" for personal use, it may make a difference whether it is personal use to satisfy a mere want or personal use to satisfy desperate need, particularly if a case can be made that society's neglect of such need is itself the ground of the injustice. Finally, it may make a difference whether the taker is attacking existing property rights purely on the basis of his own utopian theory of justice, or whether he is attacking them in the name of some alternative set of property rights that was established and existed in the society in the recent past. In his famous study *Whigs and Hunters*, E. P. Thompson notes that a lot of what was condemned in eighteenth century England as poaching, stealing and trespass was regarded by the perpetrators as the vindication of traditional property: [10]

> "What was often at issue was not property, supported by law, against no-property; it was alternative definitions of property-rights: for the landowner, enclosure—for the cottager, common rights; for the forest officialdom, 'preserved grounds' for the deer; for the foresters the right to take turf".

In this context, and equally in the context of some occupations of contested land in New Zealand, the defenders of traditional or aboriginal rights would not necessarily regard themselves as thieves or trespassers nor their taking as dishonest, however much their opponents tried to stigmatise them in those terms.

II. THE CONCEPT OF NORMATIVE RESISTANCE

We are imagining that something which is officially regarded as X's private property is taken by another individual Y, without X's consent, in circumstances where there is reason to question the justice of the official distribution.

In each of the aspects I have mentioned—manner, motive, need, extent of the background injustice, reference to an alternative set of aboriginal or traditional rights—one can imagine a sort of scale. For example, one might locate a given taking on a scale that runs from completely deceitful takings through various degrees of furtiveness in the direction of takings that are unabashedly open and public. Although there may be a point in this openness scale at which a taking ceases to be regarded as dishonest (or ceases even to be regarded as theft), there is also likely to be a range of points on the scale at which the action *would* be

[10] See E. P. Thompson, *Whigs and Hunters: the Origin of the Black Act* (Harmondsworth, Penguin Books, 1977), p. 261.

regarded as dishonest, notwithstanding the question about injustice. In some circumstances, it is dishonest to openly take property that is unjustly held. Or, to put it more carefully, there is a range of cases in which the condemnation of an open taking as dishonest does not depend on any judgement about the justification of the property right in question. One may withhold judgement on the latter issue, but still unequivocally condemn the taking as dishonest, in the cases within this range. The existence of such a range of cases, I shall call, *"the normative resilience of property"*.[11]

Normative resilience refers here to the way in which certain normative judgements (such as judgements about honesty and dishonesty) by which property rights are upheld are insulated from other normative judgements about the property rights (such as judgements about their justice or injustice, their justification or lack of justification). The concept of normative resilience points to a discontinuity between two types of normative judgement associated with an institution: (1) judgements concerning the justification of the institution, and (2) judgements concerning individual conduct in relation to the institution. Resilience is the phenomenon whereby judgements of type 2, although they are predicated upon the institution, nevertheless remain unaffected by judgements of type 1 that are adverse to the institution. A resilient institution continues to exert itself normatively through its type 2 judgements, notwithstanding the fact that it is discredited at the type 1 level.

Let me make a few general points to clarify the concept of normative resilience. First, the phenomenon does not depend on there being different communities making the judgements of type 1 and type 2, respectively. Of course that is very common: the people who condemn the taking as dishonest are not the same as those who condemn the property system as unjust. But I am interested, under the heading of "resilience", in cases where judgements of both types are made by the same people. Moreover, I'm interested in cases where this is arguably not a simple logical mistake, that is, not a failure of inference. A person may believe that all theft is dishonourable but fail to draw the conclusion that burglary is dishonourable (because they forget that burglary is a form of theft). Now maybe in the end that is the proper explanation of normative resilience—too many people are failing to draw appropriate conclusions from the judgements of type 1 that they make. But it is not the best explanation: it is possible or arguable that there is really a logical gap between judgements of type 1 and judgements of type 2. An exploration of normative resilience is an exploration of that hypothesis (and what would follow from it if it were true).

Secondly, the judgements of type 1 that interest us here may be either general judgements or particular judgements. (Depending on which they are, the relevant set of type 2 judgements will vary accordingly.) In his book *Punishment and Responsibility,* H. L. A. Hart distinguished between the general justifying aim

---

[11] I used the phrase "institutional resilience" to refer to something similar in J. Waldron, "Property, Justification and Need", (1993) 6 *Canadian Journal of Law and Jurisprudence* 185, 186–189, 205–206.

of an institution and the particular distributive rules by which it operates. He thought for example that an institution of punishment might be utilitarian in its general justifying aim but still operate by retributive principles. And he offered a similar analysis of property:[12]

> "[I]n the case of property we should distinguish between the question why and in what circumstances it is a good institution to maintain, and the question in what ways individuals may become entitled to acquire property, and how much they should be allowed to acquire".

Hart criticised John Locke—unfairly in my view[13]—for thinking that the same considerations ("the labour theory") could be used to answer both questions. The interdependence or otherwise of these two questions in the case of property is an interesting issue (as it is also in the case of punishment),[14] but it is not this that interests me under the heading of "normative resilience". For these purposes I am classifying both of Hart's questions under type 1. That is I am interested in the way in which judgements of honesty and dishonesty are insulated not only from a general judgement that a whole system of property is unjustified (a communist argument, for example, against private property) or from a general judgement that the distribution of private property in a particular society is inequitable, but also from a particular judgement that the distribution of some specific object or resource is unjust.

This explains why a famous passage from David Hume should not be regarded as an illustration of normative resilience. Hume asked us to consider that: [15]

> "A single act of justice is frequently contrary to public interest; and were it to stand alone, without being followed by other acts, may, in itself, be very prejudicial to society. When a man of merit, of a beneficent disposition, restores a great fortune to a miser, or a seditious bigot, he has acted justly and laudably, but the public is the real sufferer. But however single acts of justice may be contrary, either to public or private interest, 'tis certain, that the whole plan or scheme is highly conducive, or indeed absolutely requisite, both to the support of society, and the well-being of every individual. 'Tis impossible to separate the good from the ill".

Certainly Hume will figure in the account I want to offer (in section IV). But this passage concerns the sort of looseness between general and particular justificatory judgements that Hart was talking about, not the sort of looseness between justificatory judgements, on the one hand, and judgements (like honesty and dishonesty) pertaining to individual conduct on the other. Hume's case would be a case of normative resilience if one were to conclude that there is in

---

[12] H. L. A. Hart, *Punishment and Responsibility: Essays in the Philosophy of Law* (Oxford, Clarendon Press, 1968), p. 4.

[13] See Waldron, *The Right to Private Property,* above n. 2, at pp. 331–332.

[14] See ibid., 323–342.

[15] D. Hume, *A Treatise of Human Nature* L. A. Selby-Bigge (ed.), (Oxford, Clarendon Press, 1888), p. 497.

fact *no* justification for returning the fortune to the miser, but *still* felt dishonest about keeping it.

Thirdly, although I have concentrated so far on the relation between justificatory judgements directed towards an institution (what I call type 1 judgements) and judgements that relate to the conduct or character of those who are constrained by the institution (what I call type 2 judgements), the latter class is broader than I have so far indicated. Under the type 2 heading, I am interested in any judgements that pertain to individual conduct, character or condition which appear to be derived (in some sense) from an institutional arrangement like property, but which exhibit a certain looseness in that derivation which enables them to survive despite the discrediting of the institutional arrangement from which they are supposedly derived. "Honest" and "dishonest" have been our paradigms of type 2 judgements in relation to the institution of private property. Terms like "theft", "thief", "stealing", "pilfering", and so on, fall into the same class: like "dishonest" they seem appropriately to characterise actions which violate property rules even when those property rules are thought to lack moral justification. But it is not only terms of condemnation that have this resilience. Also some of the terms connoting ownership seem to work this way as well. I may think of a piece of land as "mine" or as "belonging to me", and think of myself as its "owner", without thinking that the rules which designate me as the owner have any moral justification.

The general characteristic of type 2 judgements is that they apply to individuals (or their actions, relations or circumstances) what are sometimes referred to as "thick" moral predicates—in this case predicates whose descriptive meaning is related to certain institutional arrangements.[16] We have been working with such predicates associated with property. But we can list other such predicates related to other institutions. For example, see Table 8.1.

In each case the type 2 predicates cannot be understood without reference to the institution denoted in the type 1 judgements. Yet in each case it is an open question how resilient the type 2 judgements are, that is, the extent to which their proper use does not depend upon the speaker's acceptance of (something like) the corresponding type 1 judgement. In group III, for example, the judgement that someone is a heretic does *not* seem to be normatively resilient. It is not a judgement that would be made except by someone who accepted the truth of the orthodoxy relative to which the alleged "heresy" was defined. Sometimes one term associated with a given institution may figure in resilient judgements while others do not. In group V, for example, a person who rejected the legitimacy of the aristocratic class system, might well refuse to talk of someone's "not

---

[16] Not all thick moral predicates have these institutional connections. In some, the descriptive element refers to types of actions and responses to situations that are being commended or condemned (e.g., virtue words like "courage"). For doubts about the ability to isolate the descriptive meaning of a thick term from its normative force, see J. McDowell, "Non-cognitivism and Rule-Following" in S. Holtzman and C. Leich (eds), *Wittgenstein: To Follow a Rule* (London, Routledge, 1981), p. 144 et seq. and the response in the same volume by Simon Blackburn.

Table 8.1: Predicates

Type 1	*Type 2*
I. *Private property* is morally justified.	Y is a thief, *dishonest*, etc. Object O *belongs* to X.
II. There is a moral justification for *the state*.	Y is a *traitor*, or a *terrorist*. X has *authority*.
III. C is the *true religion*.	Y is a *heretic*.
IV. *Traditional marriage* is a good institution.	S is a *fornicator*. H is an *adulterer*. H *deserted* W.
V. There is a justification for *aristocracy*.	X is of *noble birth*. That man is not X; he is *Sir X*. Y does not know *his place*.
VI. There is a justification for *military discipline*.	X *order* Y to do A. Y is *insubordinate*.
VII. The *criminal justice* system works fairly.	Y is a *crook*. Y is *innocent*.

knowing his place", but he might continue nevertheless to refer to a person who has been knighted as "Sir John" or whatever.

The other point I want to stress at this stage is that the type 2 predicates that interest us are normative or evaluative predicates used in a way that carries their ordinary normative or evaluative force. I am not interested in ironic or what are sometimes referred to as "inverted-commas" uses of type 2 predicates:[17] as when Martin Luther talks of "we heretics" or a social rebel acknowledges with bitter irony that he has forgotten "his place". The resilience of ironic or inverted commas uses of type 2 predicates is definitional and uninteresting. What is challenging, however, is a type 2 judgement retaining its ordinary evaluative force in circumstances where the corresponding type 1 judgement has been repudiated or discredited.

Notice I say *"ordinary"* evaluative force; I don't say that the evaluation implicit in the type 2 judgement must be conclusory. One could judge some action "dishonest" without concluding that it was the wrong thing to do, all things considered. Maybe there are circumstances in which one *ought* to be thief. There is some complication here depending on how one analyses prima facie judgements and moral conflict. For example, consider the four judgements in Table 8.2.

---

[17] See R. M. Hare, *The Language of Morals* (Oxford, Oxford University Press, 1952), pp. 124 and 167 et seq.

Table 8.2: Four judgements

---

(1)   The private property system around here is just.
(2)   Taking that food would be stealing.
(3)   Y's baby needs that food or it will die.
(4)   All things considered, Y ought to take the food.

Normative resilience concerns the relation between 1 and 2. Somebody who rejects 1 might nevertheless accept 2; but such a person may also accept 4. There are two ways to understand the relation between 2 and 4. First, one might say that the evaluative force of 2 is merely provisional, pending the final judgement 4; once 4 is adopted, one abandons the condemnation implicit in 2. Alternatively, one might say that even if 4 is adopted, still 2 retains some of its evaluative force. Moral conflicts such as those between 2 and 4 are not always neatly resolved, without moral remainder, so to speak.[18] One may appropriately feel bad about doing A, even while acknowledging that A is, all things considered, the appropriate thing to do. On this second analysis, there is no particular problem in specifying "ordinary evaluative force" so far as normative resilience is concerned. The ordinary moral force of "stealing" includes *inter alia* its propensity to hang-over as a moral remainder in conflicts such as that in our example. But suppose one adopts the first pattern of analysis, giving evaluative force 2 only provisionally, pending the final judgement 4. Then whether 2 should be regarded as normatively resilient in our sense depends on whether the rejection of 1 is decisive in yielding 4. If one says "On the one hand this would be stealing, but on the other hand, the system of property is unjust; therefore 4", then 2 is not normatively resilient. But if 4 is based on something like 3, understood as a moral consideration of independent force, then what I have called the resilience of 2 is undefeated. Its resilience consists, on this analysis, not in its always having evaluative force, but in its evaluative force being liable, so to speak, to be cancelled only by independent considerations of a certain weight.

Also, resilience and normative force may be matters of degree. I have talked about the *independence* of type 1 and type 2 judgements. But remember that in the first paragraph of section III, I stressed the existence of a *range* of cases in which the force of a type 2 judgement might vary, dwindle and finally peter out, depending on factors like motivation, openness, and so on. Some of these scalar considerations are independent of the relevant type 1 judgement. (They concern, for example, the manner in which the conduct in question is performed.) Others may *not* be independent of the type 1 judgement: we might say for example that if the injustice of the institution is really egregious, then the corresponding type 2 judgement must eventually be withdrawn. Thus it is possible that the evalua-

---

[18]   See B. Williams, "Ethical Consistency" in *Problems of the Self: Philosophical Papers 1956–1972* (Cambridge, Cambridge University Press, 1973), pp. 166–186.

Figure 8.1: Resilience and normative force

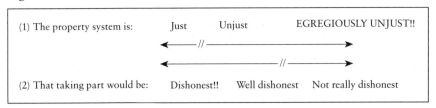

tive force of the type 2 judgement does vary in a way that depends on variations in the type 1 judgement. But the type 2 judgement may *still* be regarded as resilient if the two scales fail to line up perfectly, as, for example, in Figure 8.1.

In Figure 8.1, the judgement about dishonesty is somewhat resilient, because although it fades depending on how unjust the property system is, it is not simply abandoned as soon as the property system is condemned.

III. NORMATIVE RESILIENCE AND POSITIVISM

The examples given in Table 8.1 included many in which the type 1 institution is a legal institution. And the analysis we are giving raises certain issues in regard to our understanding of the normative ramifications of positive law. Consider, for example, the judgements in Table 8.3:

Table 8.3: Normative force of positive law

Type1	*Type 2*
VII A: Our *laws* are in general just. VII B: It is good to have a *legal system*.	This case is a *binding precedent*. That act would be *illegal*. This is a *valid* will. *Properly interpreted*, the statute means … . Y is a *criminal*.

Clearly the type 2 judgements in Table 8.3 are in *some* sense resilient, relative to judgements like VII A. Even in a legal system most of whose provisions are unjust, we can still distinguish (by the system's own lights) between valid and invalid wills, binding and non-binding precedents, lawful and unlawful acts, and proper and improper interpretations of legal sources.[19]

In a rather crude sense of legal positivism, normative resilience is simply a consequence of positivism. Legal positivism is often caricatured as the thesis that human laws have a claim to our respect simply because of their existence as

---

[19] Cf. R. Dworkin, *Law's Empire* (Cambridge, Harvard University Press, 1986). pp. 101–108.

social phenomena. Existing positive law is to be obeyed, whether we judge it morally right or wrong, according to this (caricatural) version. To discover that something is *the law*, on this account, is to discover something that has immediate normative consequences for action, whatever independent judgement we might make about it from a moral point of view. Most modern positivists do not hold this version. They know that it is a theory attributed to them by some of their opponents, but they think that in general their opponents err (both in the opponents' own jurisprudence and in the theories they attribute to the positivists) by investing concepts like "law" and "legal validity" with too much moral weight. Critiques of positivism, said H. L. A. Hart, are often based on "an enormous overvaluation of the importance of the bare fact that a rule may be said to be a valid rule of law".[20] The implication of a positivist jurisprudence, on Hart's view, is not that propositions are to be *respected* or *deferred to* as law by virtue of their social existence, but that they are to be *identified* as law on that basis, leaving it a further question—an independent moral question—what respect, if any, is due to them on that ground or any other.

It follows that although sophisticated legal positivists in the Hart camp might accept the resilience of the type 2 judgements in Table 8.3, some of them might want to deny that this is to be understood as *normative* resilience. They might say that the type 2 judgements have no normative force whatsoever. They tell us about the law, or they express legal conclusions, but they are not used to commend, condemn, evaluate, or prescribe. The positivist's judgement that some action is illegal, for example, tells us nothing about whether he thinks that, from the moral point of view, it ought to be done. Moreover, to use it in this purely descriptive way—to say what the law is—is not to use the term "illegal" ironically or in inverted commas or in any other way that varies from its ordinary use. The claim of these positivists is that terms like this are not ordinarily used to express moral judgements at all.

Four issues need to be untangled here. First, it is arguable that some of the judgements that I have listed on the right-hand side of Table 8.3 as type 2 judgements in fact belong on the left (with the type 1 judgements). They may stand in the same relation to VII A or VII B as principles of property distribution (or particular distributions) stand to the general justifying aim of property.[21]

Secondly, although it is true that terms like "illegal" are not normally used to express moral judgements, that does not mean that their use has no normative aspect at all. Participants in a legal system usually deploy type 2 judgements in a conduct-guiding way, by which I mean that there is characteristically what H. L. A. Hart called an *internal aspect* associated with the use of terms like "illegal", "valid", etc. And that aspect is certainly normative.[22] An outsider—an

---

[20] See H. L. A. Hart, "Positivism and the Separation of Law and Morals" reprinted in his collection *Essays in Jurisprudence and Philosophy* (Oxford, Clarendon Press, 1983), p. 75 (criticising Lon Fuller's jurisprudence). See also H. L. A. Hart, *The Concept of Law* 2nd edn. (Oxford, Clarendon Press, 1994), pp. 203–207.

[21] Compare the discussion in the text accompanying nn. 11–14, above.

[22] See Hart, *The Concept of Law*, above n. 19, at p. 88 et seq.

anthropologist or a comparative lawyer, for example—may not use these terms normatively. But they could not function in legal judgements unless they were used normatively by a community of participants in the legal system;[23] and the anthropologist and comparative lawyer could not infer that they were legal terms unless they noticed them being used normatively in such a community.

Thirdly, some modern legal positivists hold a view that is called "*normative positivism*". They believe that it is (morally) a good thing that judgements of legal validity and invalidity and lawful and unlawful conduct should be able to be made without using moral judgement.[24] (Jeremy Bentham certainly fell into this category, and so I think did Thomas Hobbes.) That belief is presumably dependent upon a type 1 judgement such as VII B in Table 8.3. The normative positive view is roughly this: it is (morally speaking) a good thing that we have a system of positive law, for that enables us to judge statutes, wills, and the like, as valid or invalid without making moral judgements. Now it is unlikely that type 2 judgements grounded in *this* way would be very resilient. If one were to abandon VII B, one would also be likely to divest the type 2 judgements in Table 3 of any specifically moral content. If they had any normative content at all, it would be that discussed in the previous paragraph (that is, their ordinary internal aspect).

Fourthly, whether we are talking about the normativity associated with the internal aspect of law, or the moral normativity that is associated with legal judgements in a jurisprudence of normative positivism, it is unlikely to be an all-things-considered normativity. There will be a further question of how much respect, ultimately, is owed to the law as such.[25] In other words, the issues that arose with regard to the judgements set out in Table 8.2 will also arise with regard to those set out in Table 8.3. Consider for example the variation on Table 8.2, in Table 8.4.

Table 8.4: Four further judgements

(1)   Our laws are just and it is a good thing that we have a legal system.
(2)   Action A is illegal.
(3)   Action A is required by my religion.
(4)   All things considered, I ought to perform action A.

Someone may accept 1 and 2, and yet follow 4 because of 3. Or someone may accept 2 but not 1, and yet still follow 4 because of 3. The hypothesis of normative resilience with regard to positive law would require that, in this sort of case,

[23] Ibid., pp. 110–117. But as Hart emphasises, they need not be used normatively by *all* participants in the legal system. Their normative use among a corps of officials may be sufficient (ibid., pp. 116–117).

[24] For "normative positivism", see G. J. Postema, *Bentham and the Common Law Tradition* (Oxford, Clarendon Press, 1986), pp. 328–336. (This is not the caricatural view referred to above.)

[25] See Dworkin, above n. 18, at pp. 96–98 and pp. 108–113.

there must be a looseness between 1 and 2 which is quite independent of whatever looseness there is between 2 and 4. For someone who accepts 4, 2 can have a normative force independent of 1 only if 4 is based on 3 and 3 is not the reason for rejecting 1.

This tangle of considerations—particularly the third consideration (about normative positivism etc)[26] has convinced me that it would be unwise to attempt to establish any *general* hypothesis of the normative resilience of legal judgements. It seems that some legal or legally-based judgements are normatively more resilient than others. In Table 8.1, for instance, the difference we noted between example I ("justified property"/"honesty") and example III ("true religion"/"heresy") would seem to work whether or not law is involved. Even in countries with a legally established orthodoxy, religious dissenters did not regard themselves as heretics, and probably not even as "guilty of heresy". Similarly with example II: in countries with anti-terrorist legislation, those whom legal officials designate as terrorists usually regard themselves as "freedom fighters" not terrorists, once they reject the legitimacy of the existing state and legal system.

In the present chapter I want to concentrate particularly on the normative resilience of judgements associated with property. Although private property is a legal institution and has a legal existence, and although the resilience (such as it is) of positive law no doubt contributes something to the resilience of the judgements about "stealing", "dishonesty", and "belonging", there seems to be something particular about property that lends it extra resilience in a way that is not associated with all legal institutions or all the normative judgements that they generate. Still, it is in the end an issue about positive law: for what I am exploring is the ethical significance not of the justification but of the *positive presence* in a society of a legal institution such as property.

IV. JUSTIFICATION

In this section, I shall explore a possible line of justification for the normative resilience of property, a line of justification that may also help explain the distinction noted above between property and some of the other legal examples we have been considering. In the final section—section V—I shall consider what (justified) normative resilience would imply in regard to the overall enterprise of type 1 justification in legal and political philosophy.

First, a preliminary point about justification, explanation and ideology. An explanation of the normative resilience of property may or may not justify property. The explanation may be purely psychological, in which case what appears to be normative resilience will still seem like a sort of mistake unless some other, justifying, explanation is forthcoming. A purely psychological account may tell

---

[26] See above n. 23, and accompanying text.

us something about the way an ideology works; but it will tell us nothing in itself about the rights and wrongs of property. However, it is also possible that a psychological explanation—though in itself incomplete as a justification—is nevertheless part of an account which justifies normative resilience. Alternatively it is possible that a psychological account of what appears to be normative resilience tells us something about the tasks of justificatory theory in political philosophy. It may tell us that those tasks are impossible and fatuous, perhaps because almost everything that we think of as "justification" turns out to be the psychological residue of ideology. It may tell us that social justification proceeds not institution by institution but *via* a general obligation to respect positive law, in a way that is not dependent on the justice of its content. Or (as I shall argue at the very end of the chapter) it may tell us that the burden of justification is actually heavier than we thought and the task of justifying such an institution against its critics harder than that of justifying an institution that lacks this apparent resilience. That is, the more resilient an institution, the more harm it may do if it is unjust; so the heavier the burden that must be discharged in its initial justification. That will be my thesis.

It is not hard to think of a psychological explanation for the resilience of a judgement like "This farm belongs to me". Someone who has been officially designated as the owner of a given piece of land is likely to have actual control of the land; he will know it intimately, he may inhabit it with his family, cultivate it, earn his living from it, care about it, and regard it as part of the wealth that he relies on for his own security and that of his descendants. He will be able to point to features of the land where his work and his initiative have made a difference, so that the land will not only seem like his; it may even look like his (in the way that a work of art looks like the artist's). These effects are likely to accrue to him by virtue of the operation of the system of property as positive law quite independently of whether it is just or unjust, or whether he or anyone else regards it as just or unjust.[27]

This is some interesting discussion of the phenomenon in David Hume's *Treatise of Human Nature*. We tend to think that the resilience of *mine and thine* is motivated simply by a greedy desire to hang on to what one actually possesses. In Book III of the *Treatise*, Hume noted that greed cannot be the whole story. The effects we have just been discussing, he says, are likely to produce something like a sense of *mine and thine* which is not simply a cloak for mere utility or advantage:[28]

"Such is the effect of custom, that it not only reconciles us to anything we have long enjoy'd, but even gives us an affection for it, and makes us prefer it to other objects,

---

[27] These effects are probably less likely to accrue, however, or likely to accrue to a lesser extent, if the property system seems precarious on account of its (perceived) injustice—this is, if its (perceived) injustice means that some officials are beginning not to treat the provisions of positive law, in this regard, as normative for them in any sense at all. This may happen in an advanced revolutionary situation, where crucial players are beginning to defect from the established legal system.

[28] Hume, above n. 14, at p. 503.

which may be more valuable, but are less known to us. What has long lain·under our eye, and has often been employ'd to our advantage, that we are always the most unwilling to part with; but can easily live without possessions, which we never have enjoy'd, and are not accustom'd to."

This phenomenon is, as one would expect Hume to say, a matter of constant conjunction and its effect on the imagination:[29]

"When two objects appear in close relation to each other, the mind is apt to ascribe to them any additional relation, in order to compleat the union; and this inclination is so strong, as often to make us run into errors (such as that of the conjunction of thought and matter) if we find that they can serve that purpose. Since, therefore, we can feign a new relation, and even an absurd one, in order to compleat any union, 'twill easily be imagined, that if there be any relations which depend on the mind, 'twill readily conjoin them to any preceding relation, and unite, by a new bond, such objects as have already an union in the fancy".

Hume uses this in the *Treatise* to explain why it is natural to associate the artificial relation of property to the relation between a person and thing established by mere possession and occupancy in a state of nature.[30] But it may also be used to explain why a relation of affection established by law (without regard to the law's moral content) may also be associated with—or, in Hume's terms, be completed by—a sense of righteous possession (a sense which more appropriately goes together with property systems when they *are* morally justified).[31]

Jeremy Bentham noticed something similar, which he thought was very important for public policy. He used it, for example, to ground certain proposals to reform the law of succession and inheritance. To explain why a system of escheat (which he favoured) was better, psychologically, for those who suffered under it than a system of estate duties, Bentham argued as follows: [32]

"Under a tax on successions, a man is led in the first place to look upon the whole in a general view as his own: He is then called upon to give up a part. His imagination thus begins with embracing the whole: then comes the law putting in for its part, and forcing him to quit his hold. This he cannot do without pain".

---

[29] Hume, above n. 14, p. 504n.

[30] Ibid., pp. 504–505: "And as property forms a relation betwixt a person and an object, 'tis natural to found it on some preceding relation; and as property is nothing but a constant possession, secured by the laws of society, 'tis natural to add it to the present possession, which is a relation that resembles it". (See also J. Waldron, "The Advantages and Difficulties of the Humean Theory of Property", (1994) 11 *Social Philosophy and Policy* 85–123.)

[31] See also Hume's observation in Book II: "If justice ... be a virtue, which has a natural and original influence upon the human mind, property may be looked upon as a particular species of *causation*; whether we consider the liberty it gives the proprietor to operate as he please upon the object, or the advantages, which he reaps from it. 'Tis the same case, if justice, according to the system of certain philosophers, should be esteem'd an artificial and not a natural virtue. For then honour, and custom and civil laws supply the place of natural conscience, and produce, in some degree, the same effects" (Hume, above n. 14, at p. 310.)

[32] J. Bentham, "Supply without Burthen" in W Stark (ed.), *Jeremy Bentham's Economic Writings* (London, George Allen and Unwin, 1952, vol. 1, p. 291.

If, on the other hand, we "keep from him the whole, so keeping it from him that there shall never have been a time when he expected to receive it", then there is no disappointment and no hardship.[33] "Try the experiment on a hungry child", Bentham says (though he does not say where we are supposed to find a hungry child, or how we are to ensure that the poor little wretch is properly starved to begin with):[34]

"Try the experiment on a hungry child: give him a small cake, telling him after he has got it, or even before, that he is to give back part of it. Another time give him a whole cake, equal to what was left to him of the other and no more, and let him enjoy it undiminished—will there be a doubt which cake afforded him the purest pleasure?"

In Bentham's discussion, we begin to edge the psychological account in the direction of justification. For Bentham, it is not just a matter of the imagination embracing what positive law guarantees; it is also a matter of pleasure and pain, which of course are the currency of moral justification in Bentham's utilitarianism. The child with the smaller cake gets more pleasure than the child with a larger cake that is vulnerable to confiscation. The person who has to give up what he expected to hold cannot do so, Bentham says, without pain. And that pain accrues whether or not the giving-up is morally required. What matters is that he expected to be able to hold it; that is what hurts when property is overturned. We are dealing here, in other words, with expectations—utilities projected into the future:

"[W]e must consider that man is not like the animals, limited to the present, whether as respects suffering or enjoyment, but that he is susceptible of pains and pleasures by anticipation; and that it is not enough to secure him from actual loss, but it is necessary also to guarantee him, as far as possible, against future loss".[35]

Property, says Bentham, is entirely a matter of expectations:

"In matters of property in general hardship depends upon disappointment; disappointment upon expectation; expectation upon the dispensations, meaning the known dispensations of the law."[36]

Thus the justifiable edge of Bentham's argument works as follows. The pains of disappointment that are likely to ensue when something a person has regarded as his property is taken away are much greater than the corresponding

---

[33] Ibid.

[34] Ibid., at p. 292n.

[35] J. Bentham, "Security and Equality of Property", an extract from J. Bentham, *Principles of the Civil Code*, excerpted in C. B. Macpherson (ed.), *Property: Mainstream and Critical Positions* (Oxford, Basil Blackwell, 1978), pp. 50. See also S. R. Munzer, *A Theory of Property* (Cambridge, Cambridge University Press, 1990), pp. 194–195 and A. Ryan, *Property and Political Theory* (Oxford, Blackwell, 1984), p. 98.

[36] Bentham, "Supply without Burthen", above n. 31, at p. 291. Bentham also ventures this observation in "Security and Equality of Property", above n. 34, at p. 51: "It is proof of great confusion in the ideas of lawyers, that they have never given any particular attention to a sentiment which exercises so powerful an influence upon human life. The word *expectation* is scarcely found in their vocabulary".

pleasures that someone receives when the property is redistributed fairly. Sure, the new owner gets some enjoyment from the resource; but then the old owner lost his enjoyment. Sure, the new owner's enjoyment may be greater than that of the old owner, if we have moved in the direction of a more equal distribution: the law of diminishing marginal utility shows that that is probable.[37] But that extra utility has to be balanced against the specific pains of disappointment, coupled with the impact of the redistribution on others' enjoyment of other resources, which is rendered correspondingly less secure:[38]

> "To regret for what we have lost is joined inquietude as to what we possess, and even as to what we may acquire. When insecurity reaches a certain point, the fear of losing prevents us from enjoying what we possess already. The care of preserving condemns us to a thousand sad and painful precautions, which yet are always liable to fail of their end. Treasures are hidden or conveyed away. Enjoyment becomes sombre, furtive, and solitary. It fears to show itself, lest cupidity should be informed of a chance to plunder".

As a result, industry is deadened, incentives collapse, and long-term schemes of production become psychologically impossible. It follows, says Bentham, that from a utilitarian point of view, existing property rights must be respected no matter how unjust or unequal they appear: [39]

> "When security and equality are in conflict, it will not do to hesitate a moment. Equality must yield. The first is the foundation of life; subsistence, abundance, happiness, everything depends upon it. Equality produces only a certain portion of good. If property should be overturned with the direct intention of establishing an equality of possessions, the evil would be irreparable. No more security, no more industry, no more abundance! Society would return to the savage state whence it emerged".

So we get a dissonance of the sort we are looking for—between type 2 judgments that are dependent on existing property arrangements, and type 1 judgements which hold that those arrangements are unjust. A system of property may be unjust in the sense that it was an outrage to justice when it was set up, unjust in the sense that it ought to have been set up on a different basis. But once established, the rights and relations it generates take on a moral life of their own. Now it becomes morally wrong to interfere with them, even though it would not have been morally wrong to set up the system of property on a different basis altogether.

Someone might object that Bentham's argument goes further than driving this wedge between type 1 and type 2 judgements about property. It not only gives type 2 judgements independent support; it establishes in fact a different sort of type 1 argument in favour of existing arrangements, namely a conservative argument. For surely conservative arguments are one class of type 1 argument.

---

[37] For Bentham's discussion of the utilitarian case for equality, see Bentham, "Security and Equality of Property", above n. 34, at pp. 46–47.

[38] Ibid., p. 54.

[39] Ibid., p. 57.

Some theories of property are inherently conservative. They argue that private property holdings ought to be respected, not because this is the most efficient way of dealing with material resource, nor because it is an appropriate way of rewarding moral desert, nor because it is required by respect for Lockean entitlements, but because any attempt to change the existing system would be profoundly disruptive. There is something to this. Certainly, the propositions supported by Bentham's principle of respecting established expectations are propositions that apply to governments, legislators, and would-be reformers, and not just to the ordinary beneficiaries of the property system or other private individuals constrained by its rules: [40]

> "[W]hat ought the legislator to decree respecting the great mass of property already existing? He ought to maintain the distribution as it is actually established. It is this which, under the name of justice, is regarded as his first duty. This is a general and simple rule which applies itself to all states; and which adapts itself to all places, even those of the most opposite character. There is nothing more different than the state of property in America, in England, in Hungary, and in Russia. Generally, in the first of these countries, the cultivator is the proprietor; in the second, a tenant; in the third, attached to the glebe; in the fourth, a slave. However, the supreme principle of security commands the preservation of all these distributions, though their nature is so different, and though they do not produce the same sum of happiness. How make another distribution with taking away from each that which he has? And how despoil any without attacking the security of all?"

Still, there is a significant difference between Bentham's position and a purely conservative position. When the opportunity arises to vary property arrangements in a way that does not produce pains of disappointment, Bentham is in favour of doing so, and doing so on the basis of principles of justice that are not conservative at all. His proposal to abolish collateral inheritance is a clear example of this;[41] and Bentham was infuriated by any suggestion that his plan would be opposed on the grounds of a more pervasive conservatism.

The account we have given is purely utilitarian. But one could imagine developing a similar account using non-utilitarian ideas. In a number of influential essays, Margaret Radin has argued that respect for existing property rights is bound up with respect for persons: [42]

> "Most people possess certain objects they feel are almost part of themselves. These objects are closely bound up with personhood because they are part of the way we constitute ourselves as continuing personal entities in the world".

Radin uses the idea to distinguish between claims to property of different kinds—the claims of landlords and tenants, for example, in disputes about

[40] Ibid., p. 57.
[41] See Bentham, "Supply Without Burthen", above n. 31. For a discussion of this proposal, see also J. Waldron, "Supply Without Burthen Revisited", (1997) *Iowa Law Review* 1467–1485.
[42] M. J. Radin, "Property and Personhood", reprinted in her collection *Reinterpreting Property* (Chicago, University of Chicago Press, 1993), p. 36. Note that Radin's account also includes a discussion of the fetishistic implications of this: ibid., 43–44.

residential rent control.[43] But clearly it can be used also as an account of normative resilience: in Radin's example, even if a system of residential rent control is unjust, particular persons may be so bound up with the tenancies which they have established on this basis that it would be disrespectful now to them as persons to expose that identification (of them with their homes) to the vicissitudes of market pricing. And Radin's argument would have the additional interesting feature that, if the link between property and personhood is established by something long-lived and intimate like residential occupation, landlords cannot claim the benefit of similar resilience for the property rights that they have at stake in the matter.[44]

Radin seems to think that this personhood argument is Hegelian in provenance:[45] it is an application, she says, of Hegel's argument in the *Philosophy of Right* about the importance of embodying one's freedom in the external world.[46] I am not so sure about that. I have argued elsewhere that Hegel's discussion is more like a type 1 argument about property.[47] But clearly there is enough of a conservative edge to Hegel's political philosophy in general (and enough doubt expressed in his work about the whole business of mounting type 1 arguments), that it would be wrong to neglect this connection.[48] (We will return to Hegel in section V.)

Intriguingly, there is room for a similar argument about personhood in the utilitarian tradition. David Hume pointed out in Book II of the *Treatise,* that "the mention of property naturally carries our thought to the proprietor",[49] and the constant conjunction account of possession that we considered earlier[50] can easily be associated with Hume's account of personal identity.[51] The connection is made explicit in Bentham's discussion. Expectation, for Bentham, is not just a matter of pleasure or pain projected forward into the future. It is crucial to our being, as selves extended in time: [52]

> "It is hence that we have the power of forming a general plan of conduct; it is hence that the successive instants which compose the duration of life are not like isolated and independent points, but become continuous parts of a whole. Expectation is a chain which unites our present existence to our future existence".

And he continues, in language worthy of Radin's account or that of Radin's Hegel: [53]

---

[43] M. J. Radin, "Residential Rent Control" in Radin, *Reinterpreting Property,* above n. 41.
[44] Ibid., p. 79.
[45] Radin, "Property and Personhood", above n. 41, at pp. 44–48
[46] G. W. F. Hegel, *Elements of the Philosophy of Right* A Wood (ed.), (Cambridge, Cambridge University Press, 1991), p. 73 et seq. (esp paras. 41–64).
[47] See Waldron, *The Right to Private Property,* above n. 2, at ch 10, esp 344–351.
[48] See Hegel, *Elements of the Philosophy of Right,* above n. 45, at Preface, 9–23.
[49] Hume, above n. 14, at p. 310.
[50] See above n. 28 and the accompanying text.
[51] See Hume, above n. 14, at p. 251 et seq. and 277 et seq.
[52] Bentham, "Security and Equality of Property", above n. 34, at p. 51.
[53] Ibid., p. 54.

"Everything which I possess, or to which I have a title, I consider in my own mind as destined always to belong to me. I make it the basis of my expectations, and of the hopes of those dependent upon me; and I form my plan of life accordingly. Every part of my property may have, in my estimation, besides its intrinsic value, a value of affection—as an inheritance from my ancestors, as the reward of my own labor, or as the future dependence of my children. Everything about it represents to my eye that part of myself which I have put into it—those cares, that industry, that economy which denied itself present pleasures to make provision for the future. Thus our property becomes part of our being, and cannot be torn from us without rending us to the quick".

Once again, property arrangements will continue to have this effect in constituting people's sense of themselves, whether or not they are justified. It is enough that the rights in question are established and officially supported. Once that is the case, people will tend to think of the things assigned to them (even the things assigned unjustly to them) as *theirs* and as *belonging to them*. As those claims will seem to the people concerned not just echoes of the positive law, but claims with independent moral force inasmuch as positive property rights have become connected with the basis of their personhood.

So far in this section we have concentrated on a particular type 2 judgement about property—namely, possessors' judgements of things *belonging* to them. What about the other end of the stick—people's sense of the distinction between honesty and dishonesty, and the wrongness of stealing? How do we explain and justify the resilience of these judgements in relation to a set of perhaps unjustified property rights?

David Hume offered an account of sorts. Considerations like the ones outlined earlier in this section will explain why those who benefit from existing property rights will develop various terms and modes of vehement condemnation of acts that tend to interfere with those rights. Others will join them in that, to the extent that they foresee what they have to lose from any general deadening of industry consequent upon such violations (along the lines that Bentham indicated). That will happen whether or not the system of property was initially justified. Beyond that, Hume reckoned, even when the violation and its effect are quite remote, "it still displeases us; because we consider it as prejudicial to human society, and pernicious to every one that approaches the person guilty of it. We partake of their uneasiness by sympathy".[54] Together interest and sympathy will explain the development of virtue-and-vice concepts whose role it is to sustain the existing order of property.

Hume considers the extent to which this may be supplemented by purely political indoctrination. He doubts that that does much work on its own:[55]

"Any artifice of politicians may assist nature in the producing of those sentiments, which she suggests to us, and may even on some occasions, produce alone an

---

[54] Hume, above n. 14, at p. 499.
[55] Ibid., p. 500.

approbation or esteem for any particular action; but 'tis impossible it should be the sole cause of the distinction we make betwixt vice and virtue. For if nature did not aid us in this particular, 'twou'd be in vain for politicians to talk of honourable or dishonourable, praiseworthy or blameable. The utmost politicians can perform, is, to extend the natural sentiments beyond their original bounds; but still nature must furnish the materials, and give us some notion of moral distinctions."

The connection between particular property rights and our natural sympathies is for Hume the best explanation of our tendency to mould our own sentiments and those of our children into dispositions of probity and honesty.

Of course we need not accept Hume's particular psychological account of the origin of moral distinctions. Maybe they are developed not merely by interest and sympathy, but by all sorts of methods of social construction, according to the direct power of the moral considerations at stake. So, for example, if Bentham is right, one might expect moral concepts like those used in type 2 judgements condemning theft, dishonesty, and expropriation to be forthcoming in society, just as one expects that in general, moral ideals will follow considerations of social utility. And the same sort of case may be made on Radin's account. Any sensibility that values respect for persons will tend to develop modes of evaluation appropriate to the specific vulnerability of personhood in relation to existing property rights and—this is the important point—to develop them in a way that does not connect them too tightly to the modes of evaluation used for the overall assessment of the property regime.

One further point. At the very beginning of this chapter, I noted that "honest" tends to be a quite general term of moral approbation. It used to mean virtue and honour of all sorts, encompassing chastity, generosity, and decorum; and even now it includes "uprightness of disposition and conduct; integrity, truthfulness, straightforwardness" as well as "the quality opposed to lying, cheating, or stealing". [56] More than almost any other virtue word, "honesty" connotes a thesis about the unity of the virtues in social life; it connects refraining from others' property with a general willingness to act truthfully, rightfully, and straightforwardly. It connects with virtues like industriousness, as when we talk of "an honest day's work". It connotes incorruptibility ("honest politicians"), neutrality ("honest broker"), sexual respectability ("make an honest woman of her"), and genuineness ("honest-to-God goodness"). These are not just ambiguities. There is a real tendency to think that someone is honest in any of these regards is more likely to be honest in the others as well. The fact that honesty has all these ramifications is interesting, for it echoes what we might think of as *the social pervasiveness of property*. An established system of property is not simply one aspect, among others, of the social structure. It is quite all-encompassing, for it establishes much of the context in which we deal with others, relate to them, trade with them, work for them, and compete with them. Whether we like it or not, we all have to learn how to get by in the prevailing

[56] See above n. 2.

system of property.[57] We have to learn which things are "ours" and which not; how to acquire something we don't already possess; under what circumstances we will gain the benefit of others' work with the resources *they* possess; and in general how industry, commerce, and social intercourse are carried on in a world composed of objects and places designated as items of property. One who shows himself incompetent in this regard, even in one instance, is liable to be suspected as a kind of *general* menace: if he doesn't take property seriously *here*, we may say, he may not take it seriously anywhere. (After all, we do rely to an enormous extent on people's voluntary willingness not to just run off with things they covet or break into whatever places they like.) And if this person doesn't take this part of the social fabric seriously—why, he may not take any of it seriously. If we can't trust him not to steal a towel from a hotel, can we trust him with our accounts or with our children? Can we trust him to tell the truth or keep his engagements or do the work that he promises to do?

Once again, all this holds whether or not the established system of property is itself morally justifiable. If it is *the established system*, then it is the pervasive basis of social context in the way I have been describing. It is not surprising, then, we would develop concepts like "honesty" and "dishonesty" whose purpose it is to convey this holistic point, that someone who violates existing property rules in one regard is *in general* not to be trusted. It is not surprising, either, that these concepts would develop rather independently of any thoughts about overall justification. There may be innumerable just alternatives to the existing system of property, many of them much more just than the one that presently exists. But there is room for only one of them to be established, and it is within the framework of the one that is established that we all have to make our lives, for better or for worse.

Incidentally I think this also explains a couple of the connections that were explored in section II. There I said there is a connection between honesty and actions done in the open (and that therefore an open infringement of a property rule is less likely to be stigmatised as dishonest than a covert or furtive one). An action done in the open is one that can stand scrutiny in the sight of others with whom we share a social framework: one puts oneself on display, as it were, as one who has no reason to expect that he will not be trusted in general on account of the current infringement. (The logic is similar to that of the general law-abidingness which is displayed—paradoxically—in open acts of civil disobedience.) Similarly, someone whose challenge to contemporary property is grounded in some set of traditional property rights may seem less threatening to the social fabric, insofar as his deference to a tradition of property rights shows that he does at least take seriously the idea of social fabric.

If I am right in this hunch that the normative resilience of terms like "honesty" and "dishonesty" is explained in part by the social pervasiveness of property,

---

[57] Cf. the account of "Layman's Property" in B. Ackerman, *Private Property and the Constitution* (New Haven, Yale University Press, 1977), p. 116 et seq. See also Waldron, *The Right to Private Property,* above n. 2, at pp. 42–43.

Table 8.5: Lower scale of normative resilience

Institution	Type 2 Predicate
The state	terrorist
True religion	heretic
Traditional marriage	fornicator
Aristocracy	lack of noble birth

then we might have a way of explaining some of the distinctions we found when we scrutinised Table 8.1. Remember that I said that some of the examples there exhibited normative resilience while others did not. For example, there does not seem to be the same normative resilience among the pairs shown in Table 8.5. as there is between private property and honesty. The explanation may be that those to whom the type 2 epithets in Table 8.5 are likely to be applied, share, for the most part, a social world with those who agree with them that the institutions on the left of the table are unjustified. For example, those whom proponents of traditional marriage would condemn as fornicators tend to share a social world with people who deny that sex outside marriage is always wrong; and those whom defenders of the state label terrorists, often have no choice but to confine their social relations to a small corps of trusted fellow insurgents, who of course agree with them in repudiating current state arrangements. In the case of property, by contrast, one has to be a very fortunate opponent of current property arrangements to live surrounded only by like-minded individuals. Maybe the members of extreme socialist sects can do this (though even Karl Marx paid his rent in London, and Engels inherited industrial wealth from his family); or maybe the members of utopian communities can (like the Robert Owen community in Edinburgh). But most opponents of existing property arrangements, no matter how deeply they feel about the issue, have to make a living and share a world with others who support those arrangements in the framework they constitute.

V. THE JUSTIFICATION ENTERPRISE

So there may be something to the normative resilience of property. It may not be inappropriate to condemn theft, commend honesty, and respond sympathetically to claims of "belonging" in the context of an unjust system of property rights. What follows from this? What does it tell us about the enterprise of justificatory argument in political philosophy?

It may be thought that the normative resilience of property argues for a rather gloomy prospect for grand theorising in political philosophy. By indicating the enduring importance of judgements based on existing property rights whether the property system in general is justified or not, it may be thought to weaken the case for the more general inquiry. Since we are morally bound by existing property rights anyway, what is the point of asking whether the property system is just or unjust? Perhaps normative resilience hooks up with a more general Hegelianism, which maintains that (in some suitably nuanced sense) everything is alright as it is, and philosophers should stop going around indicting existing institutions for failing to conform to their theories and, as Hegel puts it scathingly, "issuing instructions on how the world ought to be".[58] Philosophers should stop worrying that legal reality lacks a moral justification; instead they should concentrate their energies on uncovering the rationality and justification which the normative resilience of existing arrangements shows is undoubtedly present already.

A somewhat different argument, though to a similar effect, may be made by a Marxist. The resilience of type 2 judgements—the Marxist may say—is to be explained ultimately in terms of social psychology. It is an instance of ideological power—that is, an indication of the ability, which prevailing institutions have, to infect not just the lives, but the consciousness of those who suffer under them. It is not enough that the system of capitalist property expropriates and exploits the proletariat. It also inoculates them against any form of rebellion or resistance by stigmatising any infringement of prevailing property rules with the shame and dishonour of "dishonesty". Ideologically, an established system of property may have the effect that the proprietorial sentiments of the advantaged actually evoke an empathy and respect from the disadvantaged which is quite isolated from the latter's opinion about the justice or injustice of the property-holding in question. This, if you like, gives an ideological spin to the Bentham/Radin thesis about the connection between property and personality. We make it *as though* attacking P's property is attacking P herself; and since clearly it would be wrong to attack P herself (whatever the distributive situation), that sense of wrongness is projected onto any encroachment on P's property even though such encroachment considered on its own merits, might be quite justifiable. In its ideological aspect, the normative resilience of property may also be connected with myths of opportunity and the equality or reciprocity of rights. We bring our children up to believe that in respecting P's property, they are according no greater respect to her than she is required to accord to them, and that if P has property (and they have none), this has to do with the way she succeeded (while they failed) in consummating opportunities that were available equally to everyone. We know all too well that such sentiments may persist, and surface in the phenomena of shame and the sense of dishonesty I have mentioned, long after the economic conditions of opportunity, equality, and reciprocal respect have evaporated. On this account, the quest for a general justification (or critique of property) is not so much pre-empted (as it is on the

---

[58] Hegel, above n. 45, at p. 21.

Hegelian approach) as hopeless. Since the ideology of property is already firmly in possession of all the space in moral consciousness that an effective justificatory theory could possibly occupy, we should abandon the futile business of challenging that ideology on moral grounds. The normative resilience of property—as an ideological product—shows that we are bound to lose that battle. If we oppose property, we should devote ourselves to the direct task of overthrowing it, rather than waste effort in a futile endeavour to discredit it first.

I find neither of these lines of argument convincing, however, and I don't believe we should use the normative resilience of property as a basis for inferring pessimistic conclusions so far as the justificatory enterprise is concerned. There are a number of responses that I want to make.

First, and most obviously, any Hegelian account of the social and legal world would be inadequate if it did not mention *our existing practice of engaging in general justificatory discourse*—for that's part of reality too!—and if we did not give that a place in the overall system of social practice that is "alright as it is". Secondly—so far as the Marxist argument is concerned—unless we adopt a very deterministic understanding of the ideology, we should understand that something is in fact being fought out at the level of moral argument which is not simply foreordained by the victory of capitalist property at a more material "level". Ideological structures have a certain autonomy from material forms that mean they are not the mere reflex of existing arrangements. Since, as we have seen, the normative resilience of property is neither perfect nor comprehensive but varies in several dimensions (for example, according to the extent to which the system as a whole is condemned), the mere fact of resilience does not show that broader justificatory inquiry is completely futile.

Thirdly, even if we acknowledge that the normative resilience of existing private property arrangements is a sign of their ability to survive moral or philosophical critique, it doesn't follow that critique has no effect in the world or that it is morally insignificant. For it is important not only what we bring about in the world but also *how we inhabit the world*. Even if we are pessimistic about the likely effects on institutions of our justificatory discourse, still we need to consider justificatory arguments to ascertain whether we are entitled to live comfortably with the institutions that surround us. From this point of view, we are not entitled to assume in advance (on, for example, Hegelian grounds) that everything is alright in the sense that we may live at our ease in modern society. Surely the upshot of a justificatory enquiry may be sadness and shame, concerning the institutions of our society, rather than the reconciliation that Hegel was looking for. That the resilience of certain institutions is *lamentable*, rather than something to which reason can be reconciled, is a familiar and perfectly respectable position for philosophers to adopt: it is the attitude of Plato to democratic politics in books Six and Seven of *The Republic*, of de Tocqueville to banal egalitarianism in volume II of *Democracy in America*, of Max Weber to the "iron cage" of bureaucratic rationality, and of Hannah Arendt to the modern's state's preoccupation with life and labour. Though these theorists do not think there is much to be done about what they lament, and though they may accept (and even explain) the fact of resilience, that does not diminish the importance of their evaluative arguments.

A smaller-scale example may help here. Many people believe that the abolition of capital punishment is a political impossibility in the USA for the foreseeable future at least so long as fear of crime is bound up with racial antipathy. But they nevertheless regard the debate about its justification as a live and important one, inasmuch as it determines whether, as moral beings, we may live *comfortably* in a society of which popular enthusiasm for judicial killing is an ineradicable feature. Moreover, that question—reconciliation or discomfort—is not seen as an indulgent matter of posture, but as an issue of authenticity and understanding. So long as this is recognised, the strictures of justificatory debate lose none of their importance in view of the resilience of the institutions we are evaluating.

The fourth point I want to make is the most important, it is the point I intimated earlier (at the beginning of section IV). It seems to me that if an institution has the sort of resilience that we have been talking about, if it has or is likely to have this sort of presence in any society in which it is established, if it carries this kind of psychological baggage, if the mere fact of its positive existence is going to generate and sustain resilient type 2 judgements, then that does not diminish the burden of justification so far as an institution of this kind is concerned: instead it increases it. It means that if we do have any opportunity to make our justificatory discourse effective—we are poised, for example, to introduce a new system of property (as governments have been over the last decade in Eastern Europe)—then we should think very carefully, because the likely resilience of what we are instituting means that it is liable to do much more damage and be much harder to eradicate if we make a wrong choice at this stage than would be the case with a non-resilient institution.

Again an analogy may help. Consider the choices faced by a religious teacher who wants to address the question of sex with his pupils. Clearly it is important for him to tell them the truth, to get it right, and to communicate that truth in a way that will do the most good. If he makes a mistake (or, worse, tell his pupils lies), he does them a great disservice—depriving them of harmless pleasures, leaving them ill-equipped to deal with the dangers of pregnancy or sexually-transmitted diseases, making them ashamed of things they need not be ashamed of. To some extent, this damage may be reversible in later life, as they discover what they were taught was untrue. But if his sex education teaching is resilient in the consciousness of his pupils, in the way that religious sex education often is, it will not be enough for the pupils to later become aware of his errors. Even if they are rightly convinced that he misled them (say about homosexuality or masturbation) the stigmatisation of these activities as "wrong" or "dirty" might remain, resiliently, long after the underlying theories that have been discredited. If this is a possibility—and I take it that one can figure out in advance that it is—

then that is a reason for the teacher to approach his task more carefully, rather than less carefully. He should think to himself, "I had better be very sure that I have got this right, because to a certain extent my teachings will be resilient and incorrectable if I am wrong". He certainly should not think (though no doubt many sex educators do), "It doesn't matter whether I am right or wrong, for even if my lies are uncovered, they will still have the psychological effect that I desire". And that would be the analogue of inferring a diminution of the justificatory burden from the normative resilience of property. In other words, the normative resilience of property may properly be said to diminish our sense of when justificatory discourse can have any effect in the real world; but just because of that, it increases the burden of justification we are under for those occasions when justificatory discourse *can* have some effect.

The same, finally, may be said not just about the institution of a new set of property arrangements, but also about occasions of injustice that are likely to become entrenched or established. Part of what was wrong about (say) the expropriation of aboriginal lands in New Zealand, Australia and the USA in the nineteenth century, was of course the immediate injustice, loss, and suffering endured by those who were the victims of expropriation. But part of the cost also is that that injustice is now not easily correctible, and that it persists, resiliently, both in the consciousness of the victims' descendants that they are somehow cheating or being dishonest in demanding the land back, and in the real pain and sense of deprivation that would be suffered by those who have become (perhaps through no fault of their own) the modern-day beneficiaries of that injustice. To that extent, the fact of resilience means that an injustice of this sort—in property arrangements—is a much worse thing to inflict on a people than an injustice in some area of life where resilience is not an issue. Resilience muddies the water; it makes the injustice that much more difficult to clear up; it lays a kind of curse on a land so that even good-hearted members of later generations may be genuinely at a loss as to how to make things better. That means, historically, that the original expropriation is all the more regrettable. But it also indicates a lesson for us so far as current issues of justice and injustice are concerned. For if we act unjustly now, in an area of life or law which exhibits this resilience, we should be aware that we are not just injuring the immediate victims, but we are poisoning the ground for any future attempt to make thing better, and leaving for our children and grandchildren to sort out a more hideous tangle of shame and loss and disorientation.

9

Normative Resilience–A Response to Waldron

M M GOLDSMITH

Jeremy Waldron has identified a phenomenon, which he has dubbed "the normative resilience of property".[1] What I intend to do is to examine this apparent resilience of property rights and to see whether we should be surprised by it in relation to some more general theories of legal authority.

Let's begin with a familiar distinction between justifying a practice or institution and justifying a particular action under that institution. It is a distinction which has been used both by Herbert Hart and John Rawls.[2] Rawls argued that making this distinction could be used to defend utilitarianism against some common criticisms of it, especially the accusations that it justified 'punishing' the innocent if that would produce overall social benefit and that it could not account for the obligatory character of promises. He related the distinction to two different offices: that of the legislator looking at the desirability of a practice or institution in terms of its overall future consequences and that of the judge deciding in a particular case by looking at past events. Justifying punishment and promising as social institutions required distinguishing between two different conceptions of rules. On the first conception, typical of the type of consequentialist theories in which the actor aims at achieving the best result possible under the circumstances, rules are summaries, condensed guides to what is likely to be the best thing to do under particular conditions. The other conception takes rules to be authoritative, to bind the actor to follow the rule without calculating (short of disaster) the desirability of the consequences.[3]

Hart pointed out that much confusion could be avoided if the definition of punishment and its general justification were kept distinct from each other and from the rules about how punishment should be distributed. Particular

---

[1] J. Waldron, "The Normative Resilience of Property", Chapter 8 above.

[2] J. Rawls, "Two Concepts of Rules", (1955) 64 *Philosophical Review* 3–32; H. L. A. Hart, *Punishment and Responsibility: Essays in the Philosophy of Law* (Oxford, Clarendon Press, 1968), pp. 3–11.

[3] Rawls, "Two Concepts" at 17–18, takes the view that deliberation in particular cases is confined to whether "the various excuses, exceptions and defenses, which are understood by, and which constitute an important part of, the practice, apply to one's own case". Nevertheless, that the consequences "would have been extremely severe" may be among those defences.

instances of punishment, who was to have it and how much, might be arranged retributively even if a retributive justification of the institution itself were rejected.

The same distinction between justifying a practice and justifying particular conduct within a practice underlies normative resilience: [4]

> "The concept of normative resilience points to a discontinuity between two types of normative judgment associated with an institution: (1) judgements concerning the justification of the institution, and (2) judgements concerning individual conduct in relation to the institution. Resilience is the phenomenon whereby judgements of type 2, although they are predicated upon the institution, nevertheless remain unaffected by judgements of type 1 that are adverse to the institution."

So the idea is that type 2 judgements about conduct, such as "she is innocent of dangerous driving", "he is a thief", "that action was dishonest", are warranted as justified or unjustified by appealing to the criteria embodied in the rules of an institution. They are authorised or not authorised by its rules (which make those statements either true or false). In making these type 2 judgements, individuals invoke the authority of the practice; they do not revert to the values which ultimately justify the practice itself or its rules. [5]

Thus the warrant for particular judgements about conduct is produced by appealing to the rules of an institution. [6] If institution C is justified and conduct c is an action properly carried out according to the rules of C, then conduct c is justified. If conduct c is not an action properly carried out according to the rules of C, then conduct c is not justified by institution C. If conduct c is contrary to the rules of institution C then the judgment that c is wrong is justified by the rules of institution C. Judgements about c in all these cases are warranted by appealing to the rules of institution C.

But what if C itself is not justified? That would seem to remove normative support for judgements about c being justified or not justified. The warranting appeals might persist, but what status would the resulting judgements have? They seem to be undermined, perhaps their status becomes indeterminate, neither true nor false. Nevertheless, it may still be felt that such judgements have normative force: they are normatively resilient.

Let's suppose that C is a legal system. Legal positivism seems to cash out into the claims that: (1) If the legal system is justified, then it warrants judgements about conduct under the rules and institutions of that system, and (2) a legal sys-

---

[4] Waldron, "Normative Resilience" Chapter 8 above at p. 174.

[5] Indeed it may be the case for a practice to be authoritative that judgements under the practice replace the considerations which are otherwise the reasons individuals have for actions and foreclose appeals to those reasons and values, that is, they provide "exclusionary reasons": see J. Raz, *Practical Reason and Norms* (London, Hutchinson, 1975), pp. 35–48, 62–65; *The Morality of Freedom* (Oxford, Clarendon Press, 1986), pp. 38–69.

[6] I shall use the terms "warranted" and "warrant" to refer to the process of validation as distinct from "justified" or "unjustified" as referring to the success or failure of the process.

tem is justified by virtue of its being an operating, socially established system.[7] Legal normative validity does not depend on the conformity of the system to substantive moral norms. The moral question is a separate one from whether there is an operating legal system and from the legal status of laws within a legal system: what is legally valid is always open to moral criticism. Legal positivism thus accepts that law is not necessarily morally good. Legal positivism does not deny that legal systems often include laws which embody what is regarded as morally right in a society, but it does claim that there is a gap between 'legally valid' and 'morally right' in the sense that the former does not entail the latter. That something is right morally is neither a necessary nor a sufficient condition for it to be valid law.

A coincidence of legal validity and moral rightness will not provide normative resilience. There are situations in which there would be good moral reasons for doing *c* even if *c* were not legally required (or not doing *c* even if it were not legally prohibited). These reasons would still carry some weight even if they were outweighed by other reasons making *c* wrong (or right). This would not be normative resilience for the very reason given by Waldron: the considerations which make *c* ultimately the wrong, rather than the right, thing to do come from other independent moral considerations, which in the end outweigh the reasons in favour of *c* despite those reasons retaining their force.[8]

The concept of 'moral resilience' applies when a type 2 judgement persists despite its failing to be justified by type 1 backing. Suppose that the law includes a morally unjust property arrangement, say, gross partiality toward landlords in relation to tenants' sub-tenanting a rented property. A tenant evades the provisions about sub-tenanting, enabling a friend to live in the property because the friend desperately needs a place to live and cannot otherwise find a suitable place. In case i, the tenant accepts that the action is legally wrong but feels that the dishonesty is overridden by other moral considerations such as the obligations of friendship, or the welfare of the friend, and so feels justified. In the alternative case ii, the tenant holds that the law is unfair but still feels dishonest in breaking it. In situations where the law is extremely unjust, say slavery, the situation may be somewhat different. In case iii, it is recognized that helping a slave escape to freedom is legally wrong, but whatever dishonesty involved in breaking the law by doing so is overridden by other moral considerations, such as the right of humans to be free, or the well-being of the escaped slave. In the

---

[7] The thought here is that legitimation, legal validity or authorisation is transitive. If x legitimates y and y legitimates z then x legitimates z; similarly, if z is authorised by y and y is authorised by x, then z is authorised by x. Thus the legal system authorises legal institutions and the rules of those institutions authorise conduct. The hierarchical arrangement of legitimising authority follows the pattern of a legal system composed of an ultimate rule of recognition, authority conferring rules and primary rules of conduct as outlined by H. L. A. Hart in *The Concept of Law* (Oxford, Clarendon Press, 1961), pp. 77–120, or an hierarchy of norms as propounded by H. Kelsen, *General Theory of Law and State* (New York, Russell & Russell, 1961). For a similar conception of authority in relation to sovereignty, see I. Wilks, "A Note on Sovereignty", (1955) 5 *Philosophical Quarterly* 342–347.

[8] Waldron, "Normative Resilience" Chapter 8 above at p. 178–179.

alternative version, case iv, it is recognised that slavery is morally wrong, but there will at most be a very slight resilience, perhaps only a slight regret at breaking the law rather than the stronger feeling that it is dishonest to do so.[9] In so far as normative resilience occurs in these cases, it occurs in ii and iv and not in i and iii.

To what extent is normative resilience a consequence of legal positivism or even compatible with it? It seems that what one would need here is a theory which justified attributing some moral force to legality. Such a theory would have to contend that the very fact of something being legally required or legally forbidden made a difference to the moral reasons for or against doing it. These would have to be reasons which were independent of other substantive moral reasons. It would not be enough, for example, if it were in any case morally wrong to disappoint expectations or frustrate interests, that legal validity created interests that would be frustrated or expectations that would be disappointed. In that case the wrongness would come not from the law but independently from what was morally right or wrong. What would be required is a theory in which the very fact of 'legality' provided some moral force, that is, a theory in which something being a law carried some moral weight even if it were a bad or evil law. If that were the case then 'legality' would provide some '*pro tanto*' moral force even in cases in which other moral considerations outweighed legality.

One might suggest that Herbert Hart's version of legal positivism does provide that kind of status for legality. Hart criticised Austin's theory of law for confusing two senses of 'obliged'. In the first sense, rules are taken to oblige when there is serious social pressure to conform to them. The serious pressure may be applied by identifiable persons holding official positions in the society or by undifferentiated members of the public; the types of social pressure may range from verbal disapproval to physical sanctions. It is possible to identify these rules empirically or 'externally': an observer can predict that certain kinds of actions will tend to evoke this kind of serious pressure:[10]

> "After a time the external observer may, on the basis of the regularities observed, correlate deviation with hostile reaction, and be able to predict with a fair measure of success, and to assess the chances that a deviation from the group's normal behaviour will meet with hostile reaction or punishment. If, however, the observer really keeps austerely to this extreme external point of view and does not give any account of the manner in which members of the group who accept the rules view their own regular behaviour, his description of their life cannot be in terms of rules at all, and so not in the terms of the rule-dependent notions of obligation or duty."

Hart uses the example of a red traffic light to illustrate what the external observer misses. The external observer can predict the incidence of cars stopping when the light turns red; the probability of that happening can be calcu-

---

[9] Waldron, "Normative Resilience" Chapter 8 above at pp. 179–180.
[10] Hart, *Concept of Law*, above n. 7, p. 87.

lated. But the external observer cannot treat the red light as a signal to stop or take the red light as a reason for stopping. For those who take the "internal point of view" the rules establish obligations; they "provide guides to the conduct of social life".[11]

But it seems to me by no means clear that Hart's theory does provide moral weight for law just because it is law and so explains normative resilience. It cannot be the internal point of view towards the system of law as a whole which gives the moral weight to the type 2 judgements which are resilient, because the case which we're considering is one in which the type 2 judgment persists despite the rejection of the type 1 judgement, that the system is justified. Under these circumstances it seems as if the type 2 judgement would no longer express or presuppose the internal point of view, but would shift to an external point of view. Thus, if we were rejecting the system or some part of it, instead of saying, "John committed a crime", it would seem that we would say, "According to the law as it now stands, John committed a crime".[12] Such a shift would at least hint that legal validity carried no implied moral rightness.

Moreover, there is at least one instance in Hart's writing where he comes close to considering this problem. In defending the distinction between "law as it is" and "law as it ought to be", he discussed the revival of natural law in Germany in the post-Second World War period. In 1949 a woman was prosecuted under an 1871 statute for the offence of illegally depriving a person of his liberty. In 1944 she had reported her husband to the authorities for remarks denigrating Hitler while he was home on leave from the army. He was sentenced under a statute of 1934 making it illegal to make statements inimical to the welfare of the Third Reich. Although the sentence was not carried out, he was sent to the front. On the basis of the 1934 statute, she claimed that she had committed no crime. Should the Court of Appeal allow her conviction on the grounds that the 1934 statute could not be valid law because it was contrary to natural law?[13]

Hart discussed the problem twice, in slightly different but compatible ways. In "Positivism and the Separation of Law and Morals" (1958), he claimed that the court was presented with a choice between evils. One evil would have been to allow the woman to take advantage of an iniquitous deed allowed by an evil law and profit from her action; the other evil would have been to punish someone for action which was legal when it took place. Although retrospectively making something a crime and punishing someone for committing it would be "odious", Hart preferred an open recognition that this was involved to the more veiled voiding of a law which had plainly been in force at the time the act took

---

[11] Ibid., pp. 84–88; see also pp. 55–57.

[12] See Hart, *Concept of Law*, above n. 7, p. 99, for an example of this kind of contrast in locution between the internal and external points of view.

[13] See H. L. A. Hart, "Positivism and the Separation of Law and Morals", (1958) 71 *Harvard Law Review* 593, 618–621; *Concept of Law*, above n. 7, pp. 203–207; see also pp. 254–255 for Hart's correction of the actual decision of the German court in the case.

place. In *The Concept of Law*, Hart's emphasis is on considering which of two conceptions of what counts as law is preferable: the wider (positivist) conception or the narrower (natural law) conception. In both discussions, the problem for Hart has both moral and conceptual elements. What should one do when faced with iniquitous laws? This decision is a moral one. Is it intellectually and practically desirable to take the position that no evil law can truly be law? Or is it better to accept that laws can be evil? Which position will lead to fewer bad consequences in terms of obedience to evil laws? But there is no suggestion that he takes the view that the existence of something as valid law itself provides a moral reason for obeying it.

Natural law theories tend to deal with the problem in a different way. They take what Hart called a "narrower" view of legal validity in which the criterion of legal validity is not content independent. According to such theories, quoting Augustine, "A law that is not just, seems to be no law at all".[14] Nevertheless it would be too simple to conclude that natural law theories treat unjust laws as simply non-existent or void.

There are two types of criteria on which laws may not be just: formal and substantive. Perhaps the best known natural law theory is that of Thomas Aquinas. According to his definition law has four characteristics: it is an ordinance of reason, aimed at the common good of a community, made by the community or the person who has care of the community, and promulgated.[15] That the law aim at the common good is a substantive criterion; that it be promulgated is a formal one. The other two criteria mix formal and substantive elements. As an "ordinance" of reason law provides a guide for those subject to it—a formal requirement. But being an ordinance of "reason" also seems to refer to a substantive element since Aquinas is concerned to reject a "command theory" of law as embodied in *Digest* 1, 4, 1: *quod princeps placuit legis habet vigorem*.[16] The will of the ruler need not be deficient in providing a guide for action so there seems to be some further element required. That the law be made by the community or the person in charge of it combines the formal criterion of proper procedure with the substantive standard that the purported legislator have legitimate authority.

By failing to meet any one of these criteria, a law fails to be what a law should be. But what does that failure imply? For Aquinas the consequence is not straightforwardly that such laws do not exist, nor even that they be disregarded and not obeyed. His view is more subtle and qualified: unjust laws do not bind in conscience, except perhaps to avoid scandal or disturbance. There are some laws which must not be obeyed. These are laws which are contrary to God's laws: for example, a law commanding the worship of idols should be disobeyed. But in other cases it seems that the subject must consider the consequences of

---

[14] Augustine, *De Libero Arbitrio*, I, v, 11.
[15] T. Aquinas, *Summa Theologiae* I-II, question 90, art. 1–4, esp art. 4. For a similar definition see J. Finnis, *Natural Law and Natural Rights* (Oxford, Clarendon Press, 1980), pp. 273–281.
[16] Aquinas, *Summa Theologiae* I-II, question 90, art. 1.

obedience and disobedience. Indeed it looks as if the subject will usually have to obey since disobedience will always cause some disturbance.[17]

A different version of a natural law theory is that of Lon Fuller. In *The Morality of Law* he contends that law has an 'internal morality'. This turns out to be a set of eight characteristics which law must have to a greater or lesser extent in order to qualify as law.[18] The characteristics are formal ones. Failure to reach a certain level of various of these qualities will undermine a purported legal system so that it cannot operate as 'law'. For example, high degrees of lack of clarity in the rules, retroactivity, frequent change or incongruity between the rules and their administration will affect the capacity of the system to provide guidelines for conduct to those subject to the system. The theory does not raise a problem of legal validity or invalidity, and so of normative resilience, but rather suggests that there is a threshold level below which a system becomes incapable of doing what law is meant to do.

But if Fuller's theory escapes the problem of normative resilience, do theories on the Aquinas model also do so? The answer to this question seems to depend on how one interprets the contention that unjust laws do not bind in conscience. Just laws ought to be obeyed; they fulfil the substantive as well as the formal criterion for law. But the substantive criterion is that their content is justified by natural law, which is the participation through reason of human beings in God's law for the creation. The laws of particular societies, human laws, are subordinate to natural law. The obligation to obey those laws is derived from natural law. But it isn't the case that human law is something like a mere transcription, not requiring any adaptation or intellectual effort. Natural law provides general principles; human law relates to it as either specification of generalities or deduction from premises.[19] Putting aside the theological premises and language, the idea is that practical reason provides principles which direct human beings to their natural ends, to the fulfilment of the values which ought to be realised in life. The law of a particular society is proper law when it further adapts those general principles for that society, for example, by setting out what actions are harmful to others by endangering life or health, or by specifying speed limits and other rules of the road.

Thus on this type of natural law theory, just laws derive their obligatory character from their source in practical reason (natural law) not their enactment as positive law. Because of that derivation they are morally binding. Other seeming laws are "not truly" laws although they have the "form of law". To be morally binding is to bind in conscience. What does not bind in conscience has no moral force. Whatever moral reasons there may be for not disobeying those

[17] Aquinas, *Summa Theologiae* I-II, question 96, art. 4; see also *Summa Theologiae* II-II, question 42, art. 2, question 104, arts. 1–6; *Commentary on the Sentences of Peter Lombard*, Distinction 44, question 2, art. 2. See also Finnis, above n. 15, at 363–366, emphasising the qualifications on the simple principle that an unjust law is not a law.

[18] L. L. Fuller, *The Morality of Law* (New Haven, Yale University Press, 1964), pp. 33–94.

[19] Aquinas, *Summa Theologiae* I-II, question 91, art. 3; question 95, art. 2.

laws, or for obeying them, cannot derive from their having moral weight by virtue of having been legally enacted. If there are reasons for not disobeying those laws, those reasons must come from some other moral or prudential consideration—for example, Aquinas mentions causing disturbance or scandal, both bad things.[20] Consequently it seems that this type of natural law theory does not attribute moral weight to the fact of (wide) legal validity and so does not provide a basis for normative resilience.

It seems to me that the same considerations will apply whether we are looking at the system as a whole or some part of it. If the system is not just then it can provide no moral force to institutions or laws or determinations within it; if an institution is not just then it can provide no moral force to laws or determinations under it. If there are moral reasons for respecting such determinations, laws or institutions, they must come from an independent source.

Let us suppose that "having a legal system is a good thing" is both true and widely agreed within a society. What is not agreed is that the established system is a morally just one: the system exists but it lacks full justification. Like many societies, it is not a "well-ordered society".[21] There are at least two cases: (1) the evil society; (2) the partly flawed system. By an evil society I mean one which is tyrannical, oppressive, perhaps even murderous toward its citizens and subjects. There are all too many recent examples of societies which had or have morally rotten justificatory foundations. But even in such a society many laws and institutions will continue to operate as they had done before the advent of the evil. Consider the example of Nazi Germany. Despite the *Führerprinzip* being the basis of authority and the rule of law being subverted in a number of ways: the notion that judges were to interpret law in accordance with party ideology, the enunciations of the Führer and the sound feelings of the folk; the extensive introduction of special privileges, liabilities and jurisdictions; and arbitrary action against persons deemed hostile to the régime—all of which undermined legal regularity and certainty—a completely new and Nazi codification never occurred.[22] Much of the ordinary arrangements in the society went on as before: property rights persisted, as did much commercial intercourse. Trivially, people bought and sold groceries, rents and wages were paid and so on. Notwithstanding the system's lack of overall justification, many standard type 2 judgements will continue to be made and warranted in the normal way. Those judgements will be justified both for those who live under the régime and mistakenly accept it as a good régime and for those who come afterward and

---

[20] For a different analysis, see Finnis, above n. 14, at pp. 354–362.

[21] J. Rawls, *A Theory of Justice* (Oxford, Clarendon Press, 1972), pp. 4–5: "a society is well-ordered when it is not only designed to advance the good of its members but when it is also effectively regulated by a public conception of justice. That is, it is a society in which (1) everyone accepts and knows that others accept the same principles of justice, and (2) the basic social institutions generally satisfy and are generally known to satisfy these principles". For a fuller account see ibid., pp. 453–462.

[22] See J. Noakes and G. Pridham (eds.), *Nazism 1919–1945, Vol. 2: State, Economy and Society, 1933–1939: A Documentary Reader* (Exeter, University of Exeter, 1984), pp. 471–489.

denounce it as evil. For the grossly evil parts of the system, the situation will be different. Supporters of the régime will not make type 1 judgements which are adverse to the system; those who reject it will not feel that type 2 judgements in these areas have any moral weight. Normative resilience seems not to apply.

The second situation is that of a partly flawed system. Here we may indeed feel the kind of tension involved in normative resilience. The system as a whole is not evil, but some parts of it are bad. So the judgement that the institution lacks full justification along with some element of persistence in type 2 judgements under it may occur—as we supposed it might in the examples given above of the sub-tenanting arrangement and of slavery.

Nevertheless it seems to me that there remains a possibility that normative resilience does not provide the true explanation of the phenomenon involved. Throughout the discussion, the assumption has been of an hierarchical scheme such that the justification of particular judgements depends on and is derived from the justification of the institutions under which they are made and the justification of the institutions depends on and is derived from the justification of the system. The scheme involves an hierarchy of authority, each level being subordinate to the level above. That arrangement provides a useful way of explaining the structure of a legal system, for example, as Hart does, in terms of primary and secondary rules.[23] But the hierarchical scheme of authorities, designated by "rules of recognition", may mislead us in thinking that mere legal validity in itself carries moral weight, the idea which is required for the concept of "normative resilience".

There is an alternative explanation. Given the usual circumstances of human life, there may be some conventions, which are so basic to humans associating with each other that it is virtually inconceivable that any society could exist without some version of them. Among these conventions will be ones providing some arrangements for personal security and others establishing security of possessions, their transfer by consent and the obligation of promises.[24] Of course specific rules and arrangements may vary considerably. When a society formalises itself so that it has a legal system, that is a scheme of rules of recognition and authorities, its version of these basic conventions will be embodied in its law. The conventions will be further altered by the recognised authorities.[25] It will look as if the justification of these arrangements depends on the justification of the system. But despite appearances, it will be a misreading to attribute the basis and persistence of the conventions to their status as law.

Whether there is normative resilience or merely the persistence of the established version of conventions of certain types, changing the existing rules and the rights established by them will disrupt settled expectations and rights. Nor

[23] See Hart, *Concept of Law*, above n. 7, pp. 77–96.
[24] See Hart, *Concept of Law*, above n. 7, pp. 188–195. See D Hume, *A Treatise of Human Nature*, Book III, part ii, ss.1–6.
[25] See Hart, *Concept of Law*, above n. 7, pp. 89–92; Hume, *Treatise*, above n. 7, pp. Book III part ii, s. 7.

can it be guaranteed that changes will be successful and make things better. It is sometimes claimed that abolishing slavery in the USA destroyed a way of life established in the southern states; it certainly altered property rights in those states. No doubt the implementation of the civil rights laws in the USA in the 1960s and 1970s was also disruptive, as has been the ending of apartheid in South Africa. That there may be such disruption provides an argument for care and thought in making changes, as does the likelihood that the changes made will themselves become similarly entrenched. It may usually be desirable to maintain established rights, but once we become convinced that what is established is seriously wrong, neither some disruption nor the dangers of a new entrenchment can provide an irrebutable argument for leaving established wrong untouched.

10

A Constitutional Property Settlement Between Ngai Tahu and the New Zealand Crown

JOHN DAWSON

I. INTRODUCTION

The question considered in this chapter, through the study of an example, is the extent to which it is possible, using ordinary legislation, to bring within a state legal system the previously unrecognised property claims or property conceptions of an indigenous people and so to produce within the state a new distribution of power. As we know, power follows property and property signifies power, so any major reallocation of property will have consequences for state power or state governance and nowhere is this more true than in New Zealand in the Treaty of Waitangi settlement domain. Through these negotiated settlements between the New Zealand Crown and certain Maori tribes, various forms of property, removed from Maori in breach of the Treaty,[1] are being restored to the tribes, with the result that tribal capacity to participate in public affairs is progressively enhanced.[2]

Ngai Tahu are a southern tribe or iwi, with a current membership of about 25,000 people. Their Takiwa, or region of authority, covers the lower four-fifths of the South Island.[3] This is about half the land surface of New Zealand and there is an equivalent area of coastal sea. This chapter describes how the Ngai Tahu settlement approaches the task of incorporating the property conceptions of this iwi within New Zealand's state legal system.

---

[1] The official text of the Treaty of Waitangi, in the Maori and English versions, is published as a Schedule to the Treaty of Waitangi Act 1975 (NZ). See generally, P. McHugh, *The Maori Magna Carta* (Auckland, Oxford University Press, 1991); H. Kawharu (ed.), *Waitangi: Maori and Pakeha Perspectives of the Treaty of Waitangi* (Auckland, Oxford University Press, 1989); A. Sharp, *Justice and the Maori*, 2nd edn. (Auckland, Oxford University Press, 1997); M. Durie, *Te Mana, Te Kawanatanga: The Politics of Maori Self-Determination* (Auckland, Oxford University Press, 1998).

[2] For another settlement, given effect by legislation, see the Waikato (Raupatu Claims Settlement) Act 1996.

[3] Te Runanga o Ngai Tahu Act 1996 (NZ), s. 5 and First Schedule.

Consider, as an initial example, Ngai Tahu's associations with Aoraki/Mt Cook, the highest peak in the country. Ngai Tahu see their ancestors in that mountain or in the chain of mountains of which it is a part. This is captured in tribal waiata or song:

> Aoraki taku maunga
> Waitaki te awa
> Ko Tahu Potiki te tangata
> Ko Kai Tahu te iwi whanui o te Waipounamu e
> Tenei ra te whanau o Otakou.
>
> Aoraki is my mountain,
> Waitaki the river
> Tahu Potiki the ancestor.
> Kai Tahu are the federated peoples
> of the Greenstone Isle.
> These are the family of Otago.

This is a statement of tribal identity in which a mountain stands at the centre of the gaze. A relationship with this mountain constitutes in part what it means to be Ngai Tahu. For the Waikato or the Wanganui iwi it is a river, perhaps, that is the measure of identity. Ancestors, land, history, authority and communal identity are bound in an integrated system of reference. As Justice Durie puts it, for traditional Maori, "land and ancestors were fused".[4]

The Minister for Treaty Negotiations, the Hon. Doug Graham, was discussing how we may fit such conceptions within the state legal system, in a speech to the Ruapehu Federated Farmers (not an easy group to speak to on this subject), when he said:[5]

> "how difficult it is to give recognition to values and traditions which are unique to Maori in today's world. If we are to live together with goodwill we have to recognise these intangible elements in some way which fits in with current needs. In the Ngai Tahu negotiations, many months have been spent with much lateral thinking trying to devise new concepts which will do this".

In relation to Aoraki/Mt Cook this recognition is attempted, in the Ngai Tahu settlement, in the following ways: by ensuring the mountain is referred to officially by its Maori name; by vesting symbolic title in the mountain in Ngai Tahu; by ensuring the iwi is involved in formulating management plans concerning the area; by ensuring refuse is removed from the mountain; and by

---

[4] E. Durie, "Will the Settlers Settle? Cultural Conciliation and the Law", (1996) 8 *Otago LR* 449, 452. Justice Durie is the chairperson of the Waitangi Tribunal, which hears claims against the Crown concerning breaches of the principles of the Treaty of Waitangi, under the Treaty of Waitangi Act 1975. See W Oliver, *Claims to the Waitangi Tribunal* (Wellington, Department of Justice, 1991); E. Durie and G. Orr, "The Role of the Waitangi Tribunal and the Development of a Bicultural Jurisprudence", (1990) 14 *NZULR* 62; E. Durie, "Background Paper", (1995) 25 *VUWLR* 97; *Te Runanga o Muriwhenua Inc* v. *A-G* [1990] 2 NZLR 641 (CA); the numerous reports of the Waitangi Tribunal on particular claims; and the *National Overview* or *Rangihaua Whanui* series of Tribunal reports, commenced in 1997.

[5] Ruapehu Federated Farmers AGM, Taumaranui, 29 May 1997; see *Maori LR*, June 1997, 1–2.

giving those who climb it a statement of Ngai Tahu's associations with the mountain, including the suggestion that they do not stand on its head.

These changes will be facilitated by legislation. The name of the Mt Cook National Park, for instance, is changed to the Aoraki/Mt Cook National Park.[6] Ngai Tahu representatives are placed on the Conservation Board with jurisdiction over the area.[7] Several innovative forms of statutory instrument are created which will apply to the management of the area, called Statutory Acknowledgments, Deeds of Recognition,[8] and Topuni or statutory cloaks.[9] In addition, Ngai Tahu are declared to be a Statutory Adviser to certain administrative bodies[10] for particular purposes, such as advising Fish and Game Councils concerning the management of native birdlife.[11]

The general effect of these new statutory instruments will be to involve Ngai Tahu to a greater extent in resource management decision-making, often by specifying that a particular statutory body must "have particular regard to" their tribal connections with a feature of the environment or with a species of flora or fauna;[12] or by authorising the iwi to appoint representatives to participate in the decision-making of a designated body—to sit on the NZ Conservation Authority, for instance, a body which advises the Minister of Conservation on national conservation policies.[13] In effect, joint decision-making procedures will be established, particularly in the areas of land and water use and in the management of wildlife. Consultation between the iwi and government agencies will be required and Ngai Tahu concerns will be mandatory relevant considerations in the administrative process.

The concept of the Topuni, or statutory cloak, provides an example. A cloak of iwi values and associations is thrown by law over Aoraki/Mt Cook, ensuring Ngai Tahu's concerns will be heard in the resource management decisions

---

[6] Ngai Tahu Claims Settlement Act 1998 (NZ), s. 162; and see s. 269 and Sch. 96 which give effect to numerous other name changes. Hereafter all references to legislative provisions and Schedules are to the Ngai Tahu Claims Settlement Act 1998 (NZ) unless the context indicates otherwise.

[7] Section 273 guarantees Ngai Tahu representation on all Conservation Boards within their region. Conservation Boards are established by the Conservation Act 1987 (NZ), ss. 6L–6W. Their powers include recommending conservation management strategies, approving conservation management plans, advising on proposals for walkways, and liaising with Fish and Game Councils. Ngai Tahu will also be guaranteed representation on numerous other statutory bodies: e.g., NZ Conservation Authority, s. 272; the Guardians of Lakes Manapouri, Monowai, Te Anau and Wanaka, ss 274, 275; New Zealand Geographic Board, s. 276; and Te Runanga o Ngai Tahu is appointed as the statutory adviser to the local Fish and Game Councils, which "must have particular regard to that advice": ss. 278–280.

[8] Sections 205–220 and associated Schedules.

[9] Sections 237–253 and associated Schedules.

[10] E.g., ss. 230–236 and associated Schedules.

[11] Sections 277–280 and associated Schedules.

[12] E.g., s. 241 provides that the NZ Conservation Authority "must have particular regard to The Ngai Tahu values" associated with designated features of the environment in the formulation of national conservation policies.

[13] Conservation Act 1987 (NZ), ss. 6A-6K.

concerning the mountain and the surrounding area.[14] Ngai Tahu do not get exclusive possession of the mountain, nor veto powers in national park management decisions, nor are mountaineers prevented from climbing the peak. There will be no Maori warden at the top to see if climbers do stand on its head. This is certainly less than full Ngai Tahu authority over the area. But Ngai Tahu concerns and representatives are integrated into joint decision-making regimes.

This indicates the general shape of the settlement as whole. It provides administrative and property law solutions to constitutional problems. It will operate at the level of the micro-constitution, the only level at which settlement currently seems feasible. The settlement proceeds not through the entrenchment of a constitution, nor through redesign of Parliament, but through ordinary statutes and via regional and agency arrangements that bear on specific items of cultural property. At this level, however, matters are addressed in far greater detail than has ever been attempted in the Treaty field before. This is the kind of settlement that is possible and it seems capable of meeting Ngai Tahu's fundamental concerns.

Overall, a model of governance is established that goes some way to remedy the great deficiency in the Treaty of Waitangi itself, identified by Sir Hugh Kawharu in 1989, which is its "lack of a conceptual framework that could accommodate the two cultures, and an administrative infrastructure for devising coherent policies and programmes that balance obligations of sovereignty against those of rangatiratanga" (or Maori self-governance).[15] The Ngai Tahu settlement legislation helps put those infrastructures in place with regard to resources of particular significance to Ngai Tahu within their region. As a whole, it is best described as a constitutional property settlement, because the property arrangements, the constitutional provisions and the process of negotiation through which the settlement has been reached all signify the same thing— the beginning of a new era of equality of mana between Ngai Tahu and the Crown.

II. AN OVERVIEW OF THE NGAI TAHU SETTLEMENT

The Ngai Tahu claims relate to breaches by the Crown of the Treaty of Waitangi which was signed by Ngai Tahu representatives in May and June of 1840.[16] In particular, the claims relate to failure by the Crown to honour the conditions upon which Ngai Tahu lands were purchased, to over-exploitation and then expropriation of Ngai Tahu fisheries, and to destruction of Ngai Tahu food gathering practices and places, which are known as the mahinga kai (literally, food-workings).

---

[14] Schedule 80.

[15] H. Kawharu, Introduction to *Waitangi,* above n. 1 at p. x; see also the essay in that volume by the Ngai Tahu leader, Sir Tipene O'Regan, "The Ngai Tahu Claim" at p. 234.

[16] See the Waitangi Tribunal's *Ngai Tahu Report 1991* (Wai 27), vol. 2, Ch. 4 (hereafter *Ngai Tahu Report*).

Through negotiation and purchase by deed the Crown acquired from Ngai Tahu, in eight blocks, between 1844 and 1865, half the land surface of New Zealand for 14,750 pounds. 500,000 acres of Otago land were bought for 2,400 pounds, more than a million acres of North Canterbury for 500 pounds.[17] Nevertheless, the claims relate not so much to the prices paid, but to failure by the Crown to honour the conditions upon which these purchases were made. The Crown failed to leave with Ngai Tahu sufficient lands for tribal self-sufficiency;[18] it failed to set aside specific reserves;[19] it did not meet adequately its promises concerning schools and hospitals;[20] nor did it preserve to Ngai Tahu their pounamu (or greenstone) resources[21] or their mahinga kai.[22] In addition, there are claims to sea fisheries plus more than a hundred ancillary claims made by smaller social units—by hapu or whanau—concerning particular blocks of land, for instance, that should have been set aside.

All of these claims have now been settled through a process of research, inquiry and negotiation, and then by agreement in a Deed of Settlement, and that Deed has been given effect through legislation, so far as legislation was required.[23] The modern history of the claims began in 1985 with the extension of the jurisdiction of the Waitangi Tribunal back to 1840.[24] The Ngai Tahu claims were then researched and presented to the Waitangi Tribunal over a two and a half-year period between 1987 and 1989. The formal hearings covered 24 weeks.[25] The Tribunal reported in 3 phases. The findings on the land-related claims were released in 1991, along with a supplementary report which recommended the creation by statute of a representative tribal body for Ngai Tahu which would be the holder of the settlement assets on behalf of the iwi.[26] The Ngai Tahu Sea Fisheries Report was released in 1992,[27] before the pan-Maori fisheries settlement.[28] The Ancillary Claims Report followed in 1995.[29]

[17] See H. Evison, *The Long Dispute: Maori Land Rights and European Colonisation in Southern New Zealand* (Christchurch, Canterbury University Press, 1997); H. Evison, *Ngai Tahu Land Rights and the Crown Pastoral Lease Lands in the South Island of New Zealand*, 3rd edn. (Christchurch, Ngai Tahu Maori Trust Board, 1987); and the *Ngai Tahu Report*, especially vol. 2 and vol. 3, Ch. 16.

[18] *Ngai Tahu Report*, above n. 16, especially Vol. 3, Ch. 16, 18.

[19] *Ngai Tahu Report* above n. 16. Concerning the promised Arahura Reserve, see e.g., *Ngai Tahu Report*, vol. 3, para. 13.5.11.

[20] *Ngai Tahu Report*, above n. 16, vol. 3, Ch. 19.

[21] *Ibid.*, vol. 3, Ch. 13.

[22] *Ibid.*, vol. 3, Ch. 17.

[23] Some major aspects of the agreement can be given effect without specific legislation, such as the payment to Ngai Tahu of the cash settlement sum of NZ$170 million.

[24] By the Treaty of Waitangi Amendment Act 1985 (NZ).

[25] For a description of the hearing process see *Ngai Tahu Report* above n. 16, vol. 3, Appendices 6–9.

[26] *Ngai Tahu Report*, above n. 16.

[27] *Ngai Tahu Sea Fisheries Report 1992* (Wai 27).

[28] See Treaty of Waitangi (Fisheries Claims) Settlement Act 1992 (NZ); Waitangi Tribunal, *Fisheries Settlement Report 1992* (Wai 307); J. Munro, "The Treaty of Waitangi and the Sealord Deal", (1994) 24 *VUWLR* 389; M. Durie, *Te Mana, Te Kawanatanga*, above n. 1, ch. 6; *Te Runanga o Wharekauri Rekohu Inc v. A-G* [1993] 2 NZLR 301 (CA).

[29] *Ngai Tahu Ancillary Claims Report 1995* (Wai 27) .

Not all of Ngai Tahu's claims were upheld by the Tribunal, but their substantial merits were, and the Tribunal's general findings were accepted by the Crown.[30] The Tribunal concluded:[31]

> "many of the claimants' grievances arising out of the eight Crown purchases, including those relating to mahinga kai, have been established. Indeed the Crown has properly conceded that it failed to ensure Ngai Tahu were left with ample lands for their present and future needs. The Tribunal cannot avoid the conclusion that in acquiring from Ngai Tahu 34.5 million acres, more than half the land mass of New Zealand, and leaving them with only 35,757 acres, the Crown acted unconscionably and in repeated breach of the Treaty of Waitangi. The evidence further establishes that subsequent efforts by the Crown to make good Ngai Tahu's loss were few, extremely dilatory, and largely ineffectual. As a consequence Ngai Tahu has suffered grave injustices over more than 140 years. The tribe is clearly entitled to very substantial redress from the Crown".

The ancillary claims were also substantially upheld.[32] In its findings on the sea fisheries claim the Tribunal concluded: "there is a fundamental conflict between Maori fishing rights under the Treaty and the quota management scheme".[33] That scheme, in granting exclusive rights to fish commercially to holders of fishing quota, "effectively guaranteed to [quota holders] (almost all of whom were non-Maori), the full exclusive and undisturbed possession of the property rights in fishing that the Crown had already guaranteed to Maori".[34] The implementation of the quota management system, said the Tribunal, was based on the mistaken premise "that no fisheries subject to the quota belonged to Maori but all to the Crown".[35] These findings repeated the Tribunal's conclusions concerning fisheries in the far north of New Zealand in the Muriwhenua claim.[36]

By and large, the Tribunal ended its involvement with the Ngai Tahu claim when its findings were made. By agreement, it did not make detailed recommendations for redress. This was left to be negotiated between the iwi and the Crown.[37] Negotiations commenced in 1991. They proceeded fitfully, breaking down for a year or more around 1995. Finally in 1996–1997 an agreement was reached and ratified after a postal ballot of Ngai Tahu's members.[38] The Deed

---

[30] The Background Statement (or preamble) in the Settlement Act records, in the English version, that the Crown "accepted the thrust of the 1991 Waitangi Tribunal report, and, in consequence of that acceptance, in September 1991 the Crown and Ngai Tahu entered into negotiations to seek resolution of Ngai Tahu's grievances".

[31] *Ngai Tahu Report,* above n. 16, vol. 3, para. 24.1.

[32] *Ngai Tahu Ancillary Claims Report 1995.*

[33] *Ngai Tahu Sea Fisheries Report 1992,* para 12.5.4.

[34] Ibid.

[35] Ibid.

[36] *Muriwhenua Fisheries Report 1988* (Wai 22).

[37] *Ngai Tahu Report,* above n. 16, vol. 3 at para. 24.1.

[38] See *Crown Settlement Offer,* Te Karaka Special Edition (Ngai Tahu Publications, 1997), p. 16 (the document explaining the Crown's settlement offer to Ngai Tahu's members); available on Ngai Tahu's website at http://www. ngai.tahu.iwi.nz.

of Settlement was entered, 1,800 pages, on 21 November 1997. The Settlement Bill, to give it legislative effect, was introduced to the NZ House of Representatives in March 1998. It was enacted by the House in September and came into force in October 1998, following compliance with section 1.[39]

III. REDRESS

In the Ngai Tahu Claims Settlement Act the Crown apologises to Ngai Tahu for repeated breaches of the Treaty of Waitangi;[40] and Ngai Tahu are affirmed as the tangata whenua, or the indigenous people, of their lands.[41] In particular, the Crown acknowledges that it failed to protect Ngai Tahu authority or mana over their land and other cultural properties, causing them suffering and hardship, thereby keeping "the tribe for several generations in a state of poverty".[42]

The Act provides a complex texture of redress, virtually all of it property related. Significant tracts of rural and urban land will be returned, including several high country runs with tourism potential and some important commercial properties.[43] All pounamu, or jade, in its natural state within Ngai Tahu's region is vested in the tribe.[44] Certain islands,[45] reserves,[46] wetlands,[47] eeling grounds, shares in airports, possibly a hydroelectric power station,[48] and Aoraki/Mt Cook—all will find their way into Ngai Tahu ownership or control. In addition, there will be redress to Ngai Tahu through new administrative arrangements, at regional and national levels.

Ngai Tahu for their part accept these apologies and acknowledgements and properties and the new administrative arrangements as sufficient for their claims to be quietened and for a new era of co-operation to begin.[49]

One development which occurred during the negotiations deserves special mention and that is the establishment of the Crown Land Bank as an indication of good faith on the part of the Crown. Surplus Crown lands, that might otherwise have been sold, were placed in this Bank, from where they could be drawn later for restoration to the tribe. This has minimised the impact of the settlement on the general public.

---

[39] See below.
[40] See s. 6.
[41] Ibid.
[42] Ibid.
[43] Parts 4–11.
[44] Ngai Tahu (Pounamu Vesting) Act 1997 (NZ).
[45] E.g., the Titi Islands: ss. 333–337.
[46] E.g., ss. 146–161.
[47] Ngai Tahu (Tutaepatu Lagoon Vesting) Act 1998 (NZ).
[48] These are Crown assets that may be chosen by Ngai Tahu under the Deferred Selection Process: see n. 51 below and associated text.
[49] See particularly Part 16 where the Ngai Tahu Claims are declared to be finally settled, all future progress on the claims is statute-barred and any associated litigation is discontinued.

Ngai Tahu will now be able to use the $170 million cash settlement they have received, and any other funds they can find, to purchase from the Crown properties of their choice up to a total value of $250 million, under what is known as the Deferred Selection Process.[50] This gives the iwi a year to select the Crown properties or assets they will take. Beyond that Ngai Tahu will have a permanent right of first refusal should the Crown put any of those properties on the market.[51] This has been described as putting the Crown's right of pre-emption under Article II of the Treaty of Waitangi in reverse.[52] Through these mechanisms Ngai Tahu will be able to extract significant added value beyond the limits of their cash settlement.

Brian Kennedy of Ngai Tahu said in July 1998 that by the year 2003 the iwi will have an asset value of around $500 million, from a zero base in 1990.[53] Ngai Tahu will become a major force in the South Island economy and they will be in a position to respond to the demands placed upon them by the new administrative regimes.

With regard to fisheries, very significant quantities of commercial fishing quota will eventually vest in the tribe.[54] Customary sea fisheries regulations have been issued for the South Island[55] and customary freshwater fishing regulations will be issued.[56] Several indigenous species of freshwater fish are to be deemed "taonga fish species".[57] Some stretches of riverbank, to be known as Fenton entitlements, will be set aside for specific descent groups "to occupy temporarily land close to waterways for lawful fishing and gathering of other natural resources" and these will be linked to customary fishing entitlements.[58] Some 72 nohonga, or camping sites, will be created, up to two hectares in size. On these the iwi generally will have exclusive rights to camp adjacent to certain rivers and lakes, during the warmer months, for food gathering purposes. They are to be sited back from the water and general riparian and public access rights are not to be impaired.[59] Along with the vesting in Ngai Tahu of the Titi

---

[50] Parts 4–7.

[51] Part 9.

[52] The latter part of Art. II of the Treaty of Waitangi provides, in the English version: "the Chiefs . . . yield to Her Majesty the exclusive right of Preemption over such lands as the proprietors thereof may be disposed to alienate at such prices as may be agreed upon between the respective Proprietors and persons appointed by Her Majesty to treat with them in that behalf", above n. 1.

[53] "Ngai Tahu 'family trust' plans financial strategy", *Otago Daily Times*, Dunedin, 9 July 1998.

[54] Substantial commercial fishing assets belonging to all Maori have been vested in the Treaty of Waitangi Fisheries Commission by the Maori Fisheries Act 1989 and the Treaty of Waitangi (Fisheries Claims) Settlement Act 1992, but the distribution of those assets to iwi has been dogged by controversy and litigation: *Te Runanga o Muriwhenua* v. *Te Runanganui o Te Upoko o Te Ika Association* [1996] 3 NZLR 10 (CA); *Treaty Tribes Coalition* v. *Urban Maori Authorities* [1997] 1 NZLR 513 (PC); *Te Waka Hi Ika o Te Arawa* v. *Treaty of Waitangi Fisheries Commission*, unreported, Anderson J, HC, Auckland, 4 August 1998; Waitangi Tribunal, *Sea Fisheries Report 1992* (Wai 307).

[55] Fisheries (South Island Customary Fisheries) Regulations 1998 (NZ).

[56] Section 305.

[57] Sections 297–306 and Sch. 98.

[58] Sections 354–386.

[59] Sections 255–268 and associated Schedules.

Islands,[60] where muttonbirds are collected, and the vesting of the beds of several lakes and wetlands,[61] these forms of redress in the area of fishing recognise the significance to Ngai Tahu of their customary food gathering practices and their annual harvesting round.

This gives some idea of the redistribution of resources towards Ngai Tahu, or the redistribution of authority in relation to the management of resources, that is to occur. Not all of these developments are easily quantifiable in monetary terms, but for a small country there is clearly a significant redistribution of property within the state. This will enhance Ngai Tahu's mana and permit the restoration of a tribal community.[62] It will provide the resources necessary for the iwi to participate in public decisions and it will return to them cultural properties of special significance, recognising their traditional economy and way of life. There is both symbolic and material property exchange.

Nowhere is the symbolism of property and power more clearly visible than in the arrangements concerning that mountain, itself rarely seen, which is now to be known as Aoraki/Mt Cook.

IV. AORAKI/MT COOK

Here equality of mana between Ngai Tahu and the Crown is most fully expressed in the form of a property exchange. The legislation facilitates a double transfer in ownership of the mountain. First, title to the mountain is to be returned by the Crown to Ngai Tahu.[63] Then, within seven days, it will be gifted back by Ngai Tahu to "the Crown on behalf of the people of New Zealand".[64] There will be an exchange of taonga, of valued property, whose aim is to quieten the enduring grievances of the past—an attempt at restorative justice writ 3,700 metres high.

There is an insurance scheme to make sure Ngai Tahu proceed with the deal. Before the mountain is transferred to the tribe, they must deposit with an escrow agent an "executed counterpart" of the deed through which the mountain will be gifted back to the Crown, and the Crown may act on that copy if Ngai Tahu do not deliver the original by the appointed hour.[65]

The iwi say of this exchange, that return to them of Aoraki: [66]

---

[60] Sections 333–337.

[61] E.g., s. 123, Sinclair Wetlands; s. 168, bed of Lake Waihora; s. 184, bed of Muriwai; s. 192, bed of Lake Mahinapua; and Ngai Tahu (Tutaepatu Lagoon Vesting) Act 1998 (NZ).

[62] The Waitangi Tribunal has repeatedly emphasised the need for the Crown to take steps to assist the restoration of tribal mana and authority as the principal form of redress for established breaches of the Treaty: see *Orakei Report 1991* (Wai 9), para. 14.2.3; *Ngai Tahu Report*, above n. 16, vol. 3, para. 24.2; *Turangi Township Report 1998* (Wai 84), para. 2.6.3.

[63] Section 15.

[64] Section 16(2).

[65] Section 16(3), (4).

[66] *Crown Settlement Offer*, above n. 38, at p. 16.

"will confirm Ngai Tahu's special relationship with the mountain and all that it represents, and in particular Aoraki's pivotal role in our southern creation stories".

The gifting back of the mountain to all the people confirms that Ngai Tahu have "the mana, or power" to make that gift;[67] and it will be "an enduring symbol of the tribe's commitment to the co-management of the areas of high historical, cultural and conservation value with the Crown".[68] That commitment is underpinned by the mechanisms of administrative redress.

V. THE NEW STATUTORY INSTRUMENTS AND CO-MANAGEMENT REGIMES

The novelty of the new statutory instruments, as a means of bringing Ngai Tahu conceptions within the legal system, is best captured in the language of the schedules which create them. The Statutory Acknowledgement concerning Aoraki/Mt Cook, for example, includes the following recital:[69]

"To Ngai Tahu, Aoraki represents the most sacred of ancestors, from whom Ngai Tahu descend and who provides the iwi with its sense of communal identity, solidarity, and purpose. It follows that the ancestor embodied in the mountain remains the physical manifestation of Aoraki, the link between the supernatural and the natural world. The tapu associated with Aoraki is a significant dimension of the tribal value, and is the source of the power over life and death which the mountain possesses".

The Crown then "acknowledges" this statement of Ngai Tahu associations with the mountain and undertakes to recognise and promote these within the administrative and resource management regimes. In effect, the Statutory Acknowledgements bind Ngai Tahu interests to the existing management structures concerning particular features of the environment. There are 63 Acknowledgements listed in Schedules which cover 140 pages of the Settlement Act. These all have a similar form. They locate the natural feature—river, lake, mountain—by reference to official maps, using the Maori name. They then declare that the Crown acknowledges the attached statement by Ngai Tahu of their "cultural, spiritual, historic, and traditional association" with that feature;[70] and those associations are narrated, in a blend of creation stories, genealogical connections and descriptions of specific events in the history of the tribe. The sites of settlements are recounted and food gathering practices and areas of traditional knowledge are described.

Each narrative concludes with observations on the values or environmental ethics of the iwi. Reference is made to the mauri or vital essence of the features of the natural world, a concept "that binds the physical and spiritual elements

---

[67] *Crown Settlement Offer*, above n. 38, at p. 16.

[68] Ibid.

[69] Schedule 14.

[70] The quotations in the next few paragraphs are drawn from the Statutory Acknowledgement for Aoraki/Mt Cook, in Sch. 14.

of all things together, generating and upholding all life". Mauri is said to be "a critical element of the spiritual relationship of Ngai Tahu" with the natural world. There is a blending here of the physical and the metaphysical, of whaka-papa (genealogy), journeying and methods of survival. We are presented, in effect, with a public memory of the tribe, a history jointly acknowledged, which may form the ground of reconciliation.[71]

The legal effects of each statutory acknowledgement are then specified in detail. In general, their effect will be to require resource consent authorities to forward summaries of all consent applications to Ngai Tahu to permit them to respond; and those authorities, along with other named bodies, like the Environment Court and the Historic Places Trust, must "have regard to" the Statutory Acknowledgement in their decision-making.[72] In addition, the Minister responsible for management of the particular feature is authorised to enter into a further Deed of Recognition in relation to that area or river or land form.[73] This will have additional consequences, such as involving Ngai Tahu at the earliest stages in the preparation of resource management plans.

Any member of Ngai Tahu may cite an Acknowledgement in resource man-agement proceedings "as evidence of Ngai Tahu's associations" with the feature named.[74] The content of the Statutory Acknowledgment is not "binding as deemed fact" upon consent authorities, or on others who participate in their proceedings, but it "may be taken into account" by them.[75]

The effect of the Acknowledgement is expressly limited to the consequences specified in the statute.[76] It is said to have no wider, implied effects on decision-makers' powers, nor consequences for the "lawful rights or interests of any per-son who is not a party to the deed of settlement";[77] and "except as expressly provided" in the Act an Acknowledgement does not of itself have "the effect of granting, creating, or providing evidence of any estate or interest in, or any rights of any kind whatsoever relating to" the river, lake, mountain, wetland or other feature that is named.[78] This indicates the careful compromises reached between Ngai Tahu and the Crown.

This detailed material is pitched at the other end of the codification spectrum from the early attempts to incorporate Treaty principles into resource manage-ment law, attempts like section 4 of the Conservation Act 1987, which simply

---

[71] See the comments on the role of the Truth and Reconciliation Commission in South Africa in uncovering and recording the recent history of that nation, in K. Kasmal, L. Asmal and R. Roberts, *Reconciliation Through Truth* (Johannesburg, David Philip Publishers, 1996); and see M. Sorrenson, "Towards a Radical Reinterpretation of NZ History: the Role of the Waitangi Tribunal" in Kawharu (ed.), *Waitangi*, above n. 1, at p. 158.

[72] Sections 207–210, 215.

[73] Section 212.

[74] Section 211(1).

[75] Section 211(2).

[76] See ss. 216–219.

[77] Section 218.

[78] Section 219.

states of the entire legislation: "This Act shall be so interpreted and adminis-
tered as to give effect to the principles of the Treaty of Waitangi".

Another novel statutory instrument is the Topuni. There are 14 of these,
relating to features of exceptional significance to Ngai Tahu, and these may
apply to the same feature as a Statutory Acknowledgement. Ngai Tahu's
account of the Topuni is as follows:[79]

> "The concept of the Topuni derives from the traditional Ngai Tahu tikanga (custom)
> of persons of rangatira (chiefly) status extending their mana and protection over a per-
> son or area by placing their cloak over them or it. In its new application, a Topuni
> confirms and places an 'overlay' of Ngai Tahu values on specific pieces of land man-
> aged by [the Department of Conservation]. A Topuni does not override or alter the
> existing status of the land (for example, national park status), but ensures that Ngai
> Tahu values are also recognised, acknowledged and provided for".

Ngai Tahu's account of each feature under a Topuni is recorded in a Schedule
and acknowledged by the Crown.[80] The Topuni must "be identified and
described in the relevant conservation management strategies, conservation
management plans and national park management plans";[81] and specified statutory bodies, such as the New Zealand Conservation Authority, must then "have
particular regard to" the Ngai Tahu values described in that instrument.[82]

The Crown and the iwi may then agree to statements of principles concerning Department of Conservation (DoC) conduct on that land, and those principles will be notified to the public.[83] DoC is further empowered to take
discretionary action to uphold those principles, by issuing bylaws or regulations, for instance.[84] These might relate to information concerning Ngai Tahu
associations to be provided to people who use the land, to the siting of mountain huts or roads, or to archeological sites.

In specific, though limited, areas, Ngai Tahu will be granted full authority to
regulate, and even exclusive possession of, a specific resource. In regard to the
Titi Islands, for example, in the far south, where muttonbirds are collected,
ownership of the islands is vested in Te Runanga o Ngai Tahu,[85] and that
Runanga (or Council), in conjunction with the Rakiura or Stewart Island hapu
of the iwi, will be responsible for formulating and implementing their own management plan.[86] These will be Ngai Tahu islands under Ngai Tahu control. The
same can be said of pounamu. But these are the exceptions.

In general the emphasis throughout is on joint participation in resource management procedures and on formalised mechanisms for sharing information. In

---

[79] Above n. 38, at 35.
[80] See ss. 237–252 and Schs. 80–93.
[81] Section 243.
[82] Section 241.
[83] Sections 240, 244.
[84] Sections 245, 246.
[85] Section 334.
[86] Section 336 and Schs. 109, 110.

effect, the settlement will extend the scope of negotiations beyond the narrow terrain of relations between the iwi and the legal Crown to cover relations between Ngai Tahu and all resource managers who have the capacity to affect the iwi's interests. Thus the perceived deficiencies of the Resource Management Act 1991, in particular its failure to bind resource planners to Treaty principles,[87] will be partially remedied within Ngai Tahu's Takiwa.

The relevant statutory agencies are directly fixed with the legal obligation to consider Ngai Tahu's associations with their environment, and the precise nature of those interests is specified in relation to scores of natural features of the land. We are not left wondering how general Treaty principles apply to the Crown, or whether the NZ Conservation Board is to be considered part of the Crown, or what "the principles of the Treaty" might mean when applied to a particular action of that Board, for instance. The Board is directly fixed with particular legal obligations and the matters it must consider are expressly codified in the statute.

VI. THE CORPORATE IWI

A further important aspect of the settlement process has been the constitution of Ngai Tahu as a corporate iwi and the recognition by statute of Te Runanga o Ngai Tahu as the legal representative and property-holding entity for the tribe. It has been the Crown's policy to encourage the evolution of what might be called Ngai Tahu Incorporated. This has involved the transformation through statute of the iwi's governing organ, from a Maori Trust Board, accountable to the Minister of Maori Affairs,[88] into an incorporated body, accountable to the members of the tribe. Agreement on these developments appears to have been an important area of common ground.

Through Te Runanga o Ngai Tahu Act 1996, passed at the request of the iwi, a corporation sole of that name was recognised by statute as the representative of the iwi for all legal purposes and a skeletal structure was established within which the Runanga (or Council) of the iwi must operate. The flesh around that structure is then formed through Ngai Tahu's Charter,[89] which is akin to its articles of association, and through the formation of a charitable trust and various companies under general legislation.

The Crown's general policies in this area were described in a discussion paper published by Te Puni Kokiri (the Ministry of Maori Development) in 1996.[90]

---

[87] Resource Management Act 1991 (NZ), s. 8 provides only that resource planners shall "take into account" Treaty principles as one relevant consideration among others, with no priority given to those principles.

[88] Maori Trust Boards Act 1955 (NZ).

[89] *The Charter of Te Runanga o Ngai Tahu*; see Te Runanga o Ngai Tahu Act 1996 (NZ), ss. 16–18.

[90] *Reform of the Maori Trust Boards Act 1955*, (Te Puni Kokiri, 1996); see also T. O'Regan, "The Ngai Tahu Claim" in Kawharu (ed.), *Waitangi*, above n. 1; *Te Waka Hi Ika o Te Arawa* v. *Treaty of Waitangi Fisheries Commission*, unreported, Anderson J, HC, Auckland, 4 August 1998; Waitangi Tribunal, *Sea Fisheries Report* (Wai 307) (1992); A. Irwin, *Aboriginal Autonomy and Legislative Reform*, LLB(Hons) dissertation, University of Otago, 1997.

The government, it says, is attempting "to grapple with the issues of tribal restructuring and iwi identification".[91] There is a need for "more appropriate structures for the better management of assets and governance of iwi".[92] These matters are becoming "particularly urgent as the settlement process progresses".[93] The essential aims, it is said, are that the body which receives assets in settlement of a claim should be properly constituted; it should represent a clearly defined Maori group or groups; it should have the mandate of those it purports to represent; it should be accountable to them; and it should have the capacity to manage tribal activities, particularly commercial activity.[94]

A similar point was made by the Royal Commission on Aboriginal Peoples in Canada: that if negotiations between the government and indigenous peoples are to proceed to successful conclusions then indigenous peoples must develop administrative and representative structures which facilitate that process, and which are still acceptable to them.[95] These are the purposes for which Te Runanga o Ngai Tahu Act was passed.[96]

In enacting such legislation Parliament is influencing the social and political organisation of the iwi. Particularly it influences the iwi's internal configuration, by empowering one entity, in this case at a centralised level, to be the legal representative and voice of the tribe, over the heads, in a sense, of the particular hapu or other local descent groups. This selection by the government of a particular level of tribal society as the one with which it will deal in reaching Treaty settlements has created tensions within southern Maori which were still being played out in litigation[97] and within the Parliamentary process in the final stages of the passage of the Settlement legislation. Some groups of southern Maori, who might be brought under the broad banner of Ngai Tahu by reason of their intermingled genealogy, still object to that designation, while claiming the status of an independent tribe. Other groups have objected to the placement in central tribal ownership of certain resources, such as pounamu, which were traditionally managed at the local or hapu level of control.[98]

---

[91] *Reform of the Maori Trust Boards Act 1955*, above n. 90, at p. 12.

[92] Ibid.

[93] Ibid.

[94] Ibid.

[95] *Canadian Royal Commission on Aboriginal Peoples*, 5 vols (1996); and see J. Tully, "A Fair and Just Relationship: the Vision of the Canadian Royal Commission on Aboriginal Peoples", (1998) 57 *Meanjin* 146.

[96] See also the Runanga Iwi Act 1990 (NZ), which was repealed the following year.

[97] *Waitaha Taiwhenua o Waitaki Trust* v. *Te Runanga o Ngai Tahu*, unreported, Panckhurst J, HC, Christchurch, CP 41/98, 17 June 1998.

[98] E. Durie, for instance, writes of traditional Maori property rights: "the underlying or radical title was vested in the hapu [local descent group]. This served to prevent a transfer of use rights outside the descent group without general hapu approval. In addition the allocation of use rights within the group was regularly adjusted by the rangatira (chiefs). The essential point . . . is that the land of an area remained in the control and authority of an associated ancestral descent group and, like fee tail, neither the land as a whole, nor a use right within it, could pass permanently outside the bloodline. Land and ancestors were fused": "Will the Settlers Settle?" above n. 4, at 452. Corporate control of assets at a centralised tribal level may not sit easily with these traditional principles.

The Ngai Tahu legislation records that Te Runanga o Ngai Tahu is composed of the 18 marae-based papatipu runanga, or local councils, of the iwi;[99] and those local councils are composed of their members, who are the individuals of the various hapu, whose tipuna or ancestors are among those with the necessary whakapapa, listed in a named genealogical book, whose existence and use for this purpose is affirmed by the statute.[100] Custody and management of that book and the iwi's membership rolls lie within the control of Ngai Tahu, though appeals concerning membership go to the Maori Land Court.[101] Ngai Tahu maintain computerised rolls of their membership, which is rapidly expanding, and whakapapa may be checked on the phone.

Te Runanga o Ngai Tahu's institutional arrangements therefore look like a set of circles within circles at ascending levels of authority. The personal members of the iwi make up the local runanga and those local runanga make up Te Runanga o Ngai Tahu, in the same manner that states or provinces constitute a federation. Within these structures the authority of individuals is never established by law. Instead, authority and ownership are invariably exercised through collective forms.

This runanga structure is, in effect, the political or policy-making branch of Ngai Tahu. Beyond these structures are the commercial and the social or educational branches of the iwi. This provides the same kind of division of labour—between policy-setting, commercial and distributive functions—that is now typical of New Zealand government as a whole.

Beneath Te Runanga o Ngai Tahu sits a charitable trust for the tax advantages, and below that lie several companies.[102] There is a holding company for general asset management, and beneath it other companies run particular enterprises, like the whale-watching at Kaikoura. The Ngai Tahu Development Corporation pursues social and educational aims, making grants, for example, to university students.

In total these new arrangements achieve many important aims. The iwi attains legal personality. The communal character of property-holdings is respected, though largely through a system of centralised tribal control. The political authority of tribal leaders can be accommodated within these structures. Representation and financial accountability are assured. Iwi property conceptions and the dovetailed social systems of Maori society are brought within the legal system in a manner that permits clear communication between the iwi and the government. This in turn facilitates the restoration of property to the tribe.

---

[99] Te Runanga o Ngai Tahu Act 1996 (NZ), s. 9.
[100] Ibid., s. 7.
[101] Ibid., s. 7(5)–(6).
[102] For an explanation of these arrangements see *Crown Settlement Offer*, above n. 38.

VII.　SECTION ONE

One final example of the emergent imagery of equality between the iwi and the government (which indicates that a more horizontal legal skyline is visibly under construction here) lies in the arrangements concerning commencement of the settlement legislation provided for by section 1. These arrangements have now been complied with during September and October of 1998 in the bringing into force of the legislation.

Section 1 provides that the legislation, having been enacted by the New Zealand Parliament, would be brought into force through an Order in Council made by the Governor-General upon the recommendation of the Prime Minister. However, the Prime Minister "must not recommend the making" of that commencement order unless "advised by Te Runanga o Ngai Tahu in writing that [the] Act is acceptable".[103] When, however, Ngai Tahu have provided that advice, the Prime Minister "must recommend" that the commencement order be made.[104] In effect, the legislation was to come into force when it was enacted by Parliament and it was agreed to by Ngai Tahu. It would not be quite correct to say Ngai Tahu enacted the legislation, as if they were a second House of Parliament, but until the last moment they were able to prevent its commencement if it was amended in ways they opposed.

The Prime Minister and the Cabinet would use their control over the majority in the House to enact the legislation; and Ngai Tahu would then signify their assent to its commencement. A bicultural structure of agreement was thus created at one step below the level of the legislature, illustrating one possible solution to the Crown-iwi relationship. Perhaps this is as good an outcome as could be obtained from negotiations that had proceeded, as David Williams puts it, "in the shadow of an existing constitutional balance of power which is not based on negotiation".[105]

Nevertheless, section 1 affirms an important shift towards shared governance with regard to cultural resources of particular significance to Ngai Tahu. It reflects at the constitutional level the joint decision-making procedures in the resource management domain. Its enactment is an important rite of passage in the maturing of a post-colonial constitution for New Zealand.

VIII.　OWNERSHIP OF THE CONSTITUTION

This brings me to my final point concerning ownership of the constitution itself. The Ngai Tahu Settlement was initially recorded in a Deed of Settlement signed

---

[103] Section 1(3)
[104] Section 1(4).
[105] In commentary on I. MacDuff, "The Role of Negotiation: Negotiated Justice?", (1995) 25 *VUWLR* 144, 153.

between the iwi and the executive government. It was a compact of a political kind.[106] Parliament did not vote on it at the time the Deed was signed. But Parliament has now had the opportunity to vote on it, because that Deed has been given full legal force through the passage of an ordinary statute enacted by a representative legislature. And that legislature was itself elected on a one person, one vote principle, under a proportional system of representation.[107]

In my view, that is the best possible means through which such an agreement could be adopted, because it commits the majority now and in the future to the new arrangements. If justice cannot be delivered to indigenous peoples through majoritarian legislative processes then perhaps its delivery through entrenched constitutions and by way of judical review is better than no justice at all.[108] But how much better that justice to indigenous peoples should be done through mechanisms that involve endorsement by the majority, if that endorsement can be obtained.

This entails risks, especially the risk that the settlements may be undone by ordinary amending or repealing legislation at some time in the future. But what if that repeal never comes? What if continuing majority commitment to joint processes of governance can be obtained? Then the Treaty settlements will have a legitimacy no other method of endorsement could confer. It is the majority who will be responsible for the settlement legislation and they will have it in their hands to amend it if they wish. Yet, they may also choose not to exercise that amending power, and to leave the Treaty settlements intact. Then majority preferences and indigenous concerns will both be honoured and all New Zealanders will own the constitution. It is in the capacity of a majority government to deliver such settlements, albeit grudgingly, combined with the willingness of iwi to accept the compromises settlement of their claims entails, that the greatest hope of peaceful co-existence lies.

IX. CONCLUSION

In New Zealand there live Maori and non-Maori people, with different frames of reference, yet still ways can be found, by agreement and through ordinary legislation, to establish joint systems of governance and to incorporate several distinct conceptions of property within a single legal system.

---

[106] See *Te Runanga o Wharekauri Rekohu Inc* v. *A-G*, above n. 28, on the effect of the equivalent Deed of Settlement in the fisheries context.
[107] Electoral Act 1993 (NZ).
[108] See Canadian Constitution Act 1982, s. 35.

11

Property and the Treaty of Waitangi: A Tragedy of the Commodities?

ALEX FRAME*

I. INTRODUCTION

Dosn't thou 'ear my 'erse's legs, as they canters awaay?
Proputty, proputty, proputty—that's what I 'ears 'em saay.
Alfred, Lord Tennyson (1809–1892)
(Northern Farmer, New Style)

The justifications by which the benefit and control of external resources is reserved to particular individuals and groups to the exclusion of others present a fascinating area of study. We are fortunate to have a contribution in this collection from a leading modern scholar in that field, Jeremy Waldron, who has neatly underlined the importance of "property" to political philosophy.[1] One of the leading accounts is that of the English political philosopher, John Locke (1632–1704), who defended the appropriation of things by individuals on the basis that the expenditure of labour on an object by an individual in some way infuses that object with the personality of the individual.[2] That champion of the efficacy of the market, Adam Smith, was certainly aware of the connection between the functions of government and the institution of private property:[3]

> "Civil government, so far as it is instituted for the security of property, is in reality instituted for the defence of the rich against the poor, or of those who have property against those who have none at all".

* The author acknowledges the assistance of the New Zealand Foundation for Research, Science and Technology and its Public Good Science Fund, through the University of Waikato's "Laws and Institutions for Aotearoa/New Zealand" Programme. The views expressed are, however, those of the author only.
[1] "Kant, like Hobbes, regarded property as the thread to tug in order to unravel the mysteries of political philosophy": (J. Waldron, "Kant's legal Positivism", (1996) 109 *Harv L Rev*, 1535, 1548, n. 53).
[2] For a good account of Locke's ideas, see also K. Olivecrona, "Locke on the Origin of Property", (1974) XXXV *Journal of the History of Ideas* 211.
[3] Quoted in I. S. Ross, *The Life of Adam Smith* (Oxford, Clarendon Press, Oxford, 1995), pp. 282–283.

In a brilliant study published in 1973, the French legal philosopher Bernard Edelman traced the response of French law to the invention and development of photography in the nineteenth century. Edelman showed that the initial response of French law was to deny the photographer property in the image, in contrast to the painter, who had long been recognised as acquiring property in the "art" produced. In Lockean terms the former was just a tool, a machine through which nature (light) did its work; the painter, on the other hand projected work, "soul", and imagination on to the canvas in such a way as to satisfy the Lockean requirements. But, as the photo-industry burgeoned and as its images became valuable and the basis for loans, share-floats, and other commercial transactions, French law made a U-turn. It concluded that the photographer *was* an artist after all, and therefore could also acquire and sell property in the image.[4] Edelman's thesis, of course, was Marxian—that ideas (about art, property and so on) followed the requirements of capitalist production. Somewhat sceptical of this grand conclusion, I decided to see whether the same pattern could be found across the channel, where the common law was experiencing an identical transition of photography from eccentric hobby to commercial enterprise. To my surprise, I found the common law undergoing a very similar evolution.[5]

Another excursion led me in the 1980s to consider Polynesian, particularly Maori, accounts of obligation concerning gifts, and to compare these with John Locke's explanation for the origin of "property". My conclusion was that both made use of a similar structure—"objects in the world get 'injected' with something as a result of the actions of human beings".[6] What strikes me now about the comparison I invited between the accounts of John Locke and Tamati Ranapiri is the syntactical structure of each. For Locke, the individual legal subject exercises rights (we could elaborate in a Hohfeldian, or more correctly as I have argued, Salmondian[7] manner) over objects in the world. For Ranapiri, individuals and the physical world are *both* subjects—notice how Ranapiri's gifts or taonga, infused with the hau of the donor, want to return home and are a threat to the current holder. As Marcel Mauss says, "the obligation attached

---

[4] B. Edelman, *Le Droit Saisi Par La Photographie* (Paris, Maspero, 1973).

[5] Cf. *Nottage* v. *Jackson* [1883] 11 QBD 627, where Brett MR denied that either the photographer or the subject were "authors": "neither of them make the picture because, after all, that is done by the sun", at 632 with *Boucas* v. *Cooke* (1903) 2 KB 227, where it was decided that if the negative is taken for the sitter for valuable consideration then he has property in it.

[6] A. Frame, "Property: Some Pacific Reflections", (1992) *NZLJ* 21, also published in slightly different form in (1992) 22 *VUWLR* 21.

[7] I have suggested in *Salmond: Southern Jurist* (Wellington, Victoria University Press, 1995), pp. 61–64 that Hohfeld's account of jural relations was anticipated by Sir John Salmond in his 1893 publication, *First Principles of Jurisprudence*. An even earlier excursion into distinctions between "liberty", "power" and "right" may be found in W. E. Hearn's *The Theory of Legal Rights and Duties* (London, Trubner, 1883). Interestingly, the copy in the Law Library at Victoria University is inscribed, in Salmond's hand, "J. W. Salmond, 1892". Hearn (1826–1888) was born in Ireland but spent his most productive years at the University of Melbourne and was the founding Dean of the Faculty of Law there from 1873–1888.

to a gift itself is not inert".[8] Provisionally, however, we might say that Polynesian law does not converse in terms of human control over an inert world, but rather of reciprocal rights and obligations involving people and an animated world. I propose to return later to this tendency of Polynesian philosophy to attribute personality to objects and physical features in the world.

The Lockean syntax, on the other hand, is set by the Protestant Reformation in a manner well summarised by Harold Berman:[9]

> "The key to the renewal of law in the West from the 16th century on was the Protestant concept of the power of the individual, by God's grace, to change nature and to create new social relations through the exercise of his will. The Protestant concept of the individual will become central to the development of the modern law of property and contract. Nature became property. Economic relations became contract. Conscience became will and intent".

That syntax leads towards the selfish extremism of Blackstone's view of the right of property as:[10]

> "The sole and despotic dominion which one man claims and exercises over the external things of the world, in total exclusion of the right of any other individual in the universe".

You will think that I have not progressed much towards the Treaty of Waitangi, but thus far we have seen that claims to an exclusive benefit and control of resources can be dressed in different garb in different societies, and can change costume across time even in the same society. In fact, we might end this introduction with Carol Rose's reminder in the final sentence of her engaging book titled "Property and Persuasion":[11]

> "And that is why, with just a bit of exaggeration, I could have named this book 'Property is Persuasion.' "

II. "PROPERTY"—THE IMPERIAL EXPORT MODEL

Maitland's comment on Blackstone's *Commentaries* gives us the clue to account for its great influence, particularly on the frontiers of the British colonial empire—brevity and portability. Having recommended Blackstone as a manual for grasping the principles of property law, Maitland added: [12]

---

[8] M. Mauss, *The Gift: Forms and Functions of Exchange in Archaic Societies* (trans. Cunnison, London, Routledge and Kegan Paul, 1967), pp. 9–10. My friend and colleague Manuka Henare, is continuing the study of Tamati Ranapiri's account contained in letters to Elsdon Best held in the Turnbull Library.

[9] H. J. Berman, *The Interaction of Law and Religion* (Nashville, Abingdon Press, 1974), p. 64.

[10] W. Blackstone, *Commentaries* II, 1.

[11] C. Rose, *Property and Persuasion* (Oxford, Westview Press, 1994), p. 297.

[12] Quoted in C. H. S. Fifoot, *Frederick William Maitland: A Life* (Cambridge, Harvard University Press, 1971), p. 50.

"After all the book is not a very big one—thirty two chapters; 500 pages. One might read it easily and profitably in a fortnight and do a great many things besides".

Blackstone's account of property in land is characteristically brief: [13]

"By the law of nature and reason he who first began to use it acquired therein a kind of transient property that lasted so long as he was using it and no longer. When mankind increased in number it became necessary to entertain conceptions of more permanent dominion and to appropriate to individuals not the immediate use only, but the very substance of the thing to be used".

On Salmond's resignation in 1907 from his founding chair at Victoria College, the remarkable Richard Cockburn Maclaurin (1870–1920) took his place, simultaneously holding responsibilities for the teaching of mathematical physics. In 1898 the Waikato-raised Maclaurin had won the Yorke Prize at the University of Cambridge with his extended essay "On the Nature and Evidence of Title to Realty".[14] Sitting at the feet of Maitland, how did the field look to Maclaurin?

Blackstone's account of the origins of property in land is pronounced to be "a poor explanation of the origin of private property". In its place is set out a supposed hierarchy of agricultural development at the end of which a fully matured private property in land is declared born. Maclaurin's hierarchy looks something like this:[15]

(1) Lowest. Bushmen of South Africa. "Wandering hunters".
(2) Australian Aborigines. Clan system with defined hunting grounds "belonging to the clan".
(3) Maori of New Zealand, with "primitive agriculture", slaves, surplus goods, distinctions of rank.
(4) Village community with intensive agriculture. Arable land is divided among families but pastures are held in common.

Of course, the judgement that a fully matured property emerges only at the end of an evolutionary scale, a suggestion already contained in Blackstone's account, carries the implication that *something less* is present at earlier stages.

---

[13] W. Blackstone, *Commentaries* II, 3. Sir Henry Maine (1822–1888) discusses this "occupancy" account in his famous *Ancient Law* (first published in 1861). Maine is critical of arguments from the "state of nature", observing that "These sketches of the plight of human beings in the first ages of the world are effected by first supposing mankind to be divested of a great part of the circumstances by which they are now surrounded, and by then assuming that, in the condition thus imagined, they would preserve the same sentiments and prejudices by which they are now actuated—although, in fact, these sentiments may have been created and engendered by those very circumstances of which, by the hypothesis, they are to be stripped" (London, Oxford University Press, World's Classics ed. 1959), ch. VIII, pp. 210–211.)

[14] R. C. Maclaurin, *On the Nature and Evidence of Title to Realty* (London, Clay & Sons, 1901). For some biographical detail, see *Salmond: Southern Jurist*, above n. 7, at p. 72. It is worth noting that Maclaurin used Maori custom to illustrate his teaching of Maine's *Ancient Law*.

[15] Maclaurin's evolutionary sketch, summarised here, is set out at pp. 3 and 4 of his prize-winning work.

This we will see to be a most persistent theme in relation to Maori customary title. Indeed, it lies at the heart of the "wastelands" issue in 1846 which now calls for our attention.

III. THE "WASTELANDS" CONFUSION, 1846

Earl Grey was Secretary of State for the Colonies from 1846 to 1852.[16] Soon after assuming office, Grey sent to Governor Grey in New Zealand instructions concerning the 1846 Constitution, and in accompanying policy directions, broached the question of the extent of Maori claims to land in New Zealand. Earl Grey deprecated the view: [17]

> "that the original inhabitants of any country are the proprietors of every part of its soil of which they have been accustomed to make any use, or to which they have been accustomed to assert any title . . . This claim is represented as sacred, however ignorant such natives may be of the arts or of the habits of civilized life, however unsettled their abodes, and however imperfect or occasional the uses they make of the land".

From this doctrine Earl Grey entirely dissented, preferring the "true principle" laid down in the works of Dr Arnold, from which Earl Grey now quoted:[18]

> "Men were to subdue the earth; that is, to make it by their labour what it would not have been by itself; and with the labour so bestowed upon it came the right of property in it . . . so much does the right of property go along with labour, that civilized nations have never scrupled to take possession of countries inhabited only by tribes of savages, countries which have been hunted over, but never subdued or cultivated . . . when our fathers went to America and took possession of the mere hunting-grounds of the Indians—of lands on which man had hitherto bestowed no labour—they only exercised a right which God has inseparably united with industry and knowledge".

This blunt exposition of what Jeremy Waldron calls "plantation ideology"[19] has a Lockean flavour, but leaves out Locke's proviso requiring "enough and as good" to be left for others, and gratuitously adds the deific sanction. It led Earl Grey into attempting to reverse the acknowledged assurance of the Treaty of Waitangi that the entire territory of New Zealand was subject to a Maori right which could only be displaced with a Maori consent. Governor Grey's response to the package from London—consisting of an Act of the Westminster Parliament, Royal Instructions, and policy directions from his Minister—was

---

[16] Earl Grey (1802–1894), formerly Sir Henry George, Viscount Howick. Egerton, in *British Colonial Policy in the Twentieth Century* (London, Methuen, 1922) describes Grey as "singularly unhappy in his management of the colonies" (318). For an account of the background and fate of the 1846 Constitution, see A. H. McLintock, *Crown Colony Government in New Zealand* (Wellington, Government Printer, 1958), esp. ch. XIII, at p. 276.

[17] Earl Grey to Governor Grey, despatch of 23 December 1846.

[18] Thomas Arnold (1795–1842) was headmaster of Rugby School.

[19] Waldron, above n. 1, at 1549, n. 55. Kant's dissent from the Lockean conclusion as it applies to land is helpfully discussed there.

bold to the point of defiance. Historians tell us to treat Governor Grey's accounts of his actions with suspicion, but I know of no reason to dispute his version to Milne that: [20]

"This constitution would destroy, at one stroke, a treaty—that of Waitangi which every Maori in New Zealand held to be sacred. It was a treaty securing them in their lands ... What was I to do indeed? My instructions were not alone that of the Colonial Office; but the Constitution had been sanctioned by Parliament . . . There was one clear line for me, simply to hang up the Constitution and intimate to the home authorities my ideas about it. This I did, and fortunately, as I thought, my plea prevailed with the Colonial Secretary and with Parliament. The latter not merely went back upon its act, a quite extraordinary event in English Parliamentary history, but empowered me to draw up another constitution for New Zealand".

Governor Grey and his high-placed Auckland supporters had their way— New Zealand reverted to the understanding before Earl Grey's flutter with the dogma of Dr Arnold—*all* the territory of New Zealand was subject to a Maori right.[21] But what was the *nature* of that right?

IV. CUSTOMARY MAORI TITLE

Thoughtful New Zealanders are increasingly aware that the contractual basis for relations between the New Zealand state and its Maori citizens is—with all its difficulties—a sounder foundation than the Australian alternative which has only belatedly regarded aboriginal inhabitants as requiring recognition as right-bearing human beings at all, historically founding itself upon the *terra nullius* falsity. However self-congratulation should be modest because, on inspection, recognition proves to have been qualified. The rights recognised were limited as to their nature and I will now sketch the expression of that qualification in law—at domestic, imperial, and international levels. It will be seen that while Dr Arnold and even Locke, may have fallen by the wayside, the spirit of Blackstone's "occupancy theory" did not.

---

[20] J. Milne, *The Romance of a Pro-Consul* (London, Thos Nelson and Sons, 1911), pp. 157–158. For confirmation of Grey's account, see J. Hight and H. D. Bamford, *The Constitutional History and Law of New Zealand* (Christchurch, Whitcombe and Tombs, 1914), pp. 198–202. The role of Bishop Selwyn, Chief Justice Martin, and Attorney-General Swainson in encouraging and reinforcing Governor Grey's resistance is well set out in McLintock, above n. 16, at pp. 288–289.

[21] The debate in the House of Commons approving Governor Grey's decision is of interest, see *Hansard* (UK), vol 96 (1848), pp. 327–366. Mr Gladstone said (342): "Now, when the Treaty of Waitangi was concluded, it was universally understood that the titles of the natives were to be recognised, under that Treaty, not only to the lands they had occupied and improved by labour, but likewise to those lands from which they derived a beneficial use . . . (334) The land was not only valuable and important to the natives, as stated by Governor Grey, but it was secured to them by a treaty made by adequate and competent authorities. To this Treaty he attached much importance . . . for his part, he thought that, as far as this country was concerned, there was not a more strictly and rigorously binding treaty in existence.".

Following the proceedings at Waitangi,[22] the Land Claims Ordinance 1841 set out the relationship between Maori, the Crown, and third parties in respect of land:

"all unappropriated lands . . . subject to the rightful and necessary occupation and use by the aboriginal inhabitants . . . are and remain Crown or domain lands of Her Majesty . . . and that the sole and absolute right of pre-emption from the said aboriginal inhabitants vests in and can only be exercised by Her said Majesty".

The distinction is unmistakably made: land could be subject to Maori customary right and yet be "unappropriated". At one level, the distinction parades as enlightened cultural relativism: as for example in the Privy Council's 1921 decision in *Amodu Tijani* v. *The Secretary Southern Nigeria*, which has added importance in New Zealand by endorsement of the Court of Appeal. Viscount Haldane said of "native title":[23]

"There is a tendency, operating at times unconsciously, to render that title conceptually in terms which are appropriate only to systems which have grown up under English law. But this tendency has to be held in check closely. As a rule, in the various systems of native jurisprudence throughout the Empire, there is no such full division between property and possession as English lawyers are familiar with. A very usual form of native title is that of a usufructuary right, which is a mere qualification of or burden on the radical or final title of the Sovereign where that exists".[24]

The most recent judicial discussion of the nature of "Maori customary title" or "aboriginal title"—the terms were described as "interchangeable"—is that of the President of the New Zealand Court of Appeal in the "Dams case" in 1993.[25] The learned President stated:[26]

"The nature and incidents of aboriginal title are matters of fact dependent on the evidence in any particular case . . . At one extreme they may be treated as approaching the full rights of proprietorship of an estate in fee recognised at common law . . . At the other extreme they may be treated as at best a mere permissive and apparently arbitrarily revocable occupancy".

The President went on to find that the Article II guarantee "must have been intended to preserve . . . effectively the Maori customary title", observing that:[27]

---

[22] Readers unfamiliar with New Zealand history will need to know that the Treaty of Waitangi, signed by officials on behalf of the Queen and by over 500 chiefs of most Maori tribes in 1840, comprises three Articles. The first grants rights of Government to the Queen, the second protects Maori rights, and the third assures to Maori the rights of British subjects.

[23] [1921] 2 AC 399. The President of the New Zealand Court of Appeal, now Lord Cooke, approved the decision in *Te Runanga o Muriwhenua* v. *Attorney-General* [1990] 2 NZLR 641.

[24] [1921] 2 AC 399, 403.

[25] *Te Runanganui o te Ika Whenua Inc Society* v. *Attorney-General* [1994] 2 NZLR 20—the "Dams Case".

[26] The President, Justice Cooke, cited judgments in the Australian case *Mabo* v. *State of Queensland (No. 2)* (1992) 175 CLR 1 to support both ends of the spectrum.

[27] Dams case, above n. 25, at 24.

"however liberally Maori customary title and treaty rights may be construed, one cannot think that they were ever conceived as including the right to generate electricity by harnessing water power. Such a suggestion would have been far outside the contemplation of the Maori chiefs and Governor Hobson in 1840".

It will not comfort those who seek certainty in the law to learn that Maori customary rights are of indeterminate nature and to an extent dependent on the Court of Appeal's view of what was in the minds of the Maori chiefs and Governor Hobson at Waitangi in 1840.

The only international Court to have faced the question of the nature of the Maori right to land was the Anglo-American Pecuniary Claims Tribunal in the Webster case, finally heard in Washington in 1925.[28] The Tribunal, committed by its constitution to applying international law in its decision, doubted whether Maori custom recognised "any such thing as *dominium* over land, as it is understood in developed law", spoke of a "regime of possession", and observed that alleged purchases by the American, William Webster, directly from Maori before the Treaty of Waitangi, gave Webster:[29]

"no more than a native customary title, the content and scope of which was very uncertain and cannot be said to have extended to a full property or dominium as known to matured law".

In sum, the authorities reviewed in the section above conclude that Maori customary titles to land are qualitatively different from those of "matured law". Maori, it seems, had not discovered "property" in its fully-fledged form, and could therefore not assert or convey it without the intervention of the legal system ushered in by the Treaty of Waitangi in 1840. This strange doctrine of the white man might not have been *terra nullius*, but it was at least a distant cousin!

V. THE CROWN'S RADICAL TITLE: "THE HERITAGE OF THE WHOLE PEOPLE"

Captain (from 1848 Sir) George Grey, that perplexing figure of New Zealand history, arriving in New Zealand to begin his first term as Governor in 1846, found Auckland agitated by the land issue. The *New Zealander* of 29 May 1847 grumbled that "every man feels it his duty, so soon as he gets up in the morning, to shoulder his arguments, and to fire off his 'bullets of the brain' in all directions for the rest of the day".

Grey had a plan to settle the issue whether certificates issued by his precursor, Governor Fitzroy, purporting to waive the Crown's right of pre-emption, were effective to permit acquisition of title by direct dealings with Maori owners. The Governor's plan was to issue a grant to his Native Secretary, J. J. Symonds, over

[28] For a full discussion of the Webster case, and for evidence that the decision was substantially the work of Roscoe Pound, see *Salmond: Southern Jurist*, above n. 7, at p. 10.

[29] The decision of the Tribunal is reported in F. K. Nielsen, *American and British Claims Arbitration* (Washington, Government Printing Office, 1926, pp.) 540–546.

an island in the Hauraki Gulf purchased by C. H. McIntosh under a Fitzroy waiver.[30] The resulting test case would establish which title was effective. In June 1847 the Supreme Court gave judgment upholding Governor Grey's later grant: [31]

> "[W]henever the original Native right is ceded in respect of any portion of the soil of these Islands, the right which succeeds thereto is not the right of any individual subject of the Crown, not even of the person by whom the cession was procured, but the right of the Crown on behalf of the whole nation, on behalf of the whole body of subjects of the Crown: that the land becomes from the moment of cession not the private property of one man, but the heritage of the whole people".

This was a bold statement of a social contract theory underlying the forms of feudal tenure. But it is Sir John Salmond who specifies the legal consequences of the feudal doctrine for colonial law, in a passage which survived all 7 editions of his text on Jurisprudence for which he was responsible: [32]

> "When we say that certain lands belong to or have been acquired by the Crown, we may mean either that they are the territory of the Crown or that they are the property of the Crown. The first conception pertains to the domain of public law, the second to that of private law . . . In accordance with the principles of feudal law all England was not merely the territory but also the property of the Crown; and even when granted to subjects, those grantees are in legal theory merely tenants in perpetuity of the Crown, the legal ownership of the land remaining vested in the Crown. So, in accordance with this principle, when a new colonial possession is acquired by the Crown and is governed by English law, the title so acquired is not merely territorial, but also proprietary. When New Zealand became a British possession, it became not merely the Crown's territory, but also the Crown's property, *imperium* and *dominium* being acquired and held concurrently".

---

[30] The Island must have been either Pakatoa or an island called Taratoroa "a little to the eastward of Waiheke", or perhaps both. The *New Zealand Government Gazette* of 25 February 1845 contains a "Schedule of lands over which the Crown's right of Pre-emption has been waived under the Regulation of 26th of March 1844"—it includes "C. H. McIntosh . . . the Island called Pakatua (sic) . . . 70 acres". The *New Zealand Government Gazette* of 25 February 1847 notifies pre-emption certificate No. 84 in favour of Charles H McIntosh, Auckland, Gentleman, relating to "401 ½ acres . . . the Island called 'Taratoroa' situated in the Frith of Thames, a little to the Eastward of Waiheke . . . also a small rocky island, Motu Kahakaha containing about one acre and a half". Much useful material on the background and context of the case is to be found in D. V. Williams, "The Queen v Symonds Reconsidered", (1989) 19 *VUWLR* 385–402.

[31] *The Queen* v. *Symonds* (1847) [1840–1932] NZPCC 387, 396, per Martin CJ. The Chief Justice did not of course exclude the subsequent creation of private property: "It (the 'heritage of the whole people principle') says nothing of the fitness or unfitness of the regulations or conditions under which the State may from time to time allow this property to be distributed and appropriated to individual citizens". However, an implication is that private property in New Zealand is derived from the historically and morally prior concept of common property, and ought accordingly to serve the common interest.

[32] Sir John Salmond, *Jurisprudence*, 7th edn. (London, Sweet and Maxwell, 1924) Appendix II, "The Territory of the State", p. 554.

The stark appearance of the final sentence, which it must be observed is supported by recent judicial and academic authority,[33] is of course moderated by the proviso, fully subscribed to by Salmond,[34] that the Crown's proprietary title is *subject to* Maori customary rights. The co-habitation of these two rights, for better or for worse, has many elements, some of which I want now to consider.

The collision of the Crown's radical and proprietary title with Maori customary rights founded on the Treaty of Waitangi and common law has been buffered and contained by a range of New Zealand institutions and understandings—some legal, some political and some social. The ambivalent jurisdiction of the Native Land Courts with the later invention of the Waitangi Tribunal, the historical functioning of the Maori Affairs Committee of Parliament, and the widespread deference to the role of tangata whenua in public ceremony, are examples of each.

Although most modern historians trace the origins of the Native Land Court regime (in the 1862 and 1865 Acts) to settler pressure for the unlocking of Maori's land for sale, there was a rationale for the conceptual contradiction of requiring the Court to determine the "individual interests" of Maori in land "in accordance" with a custom which recognised no such interests. It was that Maori would exchange the limited, "usufructuary" right of occupancy for the supposedly more valuable copper-plate of Crown Grant and fee simple.

A further element in the uneasy accommodation of feudal doctrine and Maori customary rights lay in public ownership. We have seen Sir William Martin's ringing assertion that acquisition of Maori rights by the Crown created a "heritage of the whole people". Governor Grey, for example, was explicit about the point in addressing the Legislative Council on the lands issue in August 1847:[35]

"The Governor said that there appeared to be a popular error abroad on the subject of Government dealings with natives for land. The Government in all cases had bought land from the natives as trustee for the two races, and a considerable portion of the land fund had been appropriated for the benefit of the natives".

The public ownership umbrella had a double utility: first, it lay philosophically closer to Maori conceptions than did the Blackstonian individualism; second, it removed land and resources from the market.

---

[33] This support is discussed in *Salmond: Southern Jurist*, above n. 7, at pp. 124–126. In addition, I note that K. McNeil, in his challenging work, *Common Law Aboriginal Title* (Oxford, Clarendon Press, 1989) 108 at n. 3 concedes the correctness of the legal proposition, while adding that this is not inconsistent with the co-existence of customary rights.

[34] For demonstration of this proposition, see *Salmond: Southern Jurist*, above n. 7, at pp. 124–126, and Salmond's hand-written note reproduced in the illustrations after p. 134.

[35] *The Nelson Examiner*, report of proceedings in the Legislative Council, 24 August 1847.

VI. THE MODERN DISRUPTION

Common property has had a bad press in recent times. Garrett Hardin's "Tragedy of the Commons", according to which commons are degraded and destroyed for lack of disincentives to competitive overuse, has been one reason urged in favour of "enclosure", and privatisation.[36] I want to suggest in this part of this chapter that there may be a "Tragedy of the Commodities" in the New Zealand context, whereby privatisations of public land, natural resources, and other state assets, have compelled Maori to formulate and pursue claims to "ownership" of these assets. The "commodification" of the "common heritage" has provoked novel claims and awakened dormant ones in a manner destructive of New Zealand's social cohesion. Claims to water flows, electricity dams, airwaves, forests, flora and fauna, fish quota, geothermal resources, seabed, foreshore, minerals, have followed the tendency to treat these resources, previously viewed as common property, as commodities for sale to private purchasers. Not surprisingly, the Maori reaction has been: if it *is* property, then it is *our* property!

Many Maori claims to the courts and the Waitangi Tribunal are, directly or indirectly, a consequence of the attempt to disengage the Crown from control of assets and resources which had previously been regarded as belonging to the nation as a whole. The haven of state-ownership had been thought to mean that land, assets and resources were safe from sale, and that practical decisions as to their use and control could be made as the need arose, in an evolutionary and co-operative manner. Privatisations, or even talk of them, provided both the provocation and the opportunity for adversarial contests. Decisions were made quickly: at the executive and legislative levels because asset-sales programmes had tight time-lines; at the judicial level because several critical cases concerned interim remedies, granted on low burdens of proof, designed to force negotiations. With respect, haste is evident in the decisions within all three branches of Government. The result, whether one considers State-owned lands, fish, forests, broadcasting spectrum, or other publicly owned assets still in dispute, has been that a "Maori dividend" has been the price of privatisation. That in itself is no matter for regret, especially when issues of historical and contemporary equity are considered. However, that dividend has been forced into Blackstonian form, and has sometimes been a poisoned chalice for Maori, as for example in the case of fish quota.[37]

---

[36] G. Hardin, "Tragedy of the Commons", (1968) 162 *Science* 1243. For a sustained criticism, see M. Taylor, "The Economics and Politics of Property Rights and Common Pool Resources", (1992) 32 *Natural Resources Journal* 633.

[37] The interim settlement of Maori commercial fishing claims in 1989 contemplated that fish quota allocated to Maori would be held inalienably by a Commission on behalf and for the use of all Maori, see the Maori Fisheries Act 1989. The decision subsequently to amend the model to compel the distribution of the quota as transferable property to individual tribes has been divisive and the subject of protracted and as yet unresolved litigation.

What then is the answer to these problems of those who urge ever more privatisation—of water rights, even of rights to pollute? In 1992 the New Zealand Business Roundtable, a business-oriented lobby group with an aggressive view of the beneficial effects of private property and the free market, published a document called *The Public Benefit of Private Ownership*. As its title indicates, it urged further privatisation in New Zealand and set out many reasons why this would be a public good. I make no comment on those reasons except to note the complete absence of any awareness of the issue of social cohesion described in this part of this chapter. The expression "Maori" occurs only once in the document—in the context of[38] "problems (that) have arisen during the sale process. Not the least of these difficulties were Maori land claims". These problems did not merely arise "during" the sale process, but rather *because of it*, and a comprehensive and objective assessment of the "public good" ought to have taken that consequence into its reckoning. Most recently, the Business Roundtable has published a study by Professor Kenneth Minogue of the "Waitangi Process". The author, whose thesis is critical of recent efforts to give some effect to the Treaty of Waitangi, reviews the intervention of the Waitangi Tribunal in 1986 to urge the Government not to proceed with the Individual Transferable Quota fish regime and comments:[39] "Maori were generally part-time fishers whose activities had not seemed relevant to a quota system". In fact, many Maori lost their fishing permits in 1983 because they did not earn a sufficient proportion of their total income from fishing, were consequentially ineligible for quota, and were therefore expelled from the activity of commercial fishing. This was a major, and justifiable source of Maori discontent and cannot be brushed aside as a puzzling irrelevance.

Professor Minogue complains of the apparent elasticity of the concept "taonga" which is the subject of the Crown's guarantee in Article II of the Treaty:[40]

"It is clear enough that land and fish might well come into this class. What is remarkable is how much else has at one time or another been included under this term—in one instance, a land free of pornography, for example".

Indeed, but Professor Minogue might cast an eye upon the commensurate enlargement in recent times of the category "private property" where he will find conceptual gymnastics no less startling. Dr Paul McHugh has made the point well, in a paper prepared for the Ministry of Justice in 1996, that indigenous peoples "appropriate and reformulate the language of the dominant culture: in the pattern of their subjugation lies the shape of their resistance".[41]

[38] New Zealand Business Roundtable, *The Public Benefit of Private Ownership*, (Wellington 1992),p. iii.

[39] K. Minogue, *Waitangi: Morality and Reality* (Wellington, New Zealand Business Roundtable, 1998), p. 19.

[40] Ibid., p. 22.

[41] P. McHugh, "Aboriginal Identity and Relations—Models of State Practice in North America and Australasia" in K. S. Coates and P. G. McHugh, *Living Relationships/Kokiri Ngatahi: The Treaty of Waitangi in the New Millenium* (Wellington,Victoria University Press, 1998).

Indeed, the "privatisation process" has served to emphasise to Maori that "the Crown" stands not as a protector of Maori interests as contemplated by the Treaty of Waitangi, but as an opportunistic liquidator of assets without regard to Maori interests.

The "Tragedy of the Commodities" might be that as common property shrinks, and is transformed into private property held by fewer and fewer hands, the New Zealand landscape will present to many of our citizens only the property of others—and the guards acknowledged by Adam Smith as necessary to protect it. Will there not need to be more and more guards, ever more vigilant, to maintain such a disequilibrium? Early in the siege of Sarajevo there appeared on the wall of a half-ruined post office the familiar slogan "This is Serbian land!". Someone had scrawled underneath: "No, you idiot, it's a Post Office!"[42] This is what happens when the rhetoric of property supersedes that of public purpose.

I will summarise my point in this section. It is that successive governments and their advisers have paid insufficient attention to the intersections between "dry" economic theory and practice on the one hand, and the health of the unique New Zealand arrangements contemplated in the Treaty of Waitangi on the other. These intersections complicate the calculation as to the overall national advantage of any privatisation in New Zealand in a way which is absent from overseas experience and may not always be well understood by foreign advisers.

VII.   DEVELOPING A NEW ZEALAND JURISPRUDENCE ON PROPERTY

I have had occasion in recent years carefully to study the work of New Zealand's great jurist, Sir John Salmond. Salmond's analytical approach to law, far from being the straightjacket which some suppose, in fact suggests quite revolutionary and imaginative uses of legal forms to achieve utilitarian objectives. It does this by bringing a liberating clarity to legal concepts, as in the following distinction between "natural persons" and "legal persons":[43]

> "A legal person is any subject-matter to which the law attributes a merely legal or fictitious personality. This extension, for good and sufficient reasons, of the conception of personality beyond the limits of fact—this recognition of persons who are not men— is one of the most noteworthy feats of the legal imagination".

[42] Related by T. G. Ash, "Bosnia in our Future", *New York Review of Books,* 21 December, 1995.
[43] Sir John Salmond, *Jurisprudence*, 7th edn. (London, Sweet and Maxwell,1924), p. 336. Commentators have frequently noted the case of *Pramatha Nath Mullick* (1925) LR 52 Ind App 245 in which the Privy Council conceded legal personality to a Hindu idol. More recently, in *Bumper Development Corp Ltd.* v. *Commissioner of Police of the Metropolis* [1991] 4 All ER 638, 647, Purchase LJ described Salmond's treatment of legal personality as "illuminating" and observed: "Thus Salmond recognises the possibilities, which may not be far-fetched, of (say) a foreign Roman Catholic Cathedral having legal personality under the law of the country where it is situated".

Some geographical features of particular significance to Maori and to other New Zealanders, such as some rivers and mountain peaks, do not lend themselves to allocation as property without engendering feelings of dispossession and demoralisation from one or other side of the community. The status quo—of the Crown's radical title—has become uncomfortable for Maori for two reasons: first it is difficult to square with the Treaty of Waitangi; secondly, the readiness of successive governments in recent times to take that radical title as authority to privatise assets has meant that it is no longer seen as a safe haven. Some attempts to compromise the situation have proposed slicing a river, for example, into river-bed, subsoil, waterflow, and so on, and allocating different slices to different interests. It is increasingly clear that such "solutions" are not regarded as satisfactory by Maori, precisely because these important geographic features associated with tribes are seen as tupuna, as ancestors, who ought not to be dismembered in this way.

The idea that prominent geographical features have personalities is familiar to anyone with even slight knowledge of Polynesian custom—indeed, whaikorero or formal speech-making will customarily include direct address to rivers, mountains and other geographical features of special importance: "Tena koe te maunga. . ." ("There you are, mountain"). Nor is the further step of attributing rights to such features as unusual for Polynesians as it might seem to some Europeans.[44]

A possible alternative to the zero-sum difficulties of Blackstonian tussles might be to endow a river, for example, with legal personality. The river would become not the *object* of law, but a legal *subject* in its own right and with its own rights—it would not be *owned* by anyone. The real question would of course then become "who *speaks for* the river in the assertion of its rights, and what are those rights to be?": the answer might depend on which aspect of the river's legal personality, or which rights, were being asserted or challenged on any given occasion. The persons, or combinations of persons entitled to speak for the river on particular issues would need to be settled by careful investigation, negotiation, and statutory enactment.

I should immediately acknowledge the debt that this suggestion owes to the seminal work of Professor Christopher Stone in his 1972 article "Should Trees Have Standing?".[45] Stone declared:

"I am quite seriously proposing that we give legal rights to forests, oceans, rivers and other so-called natural objects in the environment . . . To say that the environment should have rights is not to say that it should have every right we can imagine, or even

---

[44] An example is provided by the evidence of a kaumatua, or elder, in recent New Zealand litigation concerning fishing in a river: "Our Iwi and Hapu have a very close relationship with the Awa (river). We are the owners of the Awa—*it owns us:*" *Taranaki Fish and Game Council* v. *McRitchie* [1997] DCR 446, 452 (evidence of Niko Tangaroa).

[45] C. D. Stone, "Should Trees Have Standing? Towards Legal Rights for Material Agents", (1972) 45 *Southern California Law Review* 450. See also Stone's revisiting of the question in "Should Trees Have Standing? Revisited: How Far Will Law and Morals Reach? A Pluralist Perspective", (1985) 59 *Southern California Law Review* 1.

the same body of rights as humans have. Nor is it to say that everything in the environment should have the same rights as every other thing in the environment".

Anticipating the objection that natural objects could not have standing because they cannot speak, Stone pointed out that: [46]

"Corporations cannot speak either; nor can states, estates, infants, incompetents, municipalities or universities. Lawyers speak for them, as they customarily do for the ordinary citizen with legal problems".

Of course, Stone's objective was different from mine. He saw several weaknesses in the conventional Western conception of the natural environment as a "thing" to be used by humans. First, the "thing" had no standing in its own right and its integrity would only be protected where it happened to be in the interests of those holding rights to assert them. Secondly, the outcome of disputes tended to turn not on the values of the environment, but on demonstrable damage to right-holders. Thirdly, any compensation awarded went not to the "thing" but to the right-holders. Stone's purpose was accordingly enhanced environmental protection. Although any gains to environmental quality will not be disdained, the proposal here is made as a small contribution to the on-going search for a New Zealand jurisprudence which reconciles rather than divides our principal cultures, and which speaks in a language close to rather than distant from Maori and Polynesian conceptions. I have the privilege of working under the leadership of a distinguished New Zealand lawyer, Judge Michael Brown, in a project based at the University of Waikato which aims to advance that search in a co-operative effort by scholars of diverse background and knowledge. It is clear that our project needs to pay close attention to the concept of "property" and to its place in New Zealand jurisprudence.

---

[46] Stone (1972), above n. 45, at 464.

12

Liberal, Democratic, and Socialist Approaches to the Public Dimensions of Private Property

MICHAEL ROBERTSON

I. INTRODUCTION

My thesis is that mainstream thinking about property exhibits characteristic limitations and blind spots resulting from the underlying structure of liberal thought. The result is that most thinking about property fails to appreciate fully the public dimensions of private property. In particular, the political role of property and the power it gives owners is rarely made central. I will argue that this is due to the liberal public/private distinction and the location of property firmly within the private zone. I will use the contributions to the conference which prompted this book as evidence to support this thesis.

Although the underlying structure of liberal thought impedes an adequate account of the public dimensions of private property, other traditions are more helpful. The democratic and the socialist traditions, although not as dominant in our culture as the liberal tradition, both have developed more insightful ways to respond to the challenge posed by the conference. A final goal of this chapter is to highlight their distinctive contributions.

II. THE UNDERLYING STRUCTURE OF LIBERAL THOUGHT

The liberal public/private distinction

One of the great innovations of liberalism was to provide a new way of dividing social space into a public zone and a private zone. Previous Western societies had a public/private distinction that reflected a division between what was open for all to see and what was hidden away (in the King's privy chamber, or the home). But what was distinctive about liberalism was a new division which separated out economic and religious life into a private zone separate from the public political realm.[1]

In pre-liberal societies the legitimate authority of the monarch was not so circumscribed, and the economic and religious lives of his subjects were within his jurisdiction. This much more unlimited potential role of the state is brought out well in these two descriptions by the economic historians Schumpeter and Heilbroner:

> "[The Monarchy of Louis XIV] was not simply a government in the sense of nineteenth-century liberalism, ie, a social agency existing for the performance of a few limited functions to be financed by a minimum of revenue. On principle, the monarchy managed everything, from consciences to the patterns of the silk fabrics at Lyons, and financially it aimed at a maximum of revenue. Though the king was never really absolute, public authority was all-comprehensive".[2]

> "[Capitalism brings] the separation of overall governance in any social order into two independent and legally divorced realms, which are at the same time mutually dependent and married for life . . . What we do not ordinarily bear in mind is that this duality of realms, with its somewhat smudgy boundaries, has no counterpart in non-capitalist societies . . . There was only one realm even in such seemingly capitalistlike societies as ancient Greece, with its flourishing international trade, or Rome, which sported a kind of stock market in the forum, or 16th century Florence with its monied life. The reason was that the governing authority of the state was legally unbounded. The idea that the material provisioning of society, gladly left to the self-motivated activities of farmers, artisans, and merchants, was not in some ultimate sense under the aegis of the state would never have occurred to Aristotle, Cicero, or Machiavelli".[3]

According to the new liberal theorists, there was no need for the state to act in its public zone to achieve desirable economic results for society, because individuals freely contracting in the private zone could achieve this public benefit so much better. Adam Smith put it this way: [4]

> "Every man, as long as he does not violate the laws of justice, is left perfectly free to pursue his own interest in any way, and to bring both his industry and his capital into competition with those of any other man, or order of men. The sovereign is completely discharged from a duty, in the attempting to perform which he must always be exposed to innumerable delusions, and for the proper performance of which no human wisdom or knowledge could ever be sufficient; the duty of superintending the industry of private people, and of directing it towards the employments most suitable to the interests of society".

[1] For an expansion of this claim, see J. B. Thompson, *Ideology and Modern Culture* (Cambridge, Polity Press, 1990), pp. 238–241.

[2] J. Schumpeter, "Capitalism, Socialism, and Democracy" (1943) in B. Sutton (ed.), *The Legitimate Corporation* (Oxford, Blackwell, 1993), p. 27.

[3] R. Heilbroner, *Twenty-First Century Capitalism* (Concord, Anansi, 1992) 50–51. See too his *Behind the Veil of Economics* (New York, Norton, 1988), pp. 43–44, 70–72, 73–74.

[4] A. Smith, *The Wealth of Nations*, quoted in Heilbroner, "Adam Smith's Capitalism" in *Behind the Veil of Economics*, above n. 3, at pp. 138–139.

The place of property in the liberal public/private distinction

Clearly, property rights are firmly ensconced in the private zone in Smith's account, just as they were for all of the major early liberal thinkers. For John Locke, private property was a right which came into existence by the unilateral act of mixing one's labour with something previously held in common. Because this act did not require the prior existence of any government or law, private property rights could arise in the state of nature. Governments were only formed later in order, *inter alia*, better to preserve these pre-existing property rights. Since these property rights did not originate from or depend upon the state, and since a main purpose of the state was to make them more secure, the state was rarely entitled to alter private property rights in the exercise of its legitimate governing function. Consequently property existed in a private zone that was generally immune from interference by the state. [5]

Utilitarian liberals like Bentham argued from different premises to reach the same result. Private property was needed to provide the incentives to get people to use assets productively. If people couldn't be sure of retaining the fruits of their labours, they wouldn't produce the surpluses that through trade would result in the maximum satisfaction of preferences. Bentham argued that any redistributions of property or changes to the existing property rules by the state would destroy this incentive to produce. Even the immediate beneficiaries of such changes would realise that if property rules could be changed in their favour today, they could be changed to their disadvantage just as easily tomorrow. Maximising utility required maximising the security of private property, and this meant that the state must not meddle with property rights. [6]

So even though classical liberalism has a number of different strands, they all speak with one voice when it comes to property. Property should be understood as belonging in the private zone where its owner decides how the asset is to be used. The state has a legitimate role in the separate public zone, but that role will only rarely require it to interfere with private property rights. Examples of this permitted interference would be tort laws, and taxation to pay for the police and courts that enforce the laws protecting property. Today the enduring influence of this classical liberal manner of thinking about property can be seen even in the views of modern liberals like Charles Reich who see a greater role for the state: [7]

"Property draws a circle around the activities of each private individual or organization. Within that circle, the owner had a greater degree of freedom than without. Outside, he must justify or explain his actions, and show his authority. Within, he is master, and the state must explain and justify any interference . . . Thus, property

---

[5] See J. Locke, *Second Treatise on Government* (Cambridge, Cambridge University Press, 1967).
[6] See J. Bentham, *Principles of the Civil Code* in C. B. Macpherson (ed.), *Property: Mainstream and Critical Positions* (Oxford, Blackwell, 1978), pp. 41–58.
[7] C. A. Reich "The New Property", (1964) 73 *Yale LJ* 733, 771.

performs the function of maintaining independence, dignity and pluralism in society by creating zones within which the majority has to yield to the owner".

The structuring effect of the public/private distinction on liberal thinking about property

The central thrust of liberalism was to constrain the state in order to safeguard individual freedom, because the state was seen as the greatest danger to that freedom. The absolutist state was to be replaced by constitutional government and the rule of law, and it was to be denied its prior role of ordering the economic and religious activities of citizens. This central thrust explains the shape of the new liberal version of the public/private distinction. The point of this distinction was to keep the state and its coercive power to a circumscribed zone, and out of a separate private zone where individual freedom could reign.

But making fundamental this dichotomy between public and private realms comes at a cost. It structures the thinking of liberals in ways that emphasise some things and render others harder to see. Property is an area where we can see the negative effects of this underlying structure of liberal thought in two ways. The first effect is that liberals find it hard to see that private property can be a source of oppressive power even more dangerous to individual freedom than the state. Because private property is categorised by them as belonging in the realm where *freedom* is safeguarded, liberals find it hard to fully absorb the way property can give owners great power to restrict the freedom of others. The second effect is that liberals find it hard to appreciate fully the public aspects of private property. Because property is categorised by them as belonging in the *private* zone, they find it hard to acknowledge the large range of ways in which it has a public dimension. Ultimately these two effects are related, because the power of private property turns out to have public dimensions and is not simply a private matter between individuals.

I don't wish to be guilty of overstatement here. My argument is not that the underlying structure of liberal thought—its use of the public/private dichotomy and its placing of property deep inside the private zone of freedom—renders liberals *unable* to see *any* public dimensions to private property. I will soon be describing some liberal thinkers who have indeed achieved such insights. But I do want to argue that the effect of the underlying structure of liberal thought is that recognising the full extent of the public and political dimensions of private property, and the ways the power of private property limits freedom, cuts against the grain of liberalism and is harder for liberals to do. The result is that the public and power dimensions are missing or de-emphasised in most liberal analyses of property. Even when these features are noted, liberal theorists don't really know how to respond to them adequately, since a remedy would require a radical reconception of private property that moves beyond the confines of liberalism.

III. THE STRUCTURING THESIS TESTED

The conference papers exhibit the structuring effect

I now want to argue that the papers delivered at the recent conference on property held in Wellington under the auspices of the New Zealand Institute of Public Law bear out my structuring thesis. The title of the conference was: "Property and the Constitution. The Public Dimension of Private Property".[8] The subtitle in particular challenged the participants to think against the grain of liberal thought and to focus on the wider public dimensions of something usually categorised as anchored deep in the private zone. However, the response of most conference participants to this challenge was not a bold one. With two exceptions, only a narrow and conventional range of "public" dimensions was considered, and the role of private property in reducing freedom was not addressed. This is consistent with my claim that the underlying structure of liberalism deflects liberal thought away from facing certain realities.

Most participants chose to focus on the one public dimension of private property noted in the main title; its constitutional implications. Thus there were a number of papers on the unresolved land issues between Maori and Pakeha at the root of New Zealand society arising out of the European colonisation of the country and the Treaty of Waitangi.[9] The other constitutional issue that loomed large was the relationship between private property and bills of rights. Bills of rights have constitutional significance in liberal societies because they are seen as important devices for constraining the state and protecting a private zone of freedom for the individual. Bills or charters of rights identify the most fundamental interests of citizens that the state must respect. Deciding whether to give private property a place among these fundamental rights is thus a constitutional issue, as is the question of how any such constitutional right is to be interpreted.

The American experience tends to cast a large shadow over any such discussions. Their Bill of Rights deals with property in the Fifth Amendment as follows: "No person shall be . . . deprived of life, liberty, or property without due process of law; nor shall private property be taken for public use, without just compensation". The American experience of working with this provision captured the attention of conference speakers in two ways. First, the Fifth Amendment has led to an extensive case law in the area of "takings" or compensation for expropriation, and the way this issue has been dealt with in the

[8] This conference was held in Wellington, New Zealand, at the Victoria University of Wellington Faculty of Law, on 17–18 July 1998.

[9] See the chapters by J. Dawson, "The Ngai Tahu Settlement", A. Frame, "Property and the Treaty of Waitangi", and J. Waldron, "The Normative Resilience of Property", Chapters 10, 11 and 8 respectively above. Waldron's chapter dealt with the issue of returning property unjustly taken long ago. See too his "Historic Injustice: Its Remembrance and Supercession" in G. Oddie and R. Perrett (eds), *Justice, Ethics, and New Zealand Society* (Auckland, Oxford University Press, 1992), p. 139.

USA and other countries prompted a number of papers.[10] Secondly, the American experience prompted a panel discussion on whether it was even a desirable thing to include private property as one of the fundamental interests protected in bills of rights.[11] Gregory Alexander's paper compared the different experiences of Germany and the USA in granting private property protection in a basic constitutional document. [12]

An objection dealt with

It might be objected here that any narrowness of focus was due not to the limiting effects of the structure of liberal thought, but rather was due to sticking to the conference topic. After all, the main topic was "Private Property and the Constitution", and so "The Public Dimension of Private Property" was only to be pursued to the extent that it involved a constitutional dimension. But this will not do, because even within the confines of liberal thought, it is possible to link property and the constitution with far wider public dimensions than the conference participants identified. The work of Charles Reich provides an example of this.

Charles Reich is famous for his 1964 article, "The New Property", in which he argued that although private property in productive assets originally served to give people independence and self-sufficiency, this is no longer commonly the case.[13] The modern world is dominated by large private commercial organisations and the large state, and there is no longer any significant place for the individual owner/producer. Most of us no longer own productive assets out of which we can support ourselves and our families, as might have been the case in colonial America. Instead we rely on wages from the large owners of productive assets, and benefits of various kinds from the large state. This has reduced our freedom and placed us in the power of these large organisations.

Reich's argument was that because the old form of private property that gave independence, security, and self-sufficiency was no longer widely available, we needed to find a new form of private property that would perform the same role in the modern world. His solution was to treat the manifold benefits flowing from state action in the economy (for example, money, benefits, services, contracts, franchises, and licences, which he called "largess") as a new form of private property right in the hands of individuals. The idea was that if this government largess was not a discretionary matter, the state could not use the

---

[10] e.g. A. van der Walt, Chapter 6 of this volume

[11] J. W. Harris's paper, "Is Property a Human Right?", Chapter 4 above, concluded that some form of private property was a human right, but didn't go on to consider whether that meant it should be included in a bill of rights.

[12] G. S. Alexander, "Constitutionalising Property: Two Experiences, Two Dilemmas", Chapter 5 above.

[13] C. A. Reich, above n. 7.

threat of withholding it to coerce individuals to behave in ways the state wanted:[14]

"Above all, the time has come for us to remember what the framers of the Constitution knew so well—that 'a power over a man's subsistence amounts to a power over his will'. We cannot safely entrust our livelihoods and our rights to the discretion of authorities, examiners, boards of control, character committees, regents, or licence commissioners . . . We must create a new property".

By 1990, in a follow-up article entitled "Beyond the New Property: An Ecological View of Due Process", Reich was taking a stronger stand.[15] He felt that liberal states had recently demonstrated that if they could, they would avoid facing up to their obligation to ensure that individual citizens had the property rights needed to be independent. His solution was to interpret the Fifth and Fourteenth Amendments in such a way as to give each citizen "a constitutional right to minimum subsistence and housing, to child care, education, employment, health insurance, retirement, and to a clean and healthy natural environment".[16]

Reich is significant because he does succeed in thinking against the grain of liberal thought to a noteworthy degree. Unlike most liberals, he stresses the dark side of private property; how in contemporary circumstances it has freedom-destroying aspects. His account of a new form of private property based on government largess, and his call for constitutionally entrenched *substantive* property rights for all citizens acknowledge public dimensions to private property that go well beyond most liberal analyses. He thus shows how the constitutional theme of the conference can indeed be linked with some of the wider issues which most liberal property theory neglects.

Why then did no conference participant pursue his approach? It is not that they were unaware of his work—some of them mention him. Nor is it because Reich has moved outside the boundaries of liberal thought entirely. Indeed, one of the interesting things about Reich is the way he fully embraces the core values of classical liberalism—the autonomy of the individual and the key role of private property in preserving that autonomy—but seeks to find a better way of realising those values in the modern world. My explanation for the failure to follow Reich's lead is that he has pushed against the structure of liberal thought to an extent which renders his work a provocative but marginal oddity to most mainstream liberal thinkers who remain more firmly embedded within that tradition.

---

[14] Ibid., 787.

[15] C. A. Reich, "Beyond the New Property: An Ecological View of Due Process", (1990) 56 *Brooklyn L Rev* 731.

[16] Ibid., 733. For another approach exploring the way in which substantive property entitlements can be a constitutional right, see F. Michelman, "Property as a Constitutional Right", (1981) 38 *Washington and Lee L Rev* 1097; "Possession vs Distribution in the Constitutional Idea of Property", (1987) 72 *Iowa L Rev* 1319.

It is also worth noting that notwithstanding the boldness of Reich's analysis, he does not completely escape the constraining effects of the structure of liberal thought. Although he recognises that the economy has changed radically, and that individual freedom and security are now threatened by both the large state and large concentrations of private economic power, when he comes to find a solution he ignores the private concentrations of economic power, and turns his attention to the state. This reflects the tendency of liberal thought to see the *state* rather than private property as the problem that needs to be dealt with when it comes to individual freedom. In Reich's solution, the state has the obligation to provide the individual with a new form of private property which gives back the independence and freedom which has been lost. Another response would have been to give individuals new types of private property rights with respect to the large commercial organisations in our economy, but that would have taken Reich too far outside the confines of liberal thought.[17]

IV. THE DEMOCRATIC TRADITION'S APPRECIATION OF THE PUBLIC DIMENSION OF PRIVATE PROPERTY

My thesis in this part of the chapter is that the democratic, rather than the liberal, tradition better highlights the public and constitutional aspects of private property. However, since the democratic tradition is less dominant in our culture than liberalism, its insights into the public dimensions of private property are more marginalised and muted.

The separation between the liberal and democratic traditions

An initial objection to this thesis may be that no such firm distinction between liberalism and democracy can be made in our culture. After all, we live in what are called "liberal democracies", which indicates that liberalism and democracy can be seamlessly merged together. But the reality is that the two traditions arose in different times and each has existed for long periods without the other. Democracy first flourished in Athens between 450 BC and 322 BC, while liberalism arose in different parts of Europe from the seventeenth century onwards. Athenian democracy was not liberal, and the first liberal societies were not democratic. It was nearly 200 years after the emergence of liberal societies that democracy reappeared on the political scene. Liberal societies embraced democracy late and initially unenthusiastically, as evidenced by the long time it took to widen the franchise.[18]

---

[17] For an example of a more radical approach which gives the individual citizen new private property rights with respect to large business enterprises, see J. Roemer, *A Future for Socialism* (London, Verso, 1994); *Equal Shares* (London, Verso, 1996).

[18] B. Parekh, "The Cultural Particularity of Liberal Democracy" in D. Held (ed.), *Prospects for Democracy* (Cambridge, Polity Press, 1993), pp. 156–157, 163–164.

Nor did the two traditions fit neatly together when they were conjoined. Liberalism focused on seeking individual satisfactions in the private zone and distrusted the public zone of state action, while democracy focused upon seeking fulfilment in the public zone through joining with others in collective discussion and decision-making. Because liberalism was the dominant partner, its structures of thought have tended to prevail. The result is that liberals do not value democracy because active and on-going participation by citizens in the public zone is seen as essential for human well-being. Rather liberals value democracy because it constrains the state. It is basically a way of making sure the existing governors can be replaced if they act in a way that attracts the disapproval of the citizenry.[19]

This separation between liberalism and democracy has been noted by a number of political theorists,[20] and an excellent short account of it is provided by Bikhu Parekh. After giving an expanded version of the argument summarised above, he concludes: [21]

"Liberal democracy, then, represents a highly complex theoretical and political construct based on an ingenious blend of liberalism and democracy. It is democracy conceptualised and structured within the limits of liberalism. . . . Although in liberal democracy liberalism is the dominant partner, democracy, which has its own independent tradition and internal logic, has from time to time revolted against the liberal constraints. . . . No liberal democracy is, or has ever been, without tensions. By and large, however, liberal democracy has managed to retain the structural design it evolved in the latter half of the nineteenth century and to keep the democratic impulse under check".

The reflection in property theory of the tension between the liberal and democratic traditions

I now want to argue that the underlying tension between the liberal and democratic traditions in our political culture that Parekh and others describe is reflected in different ways of thinking about property. The first step in recognising this is to note the presence within property theory of two competing traditions. Carol Rose, in her article "'Takings' and the Practices of Property: Property as Wealth, Property as 'Propriety'" [22] has described the first of these property traditions as "property as preference satisfaction". This amounts to the classical liberal position which Bentham articulated. Private property is said to provide the economic incentives to individuals to maximise wealth, which

---

[19] Ibid., pp. 162–163.
[20] See e.g., C. B. Macpherson, *The Life and Times of Liberal Democracy* (Oxford, Oxford University Press, 1977) and S. Bowles and H. Gintis, *Democracy and Capitalism* (New York, Basic Books, 1986).
[21] Parekh, above n. 18, at p. 165.
[22] C. Rose, *Property and Persuasion* (Oxford, Westview Press, 1994) p. 49.

ultimately serves, through free market exchanges of the property rights so generated, to maximise individual preference satisfactions. But Rose then points out that there also exists a competing tradition which is less dominant today than the classical liberal model, but which long predates it:[23]

> "All the same, this wealth-enhancing or preference satisfying conception of property is not the only one available in our Western historical tradition; there is another and far older traditional vision of property as a practical social institution . . . What is the purpose of property under this other understanding? The purpose is to accord to each person or entity what is 'proper' or 'appropriate' to him or her . . . And what is 'proper' or appropriate, on this vision of property, is that which is needed to keep good order in the commonwealth or body politic".

On this older understanding, which Rose calls "property as propriety", the central and foundational role of property is not economic, but is rather political and constitutional. The role of a system of property, on this second view, is to maintain the desirable form of political order. People are to have the type and amount of property that will enable them to play their part in the well-structured and well-functioning polity.

I think it is clear from this description that the "property as propriety" tradition is the one which most obviously addresses the topic of the conference. Unlike the more classically liberal "property as preference satisfaction" tradition, it sees property not as being purely private, but as having an important public dimension. The system of property arrangements in any society has to be consciously designed to maintain the proper form of political and social order. Such an outcome cannot be left to the blind workings of private market forces alone. The structure of property arrangements thus has a foundational public importance that can fairly be described as constitutional.

However, this general "property as propriety" conception does not decide what the proper form of social order is that the property system must maintain. At different times different orders have been championed. In the feudal societies which preceded the liberal ones in Europe, the well-structured polity was conceived to be a hierarchical and inegalitarian one. The massive land-holdings of the aristocrats were seen as necessary to enable them to play their proper parts in governing and maintaining this society. With the coming of liberalism and modernity, this feudal conception of the just social order disappeared, and the "property as propriety" conception itself was eclipsed by the classical liberal "property as preference satisfaction" conception. But the general "property as propriety" conception did not die with feudalism; it simply took on modern forms. One of these forms was modern liberalism, which departs from classical liberalism in some important respects. But there was also a modern form created when the "property as propriety" tradition flowed into the channels carved in our political culture by the democratic impulse.

---

[23] C. Rose, *Property and Persuasion* (Oxford, Westview Press, 1994) pp. 51, 58.

Modern liberals, who can trace their roots to John Stuart Mill, have a vision of the good society as one composed of independent and autonomous individuals with the resources and attributes neccessary to make substantive use of their freedom. They hold that property arrangements should be such as to produce and maintain these types of individuals and this type of society. However, modern liberals are less confident than classical liberals that simple market transactions will produce this desired result. Consequently, they move away from the "property as preference satisfaction" approach to the "property as propriety" approach. Modern liberals see a larger role for the state in allocating property entitlements outside the market to ensure that their vision of the proper society is maintained. Private property thus comes to have a public dimension for a modern liberal because of this state involvement. Property relations are no longer purely matters to be dealt with in the private realm from which the state must be excluded. We can see now that Charles Reich expresses a very radical version of the modern liberal "property as propriety" approach, but most modern liberals embrace a weaker version of the welfare state. [24]

Nevertheless, the focus for modern liberals remains the individual, and what arrangements must be in place to ensure that each individual has what is needed to pursue his or her own conception of the good life in the private zone. By contrast, the modern version of the "property as propriety" approach influenced by the democratic tradition is focused not upon individual actions in the private zone, but rather on combining people together to engage in joint reflection and decision-making in the public zone. As inflected by this democratic impulse, the central issue for the "property as propriety" tradition is discovering the forms of property arrangements which will promote democratic functioning, and encourage the growth of an engaged democratic citzenry. These democratic outcomes cannot confidently be left to the market alone. In the thinking of both Jefferson and the "civic republicans" at the end of the eighteenth century[25] and the "economic republicans" of the nineteenth century,[26] the desire to protect property forms that enhance democratic functioning is strongly evident. In our times, this democratic property project is still a vibrant and on-going one, as we shall soon see, but it is not the dominant strand in contemporary thinking about property.

Thus the tension between liberalism and democracy in property theory manifests itself in two places. The first is the clash between the general "property as preference satisfaction" and "property as propriety" conceptions. But there is also a tension within the "property as propriety" conception between the modern liberal and democratic versions. They are alike in seeing a greater public dimension to private property than the classical liberal "property as preference

---

[24] Ibid., pp. 63–64.
[25] Ibid., pp. 61–62.
[26] W. Simon, "Contract Versus Politics in Corporation Doctrine" in D. Kairys (ed.), *The Politics of Law: A Progressive Critique*, 2nd edn. (New York, Pantheon Books, 1990), p. 387, esp. pp. 394–402.

satisfaction" approach, but the democratic strand takes this insight much further. Instead of retaining the liberal focus on the private zone, albeit with a greater appreciation of the substantive barriers to freedom that can exist there, the democratic strand links private property to democratic functioning in the public zone. For democrats, the proper society is one in which citizens engage with each other in democratic discussion and self-direction, and the property system should operate so as to foster the development of such a society.

Although Carol Rose does not emphasise the tension between liberalism and democracy, and the connection between the democratic tradition and her "property as propriety" approach, I believe such a connection is there to be seen in her work. In a later paper entitled "Property as the Keystone Right?"[27] she explores arguments which "clearly look to property to do considerably more for a constitutional order than 'merely' to secure economic prosperity".[28] That is, she scrutinises arguments for property having *political* importance. Some of these arguments clearly reflect the dominant liberal tradition and its negative attitude to democracy as described by Parekh. Examples of such arguments are that private property has political importance because it "diffuses power" and because it "makes politics seem boring".[29] The thrust of both arguments is that the public zone of state action is dangerous to freedom, and it is better if that power is circumscribed, and people are not encouraged to exercise it. But other arguments Rose considers clearly see the political importance of property in how it can *encourage* democratic functioning, and thus show the merger of the "property as propriety" and democratic traditions. One example of such an argument is that private property "makes individuals independent and thus capable of self-government".[30] Another is that the dealings between private property owners inculcate the skills and temprament needed for democratic functioning—for example, lasting social bonds and civility rather than war-like passions etc.[31]

The contribution of the democratic tradition to the conference topic

It is my contention, then, that the democratic strand of the "property as propriety" conception is the one best suited to bring out the public dimensions of private property. However, only two of the conference participants even adverted to it. It is understandable on my hypothesis of the structuring effect of liberal thought why this would be the case. That structuring results from seeing property as firmly embedded in the zone of privacy and freedom. Seeing property as not simply playing a *private* economic role in promoting individual liberty and

---

[27] (1996) 71 *Notre Dame Law Review* 329.
[28] Ibid., 333.
[29] Ibid., 340, 356.
[30] Ibid., 345.
[31] Ibid., 351.

happiness, but as also playing a foundational *public* role in fostering active democratic co-operation and participation is a significant step beyond the shaping effects of this structuring. It is not surprising, therefore, that most of the conference participants neglected this public and political role of private property.

Although Kevin and Susan Gray do not mention Rose's analysis, their contribution can be seen as fitting within what she calls the "property as propriety" tradition.[32] For Gray and Gray, the significant thing about the dominant tradition of thinking about private property is not the goal of preference satisfaction or wealth generation, but the power to exclude others. It is this power of private property owners that they argue has to be constrained in the interest of "public propriety"when communal solidarity or democratic functioning would be harmed if it were allowed to be absolute or arbitrary. They do not try to describe the property arrangements which best promote community solidarity and democratic functioning, but they identify some modern arrangements that they claim clearly undermine these goals. The power to exclude undesirables from shopping malls and gated residential communities means that those who want to communicate political ideas or engage in discussion with the people congregated in these "quasi-public" spaces can be kept out, to the detriment of democracy.

In his conference paper on the differing experiences of Germany and the USA in giving property explicit constitutional protection, Gregory Alexander adverts more explicitly than Gray and Gray to the "property as propriety" and "property as preference satisfaction" traditions which Rose identified:[33]

> "Broadly speaking, property as a constitutional right may be thought to serve two quite different functions. The first is an individual, or personal function: securing a zone of freedom for the individual in the realm of economic activity. In this role, property is closely connected with individual liberty. This idea of property and liberty as intimately and functionally intertwined is quite familiar, of course, in traditional liberal theory and may be thought to constitute the core substantive meaning of property in the liberal tradition. The second function that might be recognised is social and public rather than personal and private. It is to serve the public good . . . [P]roperty is protected as a fundamental individual right insofar as it serves the purpose of providing the material foundation for maintaining the proper social order, defined according to a scheme of objective values rather than in terms of the satisfaction of individual subjective preferences".

Alexander agrees with Rose that the US Supreme Court's takings jurisprudence shows an unrecognised and unresolved tension between the pull of an individual preference-satisfaction view of property, and the competing pull of a more public "proprietarian" conception. In Germany, by contrast, the two competing pulls are given explicit recognition in the constitution, but no way of

---

[32] K. Gray and S. Gray, "Private Property and Public Propriety", Chapter 2 in this volume.

[33] G. S. Alexander, "Constitutionalising Property: Two Experiences, Two Dilemmas", Chapter 5 above at p. 89. See too his book, *Commodity and Propriety: Competing Visions of Property in American Legal Thought 1776–1970* (Chicago, University of Chicago Press, 1997).

resolving them is provided. From Alexander's description, the "proprietarian" tradition in Germany is very like the modern liberal approach I presented earlier. The stress is on the welfare state acting to ensure that individuals have the material resources to achieve self-direction, self-development, and self-respect. The emphasis is on enabling the individual to achieve autonomy and self-realisation rather than fostering collective democratic decision-making in the public realm. Hence in his conference paper, Alexander did not engage with the democratic strand of the "proprietarian" tradition beyond a few references to Harrington and the civic republicans.

However, in his other writing, Alexander has pursued the democratic contribution to the tradition in more depth. In a recent article entitled "Civic Property", he notes that: [34]

"civic life, or what de Tocqueville calls 'civil society', is in an enfeebled condition in many countries, including the traditional democracies of the West. By 'civil society', de Tocqueville meant those forms of social interaction in which individuals deliberate with each other about which actions will best contribute to creating a good society . . . These interactions need not be overtly political. Indeed, the traditional institutions of civil society were non-political; they included churches, hobby groups, fraternal organizations, and the like. While not overtly political, these institutions had political effects. Traditionally, they have been the primary place where citizens learn and develop the skills, values, and practices that are essential to maintaining a robust democracy . . . The legitimacy and stability of the formal institutions of democracy depend upon the capacity of the public to trust and cooperate with others. A society in which people are characteristically suspicious of and withdrawn from each other is one in which democracy cannot long survive".

He takes it as his project in that article to find forms of private property that will not leave people isolated from each other, or to deal with each other only via market transactions. Instead he wants to find private property forms that bring people together into a civil society which encourages the development of democratic skills and practices. He suggests limited equity housing co-operatives and a shift to the co-operative form for pension funds, rather than the existing trust form.[35] In both instances the co-operative is structured so that the members have more direct control over their lives and exercise that control via democratic discussion and decision-making.

Alexander's article is excellent at showing the connection between "private" property forms and the "public" political world of joint democratic participation. But even here, I think, we can see the effects of liberalism manifested in a reluctance to push the democratic property project too far. The private property forms which Alexander is suggesting be restructured fall into the category of property for *consumption*—homes and pension income. But what about property for *production*—the factories and businesses where most working people

---

[34] G. S. Alexander, "Civic Property", (1997) 6 *Social and Legal Studies* 217, 217–218.
[35] Ibid., 226–230.

are employed by others. Why not extend the co-operative model to them as well and increase the amount of democratic interaction in people's lives? Here we find, I think, the boundary line between liberal and socialist approaches to property. Liberal thinking tends to shy away from radical reconceptualisations of property in the means of production, even if such reconceptualisations continue to involve *private* property. Even those in liberal democracies who may feel a greater pull from the democratic than the liberal tradition, like Alexander, seem affected by this structuring of liberal thought. Socialists, by contrast, are convinced that a radical rethinking of the forms of productive property is necessary.

This socialist rethinking need not be as radical as is commonly supposed. People commonly identify the socialist approach to property in the means of production with the orthodox Marxist approach. On the Marxist approach, private property in productive assets is to be replaced by state ownership, and the free market is to be replaced by a planned economy. But the general socialist goal here is to extend democratic decision-making from the political realm into the economic realm. A better way to achieve this, rather than state ownership and direction, may be to have all the people working in an enterprise be the owners of it and share the power to direct it. This keeps private property and the free market, but just makes another group (the suppliers of work and skills rather than capital) the private property owners. This co-operative private property form brings democracy into the economic realm because all the member/workers decide the course of their shared enterprise on the basis of one person one vote, not one share one vote, as is the norm in the corporate form. The expectation is that the acquisition of democratic skills and values in the workplace will translate into enhanced democratic participation in the "public" realm too.

The co-operative is an old, pre-Marxist socialist model, and in the wake of the failure of communist economies, interest in co-operatives has reawakened. Some "market socialists" have incorporated co-operatives into their theorising, and this theorising has influenced some property theorists who identify with the Critical Legal Studies movement.[36] I see the models of property arrangements described by these Critical Legal Studies writers as fitting within the democratic strand of the "property as propriety" tradition described above. These writers are seeking to find forms of private property that enhance and foster democratic functioning in both the "public" and "private" zones of life. They differ from contributors to the tradition like Alexander, and Gray and Gray, because they are more prepared to abandon liberalism for socialism, and so are prepared to reconceive the forms private property should take in productive assets as well as in property for consumption.

---

[36] See K. Klare, "Legal Theory and Democratic Reconstruction: Reflections on 1989", (1991) 25 *University of British Columbia Law Review* 69; W. Simon, "Social-Republican Property", (1991) 38 *UCLA Law Review* 1335; M. Robertson, "Reconceiving Private Property", (1997) 24 *Journal of Law and Society* 465.

V. THE SOCIALIST TRADITION'S APPRECIATION OF THE PUBLIC
DIMENSION OF PRIVATE PROPERTY

The focus on power

The socialist tradition has more to contribute to property theory than just a more radical democratic extension of the "property as propriety" tradition. The socialist tradition brings with it an unrelenting focus on the *power* that flows from ownership or control of some forms of private property—in particular, productive assets that are worked by the wage labour of non-owners. Because they are less committed to the liberal public/private distinction, socialists are able to note features of this power that most liberals find hard to acknowledge. They are able to note how it systematically operates not to maximise freedom, but rather to allow a few to limit the freedom of many others. They are also less constrained in acknowledging the wide range of ways in which this power is so extensive as to acquire important public dimensions, and even to become a form of state-like power. By contrast, liberals tend to associate property with a freedom-enhancing role in the private zone, and so rarely make the public and negative power of private property central to their analyses.

The pervasive freedom-destroying role of private property under modern conditions of production was an important insight of Karl Marx.[37] He noted liberalism's claim to have increased individual freedom over prior social forms, with their slavery and serfdom. According to the liberal philosophers, freely chosen contracts have replaced these older forms of compulsion. Therefore, if people choose to be employees this can only be because they have rationally come to the conclusion that this is the best way to achieve maximum preference satisfaction for them. But Marx saw the hidden compulsion lurking under the surface of this cheery story. If access to productive assets is necessary to live, and if some people have managed to gain control of these productive assets, then the other people have no choice but to sell their labour to some of these owners. It is true that the compulsion no longer works at a personal level. An individual worker is no longer compelled to work for a particular person, as a slave or serf was. But that only means that the compulsion now works at a class level, for the worker has no choice but to sell his labour to some member of the owning class or other. In this sale, the owner of the means of production generally has the greater bargaining power, as Adam Smith noted:[38]

> "A landlord, farmer, a master manufacturer, or a merchant, though they did not employ a single workman, could generally live a year or two upon the stock [capital]

---

[37] See the extracts from *The Communist Manifesto* and *Capital* in C. B. Macpherson (ed.), *Property: Mainstream and Critical Positions* (Oxford, Blackwell, 1978), pp. 61–74.
[38] Quoted in R. Heilbroner, "The World of Work" in *Behind the Veil of Economics*, above n. 3, at p. 91.

which they had already acquired. Many workmen could not subsist a week, few could subsist a month, and scarce any a year without employment".

The result is that those who have managed to consolidate control of the means of production in their hands have the power to command the rest of mankind, and so limit their freedom.

The public dimensions of private power: political activity

We shall soon be considering an argument that power of the sort Marx identified is akin to state power, and so has a public dimension, but first we will consider some less radical arguments for the power of private property having public dimensions. One of these public dimensions can be seen when the huge wealth generated by corporations in the private zone is used by those who own or manage those corporations to give them greater influence in the political, public zone. This can be achieved through such things as campaign contributions, the funding of "think tanks", the employment of lobbyists, or the ability to pay for political views to be transmitted via the mass media. Many liberals see this as unproblematic; it is simply the exercise of free speech and people spending their own money as they want. But it is obviously a problem for the democratic tradition, since it allows some citizens to distort the public debate and marginalise the participation of the less wealthy. Owen Fiss has written eloquently of these concerns from a democratic position, and has concluded that only state action can negate the ability of private wealth to distort democratic functioning.[39]

But even Fiss's position reveals a limitation in conceiving of the public dimension of private property that I believe originates in the dominant liberal structures of thought. For the liberal, the public/private distinction is fundamental, and the two realms should be kept apart as much as possible. The danger of not keeping them apart is that the state may invade the private zone and threaten individual freedom. Now we have seen how a democrat can see the danger flowing the other way. Wealth generated in the private zone may invade the public zone of democratic life and damage it. But both these approaches assume the existence of the distinction, and also assume that if private property stays in the private zone and is used purely for economic purposes, it need have no public or political dimension. A more radical critique is to see how even the "private economic" use of large productive assets has a public dimension. This critique is more radical because it threatens to undermine the very public/private distinction that is fundamental for liberalism. The two zones are no longer kept neatly apart; instead they show an alarming tendency to collapse into each

---

[39] O. Fiss, "Money and Politics", (1997) 97 *Columbia Law Review* 2470; *The Irony of Free Speech* (Cambridge, Harvard University Press, 1996).

other. Because of this, I contend, it is a more difficult critique for liberals to make, although some have started down that road.

The public dimensions of private power: economic activity

Some of the public dimensions of the "merely private and economic" use of large productive assets seem hard to avoid, even for those whose vision has been structured by liberalism. The recent New Right orientation of many governments has led them not only to reduce the extent of government services, but also to seek private providers for the services they still see themselves as obliged to provide to citizens. Thus in New Zealand the government is exploring the idea of using private, profit-seeking corporations to provide some hospital, police, and prison services. Paying private corporations to step into the state's shoes in the provision of public services is an important new public dimension of private property.

A more enduring and general public dimension to the economic use of large productive assets lies in the immense public impact of such use. The way I use personal consumption property such as my house doesn't affect many other people, but the way Exxon uses its productive property affects people in many nations around the world. Pollution and environmental degradation as a result of commercial activities are clear examples of this public dimension of private property. Environmental degradation affects public safety and perhaps public survival, and has prompted a recent surge of interest in property theory.[40]

Interestingly, these environmental concerns can be tied in with the conference topic not only via the notion of a "public dimension of private property", but also via the reference to the constitution. Charles Reich achieved this in his "Beyond the New Property" article which was referred to earlier. There he uses an environmental analogy to support the conclusion that concern for the autonomy and independence of the individual requires substantive property rights that are constitutionally protected:[41]

> "The approach I take has much in common with the developing legal protection of the natural environment. The crisis of the natural environment and the crisis of the unprotected individual are similar. Both crises derive from the destructive aspects of our modern economic system . . . An ecological approach to individual economic rights would begin with the question of what kinds of habitat, nurture and protection from harm are needed to produce a healthy individual. This is the starting point for plants or animals—why not for human beings?"

Reich then proceeds to argue that property rights sufficient to give individuals economic security and the basis for a civilised life are to humans what its

---

[40] See e.g., T. Hayward and J. O'Neill (eds), *Justice, Property, and the Environment: Social and Legal Perspectives* (Aldershot, Ashgate Publishing, 1997); (1997) 50 *Oklahoma Law Review* No. 3 "Symposium: Environmental Protection and the Politics of Property Rights".

[41] Reich, above n. 15, at 734.

habitat is to an animal. We need such rights to exist as humans, to flourish, but just as the habitats of animals have been destroyed by industrialisation, so the access to those property rights have been removed for many humans. The same motivations that bring us to legislate for the protection of the environment must bring us to give constitutional protection for a basic cluster of substantive property rights, Reich concludes. Protection of the human habitat is the first and highest obligation of the state.

But the public impact of corporate behaviour is not limited to the environment. Corporate decisions on directions in research and development, and the patents they take out (or buy up and sit on) affect the technologies that shape our lives. Their marketing and advertising help structure our desires and aspirations. Whether a multi-national business corporation decides to put a plant in country A or B affects more people than just those employed by the plant. It provides tax revenue and produces infrastructure developments, and may also affect the political decision-making processes of that country. This public dimension of private property has not been ignored or downplayed by all liberal theorists. Charles Lindblom wrote that:[42]

> "corporate executives in all private enterprise systems . . . decide a nation's industrial technology, the pattern of work organization, location of industry, market structure [and] resource allocation".

Similarly Blumberg noted that:[43]

> "the decision of General Motors with respect to capital development, plant locations and closings, employment, price and wage policies represent decisions of vast implications for the countries, communities, and individuals concerned. The concentration in the major industrial companies of such formidable economic power, affecting so many persons and communities, has been described by observers . . . as constituting private governments, and it has been suggested that constitutional concepts developed with respect to traditional governmental processes might well be expanded to the leviathans of industry".

There is a final and more unnoticed way in which the power granted to those who have ownership or control of the productive assets has a public dimension. This public dimension is revealed not by looking at the "external" public effects of corporate behaviour, but rather at the "internal" workings of such organisations. What one sees there is that in its relationships with its employees, the corporation resembles a mini-state. The power it has over these employees is analogous to the power a state has over its citizens:[44]

---

[42] C. Lindblom, *Politics and Markets: The World's Political-Economic Systems* (New York, Basic Books, 1977), p. 171.

[43] P. I. Blumberg, "The Politicalization of the Corporation", (1971) 26 *Business Lawyer* 1551, 1564.

[44] D. Vogel, "The Corporation as Government: Challenges and Dilemmas", (1975) 8 *Polity* 5, 16–17.

"To suggest that the corporation not only exercises a sort of governmental authority, but in fact is an indivisible part of the political government itself, represents one perception of the corporation as a political institution. It is not, however, exhaustive. Equally significant, and in no way contradictory, is a political and ideological analysis that treats the business corporation as a political institution in its own right, regardless of its integration with government . . . General Motors is a critical and important part of the system of governance in the United States: at the same time it is also a distinctive institution that directly exercises poltical power".

Morris Cohen had put his finger on this in his 1927 "Property and Sovereignty" article when he noted that the owners of large productive assets get not just *dominion over things* through their property rights, but also, and more importantly, *sovereignty over people*. Their ability to withhold access to the means of production gave them power over their employees that was like the political power of governments—the corporation could "tax" them by taking a portion of their output, and issue commands to them.[45] Cohen here echoes Marx's insights into the nature of the power of capitalists over workers. Later authors have also seen the analogy between the corporation and its employees on the one hand, and the state and its citizens on the other. Brent Fisse notes that:[46]

"[m]ajor and even medium-sized corporations are centres of power, resemble minigovernments, have internal disciplinary processes and indeed often have de facto legal systems of their own".

Thus even the purely economic uses of large productive assets involve the exercise of power that has important and multiple public dimensions. Large corporations not only have a large public impact, they are also taking over many of the state's traditional functions, and even constitute mini-states themselves. One might have expected that a number of the conference participants would have seen the implications of this for the conference topics, but only Kevin and Susan Gray directed their paper in the general direction of the public dimension of private economic power.[47] Again, I think this bears out my hypothesis. While the structure of liberal thought does not make it impossible for liberals to see these things (as evidenced by Gray and Gray and the other people quoted above), it does make it harder. Consequently liberal theorising about property rarely puts the power issue at the centre of the analysis in the way that socialist thought does.

Gray and Gray do not share the general liberal assumption that the social world can be divided neatly into public and private zones. They argue for a continuum between these two poles, and that there exists an intermediate category

---

[45] M. Cohen, "Property and Sovereignty" in C. B. Macpherson (ed.), *Property: Mainstream and Critical Positions* (Oxford, Blackwell, 1978), p. 155, especially at pp. 159–160.

[46] B. Fisse, "Corporations, Crime, and Accountability", (1995) 6 *Current Issues in Criminal Justice*, 378, 383.

[47] K. Gray and S. Gray, "Private Property and Public Propriety", Chapter 2 above.

of "quasi-public" property. In this category, property may be private in legal form, but nevertheless have such a significant public dimension that the powers normally given to a private property owner may be constrained in the public interest. The power that most interests them is the power to exclude others, and they argue, as we have seen, that this power cannot remain arbitrary and absolute in the case of quasi-public property such as shopping malls and gated residential communities. Instead it must be subject to tests of reasonableness and natural justice that are derived from public law, and that the courts can enforce.

This is valuable as far as it goes, but the analysis is frustrating because it stops just when it was about to get really interesting. Gray and Gray talk about the injustice of private property owners excluding shabby unemployed people from congregating in shopping malls. But even if the right to exclude them from such places is denied, has that much been achieved? These people are still unemployed, they continue to suffer the far more important exclusion from access to productive assets, even as they have a right to enter the palaces of consumption to look at things they cannot afford to buy.

If the issue is the power of private property owners to exclude others, surely the most important instance of this, as both Marx and Morris Cohen recognised, is the power of those who own the productive assets to exclude those who have no productive assets of their own. The public dimensions of this power have already been noted: reduced liberty for those who can only gain access to the assets on the owner's terms, the granting of state-like power to owners, and great inequalities of wealth that translate into reduced opportunities for both self-development and democratic participation for most people. Here, I suggest, we have again run up against the structuring effect of liberal thinking about property. Even when the public dimension of the power of private property owners to exclude others is perceived by Gray and Gray, that insight closes down before it can be applied to the most important kind of property—productive assets. The validity of the employment relationship and the primacy of the suppliers of capital over the suppliers of work go too deep to be easily questioned by those for whom the liberal tradition is still more influential than the socialist tradition.

VI. MORE ADEQUATE RESPONSE TO THE NEGLECTED PUBLIC DIMENSIONS
OF PRIVATE PROPERTY

I have been arguing throughout this chapter that the liberal public/private distinction strongly influences the way liberals think about property. Once they place property firmly within their private zone, liberals have a tendency to see property as playing a primarily private economic role that is freedom enhancing. This makes it harder for them to see the public dimensions of property that come from its political role and the power over others it gives to some owners.

Of course, not all liberals suffer this structuring effect to the same degree. Although I find that the public dimensions of private property stressed by the democratic and socialist traditions are absent or marginalised in most liberal writing about property, some noteworthy exceptions exist, as I have tried to show.

These more insightful liberals have made some progress towards better ways of approaching private property. For example, Berle and Means noted that the large modern business corporation is not like the family home or even the family farm, and needs to be treated differently by society and the law.[48] Some important conceptual shifts underlie such a recognition. First there is a recognition that the factor of power can no longer languish in the background, as it does in most liberal theorising about property. Instead it has to be brought to the forefront and made the basis for new ways of categorising different types of property. I would argue that, at the least, this means that property for personal consumption, which gives no great power over others, must be seen as fundamentally different from property for production, which can lead to such power, especially if this property is worked by the labour of non-owners.

However, the radicalism of these liberals tends to run out when it comes to concrete suggestions for new ways of dealing with these corporations. Typically, the response of even non-mainstream liberals like Cohen is greater public scrutiny and regulation of corporations so that their power is not used to harm the public interest. Even this mild conclusion involves some interesting modifications of classical liberal thinking about property. In the classical picture, private property all belonged over in the private zone. But the effect of arguments like Morris Cohen's is to move a sub-set of what was conceived of as private property over into the public zone. Because private ownership of large concentrations of productive property gives the owner sovereignty over others, it is really a form of public power, and not really private at all. Therefore it can be subject to public or state regulation without attracting the liberal objections that would apply if it were genuinely private property only.

I think that a more adequate response to the neglected public dimensions of private property is to be found in a combination of the democratic and socialist traditions, rather than in the liberal tradition. I have developed this position elsewhere,[49] and so will only state it here in a summary fashion. I am attracted by the "property as propriety" approach identified by Rose and Alexander, and see the crucial task as being the designing of forms of private property and the free market which produce a more democratic, egalitarian, and solidary society. The goal here is to redesign the ground rules of private property and the market so that when people engage in economic transactions according to these new ground rules, more egalitarian, communal and democratic outcomes are natu-

---

[48] See e.g., A. Berle and G. Means, *The Modern Corporation and Private Property*, 2nd edn. (New York, Harcourt, Brace and World, 1968).

[49] See M. Robertson, "Property and Ideology", (1995) 8 *Canadian Journal of Law and Jurisprudence* 275; "Reconceiving Private Property", above n. 36.

rally produced. It may seem odd to see this as a socialist-inspired project, since socialism is associated with the abolition of private property in the means of production and the replacement of market mechanisms by state planning. But, as noted earlier, the non-Marxist market socialist tradition provides models of economies where the co-operative replaces the corporation as the predominant economic actor, yet these co-operatives are still privately owned by their members. The co-operative is an economic form for the use of productive assets in which the democratic and socialist traditions can run together and reinforce each other while seeking to avoid the disasters produced by communism. It is a form in which the public dimensions of private property which are neglected by liberal thought are openly acknowledged. Indeed, it is chosen precisely to increase democratic participation and reduce power imbalances.

This market socialist project raises a final constitutional issue. Is it within the legitimate power of the state to alter property and contract rights so as to advance a particular end-state or vision of the good society? Many liberals would tend to see this as improper, because the state is meant to be neutral regarding conceptions of the good or worthwhile life, and is not supposed to be seeking to advance one over another. The state, in deciding on the property and contract ground rules, is supposed to be constructing a neutral framework of rules within which individuals can exercise their free choices and pursue their own conceptions of the good life. The response to this is that the neutrality the liberal requires from the state here is an impossibility. Every choice of property and contract ground rules is political, not neutral, since it distributes power between groups in society and is informed by a commitment to a particular vision of what social life could and should be. Thus the public/private distinction which is so fundamental to liberalism is, at bottom, incoherent. The state cannot be excluded from the "private" zone, nor can it be confined to a mere "neutral" role while there.[50]

---

[50] For the detail of this argument, see Robertson, "Reconceiving Private Property", above n. 36, at 471–475.

Bibliography

ACKERMAN, B. A. (1977) *Private Property and the Constitution.*

—— (1997) "The Rise of World Constitutionalism" 83 *Va L Rev* 771.

ALCHIAN, A. A. and DEMSETZ, H. (1973) "The Property Rights Paradigm" 33 *Journal of Economic History* 16.

ALEXANDER, E. R. (1989) "The Canadian Charter of Rights and Freedoms in the Supreme Court of Canada" 105 *LQR* 561.

ALEXANDER, G. S. (1982) "The Concept of Property in Private and Constitutional Law: the Ideology of the Scientific Turn in Legal Analysis" 82 *Col L R* 1545.

—— (1997) *Commodity and Propriety: Competing Visions of Property in American Legal Thought.*

—— (1997) "Civic Property" 6 *Social and Legal Studies* 217.

ALLEN, T. (1993) "Constitutional Interpretation and the Opening Provisions of Bills of Rights in African Commonwealth Countries" in *Proceedings: African Society for International and Comparative Law.*

— *The Right to Property in Commonwealth Constitutions* (forthcoming).

ALVARO, A. (1991) "Why Property Rights were Excluded from the Canadian Charter of Rights and Freedoms" 24 *Can J Pol Science* 309.

ANDERSON, S. "Municipal Corporations go to Market" unpublished commentary.

ARTHURS, H. (1997) "'Mechanical Arts and Merchandise': Canadian Public Administration in the New Economy" 42 *McGill LJ* 29.

ASH, T. G. (1995) "Bosnia in our Future" *New York Review of Books.*

AUGUSTINE, P. W. (1986) "Protection of the Right to Property Under the Canadian Charter of Rights and Freedoms" 18 *Ottawa LR* 67.

AVINERI, S. and DE-SHALIT, A. (1992) *Communitarianism and Individualism.*

BAKER, C. E. (1986) "Property and Its Relation to Constitutionally Protected Liberty" 134 *U Pa L Rev* 741.

BAKER, J. H. (1990) *An Introduction to English Legal History.*

BARZEL, Y. (1989) *Economic Analysis of Property Rights.*

BAUMAN, R. W. (1992) "Property Rights in the Canadian Constitutional Context" 8 *SAJHR* 344.

BECKER, L. C. (1977) *Property Rights: Philosophic Foundations.*

—— (1980) "The Moral Basis of Property Rights" in J. R. Pennock and J. W. Chapman (eds), *Property: Nomos XXII.*

BEDDARD, R. (1993) *Human Rights and Europe.*

BENDA, E., MAIHOFER, W. and VOGEL, H.-J. (1984) "Die Menschenwürdige" *Handbuch des Verfassungsrechts.*

BENN, S. J. and GAUS, G. F. (eds) (1983) *Public and Private in Social Life.*

BENNION, F. A. R. (1997) *Statutory Interpretation: Codified, with a Critical Commentary.*

BENTHAM, J. (1830) "Principles of the Civil Code" in C. B. Macpherson (ed) (1978), *Property: Mainstream and Critical Positions.*

—— (1952) "Supply without Burthen" in W. Start (ed) *Jeremy Bentham's Economic Writings.*

BENTHAM, J. (1978) "Security and Equality of Property" in C. B. Macpherson (ed) *Property: Mainstream and Critical Positions.*

BERLE, A. and MEANS, G. (1968) *The Modern Corporation and Private Property.*

BERLIN, I. (1958) *Two Concepts of Liberty.*

BERMAN, H. J. (1974) *The Interaction of Law and Religion.*

BLACKSTONE, W. (1765–1789) *Commentaries on the Laws of England.*

BOLICK, C. (1995) "Thatcher's Revolution: Deregulation and Political Transformation" 12 *Yale J on Reg* 527.

BONYHADY, T. (1992) "Property Rights" in T. Bonyhady (ed) *Environmental Protection and Legal Change.*

BORKOWSKI, A. (1997) *Textbook on Roman Law* 2nd edn.

BORRIE, G. (1989) "The Regulation of Public and Private Power" *Public Law* 552.

BOWLES, S. and GINTIS, H. (1986) *Democracy and Capitalism.*

BRIDGE, M. (1996) *Personal Property Law.*

BUCHANAN, D. (1989) "Assessing the Communitarian Critique of Liberalism" 94 *Ethics* 852.

BUCKLE, S. (1991) *Natural Law and the Theory of Property: Grotius to Hume.*

BURKE, E. (1969) *Reflections on the Revolution in France* (C. C. O'Brien (ed)).

BUTLER, L. (1982) "The Commons Concept: An Historical Concept with Modern Relevance" 23 *Wm & Mary L R* 835.

BUTT, P. (1996) *Land Law.*

CACHALIA, A. et al (eds) (1994) *Fundamental Rights in the New Constitution.*

CALABRESI, G. and MELLAMED, A. D. (1972) "Property Rules, Liability Rules and Inalienability: One View of the Cathedral" 85 *Harv LR* 1089.

CANE, P. (1987) "Public Law and Private Law: A Study of the Analysis and Use of a Legal Concept" in J. Eekelaar and J. Dell (eds), *Oxford Essays in Jurisprudence.*

CAPPELLETTI, M. (1989) *The Judicial Process in Comparative Perspective.*

CARPENTER, G. (1995) "Internal Modifiers and Other Qualifications in Bills of Rights—Some Problems of Interpretation" 10 *SAPL* 260.

CHASKALSON, M. (1993) "The Problem with Property: Thoughts on the Constitutional Protection of Property in the United States and the Commonwealth" 9 *SAJHR* 388.

—— (1994) "The Property Clause: section 28 of the Constitution" 10 *SAJHR* 131.

—— (1995) "Stumbling Towards Section 28: Negotiation Over the Protection of Property Rights in the Interim Constitution" 2 *South African Journal on Human Rights* 222.

CHASKALSON, M. and DAVIS, D. (1996) "Constitutionalism, the Rule of Law and the First Certification Judgment: Ex Parte Chairperson of the Constitutional Assembly in re: Certificate of the Constitution of the Republic of South Africa 1996 (1996) (4) SA 744 (CC)" 13 *SAJHR* 430.

CHASKALSON, M. and LEWIS, C. H. (1996) "Property" in M. Chaskalson et al (eds), *Constitutional Law of South Africa.*

CHRISTMAN, J. (1994) *The Myth of Property.*

CLARKE, R. V. (1995) "Situational Crime Prevention" in M. Tonry and D. Farrington (eds), *Building a Safer Society: Crime and Justice: A Review of Research.*

CLAUDE, R. P. and WESTON, B. H. (eds) (1992) *Human Rights in the World Community.*

COCKRELL, A. (1998) "The Hegemony of Contract" 115 *SALJ* 286.

COHEN, G. A. (1995) *Self-ownership, Freedom and Equality.*

COHEN, M. (1978) "Property and Sovereignty" in C. B. Macpherson (ed) *Property: Mainstream and Critical Positions.*

COQUILLETTE, D. R. (1979) "Mosses From an Old Manse: Another Look at Some Historic Property Cases About the Environment" 64 *Cornell LR* 761.

CRAIG, P. (1997) "Public Law and Control over Private Power" in M. Taggart (ed), *The Province of Administrative Law*.

—— (1998) "Constitutions, Property and Regulation" *PL* 538.

CRAWFORD, M. (1992) "The World in a Shopping Mall" in M. Sorkin (ed), *Variations on a Theme Park: The New American City and the End of Public Space*.

CURRIE, D. P. (1989) "*Lochner* Abroad: Substantive Due Process and Equal Protection in the Federal Republic of Germany" *S Ct Rev* 333.

—— (1994) *The Constitution of the Federal Republic of Germany*.

DAVIES, K. (1974) "Injurious Affection and Compensation" 90 *Law Quarterly Review* 361.

DAVIS, M. (1992) "Fortress Los Angeles: The Militarization of Urban Space" in M. Sorkin (ed), *Variations on a Theme Park: The New American City and the End of Public Space*.

—— (1994) "Less Mickey Mouse, More Dirty Harry: Property, Policing and the Modern Metropolis" 5(2) *Polemic* 63.

DANTITH, T. (1979) "Regulation by Contract: The New Prerogative" *Current Legal Problems* 41.

—— (1985) "The Executive Power Today: Bargaining and Economic Control" in J. Jowell and D. Oliver, *The Changing Constitution*.

DELONG, J. V. (1997) *Property Matters: How Property Rights are Under Assault—and Why You Should Care*.

DEMSETZ, H. (1967) "Toward a Theory of Property Rights" 57 *Am Econ Rev* 347.

DHAVAN, R. (1977) *The Supreme Court of India: a Socio-legal Analysis of its Juristic Techniques*.

DOLZER, R. (1976) *Property and Environment: The Social Obligation Inherent in Ownership*.

DONNELLY, J. (1989) *Universal Human Rights in Theory and Practice*.

DUGARD, J. (1990) "A Bill of Rights for South Africa" 23 *Cornell Int LJ* 441.

DURIE, E. and ORR, G. (1990) "The Role of the Waitangi Tribunal and the Development of a Bicultural Jurisprudence" 14 *NZULR* 62.

DURIE, E. (1996) "Will the Settlers Settle? Cultural Conciliation and the Law" 8 *Otago LR* 449.

—— (1995) "Background Paper" 25 *VUWLR* 97.

DURIE, M. (1998) *Te Mana, Te Kawanatanga: The Politics of Maori Self-Determination*.

DWORKIN, R. (1986) *Law's Empire*.

EDELMAN, B. (1973) *Le Droit Saisi Par La Photographie*.

EGAN, T. (1995) "Many Seek Security in Private Communities" *NY Times* 3 September, A1.

ELLUL, J. (1984) *Histoire des institutions: 1-2/L'Antiquité*.

ELY, J. W. (1998) *The Guardian of Every Other Right: A Constitutional History of Property Rights*.

ENGLISH, R. (1998) "Wrongfooting the Lord Chancellor: Access to Justice in the High Court" 61 *Mod L R* 245.

EPSTEIN, R. A. (1979) "Possession as the Root of Title" 3 *Georgia LR* 1221.

—— (1985) *Takings: Private Property and the Power of Eminent Domain*.

—— (1995) *Simple Rules for a Complex World*.

EVISON, H. (1997) *The Long Dispute: Maori Land Rights and European Colonisation in Southern New Zealand*.

—— (1987) *Ngai Tahu Land Rights and the Crown Pastoral Lease Lands in the South Island of New Zealand*.

FARRIER, D. and MCAUSLAN, P. (1975) "Compensation, Participation and the Compulsory Acquisition of Homes" in J. F. Garner (ed), *Compensation for Compulsory Purchase: A Comparative Study*.

FIFOOT, C. H. S. (1971) *Frederick William Maitland: a Life*.

FISHER, W. W. (1993) "The Trouble with *Lucas*" 45 *Stan L Rev* 1193.

FISS, O. (1997) "Money and Politics" 97 *Columbia Law Review* 2470.

—— (1996) *The Irony of Free Speech*.

FISSE, B. (1995) "Corporations, Crime and Accountability" 6 *Current Issues in Criminal Justice* 378.

FLETCHER, G. P. (1984) "Human Dignity as a Constitutional Value" 22 *U Western Ontario L Rev* 178.

FRAME, A. (1992) "Property: Some Pacific Reflections" *NZLJ* 21.

—— (1995) *Salmond: Southern Jurist*.

FREYFOGLE, E. (1988–89) "Context and Accommodation in Modern Property Law" 41 *Stan L Rev* 1529.

FRUG, J. (1996) "The Geography of Community" 48 *Stan L Rev* 1047.

—— (1998) "City Services" 73 *NYU L Rev* 23.

FULLER, L. L. (1964) *The Morality of Law*.

GARDBAUM, S. (1992) "Law, Politics, and the Claims of Community" *Mich LR* 685.

GIBSON, D. (1986) *The Law of the Charter: General Principles*.

GOLDSTONE, D. J. (1998) "A Funny Thing Happened on the Way to the Cyber Forum: Public vs Private in Cyberspace Speech" 69 *U Colo L Rev* 1.

GÖTZ, V. (1991) "Legislative and Executive Power under the Constitutional Requirements Entailed in the Principle of the Rule of Law" in C. Starck (ed), *New Challenges to the German Basic Law* 141.

GRAHAM, C. and PROSSER, T. (1991) *Privatising Public Enterprises*.

GRAVESON, R. H. (1953) *Status in the Common Law*.

GRAY, K. J. (1991) "Property in Thin Air" 50 *Cambridge L J* 252.

—— (1993) *Elements of Land Law*.

—— (1993) "The Ambivalence of Property" in G Prins (ed) *Threats without Enemies*.

—— (1994) "Equitable Property" 47(2) *Current Legal Problems* 157.

GRAY, K. J. and GRAY S. F. (1998) "The Idea of Property in Land" in S. Bright and J. Dewar (eds), *Land Law: Themes and Perspectives*.

—— (1999) "Civil Rights, Civil Wrongs and Quasi-Public Space" *European Human Rights Law Review* 1.

GROSSI, P. (1981) *An Alternative to Private Property: Collective Property in the Juridical Consciousness of the Nineteenth Century*.

GRUNEBAUM, J. (1986) *Private Ownership*.

HALE, M. (1716) *De Jure Maris*.

—— (1787) "De Portibus Maris" in F. Hargrave (ed), *Collection of Tracts Relative to the Law of England*.

HALPÉRIN, J.-L. (1996) *Histoire du droit privé français depuis 1804*.

HANKS, P. J. (1991) *Constitutional Law in Australia*.

HARE, R. M. (1952) *The Language of Morals*.

HARLOW, C. (1980) "'Public' and 'Private' Law"43 *Mod L R* 241.

HARRIS, D. J., BOYLE, M. O. and WARBRICK, C. (1995) *Law of the European Convention on Human Rights*.

HARRIS, J. W. (1996) *Property and Justice*.

HART, H. L. A. (1968) *Punishment and Responsibility: Essays in the Philosophy of Law*.

—— (1982) *Essays on Bentham*.

—— (1983) "Positivism and the Separation of Law and Morals" reprinted in *Essays in Jurisprudence and Philosophy*.

—— (1994) *The Concept of Law*.

HARTOG, H. (1983) *Public Property and Private Power: the Corporation of the City of New York in American Law*.

HAYWARD, T. and O'NEILL, J. (eds) (1997) *Justice, Property and the Environment: Social and Legal Perspectives*.

HEARN, W. E. (1883) *The Theory of Legal Rights and Duties*.

HEGEL, G. W. F. (1991) *Elements of the Philosophy of Right* (A Wood (ed)).

HEILBRONER, R. (1988) *Behind the Veil of Economics*.

—— (1992) *Twenty-First Century Capitalism*.

HESSE, K. (1995) *Grundzüge des Verfassungsrechts der Bundesrepublik Deutschland*.

HIGHT, J. and BAMFORD, H. D. (1914) *The Constitutional History and Law of New Zealand*.

HOGG, P. W. (1989) "A Comparison of the Canadian Charter of Rights and Freedoms with the Canadian Bill of Rights" in G. A. Beaudoin and E. Ratushny (eds), *The Canadian Charter of Rights and Freedoms*.

—— (1992) *Constitutional Law of Canada*.

HOHFELD, W. N. (1919) *Fundamental Legal Conceptions as Applied in Judicial Reasoning*.

HONORÉ, A. M. (1961) "Ownership" in A. G. Guest (ed), *Oxford Essays in Jurisprudence*.

HUME, D. (1888) *A Treatise of Human Nature* (L. A. Selby Bigge (ed)).

HORWITZ, M. J. (1992) *The Transformation of American Law 1870–1960*.

HUND, J. (1989) "A Bill of Rights for South Africa" 34 *Am J Jur* 23.

HYATT, W. S. (1998) "Common Interest Communities: Evolution and Reinvention" 31 *J Marshall L Rev* 303.

IGNATIEFF, M. (1984) *The Needs of Strangers*.

IVESON, K. (1998) "Putting the Public Back into Public Space" 16(1) *Urban Policy and Research* 21.

JACOBS, F. and WHITE, R. (1996) *The European Convention on Human Rights*.

JACQUEMIN, A. and SCHRANS, G. (1982) *Le droit économique*.

JOLOWICZ, H. F. (1957) *Roman Foundations of Modern Law*.

JONES, J. W. (1940) *Historical Introduction to the Theory of Law*.

KAMENKA, E. and TAY, A. E. S. (eds) (1979) *Human Rights*.

KAMMEN, M. (1986) *Spheres of Liberty: Changing Perceptions of Liberty in American Culture*.

KANTOROWICZ, E. H. (1957) *The King's Two Bodies: A Study in Medieval Political Theology*.

KARPEN, U. (1990) *Soziale Marktwirtschaft and Grundesetz. Eine Einführung in die rechtlichen Grundlagen der sozialen Marktwirtschaft*.

—— (1991) "The Constitution in the Face of Economic and Social Progress" in C. Starck (ed), *New Challenges to the German Basic Law*.

KASMAL, K., ASMAL, L. and ROBERTS, R. (1996) *Reconcilation Through Truth*.

KAWHARU, H. (ed) (1989) *Waitangi: Maori and Pakeha Perspectives of the Treaty of Waitangi*.

KENNEDY, D. J. (1995–96) "Residential Associations as State Actors: Regulating the Impact of Gated Communities on Nonmembers" 105 *Yale LJ* 761.

KLARE, K. (1991) "Legal Theory and Democratic Reconstruction: Reflections on 1989" 25 *University of British Columbia Law Review* 69.

KLEYN, D. G. (1996) "The Constitutional Protection of Property: A Comparison Between the German and the South African Approach" 11 *SAPL* 402.

KNETSCH, J. L. (1983) *Property Rights and Compensation: Compulsory Acquisition and Other Losses*.

KODILINYE, G. (1990) "The Statutory Authority Defence in Nuisance Actions" 19 *Anglo-American L R* 72.

KOMMERS, D. P. *The Constitutional Jurisprudence of the Federal Republic of Germany*.

KOWINSKI, W. S. (1985) *The Malling of America*.

KRAUSE, P. (1982) *Eigentum an subjektiven öffentlichen Rechten*.

KUBE, H. (1997) "Private Property in Natural Resources and the Public Weal in German Law—Latent Similarities to the Public Trust Doctrine?" 37 *Natural Resources Journal* 857.

LANE, P. H. (1987) *A Manual of Australian Constitutional Law*.

LAURANT, A. (1993) *Histoire de l'individualisme*.

LAWSON, F. H. "Common Law" *International Encyclopedia of Comparative Law*.

—— "Comparative Conclusion" *International Encyclopedia of Comparative Law*

—— (1980) *Remedies of English Law*.

LAWSON, F. H. and RUDDEN B. (1982) *The Law of Property*.

LAZARUS, R. (1986) "Changing Conceptions of Property and Sovereignty in Natural Resources: Questioning the Public Trust Doctrine" 71 *Iowa LR* 631.

—— (1993) "Putting the Correct 'Spin' on *Lucas*" 45 *Stan L Rev* 1411.

LEGRAND, P. (1996) "European Legal Systems are not Converging" 45 *ICLQ* 52.

—— (1997) "Against a European Civil Code" 60 *Mod L R* 44.

LEIGH, I. and LUSTGARTEN, L. (forthcoming) "Making Rights Real—The Courts, Remedies and the Human Rights Act".

LEROUX, A. and MARCIANO, A. (1998) *La Philosophie économique*.

LÉVY, .J-P. (1972) *Histoire de la propriété*.

LEWIS, C. H. (1992) "The Right to Private Property in a New Political Dispensation in South Africa" 8 *SAJHR* 389

LINDBLOM, C. (1977) *Politics and Markets: The World's Political-Economic Systems*.

LOCKE, J. (1690) *Second Treatise on Government*.

LORD, J. D. (1985) "The Malling of the American Landscape" in J. A. Dawson and J. D. Lord (eds), *Shopping Centre Development: Policies and Prospects*.

LUKES, S. (1993) "Five Fables about Human Rights" in S. Shute and S. L. Hurley (eds) *On Human Rights: The Oxford Amnesty Lectures 1993*.

MACCORMICK, N. (1977) "Rights in Legislation" in P. M. S. Hacker and J. Raz (eds), *Law, Morality and Society*.

MACDUFF, I. (1995) "The Role of Negotiation: Negotiated Justice?" 25 *VUWLR* 144.

MACINTYRE, A. (1985) *After Virtue: a Study in Moral Theory*.

MACLAURIN, R. C. (1901) *On the Nature and Evidence of Title to Realty*.

MacPherson, C. B. (1975) "Capitalism and the Changing Concept of Property" in E. Kamenka and R. S. Neale (eds) *Feudalism, Capitalism and Beyond*.

—— (1977) *The Life and Times of Liberal Democracy*.

Maine, H. (1939) *Ancient Law*.

Mauss, M. (1966) *The Gift: Forms and Functions of Exchange in Archaic Societies*.

McDonald, F. (1985) *Novus Ordo Seclorum: The Intellectual Origins of the Constitution*.

McDowell, J. (1981) "Non-cognitivism and Rule-Following" in S. Holtzman and C. Leich (eds), *Wittgenstein: To Follow a Rule*.

McHugh, P. (1991) *The Maori Magna Carta*.

—— (1998) "Aboriginal Identity and Relations—Models of State Practice in North America and Australasia" in K. S. Coates and P. G. McHugh (eds) *Living Relationships/Kokiri Ngatahi: The Treaty of Waitangi in the New Millenium*.

McKenzie, B. (1994) *Privatopia: Homeowner Associations and the Rise of Residential Private Government*.

—— (1998) "Reinventing Common Interest Developments: Reflections on a Policy Role for the Judiciary" 31 *J Marshall L Review* 397.

McLean, J. (1996) "Contracting in the Corporatised and Privatised Environment" 7 *PLR* 223.

—— (1999) "Personality and Public Law Doctrine" 49 *U Toronto LJ* 123, reviewing D. Runciman, *Pluralism and the Personality of the State*.

McLintock, A. H. (1958) *Crown Colony Government in New Zealand*.

McNeil, K. (1989) *Common Law Aboriginal Title*.

Marx, K. (1978) *The Communist Manifesto* and *Capital* in C. B. Macpherson (ed), *Property: Mainstream and Critical Positions*.

Mestre, J.-L. (1985) *Introduction historique au droit administratif français*.

Merillat, H. C. L. (1970) *Land and the Constitution in India*.

Michelman, F. I. (1981) "Property as a Constitutional Right" 38 *Washington and Lee L Rev* 1097.

—— (1987) "Possession vs Distribution in the Constitutional Idea of Property" 72 *Iowa L R* 1319.

—— (1997) "The Common Law Baseline and Restitution for the Lost Commons: A Reply to Professor Epstein" 64 *U Chi L Rev* 57

Milne, J. (1911) *The Romance of a Pro-Consul*.

Milsom, S. F. C. (1981) *Historical Foundations of the Common Law*.

Mincke, W. (1997) "Property: Assets or Power? Objects or Relations as substrata of Property Rights" in J. W. Harris, *Property Problems: From Genes to Pension Funds*.

Minogue, K. (1998) *Waitangi: Morality and Reality*.

Munzer, S. R. (1984) *A Theory of Property*.

Murphy, J. (1992) "Insulating Land Reform from Constitutional Impugnment: an Indian case Study" 8 *SAJHR* 362.

—— (1993) "Property Rights in the New Constitution: an Analytical Framework for Constitutional Review" 26 *CILSA* 211.

—— (1995) "Interpreting the Property Clause in the Constitution Act of 1993" 10 *SAPL* 107.

Nedelsky, J. (1990) *Private Property and the Future of Constitutionalism: the Madisonian Framework and its Legacy*.

—— (1993) "Reconceiving Rights as Relationships" *Rev Const Studies* 20.

NEDELSKY, J. (1996) "Should Property be Constitutionalized? A Relational and Comparative Approach" in G. E. van Maanen and A. J. van der Walt (eds), *Property Law on the Threshold of the 21st Century.*

NIELSEN, K. (1926) *American and British Claims Arbitration.*

NINO, C. S. (1991) *The Ethics of Human Rights.*

NOZICK, R. (1974) *Anarchy, State and Utopia.*

OLIVECRONA, K. (1984) "Locke on the Origin of Property" *Journal of the History of Ideas* vol. XXXV, 211.

OLIVER, W. (1991) *Claims to the Waitangi Tribunal.*

OSSENBÜHL, F. (1988) "Economic and Occupational Rights" in U. Karpen *The Constitution of the Federal Republic.*

—— (1987) *Festschrift für Wolfgang Zeidler.*

OST, F. (1990) *Droit et intérêt: Volume 2 entre droit et non-droit: l'intérêt.*

PAPIER, H.-J. (1993) "Die Eigentumsgarantie des Art. 14 I 1 GG" in T. Maunz and G. Dürig *Grundgesetz Kommentar.*

PAREKH, B. (1993) "The Cultural Particularity of Liberal Democracy" in D. Held (ed), *Prospects for Democracy.*

PATAULT, A.-M. (1989) *Introduction historique au droit des biens.*

PENNER, J. (1996) *The Idea of Property in Law.*

PEUKERT, W. (1981) "Protection of Ownership under Article of the First Protocol to the European Convention on Human Rights", 2 *Human Rights Law Journal* 37.

PIETTRE, B. (1994) *Philosophie et science du temps.*

PINCOFFS, R. L. (1977) "Due Process, Fraternity and a Kantian Injunction" in J. R. Pennock and J. W. Chapman (eds), *Due Process.*

PLUMBERG, P. I. (1971) "The Politicalization of the Corporation" 26 *Business Lawyer* 1551.

POCOCK, J. G. A. (1975) *The Machiavellian Moment.*

—— (1991) "Time and Property in the American Civic Republican Legal Culture" 66 *NYU L Rev* 273.

POLLOCK, F. and MAITLAND, F. W. (1968) *History of English Law.*

POSTEMA, G. J. (1986) *Bentham and the Common Law Tradition.*

PÜTTNER, G. (1998) "Constitutional Limitations on Privatisation" in E. Riedel (ed), *German Reports on Public Law.*

RADIN, M. J. (1982) "Property and Personhood" 34 *Stan L Rev* 957.

—— (1993) *Reinterpreting Property.*

RAUTENBACH, I. M. (1995) *General Provisions of the South African Bill of Rights.*

RAZ, J. (1986) *The Morality of Freedom.*

REEVE, A (1985) *Property.*

REICH, C. A. (1964) "The New Property" 73 *Yale LJ* 733.

—— (1990) "Beyond the New Property: An Ecological View of Due Process" 56 *Brooklyn L Rev* 731.

RISHIKOF, H. and WOHL, A. (1996) "Private Communities or Public Governments: The State will make the Call" 30 *Valparaiso U L Rev* 509.

ROBERTSON, M. (1997) "Reconceiving Private Property" 24 *Journal of Law and Society* 465.

—— (1995) "Property and Ideology" 8 *Canadian Journal of Law and Jurisprudence* 275.

ROBINSON O. F., FERGUS, T. D. and GORDON, W. M. (1994) *European Legal History.*

ROEMER, J. (1994) *A Future for Socialism.*

—— (1996) *Equal Shares*.

Rose, C. (1984) "*Mahon* Reconstructed: Why the Takings Clause Is Still a Muddle" 57 *S Cal L Rev* 561.

—— (1985) "Public Property, Old and New" 79 *Nw ULR* 216.

—— (1986) "The Comedy of the Commons; Custom, Commerce and Inherently Public Property" 53 *U Chi L R* 711.

—— (1994) *Property and Persuasion*.

—— (1996) "Property as the Keystone Right?" 71 *Notre Dame Law Review* 329.

Rosen, M. L. (1982) "Lands Under Navigable Waters: The Governmental/ Proprietary Distinction" 34 *U Fla L Rev* 561.

Ross, I. S. (1995) *The Life of Adam Smith*.

Rothbard, M. N. (1974) "Justice and Property Rights" in S. L. Blumenfeld (ed), *Property in a Humane Economy*.

Roux, T. (1997) "Property" in D. Davis et al (eds), *Fundamental Rights in the Constitution: Commentary and Cases*.

Rudden, B. (1991) *A Source-book on French Law*.

Ryan, A. (1984) *Property and Political Theory*.

Sachs, A. (1990) "Towards a Bill of Rights in a Democratic South Africa" 6 *SAJHR* 1.

Sackville, R. and Neave, M. A. (1981) *Property Law: Cases and Materials*.

Saint-James, V. (1997) "Réflexions sur la dignité de l'être humain en tant que concept juridique du droit français" *Recueil Dalloz*, Chron 61.

Salmond, J. (1924) *Jurisprudence*.

Samuel, G. and Rinkes, J. (1996) *Law of Obligations and Legal Remedies*.

Samuel, G. (1998) "The Impact of European Integration on Private Law—A Comment" 18 *Legal Studies*, 167.

—— (1994) *The Foundations of Legal Reasoning*.

Sandel, M. J. (1982) *Liberalism and the Limits of Justice*.

Sandercock, L. (1997) "From Main Street to Fortress: The Future of Malls as Public Spaces OR 'Shut Up and Shop'" 9 *Just Policy* 27.

Sax, J. (1970) "The Public Trust Doctrine in Natural Resource Law: Effective Judicial Intervention" 68 *Mich L Rev* 471.

Schieber, H. (1984) "Public Rights and the Rule of Law in American Legal History" 72 *Calif L Rev* 217.

Schumpter, J. (1943) *Capitalism, Socialism and Democracy*, extracted in B. Sutton (ed), *The Legitimate Corporation* 27.

Schuppert, G. F. (1988) "The Right to Property" in U. Karpen (ed), *The Constitution of the Federal Republic of Germany*.

Selvin, M. (1980) "The Public Trust Doctrine in American Law and Economic Policy 1789-1920" *Wisconsin L Rev* 1403.

Sharp, A (1997) *Justice and the Maori* (2 ed).

Shearing, C. D. and Stenning, P. C. (1982-1983) "Private Security: Implications for Social Control" 30 *Social Problems* 193.

Shields, R. (1992) "The Individual, Consumption Cultures and the Fate of Community" in R. Shields (ed), *Lifestyle Shopping: The Subject of Consumption*.

Shukla, V. N. (1969) *The Constitution of India*.

Simon, W. (1990) "Contract Versus Politics in Corporation Doctrine" in D. Kairys (ed) *The Politics of Law* 387.

—— (1991) "Social-Republican Property" 38 *UCLA Law Review* 1335.

SIEGAL, S. (1990) "The Constitution and Private Government: Toward the Recognition of Constitutional Rights in Private Residential Communities Fifty Years after Marsh v. Alabama" 6 *Wm & Mary Bill of Rts J* 461.

SIMPSON, A. W. B. (1975) *A History of the Common Law of Contract.*

SONTHEIMER, K (1993) "Principles of Human Dignity in the Federal Republic" in U. Karpen (ed), *The Constitution of the Federal Republic.*

SORRENSON, M. "Towards a Radical Reinterpretation of NZ History: the Role of the Waitangi Tribunal" in H. Kawharu (ed), *Waitangi: Maori and Pakeha Perspectives of the Treaty of Waitangi.*

STEIN, P. (1984) *Legal Institutions: The Development of Dispute Settlement.*

STEINER, H. (1994) *An Essay on Rights.*

STEINGLASS, D. B. (1996) "Extending PruneYard: Citizens' Right to Demand Public Access Cable Channels" 71 *NYU L Rev* 1113.

STONE, C. D. (1972) "Should Trees Have Standing? Towards Legal Rights of Material Agents" 45 *Southern California Law Review* 4500.

—— (1985) "Should Trees Have Standing? Revisited: How Far Will Law and Morals Reach? A Pluralist Perspective" 59 *Southern California Law Review* 1.

STOREY, A. (1998) "Compensation for Banned Handguns: Indemnifying 'Old Property'" 61 *Mod LR* 188.

TAGGART, M. (1991) "Corporatisation, Privatisation and Public Law" 2 *PLR* 77.

—— (1993) "State-Owned Enterprises and Social Responsibility: a Contradiction in Terms?" *NZ Recent L Rev* 343.

—— (1993) "Book Review" of C. Graham and T. Prosser (1991) *Privatising Public Enterprises* 4 *PLR* 271.

—— (1995) "Public Utilities and Public Law" in P. Joseph, *Essays on the Constitution.*

—— (1997) *The Province of Administrative Law.*

—— (1998) "Expropriation, Public Purpose and the Constitution" in C. Forsyth and I. Hare (eds) *The Golden Metwand and the Crooked Cord: Essays on Public Law in Honour of Sir William Wade QC.*

TAYLOR, C. (1989) *Sources of the Self: The Making of the Modern Identity.*

TAYLOR, M. (1992) "The Economics and Politics of Property Rights and Common Pool Resources" 32 *Natural Resources Journal* 633.

THATCHER, M. (1993) *The Downing Street Years.*

THOMPSON, E. P. (1977) *Whigs and Hunters: the Origin of the Black Act.*

THOMPSON, J. B. (1990) *Ideology and Modern Culture.*

TREANER, W. (1985) "The Origins and Original Significance of the Just Compensation Clause of the Fifth Amendment" 94 *Yale LJ* 694.

TRIBE, L. (1988) *American Constitutional Law.*

TUCK, R. (1979) *Natural Rights Theories.*

TULLY, J. (1998) "A Fair and Just Relationship: the Vision of the Canadian Royal Commission on Aboriginal Peoples" 57 *Meanjin* 146.

ULLMANN, W. (1975) *Law and Politics in the Middle Ages.*

UNDERKUFFLER, L. S. (1990) "On Property: an Essay" 100 *Yale LJ* 127–148.

UNDERKUFFLER-FRUEND, L. S. (1996) "Takings and the Nature of Property" 9 *Can J Law & Jur* 161.

VAN ALSTYNE, W. (1977) "Cracks in the 'New Property': Adjudicative Due Process" 62 *Cornell LR* 445.

VAN CAENEGEM, R. C. (1995) *An Historical Introduction to Western Constitutional Law.*

—— (1988) "Government, Law and Society" in J. H. Burns (ed), *The Cambridge History of Medieval Political Thought c.350–c.1450.*

—— (1988) *The Birth of the English Common Law.*

VAN DER WALT, A. J. (1990) "Towards the Development of Post-apartheid Land Law: an Exploratory Survey" *De Jure* 1.

—— (1993) "Ownership and Personal Freedom: Subjectivism in Bernhard Windscheid's Theory of Ownership" 56 *THRHR* 569.

—— (1994) "Property Rights, Land Rights, and Environmental Rights" in D. H. van Wyk et al (eds), *Rights and Constitutionalism: the New South African Legal Order.*

—— (1994) "Notes on the Interpretation of the Property Clause in the New Constitution" 57 *THRHR* 181.

—— (1995) "Towards a Theory of Rights in Property: Exploratory Observations on the Paradigm of Post-apartheid Property Law" 10 *SAPL* 298.

—— (1995) "Tradition on Trial: a Critical Analysis of the Civil-law Tradition in South African Property Law" 11 *SAJHR* 169.

—— (1995) "Marginal Notes on Powerful(l) Legends: Critical Perspectives on Property Theory" 58 *THRHR* 396.

—— (1997) *The Constitutional Property Clause.*

—— (1997) "The Limits of Constitutional Property" 12 *SAPL* 274.

—— (1998) "'Double' Property Guarantees: a Structural and Comparative Analysis" 14 *SAJHR* (forthcoming).

—— (1998) "Police Power Regulation of Intangible Commercial Property and the Constitutional Property Clause: a Comparative Analysis of Case Law" vol 2.1 *Electronic Journal of Comparative Law.*

—— (1998) "Un-doing Things with Words: The Colonization of the Public Sphere by Private Property Discourse" *Acta Juridica* 235.

—— "Council of Europe" in *Constitutional Property Clauses: A Comparative Analysis* Capetown, Juta & Co.

VINOGRADOFF, P. (1920) *Outlines of Historical Jurisprudence.*

VIRIEUX-REYMOND, A. (1972) *Introduction à l'épistémologie.*

VOGEL, D. (1975) "The Corporation as Government: Challenges and Dilemmas" 8 *Polity* 5.

VOLFF, J. (1998) *Le ministère public.*

WALD, P. M. (1997) "Looking Forward to the Next Millenium: Social Previews to Legal Change" 70 *Temple L Rev* 1085.

WALDRON, J. (1988) *The Right to Private Property.*

—— (1992) "Historic Injustice: Its Remembrance and Supercession" in G. Oddie and R. Perrett (eds), *Justice, Ethics, and New Zealand Society.*

—— (1992) "Superseding Historic Injustice" 103 *Ethics* 4.

—— (1993) "Property, Justification and Need" 6 *Canadian Journal of Law and Jurisprudence* 185.

—— 1994) "The Advantages and Difficulties of the Humean Theory of Property" 11 *Social Philosophy and Policy* 85.

—— (1996) "Kant's Legal Positivism" 109 *Harvard Law Review* 1535.

—— (1997) "Supply without Burthen Revisited" *Iowa L R* 1467.

WALZER, M. (1982) *Spheres of Justice: a Defense of Pluralism and Equality.*

WELLE, B. A. (1996) "Public Service: Opting out of Public Provision: Constraints and Policy Considerations" 73 *Denv U L Rev* 1221.

WHITE, R. (1993) "Young People and the Policing of Community Space" 26(3) *ANZJ Crim* 207.

—— (1994) "Street Life: Police Practices and Youth Behaviour" in R. White and C. Alder (eds), *The Police and Young People in Australia*.

—— (1996) "No Go in the Fortress City: Young People, Inequality and Space" 14(1) *Urban Policy and Research* 37.

WHITE, R. and SUTTON, A. (1995) "Crime Prevention, Urban Space and Social Exclusion" 31(1) *Australian and New Zealand Journal of Sociology* 82.

WIEACKER, F. (1995) *A History of Private Law in Europe*.

WILLIAMS, B. (1973) "Ethical Consistency" in *Problems of the Self: Philosophical Papers 1956–1972*.

WILLIAMS, D. V. (1989) "The Queen v Symonds Reconsidered" 19 *VUWLR* 385.

WOOLF, H. (1986) "Public Law – Private Law: Why the Divide?" *Public Law* 220.

WOOLMAN, S. (1994) "Riding the Push-me Pull-you: Constructing a Test That Reconciles the Conflicting Interests Which Animate the Limitation Clause" 10 *SAJHR* 60.

—— (1997) "Out of order? Out of Balance? The Limitation Clause of the Final Constitution" 13 *SAJHR* 102.

—— (1998) "Limitation" in M. Chaskalson et al, *Constitutional Law of South Africa* (1st edn 1996, 2nd edn 1998).

ZENATI, F. and REVET, T. (1997) *Les Biens*.

Index